Rustico

REGIONAL ITALIAN COUNTRY COOKING

MICOL NEGRIN

CLARKSON POTTER/PUBLISHERS

NEW YORK

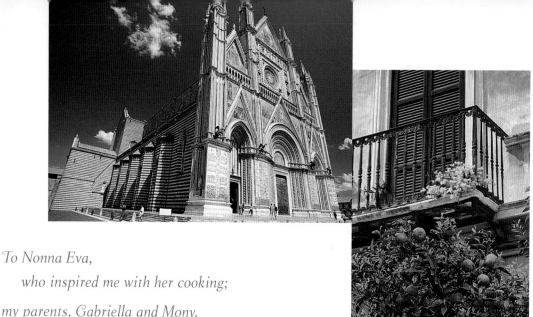

To Nonna Eva,

who inspired me with her cooking;

my parents, Gabriella and Mony,

who inspired me with their love;

and my husband, Dino,

who inspired me with his smile.

Text copyright © 2002 by Micol Negrin
Photographs of Braised Chicken with Prosciutto and Fried Eggplants, Pork Scaloppine in Caper and
Red Wine Glaze, Braised Veal Shanks with Gremolata, Veal Roast Stuffed with Spinach, Pancetta, and Frittata,
and Stuffed Escarole Bundles copyright © 2002 by Mark Ferri
All other food photographs copyright © 2002 by Jerry Ruotolo
Regional photographs copyright © 2002 by Micol Negrin and Dino De Angelis
Map on page 1 copyright © 2002 by Dino De Angelis
Certain regional photographs were originally published in *The Magazine of La Cucina Italiana* and
Italian Cooking & Living.

Published by Clarkson Potter/Publishers, New York, New York.
Member of the Crown Publishing Group, a division of Random House, Inc. www.randomhouse.com

CLARKSON N. POTTER is a trademark and POTTER and colophon are registered trademarks of
Random House, Inc.

Printed in the United States of America
Design by Maggie Hinders

Library of Congress Cataloging-in-Publication Data
Negrin, Micol. Rustico: regional Italian country cooking / Micol Negrin. 1. Cookery, Italian.   I. Title
TX723.N46   2002
641.5945—dc21   2001057793

ISBN 0-609-60944-0
10 9 8 7 6 5 4 3 2 1

First Edition

Contents

Introduction

I *grew up in a typical Italian home.* My mother, an amazing cook, prepared feasts of flavor every day, making each meal a miniature celebration. I always thought that what made our meals so essentially Italian was the freshness and the simplicity and the goodness of the food she made. But as I started formulating this book in my mind, I realized that what infused our meals with their Italianness was my mother's unconscious focus on the dishes of her region. There's nothing more Italian than the tendency to eat what you know and love—and in Italy, that's usually the food of your town, your city, your region.

OPPOSITE *Morning at the market in the Ligurian city of Rapallo.* • ABOVE LEFT *Ripe tomatoes for sale in Calabria.* • ABOVE RIGHT *A brilliant blue sky frames the cathedral of Vasto in Abruzzo.*

My mother and father grew up and lived in Milan much of their adult lives, so my mother—like all of her Milanese friends—cooked the dishes she knew best: risotto, breaded and fried veal chops, *vitello tonnato*. I don't think I ever ate a bowl of orecchiette in my parents' home: this pasta, like so many other dishes and ingredients from other parts of Italy, never made its way to our table. And the incredibly Italian thing is that we never missed it: we were too busy enjoying all the things typical of Milan.

Italians are stubborn people. When we like something, we can't imagine that it would taste better any other way. We argue for hours over whether or not garlic belongs in a particular pasta sauce, whether sage or rosemary is best for flavoring roasted veal, whether focaccia should be high and pillowy or crisp and flat. Gather three or four people from different parts of Italy around the dining room table and listen to them talk: you will hear as many opinions as there are people. From one region to the next—and in some cases from one town to the next—local preferences for food vary wildly. The same ingredients are treated in different ways depending on who is in the kitchen. Each village and town in Italy's twenty regions has its proudest specialty, its signature offering:

ABOVE LEFT *Citrus fruits, berries, and dried hot peppers from the town of Senise are offered at a roadside stand in Basilicata.* • ABOVE RIGHT *Golden arches in the regal city of Ferrara in Emilia-Romagna.*

from the saffron-tinted risotto of Milan that my mother adores to the risotto with fresh peas ritually made by Venetian cooks every spring, there are literally thousands of regional dishes that make up what is broadly called Italian cuisine.

It's amazing that a country as small as Italy—less than half the size of Texas—has such a vastly varied cuisine. Italy comprises twenty regions, five of which (Val d'Aosta, Trentino–Alto Adige, Friuli–Venezia Giulia, Sicily, and Sardinia) are autonomous, thereby enjoying greater independence as a result of their political and linguistic backgrounds. Italy's awe-inspiring gastronomic heritage is due not only to its varying climates and geography, but to its complex history of foreign invasion and domination. From the fall of the Roman Empire in 476 to 1861, Italy as a country did not exist: it was made up of small city-states, large republics, and independent regions that spent much of their time protecting their boundaries from encroaching neighbors and warring with outside intruders. In 1861, Italy was unified under its first king, Vittorio Emanuele. But the ancient rivalries and diffidence persisted; an Abruzzese felt he or she was different from an Apulian, a Tuscan considered himself a different breed from an Umbrian, and so on. Unification brought Italians together legally, but it left them with their distinct histories and traditions. Nearly 150 years after the country's formal unification, Italians still cling to their regional roots.

In general terms, Italy's northern regions—Val d'Aosta, Piedmont, Lombardy, Trentino–Alto Adige, Friuli–Venezia Giulia, the Veneto, Emilia-Romagna and, to a certain extent, Liguria—have a temperate climate, with mild summers and cold winters. Butter and lard have been the primary fats for all of these regions except Liguria, whose more Mediterranean climate has made olive oil an important product for the last two thousand years. Rice and corn thrive in the hills and plains of northern Italy, rendering dried pasta somewhat less important than it is to the south; egg pasta, however, is a much-loved staple. After the fall of the Roman Empire, these regions fell to invaders and plunderers from the north: Celts, Vikings, and Lombards. Later the Franks and Austrians—and in some regions the Spanish—arrived, contributing to the culinary palette of the land. Savory dishes laced with nutmeg or cinnamon hint at links with Byzantium and a more recent interaction with Austrians, and elaborate pastries show a central European and French flair.

Central Italy—the Marches, Tuscany, Umbria, Abruzzo, Molise, and Latium—draws its culinary inspiration from a pastoral tradition and the influence of Byzantium and the papacy. Pigs are more important than cattle, and lard is used along with olive oil to flavor and enrich many foods. Dried pasta is as essential as sheep's milk cheese, and the two are often combined to great effect. Much of the area was under Etruscan rule before the Roman Empire flourished; by the fifth century, power passed from the Romans to the Goths and Lombards and later to the Franks, Austrians, or Bourbons. A hearty, ancient form of wheat called farro is still cooked into soups and polenta, and sweet pastas remain favorite feast dishes, a holdover from medieval banquets.

Southern Italy—Apulia, Campania, Basilicata, Calabria, Sicily, and Sardinia—is decidedly Mediterranean in climate, except in the high mountains of Calabria and Basilicata. Sun-kissed vegetables and fruits form the basis of a gutsy cuisine, and pasta reigns supreme. Greek settlers and Arab invaders have left an unmistakable imprint on the foodways of these six regions: honey-drenched sweets are the norm rather than the exception, as in the days of classical Greece, and a generous hand with chili pepper and spices is a legacy of contact with Arabs. Extravagant dishes born in the Bourbon court under the Kingdom of Naples (later known as the Kingdom of the Two Sicilies) are still made. But it is the foods of poverty—pasta, vegetables, and simple sweets—that are most representative of southern Italian cuisine.

Yet breaking Italy down into three areas—northern, central, and southern—fails to do justice to its complexity and beauty. Yes, it's true that neighboring regions tend to share certain dishes; this is often because the same crops grow in adjacent areas and because bordering lands were often ruled by the same people. But the differences far outweigh the similarities, and it is precisely these differences that make Italy's twenty regions a never-ending source of fascination and wonder for the curious cook. Sometimes the differences within a region are just as marked as those across regions. The tendency to look no farther than one's own village, town, or city is known as *campanilismo* in Italian (from *campana*, a reference to the village churchbell many Italians identify with). *Campanilismo* can be either frustrating or amusing for the outsider, but when it comes to food, it has allowed a number of dishes to survive unscathed for thousands of years. If Italians had been less protective of their traditions, would the Florentines still be

baking a grape-studded flatbread as their Etruscan ancestors did three thousand years ago? Would the Modenesi still be producing Cotechino and Zampone, two pork specialties "invented" in 1511, when a town famine made them look to humbler parts of the pig for their beloved sausages? Would the Veronesi still host a yearly gnocchi festival on the last Friday of Carnevale to commemorate the day in 1500 that a generous doctor fed a famished town?

Today, Italy's super-highways facilitate communication and transport. But until a few decades ago, the situation was very different: an Apulian had little means (and often little reason, unless it was economic) to travel to Lombardy. The large-scale exchange of culinary ideas and traditions among Italians is a recent phenomenon, linked to modern roads and technology and an improved postwar economy. This too explains how Italy managed to maintain its varied cuisines into the twenty-first century. Similarly, Italy's numerous dialects thrived in their native towns and cities until recently. Not only did a Neapolitan cook differently from a Roman, he or she spoke differently too.

Just as dialects are dying out in favor of standard Italian, the various dialects of Italian cuisine are endangered. Mass communications and the global economy have taken hold of

ABOVE LEFT *A tempting selection of sheep's milk cheeses from the Marches.* • ABOVE RIGHT *A baker proudly displays his breads in Bolzano, Trentino–Alto Adige.*

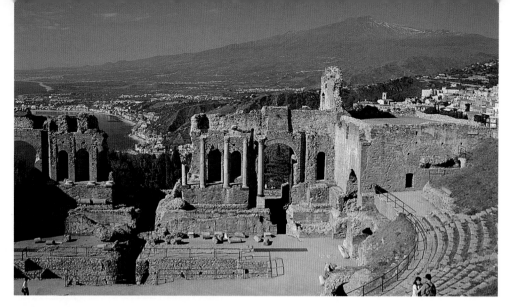

Italy, and international chains have set up camp where family businesses once stood. Many young Italians think little of the foods of their towns, cities, or regions, preferring to eat at the new American burger joint around the corner, sipping soft drinks rather than savoring wine. European Union regulations have obliterated many small-scale producers of Italy's finest artisanal foods: hand-shaped sausages, cave-ripened cheeses, heirloom fruit varieties. More and more, Italians shop, cook, and eat like the rest of the world. Ingredients that were once easy to find are vanishing, and along with them the knowledge of how best to prepare them.

Yet every region still has two or three dishes that everyone knows and most people love. Some of these "famous" recipes are included in the book, while others—by now in dozens of cookbooks—have been omitted in favor of lesser-known regional gems.

These choices were not easy—not only among which dishes to include, but among which versions to include. *Brodetto,* for example, is the seafood soup that all Marchigiani swear by; there are at least a dozen variations on it. Selecting the most representative version entailed comparing it to seafood soups from other regions to find the one that differed the most, the one with the most Marchigiano soul. *Crescia sfogliata,* on the other hand, is a Marchigiano dish few people know; yet it is one of Urbino's greatest offerings, and omitting it in order to include a more standard polenta topped with sausages (made

ABOVE *Monte Etna looms on the horizon behind the Greek Theater in Taormina, Siciliy.* • OPPOSITE *Sardinia's famed Capo d'Orso is a massive boulder said to resemble a bear.*

pretty much across Italy) would have been a shame. At times, the same dish goes by different names in different cities or regions: *maccheroni al ferretto*, a hand-rolled pasta shaped around an iron rod, is also known as *makkarones de busa, busiati,* and *ferrazzuoli.* Other times, the same name applies to different dishes: *acqua e sale* (literally, "water and salt") refers both to a tomato-topped bruschetta and to a simple country soup featuring bread; *cialledda* both to a cold bread and vegetable salad and to a hot bread and vegetable soup. The greatest diversity of names applies to pasta: after all, pasta was often the only dish eaten by peasants and farmers, who spoke dialect, giving rise to hundreds of colorful designations. With Italy's dialects as diverse as they are, the range of names for pasta is as wide as the range of pasta shapes.

BEFORE YOU START COOKING

Most of the ingredients required for the recipes are fairly easy to come by in large North American cities; specialty items can be mail-ordered from the Sources on page 372. Within each chapter I have included notes on cheeses and wines that are imported to North America and on cured meats that are either imported or produced domestically; all can be obtained through the Sources.

If you must substitute ingredients, keep in mind the nature of the dish: there is no sense in making the Gorgonzola-Topped Pizza with Sweet Onions on page 63 if you intend to substitute low-fat American blue cheese for the Gorgonzola. Substitutions can sometimes be fine; other times, they destroy the essence of the dish.

First, read the recipe all the way through before you start cooking. There may be a step that requires advance preparation, such as marinating meat or setting eggplants aside to purge. Reading the recipe thoroughly will also prevent any nasty surprises, like finding out that you don't have an essential ingredient at the last moment.

Every recipe provides you with a quantity for salt and pepper. However, except in cakes, breads, and pastries, the amount of seasoning required by any dish is personal. Different salts—iodized, sea, and kosher—have a different concentration. Before you serve a dish, taste for seasoning and adjust if needed.

Cooking times and temperatures also vary depending on the ingredients and equipment used. Watery mushrooms, for example, require higher heat to evaporate the water that will inevitably form in the pan; a gas burner responds more quickly to temperature changes than an electric range. Trust your instincts; if the recipe says to cook the onions for 15 minutes until they are soft and translucent over medium heat, but your onions are brown after 8 minutes, lower the temperature and proceed to the next step.

All the recipes in this book that call for oil rather than butter or lard specify extra-virgin olive oil (except recipes in which ingredients are to be deep-fried, in which case I suggest peanut oil as a less costly alternative). This is not only for health reasons: it is also for flavor considerations. When you buy olive oil, whatever region of Italy (or elsewhere) it is from, select a top-quality estate-bottled extra-virgin olive oil for flavoring food and drizzling raw as a condiment over salads, pastas, soups, and more.

Avoid virgin and pure olive oil, which lack the depth and intensity of extra-virgin olive oil and have a higher level of acidity; extra-virgin olive oil is required by law to have no more than 1 percent acidity, which makes it more digestible and healthier. All olive oil—whether extra-virgin, virgin, or pure—has the same number of calories: 120 per tablespoon. Steer clear of olive oils labeled "light," which have the same calories but a much blander, nondescript flavor and higher acidity.

ABOUT REGIONAL WINES, CHEESES, AND CURED MEATS

Italian regional cooking is defined as much by its use of local products such as wine, cheese, and cured meat as by the manner in which these products are transformed in the kitchen. Until 1861, when Italy was made up of independent city-states and republics, each area had to be very nearly self-sufficient, and people farmed, grew, and produced most of what they ate and drank; only the wealthy could afford to look farther than their immediate surroundings. Today, local preferences for wine, cheese, and cured meat still reflect centuries of reliance on the land.

Italy is the world's leading exporter of wine. It offers hundreds of varietals, many of which have a venerable pedigree and reflect centuries—if not millennia—of production.

Despite the country's advanced oenological practices and its reputation for producing top-quality wines, reading an Italian wine label can be frustrating. The name of the producer and origin are typically indicated, but the grape varietal may or may not be, and the place of origin can just as easily be a city as a province or a region.

Every Italian wine falls under one of four legal categories: DOC (*Denominazione di Origine Controllata*, or Denomination of Controlled Origin), DOCG (*Denominazione di Origine Controllata e Garantita*, or Denomination of Controlled and Guaranteed Origin), VdT (*Vino da Tavola*, or Table Wine), or IGT (*Identificazione Geografica Tipica*, or Typical Geographic Identification). The DOC system created in 1963 classifies Italy's arguably better wines and imposes stringent rules regarding grape varietals, production zones, vinification methods, and aging periods. DOCG is a category reserved for Italy's most prized wines, essentially super DOCs. Because the DOC and DOCG systems emphasize the use of indigenous grape varietals above all, Italian wines vinified from nontraditional grapes or according to nontraditional methods fell into the VdT category. A quirk of the DOC and DOCG systems is that a number of Italy's most prized wines —such as the high-priced super-Tuscans, vinified from international grape varietals— have been labeled VdT. To rectify the situation, the IGT designation was created in 1992.

ABOVE *A tranquil canal in Treviso, one of the Veneto's most romantic cities.*

IGT wines are considered better than VdT but do not meet DOC or DOCG regulations; as a result, many "super" wine varieties are now labeled IGT. Every Italian region offers DOC, IGT, and VdT wines; some, like Piedmont and Tuscany, are responsible for most DOCG wines.

When reading an Italian wine label, keep in mind the following descriptors: *secco* (dry), *abboccato* and *amabile* (semi-sweet), *dolce* (sweet), *liquoroso* (fortified), *passito* (raisined), *frizzante* (semi-sparkling), and *spumante* (fully sparkling).

Each region also produces cheeses that play an integral role in its cuisine. I have included a brief discussion of each region's most significant cheeses, all of which are available in North America (see Sources, page 372) and many of which enjoy DOP status. DOP (*Denominazione di Origine Protetta*, or Denomination of Protected Origin) is the cheese equivalent of the DOC system applied to wine.

Similarly, each region offers a range of cured meats (known as *salumi* in Italian) that are used in local cooking and are often featured on the regional antipasto table. Unfortunately, only a handful meet FDA guidelines and are exported to North America. Within each region, I describe the cured meats that are exported and those that are produced in North America, and provide sources for each (see page 372).

ABOVE LEFT *Massive trees and ancient Roman ruins in the town of Aquileia in Friuli–Venezia Giulia.* • ABOVE RIGHT *A field in Calabria.*

Val d'Aosta

Fonduta alla Valdostana
Creamy Fonduta over Fried Polenta

Frittelle di Fontina con Spinaci Stufati
Fontina Fritters with Wilted Spinach

Insalata di Lamponi con Polenta
Wine-Macerated Raspberries over Polenta

Seuppa Valpellinentze
Cabbage and Whole Wheat Bread Soup from Valpelline

Seuppa de Cogne
Bread, Rice, and Fontina Soup from Cogne

Costolette alla Valdostana
Fontina-Stuffed Breaded Veal Chops

Cervo Brasato con la Grappa
Braised Venison in Creamy Grappa Sauce

Insalata Verde con Pancetta Affumicata
Young Greens in Warm Bacon Dressing

Lou Mécoulen
Raisin-Studded Sweet Bread

La Coppa dell'Amicizia
The Cup of Friendship

*I*magine yourself in a lush valley. It is summer and the sun warms the grass beneath your feet. The Alpine flowers are in bloom, the air is crisp, carrying the scents of tarragon and sage, and your cows are grazing in the meadow. At nightfall, you make the two-hour journey home, the sound of cow bells announcing your arrival. Before your dinner of boiled chestnuts, a hunk of bread, and a bowl of leek soup, you milk your cows, leaving the pails of warm liquid to settle near the butter churner by the wood pile.

This was life for most Valdostani until fifty or sixty years ago: lived in rhythm with the seasons, the mountains defining not only where you could go, but what you ate and who you knew and how you earned your daily bread. Each of the valleys that coast the Dora Baltea River was isolated from the others for much of the year, and their inhabitants lived autonomously, making the most of what they could grow in the steep soil surrounding their homes and from the milk provided by their cows. They developed a subsistence cuisine that would carry them through the difficult winter, a cuisine handed down from generation to generation, much like the guillotine-shaped *copapan* used to slice the heavy, dark wheels of bread baked in communal ovens by village women.

Perhaps it's because of its geographic configuration—dizzyingly high mountains, jagged snow-capped peaks, permanent glaciers—that Val d'Aosta remains something of a mystery to the rest of Italy. The Valdostani have long lived in a state of semi-isolation, cut off from others when the region's mountain passes were covered in ice.

Val d'Aosta, Italy's smallest region, was originally settled by the Salassi, a tribe of Celts, and later annexed by the Romans, who founded its capital, Aosta, in 24 B.C.

Known as "The Rome of the Alps," Aosta and its surrounding land became part of the Burgundian and Frankish Kingdoms after the fall of the Roman Empire, then fell to the House of Savoy in the eleventh century and eventually became encompassed in Piedmont. In 1927, the province of Turin was divided, and part of it formed a new province, still under Piedmontese rule, called Aosta. Two decades later, the autonomous region of Val d'Aosta was created and bilingualism was officially instituted to preserve its uniquely French culture. Schools teach French and Italian, and most inhabitants speak a French dialect.

All of this might lead you to believe that Val d'Aosta feels like a part of France—but it doesn't. Even if the language spoken by old-timers sounds more like French than Italian and if the cuisine has more in common with nearby Savoie than Italy, there is no doubt that Val d'Aosta is Italian through and through. Just visit the city of Aosta, where a third of the population lives, and you'll instantly understand: there is a joyous exuberance, a festive atmosphere, a friendliness that is utterly Italian. Sit in a café and the noise level will let you know that you are, indeed, on Italian soil.

Milk, butter, and cheese; hearty grains like corn, buckwheat, and rye; herbs, chestnuts, mushrooms, and honey . . . these are the mainstays of the Valdostano diet. The harsh climate doesn't allow olive trees to thrive, but the Valdostani don't miss olive oil: they prefer unsalted farmhouse butter redolent of Alpine grasses and lard from the family pig to flavor their food and give their bodies energy.

Favorite Restaurants, Shops, and Places

- BERTOLIN, Via Nazionale 11, Arnad, 0125.966127. Lard of Saint Arnad and Mocetta made from beef, horse, and chamois, among other cured meats for sale.
- LA CAVE VALDÔTAINE, Via de Tillier 9, Aosta, 0165.44164. *Enoteca* where you can buy wines and liqueurs, including génepy and grappa.
- LA MAISON DE LA FONTINE BORNEY-LALE GERARD, Via de Sales 2, Aosta, 0165.35639. Fontina aged to perfection.
- LO GRAND BAOU, Località Jovençan di Vertosan, Avise. Gorgeous panorama, excellent cured meats and polenta.

- LOCANDA LA CLUSAZ, Località la Clusaz, Gignod, 0165.56075. Home of the best *seuppa valpellinentze* and an award-winning wine list.
- LOU RESSIGNON, Rue Mines de Cogne 23, Cogne, 0165.74034. Rustic mountain restaurant with exceptional meats and *seuppetta de Cogne*.
- RISTORANTE VECCHIA AOSTA, Via Porta Pretoriana 4, Aosta, 0165.361186. Restaurant dug in the old Roman walls of Aosta.

Telephone country code: 011.39

Fonduta alla Valdostana

Creamy Fonduta over Fried Polenta

This is one of Val d'Aosta's defining dishes, shared with nearby Piedmont. It is similar to French and Swiss fondue, but a few key differences give it a distinct character. First and foremost is the use of Fontina; second is that the Fontina is soaked in milk for hours before it is melted, which gives it a silky texture; third is the addition of egg yolks, beaten in at the end to ensure a velvety mouthfeel; and finally, there is the preference for pouring the fonduta over fried polenta, as below. Needless to say, you should only use Fontina from Val d'Aosta here; it has a compact texture with tiny holes and a nutty fragrance and can be identified by the mark of its consortium, which is stamped on each wheel. If the urge for truffles is there but the season has passed, drizzle the fonduta-topped polenta with white truffle oil (see Sources, page 372, for fresh truffles and truffle oil).

SERVES 8

½ recipe Polenta (page 371)
Extra-virgin olive oil for greasing the baking sheet
1½ pounds Fontina from Val d'Aosta, rind removed, cut into ¼-inch dice
2 cups whole milk
8 tablespoons (1 stick) unsalted butter
4 extra-large egg yolks
⅛ teaspoon freshly ground white pepper
2 tablespoons dry white wine (optional)
1 white truffle (optional)

Make the polenta according to instructions on page 371. Pour it while still hot onto an oiled 11 × 17-inch baking sheet, smooth with a rubber spatula, and cool until set. Cut into 3-inch triangles and set aside.

Meanwhile, place the diced Fontina in a bowl and pour on the milk; set aside at room temperature for 3 hours (or refrigerate for up to 24 hours).

Melt 2 tablespoons of the butter in a double boiler over medium heat, then whisk in the Fontina and milk; cook until the Fontina melts, about 10 minutes. Still whisking, beat in the egg yolks one at a time; the mixture should never come to a boil or it might curdle. After 3 minutes or so, the mixture will thicken. Beat in 2 tablespoons of the butter and season with the pepper. Keep warm over the lowest possible flame.

In a 12-inch skillet over medium-high heat, melt the remaining 4 tablespoons of butter until foaming. Add the reserved polenta triangles in a single layer and cook until golden and crisp on both sides, turning once, about 5 minutes per side. Divide among 8 plates.

If you are using the truffle, pour the wine on a towel and rub the truffle with it (this dislodges dirt and gives the truffle a subtle aroma). Serve the polenta hot, topped with the fonduta, shaving the truffle over it with a truffle slicer.

PREPARATION TIPS: The polenta can be cooked up to 2 days ahead, cooled, cut, and refrigerated until you are ready to fry it.

The Most and Least Exportable Specialties

Fontina, a versatile cow's milk cheese, is definitely Val d'Aosta's most exportable product. Made only from the milk of cows that have been fed fresh fodder, and aged up to four months in cellars dug in mountain rock, it derives its name not from the word *fondere* ("to melt") but rather from a grazing area known as Font, nestled between Quart and Nus. A staple in the region since the Middle Ages, it was described as "perfumed, buttery, rich, and easy to melt" in a treatise written in 1477. But if Fontina is the region's most exportable product, the honor of least exportable goes to Teutenne (also called Tetette or Tetin), a cured meat from Cogne. Historically scarce in Val d'Aosta, meat is treated with particular reverence, and no part of the animal is ever wasted—not even cows' udders. To make Teutenne, the udders are salted and marinated with sage and garlic, aged for twenty days, rinsed, and boiled. Teutenne is good, if bland, sliced paper-thin as an antipasto.

Frittelle di Fontina con Spinaci Stufati

Fontina Fritters with Wilted Spinach

When these crunchy, cheese-studded fritters are served without the accompanying spinach, they make perfect finger food for a cocktail party.

SERVES 4

3 tablespoons unsalted butter

1 pound spinach, stems on, washed thoroughly

1 teaspoon salt

¼ teaspoon freshly ground black pepper

1¼ cups fresh bread crumbs

¼ pound Fontina from Val d'Aosta, rind removed, cut into ⅛-inch dice

2 extra-large eggs

One 2-ounce slice Prosciutto Cotto, minced

2 tablespoons minced rosemary

2 tablespoons snipped chives

2 tablespoons minced basil

2 tablespoons minced Italian parsley

⅓ cup whole milk, plus extra if needed

3 tablespoons unbleached all-purpose flour, plus extra if needed

4 cups extra-virgin olive oil or peanut oil

Melt the butter over medium heat in a 12-inch sauté pan. Add the spinach, ½ teaspoon of the salt, and ⅛ teaspoon of the pepper. Cook over medium heat, covered, for 5 minutes. Uncover and cook 20 minutes more; keep warm.

Meanwhile, combine the bread crumbs, Fontina, eggs, Prosciutto, rosemary, chives, basil, parsley, milk, flour, and the remaining ½ teaspoon of salt and ⅛ teaspoon of pepper in a bowl with your hands. The mixture should hold together. If it is too dry, add a little more milk; if it is too sticky, add a little more flour. Shape with moistened hands into oval walnut-sized balls and spread out in a single layer on a floured tray.

Heat the oil in a deep 10-inch pan until it registers 350°F, or until it is hot enough to brown a cube of bread in 1 minute. Fry 6 ovals at a time until golden on both sides, turning once, about 2 minutes per side; remove with a slotted spoon to a platter lined with paper towels and blot dry. Continue in the same manner with the remaining ovals, maintaining the temperature of the oil by regulating the heat.

Mound the spinach on 4 plates, arrange the fritters around it, and serve hot.

Insalata di Lamponi con Polenta

Wine-Macerated Raspberries over Polenta

Unlike in nearby Piedmont, where pasta constitutes an important first course, in Val d'Aosta polenta and soup are predominant. Only in recent years have pasta and risotto become part of the local cooking tradition, introduced by Piedmontese merchants who settled in the valley after the Aosta-Turin railway was built. When polenta doesn't appear as a first course, it is served as a side dish to robust meat dishes. While it may sound oddly nouvelle, the recipe below is from the valley surrounding the town of Cogne: flavorful Alpine raspberries are plumped in red wine with sugar for hours, then served atop a steaming mound of polenta.

SERVES 6

2¼ pounds raspberries
½ cup sugar
1 cup dry red wine
1 recipe Polenta (page 371)
4 tablespoons (½ stick) unsalted butter
½ cup Mascarpone (preferably imported Italian)

Gently rinse the raspberries under a light spray of water, drain, and toss with the sugar and wine in a large bowl; set aside at room temperature for 2 hours.

One hour before serving, make the polenta according to instructions on page 371. When the polenta is ready, stir in the butter and Mascarpone, then mound on 6 plates. Top with the raspberries and their marinade and serve immediately.

A TYPICAL DAY IN PREWAR VAL D'AOSTA

Since cooking in Val d'Aosta is more about ingenuity and frugality than artistry and excess, typical family meals before World War II were simple affairs and did not start with an appetizer. If an antipasto was served, it usually consisted of dark bread with butter and honey, perhaps accompanied by a handful of boiled chestnuts and a few slices of cured meat. Lunch was a filling, nutritious one-dish meal, and dinner most often brought a bowl of soup followed by cheese with bread or potatoes. Desserts played a minor role, except on holidays and for celebrations, when prolific apple and pear orchards served as the basis for pies, cakes, and puddings. Today, family meals in Val d'Aosta follow the postwar Italian scheme: appetizer, first course, second course (almost always meat in Val d'Aosta), and fruit or dessert.

VAL D'AOSTA'S WINES

ESPITE ITS MOUNTAINOUS LANDSCAPE and thin layer of active soil, Val d'Aosta was already home to a number of fine wines by the early Middle Ages. The majority of vineyards are planted on either side of the Dora Baltea River and terraced into incredibly high slopes. The most important local grape varietals are Petit Rouge, Vien de Nus, and Blanc de Morgex. Yet as outstanding as some of Val d'Aosta's wines are, production is tiny and most wines are not exported to North America, with two notable exceptions: Chambave, a white with a straw-yellow color and intense aroma characteristic of Muscat, vinified in a dry and sweet raisined version; and Torrette, a dry, velvety red with hints of wild rose and a tendency to develop an almond aroma as it ages. If you visit Val d'Aosta, sample Donnas, a medium-bodied, perfumed Nebbiolo-based red; Blanc de Morgex, a white with a nuance of mountain herbs vinified at the foot of the Monte Bianco; Enfer d'Arvier, a pleasantly bitter, fruity red; and Nus Malvoisie Passito, a dried grape wine with a chestnut aftertaste.

Seuppa Valpellinentze

Cabbage and Whole Wheat Bread Soup from Valpelline

The Valdostani are so fond of soup that they are apt to recite the following proverb: "Sette cose fa la zuppa, cava fame e sete attuta, empie il ventre, netta il dente, fa dormire, fa smaltire, e la guancia fa arrossire." ("Soup does seven things, it calms hunger and quenches thirst, fills the belly, cleans the teeth, makes you sleep, makes you lean, and gives color to your cheek.") Originally conceived to serve as one-dish meals, Val d'Aosta's soups are now considered first courses. Most feature vegetables and rice or bread, like this recipe from Valpelline. To achieve the proper texture, dense country bread is a must; also important is resisting the temptation to drown the bread, cabbage, and Fontina in broth, since this is more of a thick bread porridge than a soup in the ordinary sense. This version is from Maurizio Grange, owner of Locanda La Clusaz in Gignod.*

SERVES 4

4 cups (1 quart) Beef Broth (page 368)

½ teaspoon salt

8 large Savoy cabbage leaves

5 ounces day-old whole wheat country bread, cut into ½-inch-thick slices

5 ounces day-old white country bread, cut into ½-inch-thick slices

¾ pound Fontina from Val d'Aosta, rind removed, thinly sliced

Pinch ground cinnamon

2 tablespoons (¼ stick) unsalted butter

Preheat the oven to 450°F.

Bring the broth to a boil in a medium pot and season with ¼ teaspoon of the salt. Add the cabbage leaves and cook 10 minutes. Remove with a slotted spoon to a plate (reserve the broth), cool, and cut into long, thin strips.

Meanwhile, spread out both types of bread in a single layer on an 11 × 17-inch baking sheet and toast in the preheated oven for 5 minutes, or until aromatic but not dry.

Line a shallow round 11-inch ovenproof dish with half of the slices of the whole wheat and white bread, breaking the bread as needed to fit. Top with half of the reserved cabbage and half of the Fontina, season with a pinch of salt, and repeat, making a second layer with the remaining bread, Fontina, and salt. Pour on the reserved broth, sprinkle with the cinnamon, and dot with the butter. Bake in the preheated oven for 20 minutes for a moist consistency or 30 minutes for a golden crust. Serve hot.

Seuppa de Cogne

Bread, Rice, and Fontina Soup from Cogne

This delicious soup—which in reality is more of a casserole—features both rice and whole wheat bread, two of Val d'Aosta's essential ingredients. Its success depends on the quality of the bread and Fontina: If the bread is fresh, it will fall apart in the liquid; and if the Fontina is anything but genuine, the soup will lack soul.

THE BREAD OF SUSTENANCE

The most typical bread of Val d'Aosta is round, barely yeasted, flat, and dry, baked twice or three times a year in the old days and meant for long keeping. Conceived to feed entire families, it is made of wheat or rye flour, perhaps with a few chestnuts thrown in for crunch and nutrition. Moistened in a bowl of broth, dipped into a rich sauce from braised meat, or slipped into a bowl of warm milk for breakfast, it remains the ultimate accompaniment to the cuisine of its native region.

SERVES 4

10 cups (2½ quarts) Beef Broth (page 368)
1⅓ cups Arborio rice
½ teaspoon salt
½ pound day-old whole wheat country bread, cut into 8 large but thin slices
½ pound Fontina from Val d'Aosta, rind removed, thinly sliced

Preheat the oven to 450°F.

Bring the broth to a boil in a medium pot and add the rice and salt. Cook over medium heat, uncovered and stirring often, until the rice is al dente, about 15 minutes; the rice will still be floating in broth. Strain the rice, reserving the broth.

Line a round 10-inch terra-cotta baking dish with 2 slices of the bread, breaking them as needed to fit. Top with one-quarter of the Fontina and spoon on one-quarter of the rice. Continue layering the ingredients, making 4 layers in all. Pour on the reserved broth and bake in the preheated oven for 15 minutes. Serve hot.

Costolette alla Valdostana
Fontina-Stuffed Breaded Veal Chops

Years ago in Val d'Aosta, meat was served before the soup course rather than following it like today. If the meat was not salted, smoked, or dried as a means to conserve it, it was cooked into hearty stews. Much more delicate—and recently conceived—than these robust braises are the Fontina-stuffed veal chops that appear on many Italian restaurant menus. If you feel like splurging, tuck a slice of white truffle along with the Fontina in the pocket of each chop: as the Fontina melts, the truffle lets out its inimitable aroma and the chop becomes a heavenly thing indeed.

SERVES 4

4 veal chops, bone in (1½ inches thick)
¼ pound Fontina from Val d'Aosta, rind removed, cut into 4 thin slices
½ teaspoon salt
¼ teaspoon freshly ground black pepper
½ cup unbleached all-purpose flour
1 extra-large egg, beaten
1 cup fresh bread crumbs
5 tablespoons unsalted butter

Cut a horizontal slit in each veal chop, leaving the meat attached at the bone end. Open the two flaps of each chop and place 1 slice of Fontina over the bottom flap of each chop; lay the top flap over the cheese to close. Using a meat mallet, pound each chop gently to seal the pocket. Season both sides with the salt and pepper.

Place the flour in one plate, the beaten egg in another, and the bread crumbs in a third. Dredge the veal chops in the flour and shake off the excess; dip into the beaten egg, coating both sides well; finally, dip into the bread crumbs, pressing on both sides to help them adhere.

Melt the butter in a 12-inch skillet over medium-high heat until foaming. Add the veal chops and cook until golden on both sides and still rosy inside, turning once; it should take about 5 minutes per side. Serve hot.

SWEETWATER AND SALTED FISH

Not surprisingly, given Val d'Aosta's high perch and distance from the sea, fish seldom appears on the Valdostano table. What few fish recipes there are make use of local sweetwater fish or preserved fish like cod. Typical recipes include fried trout doused with melted butter and salt cod baked with béchamel sauce and onions.

Cervo Brasato con la Grappa

Braised Venison in Creamy Grappa Sauce

Old Valdostano cookbooks offer directions for cooking game like mountain goat, bear, and marmot; one of the preferred treatments for these tougher animals is marinating the meat with onions, celery, carrots, and wine for up to a week before cooking it slowly until it becomes tender. The venison in the stew below is traditionally marinated for 3 days until it acquires the heady scent of wine and aromatic spices, then finished with a splash of cream and grappa. If time is a factor, marinating can be abbreviated, and you will still have a delicious stew. Browning the venison in olive oil is a recent adaptation; use butter for a more Alpine flavor.

Tie the parsley, bay leaves, cloves, thyme, cinnamon, and juniper berries in a piece of cheesecloth. Place in a large bowl, and add the venison, garlic, onion, carrot, celery, salt, pepper, and wine. Cover and refrigerate 3 days, tossing every 8 hours (or set aside at room temperature for 1 hour).

Remove the venison from the marinade and blot it dry on paper towels; reserve the marinade and the cheesecloth bundle. Heat the olive oil in a 14-inch sauté pan over a medium-high flame and cook the venison and any clinging vegetables until browned all over, turning to cook evenly, about 10 minutes total; you may need to do this in batches to avoid crowding the pan.

Deglaze with ½ cup of the grappa (be careful, as the grappa may flare up); when the grappa evaporates, after about 3 minutes, stir in the flour. Cook 5 minutes, stirring. Add

SERVES 6

1 bunch Italian parsley, stems included
2 bay leaves
4 cloves
1 thyme sprig
1 cinnamon stick
4 juniper berries
2 pounds boneless venison shank or
    shoulder, trimmed of fat and sinew,
    cut into 1-inch cubes
1 garlic clove, minced
1 onion, minced
1 carrot, minced
1 celery stalk, minced
1 teaspoon salt
¼ teaspoon freshly ground black pepper
2 cups full-bodied dry red wine
½ cup extra-virgin olive oil
¾ cup grappa or vodka
¼ cup unbleached all-purpose flour
4 plum tomatoes, peeled (see page 369),
    seeded, and diced
2 cups Beef Broth (page 368), plus extra if
    needed
½ cup heavy cream
1 recipe Polenta (page 371)
3 tablespoons unsalted butter
¼ cup freshly grated Parmigiano-Reggiano
6 rosemary sprigs

the reserved liquid from the marinade, the cheesecloth bundle, tomatoes, and broth. Bring to a boil, cover, and cook over medium-low heat for 2 hours, or until tender, adding broth if needed. Pour in the cream and the remaining ¼ cup of grappa; cook 5 minutes, uncovered. Discard the cheesecloth bundle.

Meanwhile, make the polenta according to instructions on page 371. When the polenta is ready, stir in the butter and Parmigiano. Serve the venison hot, mounded over the polenta and garnished with the rosemary.

PRESERVED MEAT, A WINTER STAPLE

AS IN ALL AGRICULTURAL SOCIETIES, farm animals in Val d'Aosta were only killed when they could no longer work or produce milk. The paucity of meat, combined with harsh, long winters, meant that this prized ingredient needed to be preserved for the cold season and gave rise to the salting of meat—usually beef, but sometimes goat or sheep. Meat was abundantly salted and stacked in wooden barrels with sage, rosemary, garlic, and spices for months, then boiled or roasted. Feast menus featured both a *bollito* and an *arrosto*, as an old saying implies: *"Bouli et routi, dou plat et la seuppa"* ("Boiled and roasted, two dishes and a soup"). Other ways of preserving meat called for covering it with a layer of soil or fat, or, especially in the case of pork, smoking it near the hearth.

Insalata Verde con Pancetta Affumicata

Young Greens in Warm Bacon Dressing

Similar to Savoie's bacon-topped green salads, this hearty dish is perfect for cold nights when the craving for something green and leafy strikes. Olive oil is a recent addition to the Valdostano larder; in the old days, walnut oil might have been used, as in bordering Piedmont.

4 cups young frisée lettuce, washed, dried, and torn into pieces
½ pound lean slab bacon, cut into ¼ × ¼ × 1-inch strips
Four ¼-inch-thick slices white country bread, cut into ¼-inch cubes
¼ cup red wine vinegar
½ cup extra-virgin olive oil
½ teaspoon salt
¼ teaspoon freshly ground black pepper
½ cup snipped chives

Divide the lettuce among 4 plates. Heat a 12-inch skillet over a medium-high flame; add the bacon and cook 3 minutes, or until golden. Add the bread cubes and cook 3 minutes, stirring, or until golden all over and crisp around the edges. Using a slotted spoon, remove the bacon and bread cubes and arrange on top of the lettuce.

Deglaze the skillet with the vinegar; bring to a boil and cook 1 minute, or until reduced by half, scraping the bottom of the skillet. Remove from the heat. Whisk in the olive oil, salt, and pepper (be careful of splattering). Pour over the salad, toss with the chives, and serve immediately.

THE THIRSTY CHESTNUT

A Valdostano proverb goes: *"Tsaque tsatagne, trei cou beire"* ("For every chestnut, three glasses"). Considering how many chestnuts the Valdostani eat, could there really be enough wine around to quench their thirst? The Valdostani serve boiled chestnuts with unsalted butter, lard from Saint Arnad, dried sausages, spiced Ricotta, and rye bread as an appetizer. Around the town of Arnad, a soup of milk, rice, and dried chestnuts is made on the day of the wheat threshing. In Issime and Gressoney, locals prepare soup with dried chestnuts, polenta, milk, bits of cheese, curls of butter, and crumbs of rye bread. And throughout the region, whole wheat and chestnut breads are common; in the town of Montjovet, chestnut loaves are shaped like a rooster.

MOUNTAIN MILK

LIKE MOST NORTHERN ITALIAN REGIONS, Val d'Aosta is primarily a land of cows. Artisanal dairies nestled in the mountains turn out some of Italy's greatest cow's milk cheeses; spring and summer milk, infused with the scent of the wild herbs and grasses that the cows munch on, makes the tastiest cheese of all. Fontina, a melting cheese with a smooth texture, straw-yellow color, compact flesh, and nutty flavor (page 7), is Val d'Aosta's most prized offering. Toma varieties, a family of cheeses with salty yellow flesh and a firm, thin yellow rind that darkens with age, call for raw or pasteurized milk. Somewhat smaller than Toma are Tomini—cylindrical white cheeses with a creamy texture and absence of rind—made of cow's milk or a combination of cow's and sheep's or goat's milk. Toma and Tomini are often drizzled with wine vinegar and flavored with garlic and chili. Fontina, Toma, and Tomini are available in stores across North America (see Sources, page 372).

Lou Mécoulen

Raisin-Studded Sweet Bread

This bread from Cogne is the Valdostano cousin of panettone. As good after a meal as it is dipped in sweet coffee for breakfast, it is rich, buttery, eggy, and oozing rum-soaked raisins. I tasted it in Cogne, a gorgeous little town surrounded by pristine mountains, where plump loaves are baked in old-fashioned wood-burning ovens.

SERVES 8

2⅔ cups golden raisins
½ cup rum
8¾ cups unbleached all-purpose flour,
    plus extra for the counter
1 tablespoon plus 1 teaspoon instant yeast
1⅓ cups sugar
¼ teaspoon salt
2 cups whole milk
⅓ cup heavy cream
4 extra-large eggs
8 tablespoons (1 stick) unsalted butter, cubed,
    at room temperature, plus extra for greasing
    the bowl and cake pan
Grated zest of 3 lemons

In a medium bowl, combine the raisins with the rum and allow to plump for 3 hours.

Meanwhile, combine 7 cups of the flour, the yeast, sugar, and salt in the bowl of an electric mixer. Heat the milk and cream to 110°F in a small pot; add to the flour mixture with the motor running, beating with the paddle attachment. Add the eggs, butter, and lemon zest. Continue to beat, adding as much flour as needed (about 1¼ cups) to form a soft dough that pulls away from the sides (not the bottom) of the bowl. Switch to the dough hook and beat 8 minutes, adding sprinkles of flour if needed.

Using a dough scraper, transfer to a lightly floured counter. Shape into a ball, lifting the dough from the counter with the help of the dough scraper; the dough will be sticky. Transfer to a buttered bowl and cover. Let rise at room temperature until doubled, about 3 hours.

Using a dough scraper, turn the risen dough out onto the counter. Work in the raisins and rum, adding as much flour as necessary (about ½ cup) to obtain a soft, slightly tacky dough that does not stick to the counter. Shape into a ball.

Generously butter an 8-inch springform cake pan with high sides. Place the ball of dough in it. Cover and let rise at room temperature until almost doubled, about 1½ hours.

Meanwhile, preheat the oven to 400°F.

Bake in the preheated oven for 1 hour, or until golden brown; it should sound hollow when thumped on the bottom. (If the top browns too much, cover with aluminum foil during the last 15 minutes.) Unmold and cool on a rack. Serve at room temperature.

PREPARATION TIPS: Let the dough rise in the refrigerator up to 24 hours; return to room temperature before shaping.

La Coppa dell'Amicizia
The Cup of Friendship

There is no better way to welcome a guest or demonstrate one's hospitality in Val d'Aosta than to pass a cup filled with grappa-spiked coffee around the table. A social ritual as much as an epicurean pleasure, the coppa is best sipped from a grolla, a many-spouted wooden cup made of apple or pear wood. Grolle can be purchased in most Valdostano shops, but a visit to the annual Fiera di Sant'Orso, held every January in Aosta, is your chance to see and buy some of the best in regional craftsmanship. If you don't like to share bacteria but would like to drink this bracing brew from a grolla rather than an espresso cup, you'll be happier with the single-spouted grolle now available in Val d'Aosta.

SERVES 8

1 cup brewed espresso
⅓ cup dry red wine
¼ cup grappa
⅓ cup sugar
1 strip lemon zest

Combine all the ingredients in a small pot and bring to a boil. Cook over medium heat 5 minutes, uncovered; discard the lemon zest. Remove from the heat and cool 5 minutes.

Pour into a grolla for convivial drinking Val d'Aosta-style, or ladle into 8 espresso cups. Serve hot.

MOUNTAIN DESSERTS

The simplest of Val d'Aosta's desserts take advantage of the region's famed apples: the fruit is cored, stuffed with raisins, and baked. Another sweet is *cretobleintze*: a mold is lined with rum-soaked ladyfingers, then filled with sweetened mashed potatoes. And then there are cookies called *tegole* ("roof tiles," because of their flattened, thin shape) made with ground almonds and hazelnuts, egg whites, sugar, and a whisper of flour.

DIGESTIVES AT THE FOOT OF THE GLACIERS

The most characteristic Valdostano digestive is génepy, infused with the scent of the flowers and berries that grow at the foot of imposing glaciers. Good génepy, aged for one and a half years, has a pleasantly bitter edge and decidedly herbal flavor, and is the perfect antidote to the rich mountain foods of Val d'Aosta.

Piedmont

Cipollata Rossa Monferrina
   Spicy Robiola Cheese and Scallion Spread

Peperoni Arrostiti con Bagna Caôda
   Roasted Peppers in Bagna Caôda

Crocchette di Crema Tartufata
   Custard Croquettes with White Truffles

Agnolotti ai Tre Stufati
   Three-Meat Agnolotti

Tajarin al Sugo d'Arrosto
   Egg Yolk Pasta in Veal Roast Sauce

Risotto al Barolo
   Risotto Cooked in Barolo

Trote all'Astigiana
   Baked Trout in Wine-Butter Sauce

Tasca Ripiena
   Salami-and-Scallion-Stuffed Veal

Brutti ma Buoni
   Almond Macaroons from Borgomanero

Budino Freddo Gianduja
   Decadent Hazelnut-Chocolate Pudding

Every Friday after school, my parents would load up our bright orange Volkswagen van and make the hour-long trip from our home in Milan to our country house on a hill above Lago Maggiore in Piedmont. I was two when my parents bought the land on which they built Il Poggio, as we call it, a simple white house with a brown roof and shutters and a view of Italy's largest lake after Lago di Garda.

Over the years, the house has become less simple; a second kitchen was added, a veranda erected, and a larger fireplace built. But the soul of Il Poggio remains the same, and the reason we still go there thirty years after its first brick was laid has not changed: it is a place away from the noise and bustle of the city, a place for pondering and gathering our thoughts, a place for feasting as a family.

The Italian name Piemonte means *a pie dei monti* ("at the foot of the mountains"), and indeed almost half of the region is covered in mountains: the Alps in the north and west and the Apennines in the south. Another third is hilly, planted mostly in vines, leaving a mere fifth of the land flat. Snow-topped mountains, sinuous hills, and verdant valleys each bring their own ingredients to the table, so that in reality there are three distinct Piedmontese cuisines. There is the cooking of the mountains, whose lakes offer a bounty of trout, perch, whitefish, and pike and whose climate is ideal for curing ham and aging cheese. There is the cooking of the vineyard-covered hills, where Piedmont's noblest ingredient grows: the precious *Tuber magnatum* Pico, or white truffle, essential to many Piedmontese recipes. And there is the cooking of the flatlands, where corn fields and rice paddies form the basis of a polenta and rice cuisine that is second to none.

Piedmont was already important in Roman times as a thoroughfare between Italy and the provinces of Gaul beyond the Alps; since then, the region has seen the passage of many foreign peoples, each leaving an imprint on its cuisine. Years under Lombard and Frankish rule gave Piedmont a taste for pork, sausages, cabbage, and boiled meat. Under the Savoy family, who dominated Piedmont and French Savoie, the Piedmontese became even more prosperous; the situation only improved when Turin became Italy's first capital after unification in 1861.

The link between French and Piedmontese cuisine has often been emphasized. Piedmont did belong to France from 1798 to 1814, and the nobility and politicians who led Italy's unification movement spoke French. But most Piedmontese cooking owes little to French tradition. It is only in a handful of its feast dishes, developed in the Middle Ages and Renaissance and served at important banquets—a few galantines, terrines, pastries, and sweets—that the French connection is felt.

Food in Piedmont is taken very seriously. Meals often begin with as many as four antipasti, proceed to a sumptuous first course—perhaps handmade stuffed pasta napped in ragù or risotto laced with truffles or beans—move on to a roast or stew or, if meat isn't on the menu, poached sweetwater fish in a buttery sauce, and culminate in a deliriously rich pastry or cake. In Piedmont, the cheeses are among the best in Italy, the wines among the best in the world, and there is a no-holds-barred approach to good eating.

Favorite Restaurants, Shops, and Places

- AL SORRISO, Via Roma 18, Soriso (30 miles from Novara), 0322.983228. If you can get into this exclusive culinary shrine, order the tasting menu.
- CAMBIO, Piazza Carignano 2, Turin, 011.546690. The historical restaurant where Camillo Cavour and his men discussed the future of a unified Italy.
- DEI CACCIATORI DA CESARE, Alberetto della Torre, 0173.520141. Master chef Cesare Giaccone makes vinegars from top Piedmontese wines.
- GENER NUEV, Lungotanaro Pescatori 4, Asti, 0141.557270. Try *risotto al Barolo* and *agnolotti con il plin.*

- GUFFANTI LUIGI, Via Milano 140, Arona, 0322.242038. Guffanti is one of Italy's foremost cheese experts.
- PASTICCERIA GIORDANINO, Corso Alfieri 254, Asti, 0141.53802. Buy the Moscato-laced panettone, called *monfrin.*
- SANDRINO TARTUFI, Piazza Campo del Palio, Asti, 0141.351051 or 0141.556911. Sandrino and his dog Birba find the Monferrato's best white truffles.

Telephone country code: 011.39

Cipollata Rossa Monferrina

Spicy Robiola Cheese and Scallion Spread

The pungent flavor of the spices in this creamy spread is softened by the delicate taste of Robiola. In Piedmont, cipollata is made with any one of a dozen young farmhouse Robiole or Tome available. Yet in North America, we have easy access to only one sort of fresh Robiola, that sold in plastic wrapping, usually under the Osella brand. But don't despair: cipollata is still delicious made with commercial Robiola. Although in Piedmont the pepper is not roasted before being puréed in the cipollata, I prefer the smokiness lent by roasting.

SERVES 6

1 red bell pepper, halved and seeded
2 scallions, white parts only, chopped
Pinch cayenne pepper
1 tablespoon sweet paprika
1½ tablespoons fresh lemon juice (from ½ lemon)
¼ cup plus 2 tablespoons extra-virgin olive oil
¼ teaspoon salt
½ pound fresh Robiola
Twelve ½-inch-thick slices country bread

Preheat the broiler.

Place the pepper, cut side down, on an aluminum foil–lined baking sheet. Broil in the preheated oven until the skin is blistered and blackened, about 15 minutes. Remove from the oven, wrap in the foil, and set aside 15 minutes. Unwrap, peel, and chop coarsely.

Place the roasted pepper, scallions, cayenne, paprika, lemon juice, 2 tablespoons of the olive oil, and the salt in a food processor. Process to a smooth paste. Add the Robiola and process again until smooth. Turn out into a bowl and refrigerate for 2 to 12 hours. This is the cipollata.

Heat a grill pan for 5 minutes over a high flame. Grill the bread until golden brown on both sides, turning once, about 2 minutes per side. Brush with the remaining ¼ cup of olive oil and serve with the cipollata.

THE LITTLE MONARCH'S BREADSTICKS

Grissini, Piedmont's beloved breadsticks, were born in 1679 when Turinese baker Antonio Brunero was asked by the court doctor to prepare a "long, thin, and crispy" bread for a little monarch, Duke Vittorio Amedeo of Savoy, who was ill and had no appetite. The best grissini are irregular, shaped by hand, and made only with flour, water, salt, and yeast.

Peperoni Arrostiti con Bagna Caôda

Roasted Peppers in Bagna Caôda

The warm garlic and anchovy sauce poured over roasted peppers in Piedmont is called bagna caôda, *meaning "hot bath." The Piedmontese are fond of calling their aromatic sauces by endearing names, such as bagnet verde and bagnet rosso (bagnet means "little bath"). Even though Piedmont is too cold for olive trees, olive oil is used in a number of typical recipes, since it was traded for wine with nearby Liguria; historically, however, walnut oil was used in place of olive oil in bagna caôda and other dishes. At its most expressive, bagna caôda calls for an assortment of raw and cooked vegetables: boiled potatoes, cardoons, fennel, celery, and roasted peppers. Born as a midmorning snack and communal meal for farmhands working in the vineyards, the dish has become a year-round favorite; and during truffle season, it is showered with shaved white truffles.*

SERVES 6

3 yellow bell peppers, halved and seeded
3 red bell peppers, halved and seeded
½ teaspoon salt
12 thin slices tomato (optional)
18 anchovy fillets, 6 halved lengthwise, 12 finely chopped
10 garlic cloves, 4 cut into 6 slices each, 6 minced
14 tablespoons unsalted butter
½ cup plus 2 tablespoons extra-virgin olive oil

Preheat the broiler.

Place the peppers, cut side down, on an aluminum foil–lined baking sheet. Broil until the skin is blackened and blistered, about 15 minutes. Remove from the oven, wrap in the foil, and cool to room temperature. Unwrap, then slip off the peel, trying to keep each pepper half intact.

Place 2 roasted pepper halves, one of each color, on each of 6 plates. Season with the salt and top each pepper half with 1 slice of tomato if using, half of an anchovy fillet, and 2 slices of garlic. Set aside.

Heat the butter, olive oil, and minced garlic in a small skillet over a medium-low flame until the butter melts, being careful not to let the garlic take on any color, about 5 minutes. Stir in the chopped anchovies and cook, stirring, until the anchovies dissolve and the mixture smells less pungent, about 15 minutes. Pour over the roasted pepper halves and serve immediately.

Crocchette di Crema Tartufata

Custard Croquettes with White Truffles

In Piedmont, the Marches, and Emilia-Romagna, it is customary to serve croquettes or diamond-shaped strips of fried custard alongside fried meats and vegetables as part of a fritto misto. The fried custard in Piedmont is especially enticing, since it is embellished with shaved white truffles. But even in the absence of truffles—they are a seasonal treat and a costly one—these croquettes are definitely worth trying. See Sources (page 372) to buy truffles and truffle products.

½ cup plus 1 tablespoon unbleached all-purpose flour

¼ cup semolina flour

½ cup freshly grated Parmigiano-Reggiano

⅛ teaspoon freshly grated nutmeg

½ teaspoon salt

⅛ teaspoon freshly ground white pepper

4 extra-large eggs

1 extra-large egg yolk

1½ cups whole milk

⅓ cup heavy cream

6 tablespoons (¾ stick) unsalted butter, cubed, at room temperature

2 ounces Gruyère, rind removed, coarsely grated

1 white truffle, shaved, or 2 tablespoons white truffle paste

4 cups extra-virgin olive oil or peanut oil, plus extra for greasing the plate

3 cups fresh bread crumbs

Mix the all-purpose flour, semolina flour, Parmigiano, nutmeg, salt, and pepper in a heavy-bottomed 2-quart pot. Stir in the eggs and egg yolk with a fork, then beat in the milk and cream with a whisk until smooth.

Cook over medium heat, whisking constantly, until the mixture thickens, about 15 minutes; don't allow the mixture to boil or it might curdle. Whisk in the butter. Strain through a sieve into a clean bowl and fold in the grated Gruyère and shaved truffle or paste. Spread out onto an oiled 14-inch plate and refrigerate for 6 to 24 hours; it should be quite firm.

Pour the bread crumbs on a plate. Heat the oil in a deep 10-inch pan until it registers 350°F, or is hot enough to brown a cube of bread in 1 minute. Using 2 spoons, roll a teaspoon of the mixture in the bread crumbs to coat on all sides; drop into the hot oil. Work in batches, shaping and frying 5 spoonfuls of the mixture at a time. Fry until golden brown on both sides, turning once, about 3 minutes. Remove with a slotted spoon to a plate lined with paper towels and blot dry. Continue in the same manner with the remaining mixture, maintaining the temperature of the oil by regulating the heat, and serve hot.

The White Gem of Piedmont

Every year, thousands of visitors flock to Piedmont for a taste of *Tuber magnatum* Pico, a fragrant fungus that grows spontaneously at the base of hazelnut and oak trees. Truffles have been known since antiquity and praised for their purported aphrodisiac properties for centuries, so it may not be just their exorbitant cost (approximately $1,500 per pound) that makes people's hearts race and palms sweat when they are in the presence of white truffles. Truffles first became international stars when the Savoys sent them to the King of France in the 1700s, and later to the Viennese monarchy, as a gift. The best white truffles in the world are said to be from Alba, in the Langhe area of Piedmont (although the Marchigiani might disagree, see pages 190–191), and it is here that truffle cuisine reaches its zenith. *Tuber magnatum* Pico season is from October through December, so if you're considering a trip to Piedmont, plan accordingly. And remember what Alexandre Dumas said of truffles: "They can, on certain occasions, make women more tender and men more lovable."

The Mother of all Feasts

If you have to attend only one festival in Piedmont, let it be the Festa delle Sagre in Asti, a celebration of the peasant traditions and culinary specialties of the languid hills of Monferrato. Thousands of volunteers from forty-one towns in the province of Asti join forces, proudly displaying banners with the names of their towns emblazoned on them, slipping effortlessly into their roles as farmers, carpenters, and laundresses, shedding cellular phones and jewelry in favor of drab dresses, torn jackets, and Sunday-best hats to take part in the festival's procession. Floats and wagons are decorated to evoke the atmosphere of prewar Piedmont, and gargantuan amounts of food are cooked for the two hundred thousand visitors. The Festa delle Sagre is usually held on the second Sunday of September, one week before the city's famed Palio; call 011.39.0141.530537 for more information.

Agnolotti ai Tre Stufati

Three-Meat Agnolotti

The Piedmontese only started eating significant quantities of dried pasta in the postwar boom—thanks to southern Italians who brought their culinary traditions north—so fresh pasta, polenta, and rice remain the first courses of choice. The most distinguished filled pasta is *agnolotti del plin*, made in the Langhe and Asti and named after the plin ("pinch") used to pleat the pasta and seal in the stuffing. *Agnolotti del plin* feature myriad fillings—spinach and Ricotta, melted Fontina, or braised meat—and can be boiled in water, broth, or a combination of Barolo and broth. The recipe that follows is from Ristorante Gener Neuv in Asti; the filling consists of veal, pork, and rabbit, with Savoy cabbage added for depth.

THE HUNTER'S SAUSAGES

Piedmont produces a vast array of cured meats, including a curious one dubbed Bale d'Aso ("donkey's balls," because of its shape, not its composition!), yet they are not available on North American soil. The closest one can get to purchasing Piedmontese salami is to buy the Cacciatorini ("little hunter's sausages") made in North America to emulate the small pork salami conceived as a portable snack for hunters.

SERVES 6

For the filling:
¼ cup extra-virgin olive oil
½ medium yellow onion, minced
1 garlic clove, minced
1 rosemary sprig, leaves only, minced
1 bay leaf
¼ pound boneless pork shoulder, in 1 piece
¼ pound boneless veal shoulder, in 1 piece
¼ pound boneless saddle of rabbit, in 1 piece
12 Savoy cabbage leaves, cut into thin strips
½ cup Chicken Broth or Beef Broth (page 368)
2 extra-large eggs
⅓ cup freshly grated Parmigiano-Reggiano
½ teaspoon salt
⅛ teaspoon freshly ground black pepper
⅛ teaspoon freshly grated nutmeg

For the dough:
1½ cups unbleached all-purpose flour,
    plus extra for the counter
¼ teaspoon salt
2 extra-large eggs
1 tablespoon extra-virgin olive oil

To cook and serve:
2 tablespoons salt
8 tablespoons (1 stick) unsalted butter
8 sage leaves
½ cup freshly grated Parmigiano-Reggiano

NOBLE CANNELLONI

Cannelloni alla Barbaroux are one of Piedmont's most elaborate first courses, created by Count Giuseppe Barbaroux, jurist and aide to King Carlo Alberto, in the nineteenth century. Crêpes are rolled around ground veal flavored with rosemary, sage, Prosciutto, and white wine, then swathed with besciamella (béchamel sauce) and baked until bubbling.

Make the filling: Heat the olive oil in an 8-inch sauté pan over a medium-high flame. Add the onion, garlic, rosemary, and bay leaf and cook 3 minutes. Add the pork, veal, and rabbit and cook until lightly browned on all sides, turning often, about 10 minutes. Stir in the cabbage and cook 5 minutes.

Add the broth, cover, and cook over medium-low heat for 1½ hours, or until the meats are tender.

Uncover, discard the bay leaf, and cool to room temperature. Transfer to a food processor and pulse to a chunky paste. Transfer to a large mixing bowl and stir in the eggs, Parmigiano, salt, pepper, and nutmeg.

Make the dough according to instructions on page 370 using the ingredients listed above, adding a little water if the dough is dry or a little flour if it is sticky. Knead 5 minutes, or until smooth, shape into a ball, wrap, and let rest 30 minutes.

Cut the dough into 2 pieces. Working with 1 piece at a time and keeping the other covered, roll out each piece into a nearly transparent sheet with a pasta machine. Working on the bottom half of each sheet, and starting ½ inch from the edge, place teaspoons of the filling 2 inches apart. Flip the top half of the sheet over to enclose the filling. Press with your hands between the mounds of filling to squeeze out any air pockets. Cut into 2-inch squares with a pastry wheel. Repeat with the other piece of dough. These are the agnolotti. Spread out in a single layer on a floured tray; cover with a towel.

To cook, bring 4 quarts of water to a gentle boil and add the agnolotti and the 2 table-spoons of salt. Cook until al dente, about 3 minutes, then remove with a slotted spoon to a serving platter.

Meanwhile, melt the butter with the sage in a 12-inch skillet until it is foaming. Add the agnolotti and sauté 1 minute. Serve hot, passing the Parmigiano at the table.

PREPARATION TIPS: Make the agnolotti up to 4 hours ahead, spread out in a single layer on a floured tray, and refrigerate, covered with a towel.

Tajarin al Sugo d'Arrosto
Egg Yolk Pasta in Veal Roast Sauce

In Piedmont, the leftover juices from roasted veal are married with thin, fresh egg noodles called tajarin (dialect for taglierini). Tajarin can be made following the usual flour-to-egg ratio of 100 grams (3½ ounces) of flour per egg. But when a Piedmontese cook is especially adept at making pasta, he or she may increase the number of eggs used or, best of all, add only egg yolks to the flour. Whenever you roast veal, chicken, or beef, freeze any excess pan juices; you will need about 1 cup of pan juices per pound of pasta.

Make the tajarin according to instructions on page 370 using the ingredients listed above, adding a little water if the dough is dry or a little flour if it is sticky. Knead 5 minutes, or until smooth, shape into a ball, wrap, and let rest 30 minutes.

Cut the dough into 4 pieces. Working with 1 piece at a time and keeping the others covered, roll out each piece using a pasta machine into a nearly transparent sheet. Cut each sheet into 8-inch-long rectangles. Lay the rectangles out on a floured counter to dry, uncovered, for 15 minutes. Using a taglierini attachment (about 1⁄12-inch wide), cut each rectangle into taglierini. (To cut by hand, dust each rectangle with flour, roll lengthwise, and cut into 1⁄12-inch strips using a sharp chef's knife.) Toss with flour to prevent sticking. Spread out in a single layer on a floured tray and cover with a towel.

To cook, bring 5 quarts of water to a boil. Add the tajarin and the 2 tablespoons of salt and cook until al dente, about 1 minute; drain.

Meanwhile, reduce the juices from the veal roast in a small pan to ¾ cup, about 3 minutes over medium-high heat. Toss with the cooked tajarin, butter, Parmigiano, and pepper in a platter and serve immediately, passing more Parmigiano at the table.

PREPARATION TIPS: The tajarin can be made up to 24 hours ahead, spread out in a single layer on a floured tray, and refrigerated, covered with a towel.

SERVES 6

For the tajarin:
3¼ cups unbleached all-purpose flour, plus extra for the counter
¼ teaspoon salt
16 extra-large egg yolks

To cook and for the sauce:
2 tablespoons salt
1 cup pan juices from Veal Roast Stuffed with Spinach, Pancetta, and Frittata (page 146) or other roast meat (substitute store-bought demi-glace)
4 tablespoons (½ stick) unsalted butter, cubed, at room temperature
½ cup freshly grated Parmigiano-Reggiano, plus extra for passing at the table
½ teaspoon freshly ground black pepper

Risotto al Barolo

Risotto Cooked in Barolo

Piedmont is the most important rice-producing region in Italy: every year, the rice harvest surpasses 1.3 billion pounds. The Piedmontese cook rice hundreds of ways: in paniscia, *a Novarese specialty featuring cranberry beans, Savoy cabbage, carrots, celery, tomatoes, lard, pork rind, Salami della Duja, and red wine; in* panissa, *a similar dish from Vercelli that calls for cranberry beans, pork rind, lard, Pancetta, and red wine;* alla finanziera, *with cockscombs, sweetbreads, veal marrow, and more; and with frogs, tripe, or all manner of seasonal vegetables. Giuseppina Bagliardi and her husband, Piero Fassi, owners of Gener Neuv in Asti, offered this recipe for risotto laced with Barolo, Piedmont's noble red wine. Bagliardi uses a short-grain rice variety called Carnaroli rather than the common Arborio because Carnaroli is more resistant to overcooking and has a toothier consistency even after it has absorbed plenty of broth.*

SERVES 4

¼ cup extra-virgin olive oil
3 shallots, minced
1½ cups Carnaroli rice
1½ cups Barolo
6 cups (1½ quarts) Chicken Broth or Beef Broth (page 368)
3 tablespoons unsalted butter, cubed, at room temperature
1 cup freshly grated Parmigiano-Reggiano
½ teaspoon salt

Heat the olive oil in an 8-inch sauté pan over a medium-high flame. Add the shallots and cook until wilted, about 5 minutes. Add the rice and cook, stirring with a wooden spoon, for 3 minutes. Add the Barolo and cook until it is absorbed by the rice, about 10 minutes, stirring constantly.

Meanwhile, heat the broth to just below the boiling point in a medium pot. When the Barolo has been absorbed by the rice, add the broth by the ½ cup, stirring constantly. Add more broth only when the previous addition has been incorporated. Cook in this manner, stirring and adding broth by the ½ cup, for 15 to 18 minutes, or until the rice is al dente. You may not need all the broth.

Remove the pan from the heat. Stir in the butter, Parmigiano, and salt, and serve hot.

PIEDMONT'S WINES

THE GREEKS WERE THE FIRST to plant vines in Piedmont, and by the time the Romans settled, the art of winemaking had become firmly anchored in local custom. Piedmontese wine was so good that historians have postulated that the Gauls invaded the region just to get their hands on its wine. In 1303, the first reference was made to "*una carrata de bono puro vino Nebiolo*" ("one barrel of pure Nebbiolo wine") in Canale d'Alba.

Nebbiolo remains Piedmont's most important grape varietal, and is the basis for twelve of the region's DOC and DOCG wines, big reds that include Barolo and Barbaresco. Its name is derived from the *nebbia,* or "fog," that Piedmont is blanketed with when grapes are picked for wine. Barbera and Dolcetto are Piedmont's other important red-wine varietals. Barolo, a rich, robust red, is the most potent and intense expression of Nebbiolo; it offers pronounced tannins and acidity, and is best aged five to eight years and aerated two hours before serving. The noblest red of the region is Barbaresco, dry, fleshy, intense, and austere yet velvety and slightly less muscular than Barolo. Barbera, a full-bodied, zesty, ruby red with low tannins, is better from Alba and aged two to three years.

Other great Piedmontese reds are strawberry-colored, low-acidity Brachetto d'Acqui, either fizzy or still; berry-scented, lightly tannic Freisa, vinified dry, sweet, and sparkling; high-acidity Grignolino, meant to be savored young; and Roero, from the left bank of the Tanaro River, better sipped young.

The region's reputation is built on big, bold reds, but Piedmont offers a number of outstanding whites: dry, almond-scented Arneis; world-famous sweet, aromatic Asti Spumante, produced by the Charmat method of fermentation, with a crisp acidity and ripe flavor of Muscat; fruity, perfumed, Cortese-based Gavi; and Moscato d'Asti, a slightly fizzy sweet wine made from Moscato grapes. Today, nearly 80 percent of Piedmont's wines fall under DOC designation.

Trote all'Astigiana

Baked Trout in Wine-Butter Sauce

Fish is treated simply in Piedmont: plucked fresh from clear mountain lakes and rivers, it comes to the table in a cloak of melted butter and lemon after a dip in hot oil or a moment in the oven. After all, the Piedmontese are devoted carnivores: they would rather spend hours slowly braising meat to tease out every last bit of flavor than concoct complicated fish recipes. Trout is especially popular on Piedmontese tables; served cold in a vinegary marinade, poached with raisins and celery, or stuffed with herbs and butter and baked, as below, it makes a splendid main course.

SERVES 4

4 small rainbow trout (¾ pound each), scaled, slit, and gutted
½ teaspoon salt
¼ teaspoon freshly ground black pepper
4 bay leaves
4 sage leaves
4 rosemary sprigs
6 tablespoons (¾ stick) unsalted butter
1½ cups dry white wine
Zest of 1 lemon, julienned

Preheat the oven to 400°F.

Rinse the trout and blot it dry. Rub the insides with ¼ teaspoon of the salt and ⅛ teaspoon of the pepper. Tuck 1 bay leaf, 1 sage leaf, 1 rosemary sprig, and ½ tablespoon of the butter in the cavity of each trout. Place in a single layer in a 14-inch stove-to-oven sauté pan. Season with the remaining ¼ teaspoon of salt and ⅛ teaspoon of pepper, pour on the wine, and sprinkle with the lemon zest. Top each trout with ½ tablespoon of the butter.

Place the pan over medium-high heat on the stove. As soon as the liquid in the pan comes to a boil, slip the pan into the preheated oven. Bake for 15 minutes, or until the trout are done (they should feel firm to the touch). Using 2 large spatulas, transfer the trout to a platter. Place the pan on the stove over medium-high heat and cook until the sauce thickens, about 5 minutes. Whisk in the remaining 2 tablespoons of butter, pour over the trout, and serve hot.

AN ITALIAN INSTITUTION

Every northern Italian region offers its version of bollito misto, a variety of boiled meats cooked for cold-weather indulgence. In Piedmont, bollito misto comprises seven cuts of veal plus seven ornamental meats (oxtail, beef tongue, calf's head, calf's foot, stewing hen, Cotechino sausage, and *polpettone,* or meat loaf) that are cooked until fork-tender.

Tasca Ripiena

Salami-and-Scallion-Stuffed Veal

*I*n this specialty of Monferrato—quite similar to Liguria's cima alla genovese—veal is butterflied and stuffed with a forcemeat, then tied and poached. This dish belongs to the aristocratic family of galantines.

In a food processor, process the ground veal, salami, scallions, Parmigiano, parsley, sage, garlic, egg, and ¼ teaspoon of the pepper until nearly smooth. Place the butterflied veal on a counter, smooth side down, and spread the ground veal mixture over it. Roll up jelly roll–style, tie with butcher's string, and wrap in cheesecloth, tying both ends with string.

Bring the broth to a gentle boil in a shallow, long 12-quart pot (a fish poacher is ideal). Add the veal; cook over medium-low heat for 2½ hours, covered, turning every 30 minutes. Remove from the heat, weigh the veal with 2 plates to keep it submerged, and cool to room temperature (this ensures tenderness). Remove the veal from the liquid and unwrap it. Cut into ½-inch-thick slices. Fan out the slices on a platter. Season with the salt and the remaining ¼ teaspoon of the pepper, and drizzle with the olive oil. Serve at room temperature.

SERVES 10

½ pound ground veal
½ pound mild salami, such as Genoa, thickly sliced and cut into ½-inch dice
8 scallions, white parts only, chopped
1 cup freshly grated Parmigiano-Reggiano
¼ cup Italian parsley leaves
10 sage leaves
4 garlic cloves, peeled
1 extra-large egg
½ teaspoon freshly ground black pepper
1½ pounds boneless veal top round, butterflied and pounded thin with a mallet
32 cups (8 quarts) Vegetable Broth (see box) or Chicken Broth (page 368)
½ teaspoon salt
½ cup extra-virgin olive oil

MAKING YOUR OWN VEGETABLE BROTH

Any mild, fresh vegetables can be used to make this all-purpose broth; avoid strong vegetables like turnip, cabbage, broccoli, and cauliflower. In a large pot, combine 1 yellow onion, quartered; 2 carrots, chopped; 1 celery stalk, chopped; 1 leek, halved and rinsed; 1 fennel bulb, quartered, with the stalks and fronds attached; 1 head of garlic, crushed; 1 bunch of Italian parsley, with the stems on; 8 thyme sprigs; 2 bay leaves, 1 teaspoon of black peppercorns; and 10 cups of water. Bring to a gentle boil and cook over medium-low heat, uncovered, for 1 hour. Strain through a cheesecloth-lined colander and discard the solids. Refrigerate for up to 5 days or freeze for up to 2 months. Yields 2 quarts.

Brutti ma Buoni

Almond Macaroons from Borgomanero

Ugly but good *is the literal translation of* brutti ma buoni, *homely almond maca-roons from the town of Borgomanero, near Lago Maggiore. The batter includes cinnamon and vanilla extract for aroma and is dried on the stove over low heat before baking, resulting in crispy rather than soft cookies.*

MAKES 36

2¼ cups blanched almonds
1 cup plus 1 tablespoon sugar
½ cup egg whites (about 3 large egg whites)
Pinch ground cinnamon
½ teaspoon vanilla extract
Unsalted butter for greasing the baking sheet

Preheat the oven to 375°F.

Spread out the almonds on an 11 × 17-inch baking sheet. Toast in the preheated oven for 12 minutes, or until fragrant and golden. Cool to room temperature.

Reduce the oven temperature to 275°F.

Grind the toasted almonds and sugar to a fine powder in a food processor. In an electric mixer, beat the egg whites with a whisk attachment until soft peaks form, then fold in the almond-sugar mixture, cinnamon, and vanilla with a rubber spatula. Transfer the batter to a heavy 2-quart pot and cook over low heat for 25 minutes, stirring every few minutes.

Butter the baking sheet. Using 2 spoons, transfer heaping teaspoons of the batter onto the prepared baking sheet, spacing the mounds about 1 inch apart. Bake in the 275°F oven for 45 minutes. Cool on racks and serve at room temperature.

PREPARATION TIPS: The cookies keep in airtight tins for up to 1 week.

A ONE-TON POLENTA

To know just how dearly the Piedmontese love their polenta, consider the annual festival in Monastero Bormida, in the province of Asti: for the last 175 years, a polenta weighing one ton has been prepared and garnished with 1,100 pounds of sausages, salami, Cotechino, and cod, and with a frittata weighing 90 pounds. The *festa* recalls the generosity of the Marquis Della Rovere, who, in a year of famine, fed polenta and frittata to a group of snow-blocked coppersmiths.

ESSENTIAL PIEDMONTESE CHEESES

PIEDMONT IS A PLAYGROUND for the palate when it comes to cheese. The region offers dozens of cheeses, mostly made from cow's milk or a combination of cow's, sheep's, and goat's milk. All of the following Piedmontese cheeses are available in North America (see Sources, page 372).

BETTELMATT, a cow's milk mountain cheese made from July to September, when cows graze on fresh fodder at an altitude of 6,000 feet near the Alpine town of Bettelmatt, resembles Fontina; it has a deep yellow flesh and thick gray rind, and is aged from forty days to a year.

BLU DEL MONCENISIO, a creamy, compact, large-holed blue cheese, is also made from cow's milk.

BRA is named after the city where its production is centralized; made from cow's milk (sometimes with the addition of sheep's or goat's milk), the cheese is aged from forty-five days to six months, sports a gray rind, and ranges from soft and milky to sharp and firm.

BROSS, a cow's milk cheese fermented with butter and grappa, génepy, or white wine, is so pungent that a Piedmontese saying attests: *"Mac l'amor a l'é pi fòrt che 'l Bros"* ("Only love is stronger than Bross").

CAPRINO, made of goat's milk, is typically sold fresh and meant for the grill.

CASTELMAGNO, among Italy's most ancient cheeses, is aged up to six months in caves and made from cow's milk (although sheep's or goat's milk can be added); it sports bluish streaks when mature and melts beautifully.

MACCAGNO, made of cow's milk, is pressed, salted, and aged under a layer of herbs to acquire a distinctive flavor. Magnun, a cow's milk cheese with a firm, compact texture and buttery flavor, is similar to Castelmagno.

RASCHERA is made from partly skimmed cow's milk with the possible addition of goat's or sheep's milk; aged at least one month, it is firm yet elastic, with a thin grayish-red rind, and is sometimes pressed under wood to acquire a square shape.

REBLOCHON, a full-fat cow's milk cheese, is rubbed with flour as it ages. Unfortunately, only French Reblochon from Savoie is exported to North America.

SEIRASS, a Piedmontese Ricotta, derives its name from *siero*, meaning "whey," since Ricotta is a whey cheese.

ROBIOLA describes a family of Piedmontese cheeses. Depending on where it is made, how long it is aged, and what type of milk is used, it has widely different characteristics: Sheep's milk Robiola has a reddish rind when aged; Robiola del Bec, increasingly rare, is best made from the milk of goats that have been "unmated" for a year before meeting their *becco* ("male goat"); Murazzano, a soft, white, rindless sheep's milk Robiola, can contain up to 40 percent cow's milk and is aged from four to ten days; and Robiola di Roccaverano, made near Asti from cow's, sheep's, and goat's milk, is aged only a few days and often conserved in olive oil.

TOMA, another family of Piedmontese cheeses, is aged from three to eighteen months and has a milky aroma, firm, compact flesh, and thin, yellowish rind.

Budino Freddo Gianduja

Decadent Hazelnut-Chocolate Pudding

The hills surrounding the town of Alba are known as the Langhe, and their outstanding crop of hazelnuts forms the basis for Turin's gianduja, a delicious hazelnut chocolate, and numerous hazelnut desserts. The rich hazelnut-chocolate pudding below calls for raw eggs; if you are concerned about salmonella in raw eggs, separate the whole egg, then heat the 2 egg yolks to 140°F and maintain them at that temperature for 5 minutes, and heat the egg white to 160°F to instant-kill bacteria.

SERVES 6

¼ cup hazelnuts
1 cup whipping cream
⅔ cup plus ¼ cup sugar
1 extra-large egg
1 extra-large egg yolk
¾ cup unsweetened cocoa, sifted
6 butter cookies, crumbled

Preheat the oven to 375°F.

Spread out the hazelnuts on an 11 × 17-inch baking sheet; toast in the preheated oven 12 minutes, or until fragrant and golden. Rub in a kitchen towel to peel, then chop coarsely.

In an electric mixer, beat the cream with a whisk attachment until soft peaks form; add ¼ cup of the sugar and beat until stiff peaks form. Transfer to a bowl.

Clean the mixer bowl and the whisk. Beat the egg, egg yolk, and the remaining ⅔ cup of sugar for 5 minutes, or until thick and pale. Beat in the cocoa; the mixture will be very thick. Using a rubber spatula, fold in the chopped hazelnuts, crumbled cookies, and all but ½ cup of the whipped cream. Spoon into six 6-ounce ramekins. Refrigerate for 2 to 24 hours.

Top the ramekins with the remaining ½ cup of whipped cream, piping it through a pastry bag fitted with a fluted tip, and serve.

THE ITALIAN CAPITAL OF CHOCOLATE

Belgium and Switzerland have nothing over Italy when it comes to chocolate: Piedmont's capital city of Turin has been a leader in the European chocolate industry for centuries. It was in Turin that the method for isolating cocoa butter was discovered and the first chocolate bar created. The first license to open a chocolate shop in Italy was issued in the late 1600s, and it was in this prototypical Turinese chocolate factory that the now-legendary Swiss chocolatiers Suchard and Cailler apprenticed. Not surprisingly, a number of Piedmontese sweets make use of chocolate or cocoa: Alessandria's *baci di dama* ("lady's kisses"), a pair of almond cookies joined by a coin of melted chocolate; *canestrelli di Biella,* buttery, lemon-scented wafers hugging a layer of chocolate; *cuneesi al rum,* rum-laced meringues dipped in chocolate; and *bonet,* an almond-chocolate pudding.

Liguria

Focaccia di Recco
Cheese-Stuffed Focaccia from Recco

Torta di Riso
Herbed Rice Tart

Pansotti con Salsa di Noci
Greens-Stuffed Pasta in Creamy Walnut Sauce

Testaroli al Pesto
Griddle-Baked Pasta Diamonds in Basil Pesto

Minestrina di Maggiorana Fresca
Fresh Marjoram Soup

Cappon Magro
Towering Seafood Salad

Coniglio alle Mandorle e Senape
Breaded Saddle of Rabbit with Almonds and Mustard

Polpettone di Fagiolini
String Bean Torta

La Focaccia di Luciano
Luciano's Focaccia

I Gubeletti della Signora Baj
Signora Baj's Apricot Jam Cookies

I*'ve summered in Liguria* since I could barely walk: my parents, like many Milanesi, have a house in the luxuriant hills above the Ligurian Sea only a few minutes' walk from Rapallo, and every year my husband and I make our way there for a week of sun and solace. There is something in the contrast between sea and land, the way the light plays on the blue of the water and the green of the mountains, that makes me wish I could stop time and simply sit, watch, listen, be. Liguria makes me wish every day were a holiday and I were an eternal reveler.

There are those who love Liguria for its most luxurious port town, Portofino, an exclusive harbor filled with millionaires and jet-setters and wannabes. But the real Liguria is in the small mountain towns and the tiny fishing villages, the larger cities like Rapallo, and the winding streets of old Genoa. It is in the *lungomare* of Santa Margherita, the promenade lined with palm trees. It is in the sandy bay of Paraggi, snugly enclosed between mountains, and the pebble-strewn beach aptly called Il Castello dei Sogni ("The Castle of Dreams") where families, lovers, and peace-seekers come to plunge for a late-afternoon swim, a stab at octopus fishing, or a laze on massive, sun-warmed rocks.

Settled by the Liguri as early as the sixth century B.C., Liguria was conquered by the Romans, Byzantines, Saracens, Swabians, French, Lombards, Spanish, and Austrians. Annexed to the Kingdom of Sardinia in 1815, it became part of the newly formed Kingdom of Italy in 1861. Genoa, a port that is still referred to as La Superba ("The Proud"), has been the region's capital since the fifth century B.C.; a major player in the spice trade in the Middle Ages and Renaissance, it vied with Venice and Pisa for top spot on Italy's commercial scene. Today, Genoa remains one of Italy's most important ports and has the largest medieval quarter in Europe. Its narrow alleys tell a thousand stories, the huddled houses and majestic palaces whispering secrets to one another as passersby shuffle beneath, heading to their favorite fruit vendor or their barber for a shave and a chat.

Liguria, geographically a northern Italian region, cooks like a southern Italian one: Olive oil is used abundantly; bread, pasta, vegetables, fruits, and cheese star in every meal; and fish, seafood, and meat play an ancillary role. As a maritime republic, Genoa enlisted many of its men into service; as a result, Ligurian men spent a great deal of time away from the comforts of home and the food of the land. While they were away fighting wars or obtaining precious spices and goods, they ate beans, chickpeas, twice-cooked doughnut-shaped biscuits called *galette del marinaio* ("sailor's biscuits," still made in a few Ligurian bakeries), and salted fish. When they returned to dry land, they craved fresh flavors. They wanted the taste of just-plucked herbs to fill their mouths, the scent of aromatic vegetables to fill their pots and their homes. And so the Ligurian kitchen is a celebration of vegetables, a triumph of herbs. Pesto, soups studded with herbs, stuffed baby vegetables and colorful salads, pastas filled with wild greens—these dishes were born to please the palates of men who spent most of their lives at sea.

Favorite Restaurants, Shops, and Places

- BOTTEGA DEI SESTIERI, Via Mazzini 44, Rapallo, 0185.230530. A fantastic cheese and cured meat selection with an emphasis on regional products, including Trarcantu.
- BUTTEGHINA MAGICA, Via della Maddalena 2R, Genoa, 010.296590. A kitchenware shop; *corzetti* stamps available.
- FORNO TOSSINI, Via Venezia 38, Rapallo, 0185.50415. A good selection of filled or plain focaccia.
- MANUELINA DI RECCO, Via Roma 278, Recco, 0185.75364 or 0185.720019. The birthplace of *focaccia di Recco.*
- MARINA PICCOLA, Via Discovolo 38, Manarola, 0187.920103. Outstanding *spaghetti alla scogliera* and *tagliatelle ai granchi.*
- PASTICCERIA BAJ, Via Mazzini 13, Rapallo, 0185.50440. Indulge in the *krapfen, gubeletti,* and *cannoncini.*

- PASTIFICIO DASSO, Piazza Venezia 31, Rapallo, 0185.53309. No better place to buy fresh pasta, pesto, and walnut sauce in Liguria.
- RISTORANTE FERRANDO, Via D. Carli 110, San Cipriano, Serra Riccò, Genoa, 010.751925. For *corzetti della Valpolcevera* and *frisceu.*
- RISTORANTE PUNY, Piazza Martiri dell'Olivetta 4/5, Portofino, 0185.269037. The best *cappon magro* in Liguria.
- ROMANENGO PIETRO, Via Soziglia 74, Genoa, 010.297869. Sweets have been prepared in this shop since 1780.
- WALTER DE BATTÈ, Cinque Terre, 0187.920127 (by appointment only). A small-scale winemaker whose Sciacchetrà is renowned.

Telephone country code: 011.39

Focaccia di Recco

Cheese-Stuffed Focaccia from Recco

La Manuelina, a family-run restaurant in Recco, created this now-legendary focaccia. A copper pan is best for baking it, since it transfers heat to the dough faster and prevents it from drying out in the oven. Enjoy this flatbread in Recco during the yearly focaccia festival, held on the last Sunday of May.

SERVES 4 AS A FIRST COURSE OR
8 AS AN ANTIPASTO

1½ cups unbleached all-purpose flour,
  plus extra for the counter
1½ teaspoons fine sea salt
¼ cup extra-virgin olive oil, plus extra for
  greasing the bowl and pizza pan
1 pound Stracchino or Crescenza, cubed

Place the flour, 1 teaspoon of the salt, and 2 tablespoons of the olive oil in a food processor. With the motor running, add ½ cup plus 2 tablespoons of room-temperature water; the dough should come together. Process for 45 seconds, adding water if it is dry or flour if it is sticky; it should be soft and smooth and form a ball around the blade. Turn out into an oiled bowl, shape into a ball, and wrap. Let rest 30 minutes.

Preheat the oven with a baking stone in it to 550°F.

Cut the dough into 2 pieces, 1 slightly larger, and roll out both on a lightly floured counter into nearly transparent circles; if the dough tears, patch with your fingers. Generously oil a round 16-inch pizza pan and line it with the larger piece of dough, allowing excess to hang over the sides. Scatter the Stracchino or Crescenza over the dough and cover with the smaller piece of dough. Press the edges to seal and run the rolling pin over the edge of the pan to cut off excess dough, then seal again. Brush the top with the remaining 2 tablespoons of olive oil and sprinkle it with the remaining ½ teaspoon of salt. Make 4 small tears in the dough; bake on the baking stone for 11 minutes, or until the crust is golden and puffed with brown spots; it should still be soft. Serve hot.

PREPARATION TIPS: The dough can be made up to 2 days ahead and refrigerated.

TWO UNIQUE LIGURIAN CHEESES

If ever you are in Liguria, I urge you to sample two unique cheeses: Prescinseua and Trarcantu. Prescinseua, a tangy, spreadable product halfway between cheese and soured milk, is used in pesto and sauces or spread on bread. Trarcantu, a raw cow's milk cheese created by cheesemonger Guido Porrati of Rapallo with wine producer Walter De Battè, is aged five months in barrels, doused with wine, and flavored with the lees of Sciacchetrà, a dried-grape wine vinified in the Cinque Terre; it is available in Guido's shop, La Bottega dei Sestieri (see page 43).

Torta di Riso

Herbed Rice Tart

*I*n Liguria, rice is enjoyed in various forms: in seafood or vegetable risotti, cooked into soups, and baked into savory torte. The torta below is a delicate combination of tender crust and creamy-tasting, if not creamy-textured, rice scented with marjoram.

SERVES 6 AS A FIRST COURSE OR 12 AS AN ANTIPASTO

1½ cups unbleached all-purpose flour, plus extra for the counter

1 teaspoon salt

2 tablespoons extra-virgin olive oil, plus extra for greasing the bowl and pizza pan

1 cup Arborio rice

⅓ cup plus 1 tablespoon whole milk

¼ teaspoon freshly ground black pepper

¼ pound fresh Ricotta

½ cup freshly grated Grana Padano

¼ cup marjoram leaves, minced

3 extra-large eggs, beaten

Place the flour, ½ teaspoon of the salt, and the olive oil in the bowl of a food processor. With the motor running, add ½ cup plus 1 tablespoon of room-temperature water; the dough should come together. Process for 45 seconds, adding water if the dough is dry or flour if it is sticky; the dough should be soft and smooth and form a ball around the blade. Turn out into an oiled bowl, shape into a ball, and wrap. Let rest 30 minutes.

Preheat the oven to 375°F.

Meanwhile, bring 3 cups of water to a boil. Stir in the rice and the remaining ½ teaspoon of salt; cook, covered, over medium heat until al dente, about 15 minutes. Drain into a colander set over a bowl and cool to room temperature. Transfer to a bowl and add the milk, pepper, Ricotta, Grana, marjoram, and two-thirds of the beaten eggs.

Roll out the dough on a lightly floured counter into an 18-inch circle. Generously oil a 14-inch round pizza pan and line it with the dough, then spoon in the rice. Flip the excess dough down over the rice to create a border. Pour on the remaining egg and spread it over the dough and rice with a spoon. Bake in the preheated oven for 40 minutes, or until golden on top and set. Serve hot or warm.

PREPARATION TIPS: The dough can be made up to 2 days ahead and refrigerated.

Pansotti con Salsa di Noci

Greens-Stuffed Pasta in Creamy Walnut Sauce

The name of this pasta is dialect for pan-ciuti, *meaning "having a tummy," because of the generous filling that gives it a rounded shape. In Liguria, the greens used to fill pansotti are called* preboggion *and include wild herbs like pimpernel, sow thistle, and borage. This recipe is based on one from Olga and Maurizia Dasso, owners of Pastificio Dasso in Rapallo.*

PASTAS FROM THE BIRTHPLACE OF RAVIOLI

Legend has it that Liguria was the birthplace of ravioli and that from its shores this pasta spread to other regions. Today, Liguria offers one of Italy's richest pasta repertoires. Unique Ligurian pastas include *corzetti* made in Val Polcevera shaped like full figure-eights; delicate disks called *corzetti stampati* stamped with a raised motif; tiny twirled gnocchi called *trofie*; light-as-air *mandilli di sea* ("silk handkerchiefs"); and *gnocchi dolci* made of chestnut flour.

SERVES 4

For the dough:
2¼ cups unbleached all-purpose flour, plus extra for the counter
¼ teaspoon salt
¼ cup plus 1 teaspoon dry white wine

For the filling:
¾ pound Swiss chard leaves
¾ pound spinach leaves
¼ pound arugula leaves
¼ cup packed chervil or basil leaves
¼ pound fresh Ricotta
½ cup freshly grated Parmigiano-Reggiano
2 extra-large eggs
¼ teaspoon salt
⅛ teaspoon freshly ground black pepper

For the sauce:
½ ounce crustless country bread, crumbled
¼ cup whole milk
1 cup walnut halves
½ cup pine nuts
½ cup freshly grated Parmigiano-Reggiano
½ garlic clove, peeled
¼ teaspoon salt
⅛ teaspoon freshly ground black pepper
¼ cup heavy cream
¼ cup extra-virgin olive oil

To shape and cook the pansotti:
1 extra-large egg, beaten
2 tablespoons salt

Make the dough according to instructions on page 370 using the ingredients listed above, adding as much water as needed (about ½ cup) to form a firm dough. Knead 5 minutes, or until smooth, adding a little water if the dough is dry or a little flour if it is sticky. Shape into a ball, wrap, and let rest 30 minutes.

Make the filling: Bring 4 quarts of water to a boil and cook the Swiss chard and spinach 5 minutes; add the arugula and cook 2 minutes. Drain, rinse under cold water, and squeeze dry. Chop and place in a food processor with the chervil, Ricotta, Parmigiano, eggs, salt, and pepper. Process until nearly smooth.

Make the sauce: Soak the bread in the milk for 5 minutes, then drain and squeeze it dry. In a food processor, purée the bread with the walnuts, pine nuts, Parmigiano, garlic, salt, and pepper until a paste forms. With the motor running, add the heavy cream, then the olive oil in a thin, steady stream; the sauce should be creamy.

To shape the pansotti, cut the dough into 4 pieces. Working with 1 piece at a time and keeping the others covered, roll out each piece using a pasta machine into a nearly transparent sheet. Cut into 3-inch squares. Spoon a dollop of filling over each square and brush the inside top edge with the beaten egg. Fold diagonally into a triangle, then join the two ends at the base of the triangle around your index finger, pressing to make them stick. These are the pansotti. Spread out in a single layer on a floured tray; cover with a towel.

To cook, bring 4 quarts of water to a boil. Add the pansotti and salt and cook until al dente, about 3 minutes. Remove with a slotted spoon to a bowl, reserving ⅔ cup of the pasta cooking water.

Place the sauce in a serving bowl and fold in the reserved cooking water. Gently fold in the drained pansotti with a rubber spatula and serve hot.

PREPARATION TIPS: Prepare the sauce and pansotti up to 12 hours ahead; refrigerate both, spreading out the pansotti in a single layer on a floured tray, covered with a towel.

Testaroli al Pesto

Griddle-Baked Pasta Diamonds in Basil Pesto

This pasta is a direct descendant of the porridges of the Neolithic Age that were poured onto hot stones to cook. Testaroli derive their name from the *testo* (a terra-cotta or iron pan with a concave lid) in which they are cooked and are a specialty of Lunigiana, an archaeologically rich area straddling Liguria and Tuscany. They can be made with white or whole-wheat flour; the latter have a nuttier aroma.

SERVES 6

¼ cup pine nuts
2½ cups tightly packed young basil leaves
1 garlic clove, peeled
2 tablespoons plus 1 teaspoon salt
1 cup plus 2 tablespoons extra-virgin olive oil
⅔ cup freshly grated Parmigiano-Reggiano
⅔ cup freshly grated Pecorino Romano
4¼ cups unbleached all-purpose flour
½ medium yellow onion, peeled

Heat a small skillet over a medium flame. Add the pine nuts and cook, stirring often, 5 minutes, or until golden. In a food processor, process the toasted nuts with the basil, garlic, and ½ teaspoon of the salt until a paste forms. Gradually pour in 1 cup of the olive oil with the motor running; the mixture will emulsify. Transfer this pesto to a serving bowl and stir in the Parmigiano and Pecorino.

Combine the flour and ½ teaspoon of the salt in a large mixing bowl. Pour in 4½ cups of room-temperature water, beating with a whisk all the while. The batter should be fairly liquid, similar to heavy cream; add more water if needed.

Heat a heavy 8-inch skillet over a medium-high flame for 5 minutes. Spear the onion on a fork and dip it into the remaining 2 tablespoons of olive oil. Rub the cut half over the bottom and sides of the skillet to flavor the oil. Set the onion aside and ladle ½ cup of the batter into the skillet; immediately spread it to a thickness of 1/16-inch using the back of the ladle. Cover and cook for 4 minutes, then flip, cover again, and cook 3 more minutes. Remove to a cutting board and cut into ½ × 1-inch pieces (reserve trimmings for soup). These are the testaroli. Continue in the same manner with the remaining batter, rubbing the skillet with the oiled onion before pouring in more batter.

Meanwhile, bring 5 quarts of water to a boil. Add the testaroli and the remaining 2 tablespoons of salt. Cook 1 minute; drain. Fold into the pesto in the bowl using a rubber spatula. Serve hot.

THE VIRTUES OF POUNDING

The Ligurian kitchen elevates pounding to an art form. The mortar and pestle is the Ligurian cook's most important implement, and even in this era of processors and blenders, no Ligurian home is without one. The word *pesto* comes from *pestare,* meaning "to pound," and if you've never made pesto in a mortar, try it: that's the way Ligurian *mamme* do it, and it results in a perfect texture.

Minestrina di Maggiorana Fresca

Fresh Marjoram Soup

Marjoram is used frequently in the Ligurian kitchen to perfume pasta fillings and sauces and to lend a bright note to fish and meat. Here it stars in a simple soup that takes just minutes to prepare.

SERVES 4

¼ cup plus 2 tablespoons extra-virgin olive oil
2 garlic cloves, minced
9 cups (2¼ quarts) Vegetable Broth (page 34)
1 pound ditalini or other short soup pasta
½ teaspoon salt
⅛ teaspoon freshly ground black pepper
4 extra-large eggs
½ cup plus 2 tablespoons freshly grated Grana Padano
½ cup plus 1 tablespoon marjoram leaves, minced

Heat 3 tablespoons of the olive oil in a 4-quart pot. Add the garlic and cook over medium-high heat until aromatic, about 30 seconds. Pour in the broth and bring to a boil. Stir in the ditalini, salt, and pepper and cook until the ditalini are al dente, about 8 minutes.

Beat the eggs, Grana, and marjoram in a small bowl. Pour the egg mixture into the soup. Remove from the heat; wait 30 seconds, then stir gently once or twice to scramble the eggs. Serve hot, drizzled with the remaining 3 tablespoons of olive oil.

THE PROOF IS IN THE PASTA

If there is still any doubt that pasta was an Italian staple before Marco Polo came back from the Orient, consider this: in 1279 (thirteen years before Marco Polo returned from his voyage), a Ligurian notary act mentioned *"una bariscella plena de macaronis"* ("a basket full of macaroni") among the possessions of a noble.

FROM CHICKPEA FLOUR TO BARLEY BREAD

One of the tastiest Ligurian flatbreads is a chickpea flour pancake called *farinata*. Baked since time immemorial on hot stones and regulated by law since at least the fifteenth century, it has become an autumn specialty. Barley bread, a long-keeping staple of Ligurian shepherds, is another rustic offering: still baked in the small towns of Carpassio and Badalucco, it is elliptical, dry, and so crunchy that it must be soaked in water before eating.

Cappon Magro

Towering Seafood Salad

Of all Ligurian seafood dishes, none comes close to the glamour of cappon magro, defined by Emanuele Rossi as "the queen of salads" in his nineteenth-century book, La Vera Cuciniera Genovese. A variety of boiled fish, shellfish, and vegetables is layered with crunchy, twice-baked bread called galette del marinaio (see Sources, page 372), hard-boiled eggs, and salsa verde to stunning effect. The recipe below, ideal for special occasions, is from Luigi Miroli, owner of Ristorante Puny in Portofino.

SERVES 8

2 lobsters (1½ pounds each)

1 pound boneless sea bream or red snapper fillets

2 pounds medium shrimp, shelled and deveined

2½ cups extra-virgin olive oil

3 tablespoons fresh lemon juice (from 1 lemon)

1¼ teaspoons salt

½ teaspoon freshly ground black pepper

9 extra-large eggs

3 pounds assorted vegetables (such as baby artichokes, new potatoes, string beans, cauliflower florets, baby carrots, and beets), trimmed as needed

⅓ cup plus 3 tablespoons white wine vinegar

6 galette del marinaio (see Sources, page 372) or ¼-inch-thick slices toasted bread

¾ cup packed cubed crustless white country bread

3 cups Italian parsley leaves

½ cup plus 1 tablespoon pine nuts

¼ cup plus ½ tablespoon capers, drained

3 salted anchovies, boned, gutted, and rinsed

9 pitted green oil-cured olives, such as Sicilian

1 small garlic clove, peeled

In a shallow and wide 12-quart pot, bring 6 quarts of water to a boil. Reduce the heat to medium and add the lobsters; cook 8 minutes. Add the sea bream and cook 4 minutes. Add the shrimp and cook 1 minute. With a slotted spoon, remove all the seafood and fish to a tray and cool to room temperature. Shell the lobsters and cut the tail and claw flesh into 2-inch pieces; skin the sea bream and cut into 2-inch pieces. Toss the lobster, sea bream, and shrimp with ½ cup of the olive oil, the lemon juice, ½ teaspoon of the salt, and ⅛ teaspoon of the pepper. Set aside.

Bring 4 quarts of water to a boil. Gently lower the eggs into the boiling water and cook for 12 minutes. Remove with a slotted spoon, cool, shell, and cut 6 of the hard-boiled eggs into thin slices; scoop out the yolks from the 3 remaining hard-boiled eggs (reserve the whites for other dishes). Keep the water boiling. Add the vegetables and cook over medium heat until tender when pierced with a knife, about 10 minutes depending on the variety and size of vegetables you are using; drain and cool to room temperature.

In a large mixing bowl, toss the vegetables with ½ cup of the olive oil, 3 tablespoons of the vinegar, ½ teaspoon of the salt, and ⅛ teaspoon of the pepper. Sprinkle the galette del marinaio with ¼ cup of cool water (if you are using bread, do not sprinkle it with water). Layer the cooked vegetables, fish, seafood, galette, and 6 sliced hard-boiled eggs on a large serving platter.

Place the yolks from the 3 hard-boiled eggs in a food processor. Soak the cubed bread in the remaining ⅓ cup of vinegar for 5 minutes, then squeeze dry and crumble into the food processor. Add the parsley, pine nuts, capers, anchovies, olives, and garlic, and process to a paste. Add the remaining 1½ cups of olive oil in a thin stream with the motor running until emulsified. Season with the remaining ¼ teaspoon of salt and ¼ teaspoon of pepper, and transfer to a bowl; this is the salsa verde.

Pour half of the salsa verde over the salad and serve immediately, passing the remaining salsa at the table.

PREPARATION TIPS: The salsa verde can be made up to 24 hours ahead and refrigerated; the vegetables can be boiled up to 24 hours ahead and refrigerated.

FRESH FISH, A LUXURY EVEN ON LIGURIAN TABLES

Despite Liguria's perch on the Mediterranean, its cuisine does not draw heavily on the sea. In the past, fresh fish was a luxury reserved for the wealthy; most people ate dried fish, especially salt cod. In G. B. Ratto's book *Cuciniera Genovese*, written in the 1860s, one-third of the fish recipes feature salt cod or stockfish.

Coniglio alle Mandorle e Senape

Breaded Saddle of Rabbit with Almonds and Mustard

When Ligurians eat meat, they prefer rabbit, chicken, or veal. If you have never made rabbit before, this dish from the town of San Fruttuoso is the perfect one to start you off; unbelievably easy, it highlights the subtle flavor of rabbit. Chicken scaloppine make a good substitute for the rabbit.

SERVES 6

1 pound boneless saddle of rabbit, cut into
    12 medallions and pounded into ¼-inch-thick
    scaloppine with a mallet
1 teaspoon salt
1 cup almonds (preferably with the skin on)
2 extra-large eggs
1 cup fresh bread crumbs
½ cup extra-virgin olive oil
8 sage leaves
2 tablespoons Dijon mustard
1 lemon, cut into wedges

Place the rabbit on a plate, sprinkle with ½ teaspoon of the salt, cover, and refrigerate 1 hour.

Grind the almonds in a food processor until they are smaller than peas but not powdery. Spread out on a platter.

Beat the eggs with the remaining ½ teaspoon of salt on one plate. Place the bread crumbs on a second plate. Dredge the rabbit in the eggs, coating both sides, then in the bread crumbs, again coating both sides.

Heat the olive oil with the sage in a 12-inch skillet until it is nearly smoking. Add 6 of the rabbit medallions and cook over medium heat until golden on both sides, turning once, about 2 minutes per side.

Remove the rabbit to the platter with the almonds and cover with foil to keep warm. Cook the remaining 6 rabbit medallions in the same manner in the olive oil left in the skillet; remove to the platter and serve hot, passing the mustard and lemon at the table.

THE MONKS' OLIVE OIL

In the first millennium, Benedictine monks selected Taggiasca as the olive varietal of choice in Liguria. A thousand years later, Taggiasca olives are still harvested every spring and pressed into delicate oil. Much of Liguria's olive oil production is concentrated in the province of Imperia, especially around the town of Oneglia, but every little corner that can support an olive tree does.

LIGURIA'S WINES

IGURIANS ONCE TRADED THEIR OLIVE OIL for wine with the Etruscans, but centuries of winemaking have resulted in a number of top-quality wines emerging from this tiny crescent-shaped region. Vineyards are planted on steep terraced slopes in seeming defiance of gravity. The most prolific grape varieties are Albarola, Pigato, Vermentino, Bosco, Rossese, Sangiovese, and Ormeasco, responsible for a small but qualified production of wines. The region's most notable whites are Cinqueterre, a crisp wine vinified from Bosco, Albarola, and Vermentino above the Tyrrhenian Sea; Pigato, a refreshing, somewhat fleshy, intense wine produced in dry, semi-dry, raisined, and sparkling versions; and Vermentino, a versatile wine with a deep straw color, delicate floral aroma, and grassy notes. The best-known red is Rossese di Dolceacqua; it offers a light ruby color, delicate bouquet of black currants and roses, and strawberry nose, and can age up to ten years. Sciacchetrà, or Cinqueterre Sciacchetrà, is a rare, perfumed, amber-hued dessert wine made from dried Bosco, Albarola, and Vermentino. A memorable Sciacchetrà, and the only one exported to North America, is from small-scale producer Walter De Battè (see Sources, page 373).

Polpettone di Fagiolini

String Bean Torta

It is in its multitude of stuffed vegetables and vegetable pies that the Ligurian love for the garden's bounty finds its most noble expression. This polpettone belongs to a family of dishes featuring vegetables bound with eggs, grated cheese, and bread plumped in milk. But the original polpettoni were made with meat, not vegetables: after all, polpetta means "meatball."

½ cup dried porcini mushrooms

1½ pounds string beans, ends trimmed

1 tablespoon plus ½ teaspoon salt

2 tablespoons extra-virgin olive oil, plus extra for greasing the baking dish

½ medium white onion, minced

1 garlic clove, minced

2 tablespoons marjoram leaves, minced

1 ounce crustless bread

¼ cup whole milk

¼ cup freshly grated Parmigiano-Reggiano

2 extra-large eggs

½ teaspoon freshly ground black pepper

½ cup fresh bread crumbs

1 tablespoon unsalted butter, cut into 8 pieces

Soak the porcini in cold water to cover for 30 minutes, then drain (reserve the soaking water for risotto or pasta sauces, first straining it through a cheesecloth-lined sieve to get rid of dirt). Rinse the porcini and mince.

Meanwhile, bring 6 quarts of water to a boil. Add the string beans and 1 tablespoon of the salt and cook 5 minutes. Drain, plunge into a bowl of ice water, and drain again. Cut into ⅛-inch lengths.

COOKING IN ANCIENT LIGURIA

In the Balzi Rossi caves near Grimaldi, between Ventimiglia and Montone, archaeologists discovered sculptures and paintings dating to the Paleolithic Age. It seems that the ancestors of the Ligurians were among the first to inhabit Italy—the first reference to the Liguri dates to the sixth century B.C. These ancient Ligurians drank milk and *idromele* (a slightly alcoholic drink made from barley, water, and honey) and traded honey for olive oil and Etruscan wine. Their diet was based on bread, vegetables, fruit, cheese, and a little fish, seafood, and meat. Pliny the Elder reported that in the first century, Ligurians conserved grapes for the winter by drying them in the sun, then tying them with rush reeds and placing them in terra-cotta jars.

Heat the olive oil in a deep 12-inch sauté pan over a medium flame and cook the onion 5 minutes. Add the garlic and marjoram and cook 1 minute. Fold in the string beans and minced porcini and cook 20 minutes, stirring often and adding a little water if needed to prevent sticking. Transfer to a large bowl and cool to room temperature.

Preheat the oven to 375°F.

Soak the bread in the milk for 5 minutes, squeeze dry, and crumble into the string bean mixture. Stir in the Parmigiano, eggs, the remaining ½ teaspoon of salt, and the pepper.

Generously oil a deep 7 × 10-inch baking dish, coat the bottom and sides with ¼ cup of the bread crumbs, and spoon in the string bean mixture. Sprinkle with the remaining ¼ cup of bread crumbs and compress with a flat spatula. Dot the top with the butter and bake in the preheated oven for 30 minutes, or until the top is golden. Serve hot, warm, or at room temperature.

La Focaccia di Luciano

Luciano's Focaccia

The most emblematic Ligurian food is focaccia, an oil-slicked, dimpled flatbread that frequently replaces bread on the table. Luciano Benedetti, a young baker who once worked at the Forno Tossini in Rapallo, was my guide to focaccia. Barely thirty years old, he has been baking since the age of thirteen. His trick is a water-oil bath poured over the dough so that as the focaccia bakes, the water evaporates, leaving delicious puddles of oil in the dimples pressed into the dough.

3½ cups unbleached all-purpose flour
1 teaspoon instant yeast
1 tablespoon plus 1 teaspoon fine sea salt
¼ cup extra-virgin olive oil, plus extra for greasing the bowl and pizza pan

Mix the flour, yeast, and 1 tablespoon of the salt in a food processor. With the motor running, add ¾ cup of warm (110°F) water, then pour in 2 tablespoons of the olive oil and add enough warm water (about ½ to ⅔ cup) to make a soft dough that forms a ball. Process 45 seconds, transfer to an oiled bowl, and shape into a ball. Wrap and let rise at room temperature until doubled, about 1 hour.

Transfer the dough to a generously oiled round 18-inch pizza pan and push with your fingers until it extends to the sides of the pan (you might need to wait 5 minutes for the dough to stretch more easily). Combine the remaining 2 tablespoons of olive oil and the remaining teaspoon of salt with 2 tablespoons of room-temperature water in a small bowl and pour over the focaccia. Dimple with your fingers, using the pads rather than the nails so you don't tear the dough, and let rise at room temperature 45 minutes.

Meanwhile, preheat the oven to 475°F (preferably with a baking stone in it).

Bake the focaccia on the bottom rack of the preheated oven (or directly on the baking stone) for 20 minutes, or until golden on the top and bottom and lightly crisp. Serve hot, warm, or at room temperature.

PREPARATION TIPS: Make the dough up to 24 hours ahead and let it rise in the refrigerator; return to room temperature before proceeding.

A POET ON FOCACCIA

Genoese poet Vito Elio Petrucci wrote a veritable ballad in honor of his beloved flatbread. Here is an excerpt: *"E vi dirò di più, fo paragoni con l'amigo . . . che fa le pizze co-i calzoni. Duxento pisse 'no fan unna fugassa!"* ("And I'll tell you more, I'm making comparisons . . . with the friend who makes *pizze* and *calzoni*. Two hundred pizze don't equal one focaccia!") Petrucci also suggested that focaccia must be eaten upside-down, to maximize contact between the salty-oily topping and the taste buds on the tongue.

I Gubeletti della Signora Baj

Signora Baj's Apricot Jam Cookies

These are the pastries—fat muffin-shaped butter cookies hiding a dollop of apricot jam within their golden interior—that my husband and I eat every morning in Rapallo. For some reason, gubeletti are made exclusively in Rapallo; the ultimate version is baked at Pasticceria Baj, an elegant pastry shop. This is my rendition of Baj's addictive cookies.

MAKES TWELVE 2-INCH PASTRIES

3¼ cups unbleached all-purpose flour, plus extra for the counter

½ cup sugar

¼ teaspoon salt

20 tablespoons (2½ sticks) unsalted butter, chilled and cubed, plus extra for greasing the muffin pans

¼ cup sweet Marsala

1 extra-large egg, beaten

1 cup apricot jam

Mix the flour, sugar, and salt on a counter, then work in the butter until the mixture resembles coarse meal. Work in the Marsala and add enough of the egg to form a dough; you might not need all of the egg. Gather into a ball, wrap, and refrigerate 30 minutes.

Preheat the oven to 350°F.

Butter 12 individual 2-inch muffin pans. Cut the dough into 2 pieces. Roll out 1 piece on a lightly floured counter into a ⅛-inch-thick rectangle. Line up the muffin pans on a counter next to one another, making 3 rows of 4 pans each, and drape the dough over the pans. Line each pan with the dough by pushing it gently with your fingers until it touches the bottom of the pan. Distribute the jam equally among the pans.

Roll out the second piece of dough on a lightly floured counter into a ⅙-inch-thick rectangle. Drape over the muffin pans and press the edges to seal. Place the rolling pin on the row of muffin pans closest to you and roll it over the pans away from you to trim excess dough. Place the muffin pans on an 11 × 17-inch baking sheet and bake in the preheated oven for 25 minutes, or until the crust is golden. Cool on a rack, unmold, and serve at room temperature.

PREPARATION TIPS: The dough can be made up to 24 hours ahead and refrigerated.

PANDOLCE, A CHRISTMAS TRADITION ALL YEAR LONG

If you're in Liguria, make it a point to taste pandolce, a buttery dried fruit and nut cake akin to—but drier and denser than—Milan's panettone. Traditionally baked for Christmas, it is now available year-round. Since it keeps well, you can always bring some home for a taste of Liguria on American shores.

Lombardy

Anguilla in Carpione
Fried Eel Marinated in Medieval Spices

La Pizza al Gorgonzola della Pizzaccia
Gorgonzola-Topped Pizza with Sweet Onions

Pizzoccheri della Valtellina
Buckwheat Flour Ribbons with Wilted Cabbage,
Potatoes, and Mountain Cheese

Casônsei Bresciani
Sausage and Cheese Pasta Horns from Brescia

Gnocchi di Zucca al Rosmarino
Butternut Squash Gnocchi in Rosemary Butter

Risotto alla Milanese
Saffron Risotto from Milan

Vitello Tonnato
Thinly Sliced Veal in Cold Tuna Sauce

Ossobuco alla Milanese
Braised Veal Shanks with Gremolata

Ciabatta
Slipper-Shaped Bread

Budino di Panettone
Panettone Bread Pudding

T*here are people who claim* that there is no such thing as Milanese cooking, that Milan is all about fast food, business lunches, restaurants where you can sample the best national dishes while never getting a sense of the local cuisine. I grew up in Milan, and I maintain that the opposite is true. Milan may be Italy's commercial capital, its most businesslike of business cities, but even there, in the heart of the most heavily populated Italian region, people passionately preserve their culinary roots.

The best place to sample real Milanese cuisine, of course, is at somebody's house. (This is true for every region, not just Lombardy.) The next best place is a trattoria, an unpretentious restaurant where the food mirrors the area's home cooking. Milan's venerable trattorie—and there are quite a few, some with most untrattorialike prices—still offer old-time recipes: battered and fried nuggets of salt cod; braised pig's head and pork loin with chickpeas, typically eaten on All Souls' Day; breaded and fried veal chops, an Austrian legacy known as *cotolette alla milanese* that has become synonymous with Italian cuisine as far away as Mexico; and boiled chestnuts topped with whipped cream or drowned in sweet wine. Farther out, in the vast countryside of Lombardy—the fertile plains, the narrow valleys huddled by the Alps, the Lake District—the cuisine is just as beguiling, and cooks cling to their culinary heritage just as tenaciously.

Second only to Emilia-Romagna in agricultural production, Lombardy offers the cook a wealth of ingredients: polenta and rice reign in the plains, while hearty grains like buckwheat thrive in the mountains. The Lombard appetite for meat seems insatiable: beef and veal are adored, prized pigs are grown for hams and salami, and rich stews are scented with sweet spices like nutmeg, cinnamon, and cloves, a Renaissance legacy. All across this vast, fertile region, butter and cheese are used with abandon—in fact, the feature that unifies the cooking of Lombardy's eleven provinces is their taste for rich foods.

The penchant for luxury on the Lombard table has very old roots. Increasingly prosperous since the eleventh century, when the Po River Valley made it a pivotal transit point between the Mediterranean and lands beyond the Alps, Lombardy has been occupied by the Celts, Romans, Lombards (a Germanic people who ruled from 568 to 774 and gave the region its name), Franks, Spanish, Austrians, and French. The cities of Bergamo, Brescia, Cremona, and Milan were among Europe's commercial leaders by the twelfth century; two hundred years later, Milan imposed itself as the region's most important city, a position it claims to this day. But it was during the Renaissance that Lombardy's cuisine truly flourished. Bartolomeo Sacchi, known as Platina and author of Italy's first printed cookbook, *De Honesta Voluptate et Valetitudine*, was born in Cremona in 1421. Bartolomeo Stefani, chef to the Gonzagas, who ruled Mantua from 1328 to 1627, developed a refined court cuisine in the seventeenth century. The haunting flavors and sweet-and-savory notes of the Gonzagas' Mantua are still alive in dishes like squash-stuffed tortelli and other delicate specialties whose roots lie in the Renaissance.

Favorite Restaurants, Shops, and Places

- AIMO E NADIA, Via Montecuccoli 6, Milan, 02.416886. Regional dishes cooked to perfection.
- ANTICA TRATTORIA DELLA PESA, Via Pasubio 10, Milan, 02.6555741. The place for *risotto alla milanese, ossobuco,* and more.
- COLLEONI DELL'ANGELO, Piazza Vecchia 7, Bergamo, 035.232596. Outstanding creative cuisine by Pierangelo Cornaro; try his tasting menu.
- COVA, Via Montenapoleone 8, Milan, 02.7600578. Historical pastry shop opened in 1817.
- DAL PESCATORE, Via Runate 13, Canneto Sull'Oglio, 0376.723001. Owner Nadia Santini is one of Italy's best chefs.
- FORNO COLLIVASONE, Vicolo Turati 1, Parona, 0384.91301. This is the bakery where *offelle di Parona* were born.

- LA CORTE DELL'OCA, Via Sforza 27, Mortara, 0384.98397. Goose salami, goose Prosciutto, smoked goose breast, and more.
- LA PIZZACCIA, Via San G. Boscoll 11, Milan, 02.5692094. Wood-burning oven *pizze,* including one with Gorgonzola and onions.
- PECK, Via Spadari 9, Milan, 02.860842 or 02.860843. Choose among five hundred cheeses, four hundred cured meats, and thousands of delicacies, including wine.
- TRATTORIA DEI MARTINI IL CIGNO, Piazza d'Arco 1, Mantua, 0376.327101. Historical cuisine; try the *anguilla in carpione.*

Telephone country code: 011.39

Anguilla in Carpione
Fried Eel Marinated in Medieval Spices

This appetizer, a reinterpretation of a dish created by Renaissance chef Bartolomeo Stefani for the ruler Ottavio Gonzaga, is a specialty at Gaetano and Alessandra Martini's Trattoria dei Martini in Mantua. Carpione is a northern Italian preparation in which sweetwater fish is fried, then marinated with vinegar and served at room temperature. An average (1½-pound) eel should yield the right amount for this recipe.

SERVES 4

¾ pound boneless and skinless eel, cut into 2-inch-long strips
⅓ cup unbleached all-purpose flour
¾ cup extra-virgin olive oil
1 teaspoon salt
¼ cup golden raisins
1 large yellow onion, thinly sliced
1 cup balsamic vinegar
8 cloves
3 tablespoons pine nuts
4 cups mixed baby greens, washed and dried

Dredge the eel in the flour, shaking off the excess. Heat ¼ cup of the olive oil in an 8-inch skillet over a medium-high flame and fry half of the eel until golden on both sides, about 10 minutes, turning once. Remove with a slotted spoon to a platter lined with paper towels and blot dry. Cook the remaining eel in the same manner in the olive oil that is left in the skillet. Arrange the fried eel in a single layer on a clean platter and sprinkle with ½ teaspoon of the salt.

Meanwhile, soak the raisins in water to cover for 30 minutes; drain.

Cook the onion in ¼ cup of the olive oil in a 12-inch sauté pan over medium heat for 15 minutes. Pour in all but 1 tablespoon of the vinegar; tie the cloves in a piece of cheesecloth, add to the vinegar, bring to a boil, and cook 10 minutes. Pour the vinegar-onion mixture over the fried eel and sprinkle with the plumped raisins and pine nuts. Cool to room temperature and refrigerate 2 to 4 days. Discard the cheesecloth bundle, sprinkle with the remaining tablespoon of vinegar, and bring to room temperature.

Toss the greens with the remaining ¼ cup of olive oil and ½ teaspoon of salt and mound onto 4 plates. Top with the eel and its marinade and serve.

FISH IN A LAND-LOCKED REGION

Salmon, trout, eel, and carp, already praised by the Latin poet Catullo two thousand years ago, are staples in land-locked Lombardy. Fish specialties draw on the region's many lakes and streams. One unusual dish is *misultitt,* salted and sun-dried shad eaten with polenta or draped over buttered bread in Lecco. Shad live much of their lives at sea but spawn in rivers and streams, where they are caught by Lombardy's fishermen before they return to the ocean.

La Pizza al Gorgonzola della Pizzaccia

Gorgonzola-Topped Pizza with Sweet Onions

When I was little, my family went to a pizzeria in Milan called La Pizzaccia. Pizza may not be Milan's—or Lombardy's—most emblematic dish, but the topping on this childhood favorite of mine highlights the pungent flavor of the region's famed blue cheese, Gorgonzola. It also recalls Lombardy's beloved fitascetta, a wreath-shaped focaccia topped with caramelized onions.

SERVES 4

1 recipe Yeasted Dough (page 371)
Unbleached all-purpose flour for the counter
¼ cup extra-virgin olive oil
1½ pounds Gorgonzola, rind removed, cubed
2 purple onions, thinly sliced
¼ teaspoon freshly ground black pepper

Make the dough and let it rise until doubled according to instructions on page 371.

Preheat the oven with a baking stone in it to 550°F.

Cut the dough into 4 pieces. With the palms of your hands, roll each piece into a ball on a lightly floured counter. Cover and let rest 15 minutes. Using a rolling pin (or your hands for a lighter texture), shape each ball into a 10-inch circle; the edges should be somewhat higher than the center. Place 1 disk of dough on a baking peel that has been generously sprinkled with flour.

Rub with 1 tablespoon of the olive oil, top with one-quarter of the Gorgonzola, then one-quarter of the onions, and stretch into an 11-inch circle. Transfer to the baking stone. Bake in the preheated oven for 5 minutes, or until the crust is crisp and the Gorgonzola has melted. Continue with the remaining dough and topping. (I usually bake 2 *pizze* at once; if you don't have 2 baking peels, use 2 reversed 11 × 17-inch baking sheets.) Serve each pizza as it emerges from the oven, sprinkled with a pinch of the pepper.

PREPARATION TIPS: The dough can be made up to 24 hours ahead and allowed to rise in the refrigerator; return to room temperature before proceeding.

Tired Cows, Tasty Milk

CHEESE IN LOMBARDY is something like wine in Piedmont: almost a religion. Lombardy is responsible for cow's milk cheeses with a spectacular range of aromas and textures. See Sources (page 372) to purchase in North America.

GORGONZOLA, the most renowned, is a blue-veined raw milk cheese matured two months when Dolce ("mild") and three months or longer when Piccante ("spicy").

STRACCHINO, the mold-free ancestor of Gorgonzola, derives its name from the dialect *stracco,* meaning "tired," because the cows were milked in the evening, when they were tired from a day of grazing.

CRESCENZA (whose name comes from *crescere*, meaning "to grow," because it has a tendency to swell in a warm environment) is similar to Stracchino; it is a creamy, white, spreadable cheese aged only a few days.

GRANA PADANO, the Lombard cousin to Parmigiano-Reggiano, is produced in twenty-seven provinces spanning from Cuneo in Piedmont to Venice in the Veneto, Trent in Trentino–Alto Adige, and Forlì in Emilia-Romagna. But most Grana Padano comes from the Pianura Padana (the plains around the Pò), hence its name. First made by monks in the thirteenth century, it is aged at least a year and marketed as Maggengo (summer cheese) or Vernengo (winter), with Maggengo being the most intense.

MASCARPONE, a fatty, creamy, slightly tangy cheese obtained by adding a souring agent to fresh cream and letting it ferment for a day, is often used in desserts.

TALEGGIO, born in the eleventh century, is aged about forty days and has a buttery taste and truffle-scented rind.

QUARTIROLO resembles Taleggio and is aged up to a month, becoming slightly bitter.

VALTELLINA CASERA is ivory, soft, and ripened over two months.

PROVOLONE VALPADANA belongs to the family of *pasta filata,* or "plastic curd" cheeses, of which Mozzarella is the most famous example; molded by hand into a pear shape and tied by a short noose, it is firm, mild, and melts beautifully.

Less widespread are Bagoss, a pungent, firm, nutty cheese that acquires greenish streaks when aged up to two years; Bitto, a sharp, compact cheese that can contain up to 10 percent goat's milk and is matured over two months; Pannerone (from *panna*, meaning "cream"), a soft, mild, saltless raw milk cheese with a delicately bitter aftertaste; and Scimudin, a mellow, creamy mountain cheese aged from three to four weeks.

Pizzoccheri della Valtellina

Buckwheat Flour Ribbons with Wilted Cabbage,
Potatoes, and Mountain Cheese

The Valtellina, a succession of hills at the foot of the Alps, has held on to its culinary traditions with great fervor, partly because of its isolation. Buckwheat is the Valtellina's most important grain; groats are milled into a dark, sweet, fragrant flour that forms the basis for countless *polente and this pasta.*

Make the pizzoccheri according to instructions on page 000 using the ingredients listed above, adding enough cool water (about ½ cup) to form a firm dough; add a little more water if the dough is dry or a little more flour if it is sticky. Knead 5 minutes, or until smooth, shape into a ball, wrap, and let rest 30 minutes.

Roll out the dough into a ½12-inch-thick rectangle on a floured counter. Cut into 2-inch-long rectangles. Dust the rectangles with flour, stack them, and cut into ¼-inch-wide strips. Toss with flour to prevent sticking and spread out in a single layer on a floured tray, covered with a towel.

SERVES 4

For the pizzoccheri:
1¾ cups buckwheat flour
1 cup plus 2 tablespoons unbleached all-purpose flour, plus extra for the counter
¼ teaspoon salt
2 extra-large eggs

To cook and serve:
½ pound boiling potatoes, peeled, quartered, and cut into ½-inch cubes
2 tablespoons salt
½ pound Savoy cabbage, cored, quartered, and cut into thin strips
4 tablespoons (½ stick) unsalted butter
1 medium yellow onion, minced
4 sage leaves
⅓ cup freshly grated Parmigiano-Reggiano
¼ pound Bitto, Valtellina Casera, Scimudin, or Fontina from Val d'Aosta, rind removed and cut into ¼-inch dice
½ teaspoon cracked black pepper

To cook, bring 6 quarts of water to a boil. Add the potatoes and salt and cook 5 minutes. Add the cabbage and pizzoccheri and cook until the pizzoccheri are al dente and the potatoes and cabbage are tender, about 10 minutes. Drain.

Meanwhile, melt the butter in an 8-inch skillet over medium heat. Add the onion and sage and cook 10 minutes. Layer the pizzoccheri, potatoes, and cabbage with the onion-butter mixture, Parmigiano, Bitto, and pepper in a bowl, making 2 layers of each, and serve hot.

PREPARATION TIPS: The pizzoccheri can be made up to 12 hours ahead, spread out in a single layer on a floured tray, and refrigerated, covered with a towel.

Casônsei Bresciani

Sausage and Cheese Pasta Horns from Brescia

Lombardy's plump casônsei can be crescent- or horn-shaped, and they can be stuffed with bread and sausage, greens and potatoes, beef, or boiled chicken. A pasta called casonziei or cassunziei (page 119) is also prepared in the Veneto, a legacy of Venice's four-century rule of the Lombard cities Brescia and Bergamo.

Make the dough and let it rest according to instructions on page 370.

Meanwhile, soak the bread in the milk for 5 minutes, then squeeze dry and crumble into a large bowl. Add the sausage, 1 cup of the Grana, ⅛ teaspoon of the salt, the pepper, and the nutmeg; mix with your hands until thoroughly combined.

Cut the dough into 4 pieces. Working with 1 piece at a time and keeping the others covered, roll out each using a pasta machine into a nearly transparent sheet. Cut into 2 × 3-inch rectangles. Spoon a little filling in a log shape onto each rectangle along the long side. Moisten above the filling with a touch of water, and flip the long side over the filling to enclose. Press to seal, then shape each rectangle into a horn by pulling down both corners.

SERVES 6

1 recipe Pasta Dough (page 370)
¼ pound crustless bread, torn into small pieces
½ cup whole milk
¾ pound Italian sausage, casings removed and crumbled into ⅙-inch pieces
1½ cups freshly grated Grana Padano
2 tablespoons plus ⅛ teaspoon salt
⅛ teaspoon freshly ground black pepper
⅛ teaspoon freshly grated nutmeg
Unbleached all-purpose flour for the counter
10 tablespoons (1¼ sticks) unsalted butter
12 sage leaves

These are the casônsei. Spread out in a single layer on a floured tray and cover with a towel.

Bring 6 quarts of water to a boil. Add the casônsei and the remaining 2 tablespoons of salt and cook until the casônsei are al dente, about 3 minutes. Remove with a slotted spoon to a platter.

Meanwhile, melt the butter with the sage in a 6-inch pan over medium heat. Pour the sage butter over the casônsei, sprinkle with the remaining ½ cup of Grana, and serve hot.

PREPARATION TIPS: Make the casônsei up to 12 hours ahead, spread out in a single layer on a floured tray, and refrigerate, covered with a towel.

A PASTA BEST ABSORBED

It seems that the name of one of Mantua's favorite stuffed pastas, *sorbir d'agnoli*, is derived from the indecorous manner in which it was eaten. *Sorbir d'agnoli* means "to absorb agnoli": the men who were fond of *agnolini* floating in a wine-spiked capon broth ate them without a spoon, sucking them right into their mouths from the bowl.

Gnocchi di Zucca al Rosmarino

Butternut Squash Gnocchi in Rosemary Butter

The gnocchi family in Lombardy includes potato gnocchi, spinach and ricotta mal-fatti, *and these delicate squash gnocchi.*

SERVES 4

2¼ pounds peeled and seeded butternut squash, cut into 2-inch cubes
1¼ cups freshly grated Grana Padano
Pinch freshly grated nutmeg
2 tablespoons plus ¼ teaspoon salt
½ cup unbleached all-purpose flour
10 tablespoons (1¼ sticks) unsalted butter
1 rosemary sprig
2 garlic cloves, crushed

Preheat the oven to 400°F.

Place the squash on an aluminum foil–lined 11 × 17-inch baking sheet, add 1 cup of water, and bake 1 hour, or until tender when pierced. Cool 5 minutes, then pass through a ricer twice onto the baking sheet. Return to the oven for 15 minutes to dry. Cool and place in a bowl. Stir in 1 cup of the Grana, the nutmeg, ¼ teaspoon of the salt, and enough flour to make a dough; you may not need all of the flour. Cut into 4 pieces and roll into finger-thick logs on a floured counter with well-floured hands. Cut into ½-inch pieces, toss with flour to prevent sticking, and spread out in a single layer on a floured tray. These are the gnocchi.

Bring 6 quarts of water to a boil. Add the gnocchi and the remaining 2 tablespoons of salt; cook until the gnocchi float, about 2 minutes. Remove with a slotted spoon to a platter.

Meanwhile, melt the butter with the rosemary and garlic in a 6-inch pan over medium heat. Pour over the gnocchi, sprinkle with the remaining ¼ cup of Grana, and serve hot.

PREPARATION TIPS: The gnocchi can be made up to 12 hours ahead, spread out in a single layer on a floured tray, and refrigerated, uncovered.

A PASSION FOR CORNMEAL

Lombardy is one of Italy's leading growers of corn. When polenta isn't served under a cloak of ragù, topped with Gorgonzola, layered with sausage, or grilled and partnered with porcini, it is offered alongside meat as a quiet, golden companion. But it is also baked into sweets like *torta sbrisolona,* a crumbly cake; *pan de mei,* buns flavored with elderflowers; and *pasta frolla de melgon,* a pie topped with jam. There is even *polenta e osei,* a trompe-l'oeil version of Bergamo's polenta with song birds: a cake is stuffed with apricot jam, covered with yellow marzipan resembling polenta, decorated with chocolate birds, and bathed in jam to simulate the birds' roasting juices.

Risotto alla Milanese

Saffron Risotto from Milan

In 1574, work on the Duomo, Milan's cathedral, had been under way for nearly 200 years. One of the men in charge of the stained-glass windows, known as Zafferano ("Saffron"), was so enamored of the golden hue saffron lent to his pastes that he added a little to each window he worked. He was set to marry the daughter of another glassmaker, but she was the object of another man's affections, who tried to ruin the nuptials by throwing saffron into the risotto prepared for their wedding. Everyone loved the result, however, and saffron risotto became a Milanese institution. Or so the story goes. When making this dish, cooks in Milan use Vialone Nano, a short-grain rice from Lago di Garda, instead of the more common Arborio. Vialone Nano's plump, short grains swell beautifully and release just the right amount of starch into the saffron broth.

SERVES 4

6 cups (1½ quarts) Beef Broth or Chicken Broth (page 368), or a combination
½ teaspoon saffron pistils
7 tablespoons unsalted butter, cubed, at room temperature
1 small yellow onion, minced
2 ounces beef marrow, cut into ¼-inch cubes (optional)
1½ cups Vialone Nano rice
½ cup dry white wine
½ cup freshly grated Parmigiano-Reggiano
½ teaspoon salt

Heat the broth to just below the boiling point in a 2-quart pot. Remove ½ cup of it to a bowl and dissolve the saffron in it; set aside.

Melt 3 tablespoons of the butter in a 12-inch sauté pan. Add the onion and marrow, if using, and cook over low heat 15 minutes, stirring often. Raise the heat to medium-high. Add the rice and cook, stirring with a wooden spoon, for 3 minutes. Deglaze with the wine and cook until it evaporates, stirring, about 3 minutes.

Begin adding the broth by the ½ cup and cook, stirring and adding more broth whenever the liquid has been absorbed, for 15 to 18 minutes, or until the rice is al dente. You may not need all of the broth. Strain the reserved saffron broth over the risotto through a fine sieve lined with paper towels. Fold it in along with the remaining 4 tablespoons of butter, the Parmigiano, and the salt. Remove from the heat, cover, let rest 2 minutes, and serve hot.

IN THE LAND OF RISOTTO

Nearly every Lombard town has its signature rice. In Mantua, risotto is enriched with sausage and nicknamed *alla pilota*, after the men (*piloti*) who harvest rice. In Pavia, sweetwater shrimp, peas, porcini, and tomatoes are folded into *risotto alla certosina*. In Valtellina, cranberry beans and Savoy cabbage make for a hearty risotto. And in Milan, leftover risotto is cooked *al salto*, flattened into a cake and fried in ample butter.

Vitello Tonnato

Thinly Sliced Veal in Cold Tuna Sauce

Vitello tonnato—also known as vitel tonné—is summer fare in Lombardy, as well as neighboring Piedmont. I grew up eating it, since it is one of my mother's standard cold dishes; this is an adaptation of her recipe. The twenty-four-hour marinating period is optional.

Place the veal in a large nonreactive container (such as a glass bowl) and add the carrot, onion, bay leaves, 1/2 teaspoon of the salt, 1/4 teaspoon of the pepper, and the wine. Cover and refrigerate 24 hours, turning twice.

Transfer the veal and its marinade to a 4-quart pot. Add enough water to cover the veal by 1 inch, bring to a boil, then reduce the heat to medium and cook, uncovered, for 1 1/2 hours. Cool the veal in the broth for 1 hour, then remove to a cutting board; reserve 1/2 cup of the broth and the carrot. Slice the veal very thinly and fan out the slices on a platter.

In a food processor, beat the egg yolks with 1 teaspoon of the salt and 1 teaspoon of the lemon juice for 1 minute, or until thick. Discard half of the egg yolk mixture. (It is almost impossible for ordinary food processors to properly beat a single egg yolk, which is why this recipe calls for two. You are better off wasting an egg yolk than risking not emulsifying your mayonnaise.) With the motor running, beat in the olive oil in a thin, steady stream; the mixture will emulsify. Add the remaining tablespoon of lemon juice, mix, and transfer this mayonnaise to a bowl.

Clean and dry the food processor. Process the reserved carrot, the tuna, the anchovies, 2 tablespoons of the capers, the remaining 1/2 teaspoon of salt, and the remaining 1/4 teaspoon of pepper until smooth. With the motor running, add enough of the reserved broth to dilute the sauce to a creamy coating consistency (you will need about 1/4 cup). Fold into the mayonnaise and spread over the veal. Garnish with the remaining 2 tablespoons of capers. Refrigerate for 2 hours and serve cool, the same day.

SERVES 6

1 1/2 pounds boneless veal top round

1 large carrot, chopped

1 medium yellow onion, chopped

2 bay leaves

2 teaspoons salt

1/2 teaspoon freshly ground black pepper

1 1/2 cups dry white wine

2 extra-large egg yolks, at room temperature

1 tablespoon plus 1 teaspoon fresh lemon juice (from 1/2 lemon)

1/2 cup extra-virgin olive oil

Two 6-ounce cans tuna packed in olive oil, drained

2 salted anchovies, boned, gutted, rinsed, and chopped

1/4 cup capers, drained

New Year's Sausage and More

THE ABUNDANCE OF CURED MEATS in Lombardy is in part a result of its plethora of cheeses, since the pigs' bran and corn diet is supplemented by whey leftover from cheesemaking. Most Lombard *salumi* are pork-based, but some beef, mutton, goat, horse, donkey, and goose specialties exist. The most renowned of Lombardy's cured meats is Bresaola, made in the Valtellina area from prized cuts of beef (or, less often, horse) that are salted, seasoned with pepper, cloves, cinnamon, and bay leaves, then hung to dry. A smoked version is worth seeking out in Italy, but the more common air-dried beef Bresaola is what you will find exported to North America. Italy's famed Prosciutto Cotto ("cooked ham") is largely produced in Lombardy: boneless hams are subjected to a salt brine, fla-

vored with juniper berries and other spices, then steam-baked, pressed, and shipped around the world, including North America. Sadly, none of Lombardy's sausages—including Cremona's Cotechino, a rich, fatty pork sausage typically boiled and served with lentils to ring in the New Year—meets FDA regulations; locally crafted Cotechino is sold by some American butchers (see Sources, page 372). Salame Milano, made of pork laced with grated Grana Padano and saffron and aged three months, is also produced in North America, since the original cannot be imported. If you visit Lombardy, make it a point to sample a ham called Violino; made from sheep, goat, or chamois, it earned its name because of the way it is held against the shoulder as it is sliced.

Ossobuco alla Milanese

Braised Veal Shanks with Gremolata

Literally translated, the name of this Milanese dish means "bone with a hole": the veal shank has a bone running through it, which is where the succulent marrow is found. Years ago, veal shanks were a dime a dozen. But now that the taste for them has caught on, prices have rocketed. If you can, serve *Saffron Risotto from Milan* alongside (page 68) and offer tiny spoons to extract the marrow.

FIVE MILANESE MEAT SPECIALTIES

The Milanesi have been nicknamed *busecconi,* after *busecca,* the tripe they so adore—especially when it's cooked with onions, tomatoes, cloves, and beans. Other Milanese dishes are more sophisticated, like pan-fried breaded veal chops called *cotolette alla milanese,* an Austrian legacy that has become symbolic of Italian cooking the world over; veal stuffed with sausage, chicken livers, and Pancetta, cooked in wine and broth; battered and fried calf's liver; and *fritto misto,* proof—if indeed proof is necessary— that the Milanesi have a penchant for all things battered and fried.

SERVES 4

6 tablespoons (¾ stick) unsalted butter
One ¼-pound slice Pancetta, cut into
⅛-inch cubes
4 veal shanks (½ pound each, preferably
center cut)
¼ cup unbleached all-purpose flour
½ teaspoon salt
¼ teaspoon freshly ground black pepper
1 cup dry white wine
1 carrot, minced
1 medium yellow onion, minced
1 celery stalk, minced
4 plum tomatoes, peeled (page 369), seeded,
and diced
1 cup Italian parsley leaves, minced
1 garlic clove, minced
Grated zest of 1 lemon

Melt the butter in a 12-inch sauté pan over medium-high heat. Add the Pancetta and cook until golden, about 2 minutes. Dredge the shanks in the flour, shaking off the excess, and add to the pan. Cook until lightly browned on both sides, turning once, about 5 minutes per side. Season with the salt and pepper.

Deglaze with the wine; after 5 minutes, add the carrot, onion, and celery and cook 10 minutes. Add the tomatoes, cover, and cook over medium-low heat for 1½ hours, or until tender, adding a little water if needed.

Fold in the parsley, garlic, and lemon zest; this is the gremolata. Cook 10 more minutes over medium-high heat, uncovered, adding a little water if the sauce evaporates. Serve hot.

PREPARATION TIPS: The shanks can be braised up to 2 hours ahead; warm gently and stir in the gremolata 10 minutes before serving.

Ciabatta

Slipper-Shaped Bread

The name of this rustic bread means "slipper," because that is exactly what it resembles. First baked near Lago di Como in the 1970s, ciabatta is now one of Lombardy's standard breads. Its wheaty flavor and large holes are conferred by biga, a yeasted sponge that promotes a slow rise with less yeast. If you do not have a powerful 11-cup food processor, use an electric mixer to knead the dough, or do it by hand. But the dough is so sticky that it is really best handled by a food processor.

MAKES 4 MEDIUM LOAVES

1 teaspoon instant yeast
6 cups unbleached bread flour, plus extra for the
 counter
1 tablespoon fine sea salt
Extra-virgin olive oil for greasing the bowl
1/4 cup cornmeal

Combine 1/4 teaspoon of the yeast with 2 cups of the flour in a large bowl. Add 1 cup of warm (110°F) water; stir for 2 minutes using a wooden spoon. Cover and set aside at room temperature for 6 to 24 hours. This is the biga; it will triple and then sink.

Place the remaining 4 cups of flour in a powerful 11-cup food processor with the remaining 3/4 teaspoon of yeast and the salt. Pulse to combine. Add the biga. Turn on the motor, and add enough warm (110°F) water to form a soft, sticky dough (you will need about 1 3/4 cups). Process for 45 seconds; the dough should be smooth and sticky. Place in a lightly oiled bowl, shape into a ball, cover, and let rise at room temperature until doubled, about 1 1/2 hours.

Cut the dough into 4 pieces, flatten each into a rectangle, and stretch each into a 4 × 10-inch rectangle. Place on a generously floured counter and dimple with your fingers. Cover with a towel and let rise at room temperature for 1 1/2 hours.

Meanwhile, preheat the oven with a baking stone in it to 425°F.

THE MOST TRADITIONAL COOKIES OF ALL

More than any other, one Lombard sweet embodies the devotion to tradition: *offelle di Parona,* delicate olive oil cookies baked in the town of Parona near Vigevano. Their recipe was developed in the 1800s by a baker at Forno Collivasone, who conceded it to the town council on the condition that it would continue to be made exactly as he indicated. Today, Parona's Pro Loco, an association that promotes tourism and organizes town activities, controls the production of offelle. Only a handful of local pastry shops has the original recipe, which is followed to the letter. To taste offelle in their moment of glory, attend Parona's yearly offelle festival, held every October (call 011.39.0384.253636 for more information).

Dust a baker's peel or the back of an 11 × 17-inch baking sheet with the cornmeal. Uncover the loaves, place them upside down on the peel and gently dimple the tops with your fingertips (this prevents the breads from bubbling as they bake). Dust the tops with flour. Transfer onto the baking stone and bake in the preheated oven for 10 minutes, misting every 3 minutes with water from a spray bottle and closing the oven door quickly every time. Bake 10 to 15 more minutes without misting, or until the bread is golden brown and crisp, then cool on a rack. Depending on the size of your oven and baking stone, it may be necessary to bake the bread in 2 batches, to avoid crowding on the stone.

PREPARATION TIPS: Make the dough and let it rise in the refrigerator up to 24 hours; return to room temperature before proceeding.

MOSTARDA DI CREMONA

Some foods whisper their secrets, while others call out their tales loud and strong. That's exactly what mostarda di Cremona does: it shouts of the distant past, of meals shared and feasts savored hundreds of years ago. This spicy, pungent fruit preserve laced with mustard powder (hence the name) has roots in ancient Rome, when sweet and salty concoctions were used to accompany boiled meats and vegetables. Medieval and Renaissance cooks did the same thing, providing a lift to bland foods with vibrant condiments. Made by poaching fresh fruit like pears, quince, pineapples, figs, cherries, oranges, citron, and mandarins in a simple sugar syrup with mustard powder, mostarda di Cremona is an indispensable partner to *bollito misto,* Zampone, and Cotechino, and is essential to squash stuffings for pasta.

LOMBARDY'S WINES

LOMBARDY'S LUSH VALLEYS, gentle hills, and rugged mountains yield about 42 million gallons of wine per year, with DOC wines representing more than 35 percent of total production.

The three main DOC viticultural areas are the Oltrepò Pavese, Franciacorta, and Valtellina to the far south, far east, and far north respectively. The Oltrepò is the largest of these areas, and Barbera, Croatina (locally known as Bonarda), and Uva Rara grapes (locally known as Bonarda Novarese) make up the bulk of its production.

Franciacorta, the youngest and most promising of the three viticultural areas, is responsible for a sparkling wine vinified according to the Champenoise method from a blend of Pinot Nero, Pinot Bianco, Pinot Grigio, and Chardonnay grapes, as well as still red and white wines that benefit from the mineral-rich soil, warm days, cool summer evenings, and moderating effect of Lago d'Iseo.

The Valtellina, a largely mountainous area with rocky soil, is the northernmost outpost where the Nebbiolo grape is cultivated, despite high altitudes and low median temperatures, thanks to generous sunshine. The Valtellina reds are slightly more tannic than those of Piedmont, and are often labeled by their subzones (Grumello, Inferno, Sassella, and Valgella). Valtellina also produces the prized Sforzato, a red dried-grape wine with a high alcohol content.

Lugana, a DOC wine area to the south of Lago di Garda, offers dry Trebbiano-based whites with a refreshing tang and high acidity in some vintages.

Budino di Panettone

Panettone Bread Pudding

Milan's panettone has become symbolic of Christmas the world over. This high, buttery bread is made with a natural yeast starter and studded with candied fruit and raisins. Legends concerning its origins abound: One claims that a young baker named Toni added candied fruit to a simple bread dough to increase sales at the failing bakery where he worked; another has a love-struck young baker win the heart of the bakery owner's daughter by creating this spectacular bread. Most Italians don't eat panettone after ringing in the New Year, unless it's to finish an opened one. But the Milanesi save a piece for February 3, the feast of San Biagio, protector of the throat, to ward off sore throats for the coming year. I don't save my panettone for San Biagio, but I do bake leftovers into a creamy pudding that marries perfectly with Moscato d'Asti at meal's end or hot chocolate for a winter snack.

SERVES 8

10 ounces leftover panettone, cut into 1/2-inch cubes
1/4 cup rum
1/4 cup sweet Marsala
2 cups whole milk
Grated zest of 1 orange
1 cinnamon stick
4 extra-large eggs, separated
1/2 cup sugar
Unsalted butter for greasing the cake pan

Spread out the panettone on a tray and sprinkle it with the rum and Marsala. Let rest 30 minutes.

Meanwhile, heat the milk, orange zest, and cinnamon to just below the boiling point in a 1-quart pot; discard the cinnamon and cool to room temperature. In a very large bowl, whisk the egg yolks and sugar until pale and thick, about 2 minutes. Still whisking, pour in the flavored milk.

Preheat the oven to 400°F.

In an electric mixer with a whisk attachment, beat the egg whites until stiff peaks form, then gently whisk into the bowl with the egg yolk mixture in two additions, being careful not to deflate the whites. Fold in the panettone cubes with a rubber spatula and spoon into a buttered 10-inch springform cake pan.

Place the cake pan in a 12-inch roasting pan filled halfway with warm water and bake in the preheated oven for 40 minutes, or until set and golden. Gently unmold onto a platter and serve warm or at room temperature.

Trentino–Alto Adige

Omelette di Patate
Grated Potato Pancakes

Asparagi con Salsa alla Bolzanina
Asparagus in Egg-Horseradish Sauce

Ravioli della Val Pusteria
Rye Pasta Squares Filled with Spinach and Caraway Seeds

Canederli Tirolesi
Speck-and-Chive Bread Dumplings in Aromatic Butter

Gnocchetti all'Uovo con Semi di Papavero
Fresh Egg Dumplings in Poppy Seed Butter

Strangolapreti
Swiss Chard and Bread Crumb Gnocchi

Strudel di Carne e Mele
Pork and Apple Strudel

Gulasch di Manzo
Beef, Potato, Onion, and Paprika Stew

Capriolo con Mirtilli
Braised Goat with Blueberry Compote

Palle di Prugna
Plum-Stuffed Buns

Whenever I think of Trentino–Alto Adige, I remember my first visit there: the drive through meticulously maintained countryside, winding roads leading from one valley to the next. I see rows of vines, perfectly aligned and heavy with grapes. I see thousands of peach trees standing like soldiers in the evening light. I see orchards stretching endlessly into the distance, golden apples barely discernible against the darkening sky. I remember my first taste of *canederli,* my first sip of Gewürztraminer, my first inkling that I was in Italy yet *not* in Italy.

And it wasn't just because of the food: even all those years ago, I knew better than to expect *bucatini all'amatriciana* or basil-scented seafood soups a few miles from the Austrian border. It was the feeling of the place: tidy, quiet, restrained, and—this was the clincher—buzzing with German words and accents.

Trentino–Alto Adige, decreed an autonomous region in 1948, is made up of Italian-speaking Trentino in the south and German-speaking Alto Adige in the north. It was linked to the Germanic Empire until the Hapsburg provinces absorbed it in 1801. In 1918, Austria ceded the land to Italy. But decades of Austrian rule have left the area with a distinctly Germanic feel: the food, the language, the architecture, even the window displays seem more German than Italian. It's Italy, but somehow *not* Italy.

As with Emilia-Romagna, which is home to two different cuisines, Trentino–Alto Adige is really two regions in one. Trentino is closer in spirit to Italy's Mediterranean soul. Alto Adige, by contrast, is very much as its older name implies: South Tyrol, a Germanic land with Germanic tendencies. Home to some of the highest peaks in Europe, including the Palla Bianca at more than 12,200 feet, Trentino and Alto Adige share an affinity for pure flavors and a predilection for hearty fare. As in all mountain settings, it is the valleys that are most densely populated and intensely cultivated. Grains like corn, wheat, oat, barley, rye, and buckwheat are the foundation of the cuisine, along with cow's milk cheese, cured pork, and cold-resistant vegetables like cabbage, potatoes, carrots, beets, beans, and onions. But what cooks in Trentino and cooks in Alto Adige make of this northern bounty is quite different.

Trentino developed both a survival cuisine linked to mountain life and a refined cuisine dating to the Renaissance, when the city of Trent (today's capital) was a stopover for popes, prelates, and monarchs attending the Council of Trent, a summit that defined church doctrine and fought against Lutheran reform. The chefs who cooked for the pontiffs set the stage for future cooks, who would emulate their elegant presentation and strive toward their level of sophistication.

Alto Adige, on the other hand, is the door to the Dolomites, a meeting ground for the diverse culinary traditions of Austrians, Germans, Hungarians, and Slavs. It is frontier land, the border between the German and Latin worlds, where Mitteleuropean and Mediterranean cultures come together. The Germanic world left its imprint: rigor, precision, order, and a love of pork, butter, and cream. But nearby Venice also left its mark: an eye for beauty, a passion for feasting, an affection for sweet-and-sour flavors, a fondness for anchovies. In this northern outpost of Italy, beer vies with wine for first place on the table, olive oil is rarely used, and until a few years ago, it was a challenge to find a restaurant that served pasta.

Favorite Restaurants, Shops, and Places

- EBERLE, Passeggiata S. Oswaldo 1, Santa Maddalena, 0471.976125 or 0471.978574. This is a mountain hotel and restaurant with outstanding first courses.
- FRANZISKANER, Via dei Francescani 3, Bolzano. The oldest and most famous bakery in town; try the *schüttelbrot*.
- HOTEL ELEFANTE, Via Rio Bianco 4, Bressanone, 0472.832750. A hotel and restaurant, the birthplace of the *piatto elefante*.
- PASTICCERIA MOSCHEN, Via dei Francescani, Bolzano, 0471.978776. The *torta saracena* is especially nice.

- RISTORANTE CHIESA, Parco San Marco (off Via San Marco), Trent, 0461.985577. They offer a curious apple-based menu.
- SALUMERIA MASÉ, Via Nazionale 31, Strembo, 0465.804666. Artisanal production of cured meats; try the Mocetta Rendenera and beef salami.
- TORGGLKELLER, Via Tinne 7, Chiusa, 0472.847642. A wine bar where you sip local wines as you sit inside huge wooden wine casks.
- TRATTORIA FINK, Via delle Mostre 9, Bolzano. Order the *piatto tirolese*.

Telephone country code: 011.39

Omelette di Patate

Grated Potato Pancakes

Potatoes are one of Trentino–Alto Adige's main crops, and they are cooked into a variety of pancakes. In Alto Adige, a pancake of mashed potato and beef called gröstl makes use of leftover boiled meat; in Trentino, mashed potatoes are paired with salt cod instead. But my favorite potato pancake resembles Austria and Germany's rösti: grated raw potatoes are combined with eggs and flour, then fried. Enjoy these pancakes as an antipasto, as a side dish, or, as children often do, sprinkled with confectioner's sugar as a homey dessert.

SERVES 4

1 pound boiling potatoes, peeled and
  coarsely grated
2 extra-large eggs
¼ cup unbleached all-purpose flour
½ teaspoon salt
½ cup extra-virgin olive oil

Place the potatoes in a colander over a plate for 2 hours. Squeeze dry and pat with paper towels; the potatoes will have darkened. In a medium bowl, beat the eggs; fold in the potatoes, flour, and salt.

Heat a 12-inch skillet over a medium-high flame and add the olive oil. After 3 minutes, drop in 4 spoonfuls of the potato mixture about 1 inch apart; half of the mixture will still be in the bowl. Fry until golden on the bottom, about 5 minutes. Flip and cook until golden on the other side, about 5 minutes.

Remove with a slotted spatula to a plate lined with paper towels and blot dry. Fry the remaining potato mixture in the same manner in the olive oil left in the skillet. Serve hot.

A VISIT TO THE BAKER'S

Trentino–Alto Adige has one of the richest bread repertoires in Italy; wheat, corn, rye, oat, millet, and buckwheat thrive in the Alpine climate, giving rise to an incredible variety of loaves, flatbreads, and buns. The diversity is even more marked in Alto Adige, where the Austrian and Germanic heritage have contributed a taste for dark, dense, multigrain loaves: fennel, caraway, sesame, poppy seeds, nuts, apples, raisins, Speck, saffron, onions, herbs, figs, whole wheat berries, and more are folded into bread dough. Among Alto Adige's breads, try *breatl,* a round flattened loaf. Also tasty is *brezel,* Alto Adige's pretzel, born in monasteries as a form of penance during Lent: its shape is said to symbolize hands and arms crossed over the chest. Anyone with a sweet tooth will enjoy fruit-studded *kletzenbrot,* and those seeking a crisp, wheaty accompaniment to Speck are sure to find rye flour disks called *schüttelbrot* addictive.

Asparagi con Salsa alla Bolzanina

Asparagus in Egg-Horseradish Sauce

The town of Bolzano's northerly position means that asparagus does not come into season there until May. But when it does finally arrive, it is received with pomp. Fat stalks of white asparagus, grown beneath a cover to prevent them from turning green, are especially prized. This appetizer from Eberle, a charming hotel and restaurant in Santa Maddalena, calls for two typical Austrian ingredients: fresh horseradish and chives.

SERVES 4

32 thin or 24 thick asparagus spears,
    woody ends trimmed
2 extra-large eggs
½ cup extra-virgin olive oil
2 tablespoons white wine vinegar
1 tablespoon grated fresh horseradish
    (substitute 1 teaspoon Dijon mustard)
½ cup snipped chives
½ teaspoon salt
⅛ teaspoon freshly ground black pepper

Bring 1 quart of water to a boil. Place the asparagus in a steamer basket and steam over the boiling water until crisp-tender, about 5 minutes; with tongs or a slotted spoon, remove to a bowl of ice water, drain, blot dry, and place on a platter. Keep the pot of water boiling.

Add the eggs to the boiling water and cook 8 minutes. Drain, cool, and shell. Separate the whites from the yolks; mince the whites and set aside.

Push the yolks through a sieve into a medium mixing bowl, pressing with the back of a spoon. Add the olive oil in a thin, steady stream, beating constantly with a whisk until emulsified. Beat in the vinegar, horseradish, chives, salt, pepper, and minced egg whites. Pour over the asparagus and serve within 5 minutes.

VALLEY AND MOUNTAIN VEGETABLES

Most meals in Trentino–Alto Adige include cabbage in one form or another: pickled into sauerkraut (*crauti* in Italian), shredded and sautéed with apples and Speck, or braised in red wine. The oldest and most important European mushroom market, held in Trent, offers two hundred varieties of mushrooms; chanterelles and porcini take center stage, but prized *ovoli* (edible egg-shaped *Amanita caesarea* mushrooms) and ordinary button mushrooms get their fair share of attention too. The last decade has seen the proliferation of cucumbers, celery, zucchini, radicchio, and leeks. But the most commonplace vegetables remain those that can withstand winter at the foot of the Alps, like potatoes, carrots, turnips, and kohlrabi.

Ravioli della Val Pusteria

Rye Pasta Squares Filled with Spinach and Caraway Seeds

Pasta is nearly nonexistent in Alto Adige, but it sometimes does appear as an accompaniment to meat or poultry in decidedly non-Italian style. The ravioli in this recipe are the only typical stuffed pasta of Alto Adige; the generous use of ground caraway seeds lends the dish a unique flavor.

SERVES 6

For the dough:

3 cups rye flour

¼ teaspoon salt

2 tablespoons (¼ stick) unsalted butter, melted

2 extra-large eggs

½ cup whole milk, plus extra if needed

Unbleached all-purpose flour for the counter
  and tray

For the filling:

4½ pounds spinach leaves, washed thoroughly
  and dried

4 tablespoons (½ stick) unsalted butter

2 teaspoons salt

1 teaspoon freshly grated nutmeg

2 tablespoons plus 4 teaspoons caraway seeds,
  coarsely crushed in a mortar

To cook and serve:

12 cups (3 quarts) Beef Broth (page 368) or
  water

2 tablespoons plus ¼ teaspoon salt

⅛ teaspoon freshly ground black pepper

8 tablespoons (1 stick) unsalted butter

½ cup fresh bread crumbs

½ cup freshly grated Parmigiano-Reggiano

POLENTA BOTH YELLOW AND BLACK

Trentino's corn is among the best Italy offers: golden ears are picked when the first autumn fogs drop, dried in well-ventilated rooms, and slowly ground in stone mills. One polenta recipe calls for cooking cornmeal with onions and potatoes until a purée forms; the resulting porridge is served with sausages and Speck, cheese, boiled dried cod, or fried fish. Another polenta, called *mosa* or *mus,* features cornmeal, white flour, milk, and a topping of melted butter and poppy seeds. And since buckwheat is plentiful in Trentino–Alto Adige, local cooks prepare a nutty *polenta nera* with buckwheat flour.

Make the dough according to instructions on page 370 using the ingredients listed above, adding a little milk if the dough is dry or a little flour if it is sticky. Knead 5 minutes, or until smooth, shape into a ball, wrap, and let rest 30 minutes.

Meanwhile, make the filling: Cook the spinach over medium heat in a covered 5-quart sauté pan for 5 minutes. Rinse, squeeze dry, and chop finely.

Melt the butter in the same pan over medium heat. Add the chopped spinach and cook 5 minutes. Transfer to a mixing bowl and add the salt, nutmeg, and 4 teaspoons of the caraway seeds. Allow to cool for 15 minutes.

Cut the dough into 4 pieces. Working with 1 piece at a time and keeping the others covered, roll out each piece using a pasta machine into a thin sheet (the sheets should be a little thicker than for other pastas or they might crack; the third-to-last setting on most pasta machines is ideal). Lay 1 sheet of dough on the counter, sprinkle 1 tablespoon of caraway seeds over it, and place single teaspoons of the spinach on it 2 inches apart. Brush a little water around the spinach and top with a second sheet of dough. Press between the rows of filling to squeeze out air pockets and to seal. Cut into 2-inch squares with a fluted pastry wheel. These are the ravioli. Spread out in a single layer on a floured tray. Continue in the same manner with the remaining sheets and filling.

To cook, bring the broth or water to a boil. Reduce the heat to medium, add the ravioli and 2 tablespoons of the salt, and cook until al dente, about 3 minutes; do not let the water boil vigorously or the ravioli might tear. Remove with a slotted spoon to a platter and sprinkle with the remaining ¼ teaspoon of salt and the pepper.

Meanwhile, melt the butter in an 8-inch skillet over medium-high heat and add the bread crumbs. Cook until golden, about 3 minutes, stirring. Sprinkle over the ravioli. Serve immediately, passing the Parmigiano at the table.

PREPARATION TIPS: Stuff the ravioli up to 24 hours ahead, spread out in a single layer on a floured tray, and refrigerate, covered with a towel.

WHERE PASTA IS NOT A STAPLE

Cooks in Trentino are more apt to cook pasta than their neighbors in Alto Adige. One of the mainstays is *bigoli* with sardines, as in Venice (page 118): after all, Trentino–Alto Adige was known as Venetia Tridentina until 1947. Other favorites are *tagliatelle smalzade,* tossed with cream and juices from a veal roast; ravioli stuffed with roasted meat, boiled chicken, parsley, and onions; and *pasticcio di maccheroni,* dating to the elegant repasts served during the Council of Trent, featuring maccheroni and squab ragù encased in pastry dough.

A Cow's Milk Cheese in Every Valley

EVERY VALLEY IN TRENTINO–ALTO ADIGE produces its own cheese. Compared to Piedmont's and Lombardy's cheeses, Trentino–Alto Adige's are more obscure, partly because they're produced on a smaller scale. Cows far outnumber goats and sheep, so cheeses are usually made from cow's milk. See Sources (page 372) to purchase the following varieties in North America.

GRANA TRENTINO, a firm grating cheese with a grainy structure, recalls Grana Padano and is aged at least fifteen months.

CASOLET, made at home in the old days (the word is derived from *casa,* meaning "home"), is shaped in an unusual parallelepiped form; aged from twenty to sixty days, it has a pale, smooth or slightly wrinkled rind, compact consistency with fine holes, and sweet, delicate taste.

SPRESSA, produced from winter milk, is a dark straw-yellow color with tiny holes and a rough rind, and becomes increasingly aromatic when aged two years.

PUZZONE DI MOENA ("stinky from Moena"), a potent, soft-fleshed, odorous cheese, is aged up to a year and sometimes sold under the name Spretz Tsaori.

VEZZENA, a compact, elastic cheese aged from six months to two years, owes its aroma to the fragrant herbs and grasses the cows munch on in the plateau of the Vezzene at an altitude of 3,000 feet.

GRAUKÄSE, a lean, marbled, yellow-fleshed cheese without a rind, is aged up to two weeks until it is sharp and tangy.

PRESSATO DI MERANO, a salt-brined cheese, is aged up to two years and has marvelous melting potential.

Canederli Tirolesi

Speck-and-Chive Bread Dumplings in Aromatic Butter

Trentino and Alto Adige both specialize in plump bread dumplings that float in beef broth or appear as companions to braised or roasted meat. Called canederli in Trentino and knödel in Alto Adige, they can feature nothing more than stale bread, eggs, milk, butter, onion, and parsley, or they can include bits of meat. The knödel below are of the latter variety: studded with Speck, a rosy smoked ham that is dry-salted and aged for five to six months, they make a satisfying first course on chilly evenings. Be sure to use a close-textured, dense, stale bread: if the bread is light and airy, or if it is too fresh, it will absorb too much liquid and therefore call for too much flour, resulting in leaden rather than light dumplings. You will find Speck imported only from Austria, not Trentino–Alto Adige, in North America; see Sources (page 372) to purchase it by mail.

SERVES 6

3 extra-large eggs
1 cup whole milk
½ pound crustless day-old white country bread, cut into ½-inch cubes
One ¼-pound slice Speck, cut into ⅛-inch dice
2 cups snipped chives
2 tablespoons minced Italian parsley
2 teaspoons caraway seeds
2 tablespoons plus ½ teaspoon salt
½ teaspoon freshly ground black pepper
1 cup unbleached all-purpose flour, plus extra for the counter
6 tablespoons (¾ stick) unsalted butter

Beat the eggs and milk in a large bowl. Add the bread, Speck, 1¾ cups of the chives, the parsley, caraway, ½ teaspoon of the salt, and the pepper; work with your hands until the bread breaks down. Mix in the flour with your hands until the mixture holds together and forms a gluey paste; add more flour by the tablespoon if it does not. Shape into walnut-sized balls with moistened hands and roll on a generously floured counter; spread out in a single layer on a floured tray. These are the canederli.

Meanwhile, bring 4 quarts of water to a boil. Drop in the canederli and the remaining 2 tablespoons of salt. Cook over medium heat 15 minutes, uncovered, just below the boiling point. Remove with a slotted spoon to a bowl.

Melt the butter over medium-high heat in a 12-inch skillet. Add the canederli and cook 5 minutes, or until golden all over, turning to cook evenly. Serve hot, sprinkled with the remaining ¼ cup of chives.

PREPARATION TIPS: The canederli can be made up to 6 hours ahead, spread out in a single layer on a floured tray, and refrigerated, covered with a towel.

Gnocchetti all'Uovo con Semi di Papavero
Fresh Egg Dumplings in Poppy Seed Butter

The Germans, Austrians, and Hungarians all make this delicate, eggy pasta, which is known as spaetzle. Most often served plain alongside rich meat stews, spaetzle is also lovely topped with poppy seeds and melted butter, as below. See Sources (page 372) to buy a spaetzle press.

See Sources (page 372) to buy a spaetzle press.

SOUPS WITH AUSTRIAN ROOTS

Alto Adige's soups are identifiably Austrian and German. Tripe soup is sprinkled with vinegar for an acidic tang; barley, almost extinct in other Italian regions, is cooked with carrots, celery, leeks, spinach, string beans, peas, potatoes, zucchini, and a ham bone; dried bread is topped with spleen crostini and floated in savory beef broth; and the prized wine of Terlano is combined with beef broth, egg yolks, cinnamon, and heavy cream, then poured over fried bread for a warming soup.

SERVES 2 AS A FIRST COURSE OR 4 AS A SIDE DISH

2 cups unbleached all-purpose flour
1 tablespoon plus ¼ teaspoon salt
2 extra-large eggs
¾ cup whole milk
6 tablespoons (¾ stick) unsalted butter
1 tablespoon poppy seeds

Bring 5 quarts of water to a boil.

Meanwhile, beat the flour with ¼ teaspoon of the salt and the eggs in a bowl with a wooden spoon. Beat in the milk until smooth, about 3 minutes.

Spoon the batter into a spaetzle press and place the press over the boiling water. Rub the moveable part of the press back and forth so the batter drops into the boiling water; continue until all the batter has been used. If you don't have a spaetzle press, push the batter through a large-holed colander into the boiling water with a spoon.

Add the remaining tablespoon of salt to the boiling water and stir. As soon as the spaetzle float to the surface, after about 1 minute, drain them.

Melt the butter in a 12-inch skillet over medium heat and add the poppy seeds. Stir in the spaetzle, cook 30 seconds, and serve hot.

Strangolapreti

Swiss Chard and Bread Crumb Gnocchi

The name of these gnocchi, a specialty of Trentino, means "priest stranglers." Considering the historical importance of priests and pontiffs in the area, I wonder whether locals may have found the religious presence overbearing at times; in Romagna, which was under papal rule for centuries, a different pasta goes by a similarly violent name.

Soak the bread in the milk in a medium bowl; set aside 30 minutes. Squeeze dry and crumble into a large bowl.

Meanwhile, bring 6 quarts of water to a boil. Add the Swiss chard and ¾ teaspoon of the salt and cook 5 minutes; remove with a slotted spoon to a bowl of ice water, then drain and squeeze dry, reserving ½ cup of the water you squeezed out. Keep the pot of water boiling.

In a food processor, purée the Swiss chard with the ½ cup of reserved water you squeezed from it. Add to the bowl of bread along with ¼ teaspoon of the salt, the eggs, bread crumbs, ½ cup of the Grana, and the flour. Stir until a dough forms, adding more flour if it is sticky. (Test the texture of the dough at this point: drop a ¼-inch piece into the reserved boiling water and cook until it rises to the surface. If the dough is too soft or falls apart, add more flour.)

Turn out the dough onto a lightly floured counter. Cut into 8 pieces and roll each into a finger-thick log, then cut into ¼-inch-wide pieces. Roll in flour to prevent sticking and spread out in a single layer on a floured tray. These are the strangolapreti.

Add the strangolapreti and the remaining 2 tablespoons of salt to the pot of boiling water and cook until they float to the surface, about 2 minutes. Remove with a slotted spoon to a serving platter.

Meanwhile, melt the butter with the sage over medium heat in a 6-inch skillet. Pour the sage butter over the strangolapreti in the platter and sprinkle with the remaining ¼ cup of Grana. Serve hot.

PREPARATION TIPS: Shape the strangolapreti up to 2 hours ahead, spread out in a single layer on a floured tray, and refrigerate, covered with a towel.

SERVES 4

6 ounces crustless day-old white country bread, cubed

1⅓ cups whole milk

2¼ pounds Swiss chard leaves, washed thoroughly

2 tablespoons plus 1 teaspoon salt

2 extra-large eggs

½ cup fresh bread crumbs

¾ cup freshly grated Grana Padano

1 cup unbleached all-purpose flour, plus extra for the counter

8 tablespoons (1 stick) unsalted butter

8 sage leaves

Strudel di Carne e Mele

Pork and Apple Strudel

Over forty-five varieties of apples are culti- vated in Trentino–Alto Adige, and this enticing sweet and savory strudel combines suc- culent roasted pork with pine nuts and Golden Delicious apples, the variety grown most profi- ciently in the region's orchards. If you have extra roasted pork, beef, or even veal, by all means use it in this recipe: this strudel was born as a way of finishing leftover meats.

SERVES 6

2 pounds trimmed boneless pork loin
One ¼-pound slice Pancetta, cut into 16 strips
1¼ teaspoons salt
½ teaspoon freshly ground black pepper
4 tablespoons (½ stick) unsalted butter,
    2 tablespoons cubed, 2 tablespoons melted
    and cooled
1 cup dry white wine
2 Golden Delicious apples, peeled, cored, and
    cut into ½-inch cubes
¼ cup pine nuts
1 cup plus 1 tablespoon unbleached all-purpose
    flour, plus extra for the counter
1 teaspoon sugar
1 extra-large egg

Preheat the oven to 425°F.

Make 16 small incisions in the pork with a paring knife and insert a strip of Pancetta into each incision. Season with ¾ teaspoon of the salt and ¼ teaspoon of the pepper. Place in a 12-inch roasting pan, top with the cubed butter, and roast in the preheated oven for 30 minutes.

Add the wine. Roast 30 more minutes, basting with the cooking juices every 5 minutes. Remove from the oven. Cool 15 minutes, then cut into ½-inch cubes. Place in a bowl and stir in ⅓ cup plus 1 tablespoon of the pork's cooking juices (add water if needed to make up the quantity). Add the apples, pine nuts, ¼ teaspoon of the salt, and the remaining ¼ teaspoon of pepper.

Mix the flour, sugar, and the remaining ¼ teaspoon of salt in a bowl. Work in the egg and 1 tablespoon of the melted butter, then add ¼ cup of room-temperature water. Turn out onto a floured counter. Knead into a supple dough, adding flour as needed to prevent sticking, about 5 minutes, slamming the dough on the counter a few times. Dust with flour, shape into a ball, wrap, and let rest 30 minutes.

Roll out the dough on a lightly floured counter into a 10 × 14-inch rectangle. Draping the dough over the knuckles of your two hands, stretch it until it is almost transparent into a 17 × 25-inch rectangle. Don't panic if you make a hole, since the dough will be rolled over itself.

Place the dough on a clean, dry towel. Spoon the pork mixture over the dough, leaving a 1-inch border all around. Pull the edge of the towel up to roll the dough over the filling, forming a log. Gently transfer to an 11 × 17-inch baking sheet, using the towel to help. Remove the towel, place the log seam side down, and curve into a horseshoe shape.

Glaze with the remaining tablespoon of melted butter. Bake the strudel in the preheated oven 30 minutes, or until the crust is golden and crisp, and serve hot.

PREPARATION TIPS: Shape the strudel up to 4 hours ahead, cover with plastic wrap, and refrigerate until you are ready to bake.

Gulasch di Manzo

Beef, Potato, Onion, and Paprika Stew

Except for trout, which abounds in Trentino–Alto Adige's lakes, fish plays a minor role in the region's cuisine, leaving plenty of room on the table for meat—especially beef. Beef vecchia Trento is slowly cooked until tender with vinegar and cream; salted beef is paired with boiled beans; and sauerbraten, Germany's vinegar-braised roast beef, is another specialty. Yet no meat dish is more symbolic of the Austro-Hungarian empire's legacy than gulasch, a Sunday classic of fork-tender beef in a paprika-scented sauce. Chive-scented canederli (page 85) are a heavenly accompaniment.

A DISH THAT "KILLS HUNGER"

One of Trentino's favored second courses is called *smacafam* (dialect for "kills the hunger"), once cooked only for Carnevale festivities but now enjoyed year-round: a cornmeal or buckwheat flour batter is poured into a greased roasting pan, sausages are set over the top, and the whole is baked. Recipes vary from valley to valley: some call for white flour, others for raisins, pine nuts, walnuts, anise seeds, and milk, resulting in a sweet rather than savory dish. But no matter how smacafam is flavored, it always nourishes and satisfies.

SERVES 8

6 tablespoons (¾ stick) unsalted butter

3 medium yellow onions, minced

2 tablespoons red wine vinegar

3 tablespoons sweet paprika

2 pounds boneless beef shoulder, trimmed of fat and sinew, cut into 1-inch cubes

3 plum tomatoes, peeled (page 369), seeded, and diced

1 garlic clove, crushed

2 bay leaves

1 tablespoon minced marjoram

1 teaspoon caraway seeds

Grated zest of ½ lemon

1½ cups Beef Broth (page 368), plus extra if needed

1 teaspoon salt

1½ pounds boiling potatoes, peeled and cut into 1-inch cubes

Melt the butter in a 4-quart sauté pan. Add the onions and cook over medium heat until golden, about 15 minutes. Add the vinegar and paprika and cook 2 minutes.

Stir in the beef, tomatoes, garlic, bay leaves, marjoram, caraway seeds, and lemon zest. Cook 5 minutes. Add the broth and salt and bring the liquid to a boil. Reduce the heat to medium-low and cook, covered, 3 hours, stirring once in a while and adding a little broth if needed. Add the potatoes, cover, and cook 1 more hour. Discard the garlic and bay leaves and serve hot.

PREPARATION TIPS: Cook the stew up to 3 days ahead, refrigerate, and warm over low heat before serving.

Capriolo con Mirtilli

Braised Goat with Blueberry Compote

Berries grow in profusion in Alto Adige's mountainous terrain and are cooked into chunky preserves perfect for spooning into buttery crusts or serving alongside game, as the recipe below shows. This savory and sweet pairing is not unique to Alto Adige: in Piedmont, blueberries are cooked with a hint of grappa and served with braised venison. Since you're not likely to come across mountain goat as easily as cooks in Alto Adige, opt for young goat instead; check Sources (page 372) to order, or use lamb or venison. Canederli (page 85) make an outstanding side.

SERVES 4

2 bay leaves

1 teaspoon juniper berries

2 rosemary sprigs

2 pounds boneless goat shoulder (substitute lamb or venison shoulder), trimmed of fat and sinew, cut into 1-inch cubes

1½ cups dry red wine

½ cup unbleached all-purpose flour

6 tablespoons (¾ stick) unsalted butter

1 medium yellow onion, minced

1 teaspoon salt

½ cup heavy cream

2 cups chunky blueberry preserves

Tie the bay leaves, juniper berries, and rosemary in a piece of cheesecloth. Place the goat in a deep container and add the wine and cheesecloth bundle. Refrigerate for 3 days.

Drain the goat (reserving the marinade and cheesecloth bundle) and blot dry on paper towels. Dredge in the flour, shaking off the excess. Melt the butter over medium heat in a heavy-bottomed 14-inch sauté pan. Add the onion and cook 5 minutes. Add the goat and cook, stirring often, 15 minutes. Add the reserved marinade and cheesecloth bundle, season with the salt, cover, and cook over medium-low heat 3 hours, or until the meat is tender.

Uncover the pan and bring the liquid to a boil. Add the cream and boil until the sauce reduces to a coating consistency, about 5 minutes over medium-high heat. Discard the cheesecloth bundle. Serve the goat hot, with the blueberry preserves.

TRENTINO–ALTO ADIGE'S WINES

Years ago, an ad ran on Italian television whose slogan went: *"Il Trentino è la sola regione che fa rima con vino"* ("Trentino is the only region that rhymes with *vino*"). Jingles aside, Trentino–Alto Adige is home to exceptional wines, the overwhelming majority of which has earned DOC status; in fact, Trentino–Alto Adige has the largest proportion of DOC wine production in Italy. Despite its northern location, the region does not have an excessively cool climate, making viticulture viable in its valleys and on its hillsides as heat accumulates at lower altitudes in the summer months.

The region is split into two main DOC wine areas, Trentino and Alto Adige, each divided into subzones whose wines are identified by varietal. Indigenous whites include Riesling Renano, an aristocratic wine with a pleasant bouquet, dry, fruity flavor, slight acidity, and character best appreciated within a year of vintage; slightly perfumed, fruity, soft, dry, delicate Müller-Thurgau; and delightfully aromatic, golden-hued Traminer Aromatico, or Gewürztraminer, vinified in the village of Termeno since the eleventh century.

Although it is renowned mostly for its crisp, clean, fruity white wines, Trentino–Alto Adige has recently garnered high praise for its polished reds. Schiava, the dominant grape of the area, yields a light- to medium-bodied red with hints of violets and almonds. The noblest expression of Schiava is Santa Maddalena: ruby to garnet in color, it has berry, violet, and almond aromas that become ethereal after brief aging. Other important reds are Teroldego Rotaliano, a lively, fruity wine vinified almost exclusively on the rocky soil of the Rotaliano Plain, meant to be drunk within three years of vintage; still or sparkling Marzemino, obtained from the late-ripening red-wine varietal of the same name, with a dry, herbaceous scent; and somewhat tannic, soft, velvety Lagrein Scuro. Notable dessert wines are sweet, delicate, aromatic, intense Moscato Giallo, and rose-hued Moscato Rosa. International wines of importance are Pinot Nero, Pinot Grigio, Pinot Bianco, Cabernet, Merlot, and Chardonnay; the latter accounts for the bulk of white wine production in the region.

Palle di Prugna

Plum-Stuffed Buns

Very similar to the plum- and apricot-filled gnocchi of Friuli–Venezia Giulia, which are served as a first course rather than dessert, these plum balls are a legacy of the Austro-Hungarian empire. As the dumplings boil, the plums soften, exuding a glorious nectar that seeps out when the dumplings are cut at the table. In Italy, grape-sized plums are used; each dumpling encases one plum, pit and all. Since plums in America tend to be larger, quarter and pit the plums before enrobing them in the potato dough.

SERVES 4

½ pound boiling potatoes, peeled
1 teaspoon salt
2 extra-large egg yolks
1 cup unbleached all-purpose flour, plus extra
   for the counter
3 small plums, quartered and pitted
4 tablespoons (½ stick) unsalted butter
2 tablespoons fresh bread crumbs
¼ cup sugar

Place the potatoes in a 1-quart pot with cold water to cover and ¾ teaspoon of the salt. Bring to a boil over medium heat and cook until they can be pierced with a knife, about 30 minutes. Drain and pass through a ricer onto a counter, then cool to room temperature. Work in the remaining ¼ teaspoon of salt, the egg yolks, and the flour.

Knead until a dough forms, adding a little flour if it is sticky or a little water if it is dry. Roll out on a lightly floured counter into a 12-inch circle. Cut into 4-inch disks with a cookie cutter, place a piece of plum on each, and seal the edges to form a taut ball, being careful not to tear holes in the dough as you stretch it. Gather scraps of dough, roll out again, cut into disks, and stuff with the remaining pieces of plum in the same manner; you should have 12 balls.

Meanwhile, bring 5 quarts of water to a boil. Add the plum balls and cook until they float to the surface, about 4 minutes. Remove with a slotted spoon to a plate.

Melt the butter in a 12-inch skillet over medium-high heat. Add the bread crumbs and cook 2 minutes, or until toasty. Gently add the plum balls, stir a few times, heat 30 seconds, and transfer to a platter. Sprinkle with the sugar and serve hot.

AN APPETITE FOR DESSERT

Considering the robust fare typically consumed in Trentino–Alto Adige, you would think that locals have little room for dessert by the time the sweet course rolls around. Not so: desserts in the region occupy a place of honor, partly thanks to centuries under Austrian rule. Rich chocolate cakes topped with abundant clouds of whipped cream, fruit and jam fritters, apple tarts, sweet omelets cooked in frothy butter and folded around homemade preserves, buckwheat cakes layered with raspberry jam, rich cookies swollen with dried fruit and nuts are all eaten with abandon.

Friuli–Venezia Giulia

Frico
  Crisp Montasio Cheese Pancake

Cjalzons con Ripieno di Cioccolata e Spinaci
  Chocolate-and-Spinach-Filled Pasta with Smoked Ricotta

Gnocchi con il Cacao
  Potato Gnocchi with Cocoa, Golden Raisins, and Cinnamon

Bomba di Polenta al Ragù
  Polenta Bombe with Beef Ragù

Jota
  Cranberry Bean and Sauerkraut Soup

Capesante alla Triestina
  Broiled Scallops and Oysters with Watercress

Rambasicci
  Pork-Stuffed Savoy Cabbage Bundles

Frittata alle Erbe
  Spinach, Leek, and Basil Frittata

Torta di Mandorle e Cannella
  Cinnamon-Almond Pie

Strucolo di Ricotta
  Ricotta Strudel

The foods of Friuli–Venezia Giulia are full of unexpected flavors—the savory meeting the sweet, the tart mingling with the sugary, and an abundance of herbs like tarragon and dill. But what struck me most was the presence of a hearth in most of its restaurants. The *focolar furlan,* or Friulian hearth, is the centerpiece of most homes and trattorie: just as families gather around the focolar for warmth and conversation and cook meals over its smoldering embers, patrons in the region's eateries bask in its glow and dine on meats grilled over its glowing, red-hot coals.

Exploring Friuli–Venezia Giulia's towns, mountain villages, and cosmopolitan centers, I realized that the focolar furlan is the tangible embodiment of its region's cuisine: friendly, warm, inviting, always ready to accommodate one more at the convivial table.

Invaded and plundered, raided and torn apart by ever-changing borders, Friuli–Venezia Giulia is now an autonomous region with a special statute. Bordering Austria to the north and Slovenia to the east, the region has been ruled by the Romans, Goths, Byzantines, Lombards, Franks, Hapsburgs, and the Republic of Venice; it lost part of its land to the former Yugoslavia as recently as the end of World War II, only to regain part of it a few years later. So it's not surprising that its cuisine is a melting pot of influences.

The cities of Aquileia and Cividale del Friuli, already important under the Romans, remain two of the region's most interesting destinations. The name Friuli is derived from the ancient Roman name of Cividale del Friuli, Forum Juli, meaning "Market of Julius," because the city was the site of a market which still stands. The name Venezia Giulia, meaning "Julian Venice," reflects the years that cities as far east as Udine and

Gradisca d'Isonzo belonged to the Republic of Venice; to this day, overlap with the cuisine of the Veneto is evident in seafood dishes, *risotti,* and a number of pastries.

Friuli–Venezia Giulia is split into three areas: the Carnic Alps, also known as Carnia; a hilly portion covered in vines; and the zone close to the Gulf of Venice, where the imprint of La Serenissima (as the Republic of Venice was called) is felt most strongly. Just as Furlan, the Friulian language, has Latin, Slavic, and Teutonic influences, Friulian food shows distinct Italian, Slavic, and Germanic legacies. In beer parlors, goulash is a mainstay, as are boiled pork with mustard, Prosciutto Cotto with a pungent horseradish sauce called *cren* (sometimes embellished with apples, butter, bread crumbs, and white wine, as in Alto Adige), and hearty pork and bean soups. The use of paprika with meat hints at a Hungarian influence; cinnamon, dill, lemon zest, cloves, and even ginger are added to dishes both savory and sweet, a remnant of years under Slavic rule.

Friuli–Venezia Giulia's capital, Trieste, was at the heart of a conflict with the former Yugoslavia until 1954. Called the Venice of the East, it is the ultimate Mitteleuropean city. As the most important port of the Hapsburg Empire and later the principal city of Istria (part of Yugoslavia), Trieste was a meeting ground for foreign influences, and its cuisine mirrors this international heritage. A perch on the Adriatic also means that its cooking is dominated by fish and seafood, and, indeed, memorable seafood is found here.

Favorite Restaurants, Shops, and Places

- ANTICA TRATTORIA SUBAN, Via Comici 2/D, Trieste, 040.54368. Try the *jota* and *crespelle al basilico.*
- DUCALE, Piazza Picco 18, Cividale del Friuli, 0432.730707. Pastry shop with excellent *gubana, pistum,* and *pete.*
- LA COLOMBARA, Via S. Zilli 42, Aquileia, 0431.91513. Simple Friulian fare; the *salame al sugo* is very good.
- LÀ DI MORET, Viale Tricesimo 276, Udine, 0432.46879. Good spit-roasted kid and *Musetto con brovada.*
- NONINO, Via Acquileia 104, Località Percoto, Pavia di Udine, 0432.676331. One of Italy's top distillers, best known for his single-varietal grappas.

- OSTERIA AL VECCHIO STALLO, Via Viola 7, Udine, 0432.21296. The sausage-and-herb-filled *cjalzons* are memorable.
- PASTICCERIA PIRONA, Largo Barriera Vecchia 2, Trieste, 0406.36046. James Joyce sampled the desserts at this pastry shop.
- PROLONGO GIOVANNI, Viale Trento e Trieste, San Daniele del Friuli, 0432.957161. The hams from this artisan are outstanding.
- PROSCIUTTIFICIO WOLF SAURIS, Via Vovlan 88, Sauris di Sotto, 0433.86054. Prosciutto di Sauris, Speck, Coppa, Pancetta, salami, and more.

Telephone country code: 011.39

Frico

Crisp Montasio Cheese Pancake

This antipasto was born when farm women in the Carnic Alps placed cheese crusts in a pan over the fire before bringing the herds to pasture; upon their return, they found a golden cheese pancake ready for their dinner. If aged Montasio is unavailable, try aged Asiago.

SERVES 4

1 teaspoon unsalted butter
¾ pound aged Montasio, grated

Grease an 8-inch nonstick skillet with the butter. Warm over medium-high heat 3 minutes and sprinkle in one-quarter of the Montasio, covering the skillet. Cook until crisp and golden, about 8 minutes, then tip out any fat.

Drape the warm Montasio pancake over an inverted glass and pat dry with a towel. Cool and remove to a plate. Continue with the remaining Montasio without greasing the skillet again. Serve at room temperature, to munch on before dinner or as an edible bowl for salad greens.

PREPARATION TIPS: Frico keeps up to 2 days at room temperature, uncovered.

SAN DANIELE'S PRIZED HAMS

Sit down at a trattoria in Friuli–Venezia Giulia and you'll probably start the meal with a plate of *salumi*—which, if you're anywhere near the town of San Daniele, will include the famed Prosciutto di San Daniele. San Daniele's hams are made by salting and pressing pig thighs, with the hoof still attached, so that excess moisture seeps out and a flattened shape is acquired; repeated massages of salt and pepper follow. The hams are rinsed, coated with a mixture of lard, flour, water, salt, and pepper, and aged up to eighteen months. Pinker and sweeter than Prosciutto di Parma, Prosciutto di San Daniele owes its distinct aroma to the climate of its town. San Daniele del Friuli is situated 30 miles from the sea and 6 miles from the Carnic Alps, so strong currents meet there, resulting in frequent, if brief, storms; humidity levels quickly rise and drop, "massaging" the hams. On the fourth Sunday of August, San Daniele del Friuli indulges in a town-wide pork feast: stalls sell Prosciutto, Cotechino, salami, and more, so attend if you are in the area.

Five Friulian Cow's Milk Cheeses

Just as important as pork to Friulian cooking is cheese—especially cow's milk cheese. The most widespread cow's milk cheese in Friuli–Venezia Giulia is Montasio, named after the Altopiano del Montasio in Friuli, where its production is centered. Aged from six weeks to over a year, Montasio is straw-yellow, crumbly, and firm. The whey left from the making of Montasio is turned into Ricotta Affumicata; the cheese is pressed, then smoked over juniper wood and herbs to acquire aroma, and is firm enough for grating. The Carnic Alps are home to a number of cheeses, including Formaggio Salato ("salted cheese"), a firm cheese cured in a brine of water, salt, and cream for a minimum of two months; Baita Friuli, a dense cheese with a marked scent of fresh herbs; and Carnia (also called Formaggio di Malga, or "mountain cheese"), a compact, pungent cheese that can be laced with goat's milk and has a thin, smooth, yellow rind. These cheeses are available in North America; see Sources, page 372.

Cjalzons con Ripieno di Cioccolata e Spinaci

Chocolate-and-Spinach-Filled Pasta with Smoked Ricotta

Friulians prefer soup and polenta to pasta, yet they have their fair share of pasta specialties. Cjalzons, a filled pasta from the mountains of Carnia, is usually sauced with melted butter and grated smoked Ricotta; its filling, which can call for as many as forty ingredients, and dough vary from town to town. See Sources (page 372) to buy smoked Ricotta, or substitute half each smoked Mozzarella and Ricotta Salata (salted, dry Ricotta).

Make the dough according to instructions on page 370 using the ingredients listed above, adding a little milk if the dough is dry or a little flour if it is sticky. Knead 5 minutes, or until smooth, shape into a ball, wrap, and let rest 30 minutes.

Meanwhile, make the filling: Soak the raisins in cool water to cover 30 minutes, then drain and blot dry. Set aside. While the raisins are soaking, place the spinach and parsley in a 12-inch sauté pan over medium-high heat, cover, and cook 5 minutes. Remove from the pan, rinse, squeeze dry, and mince. In a large mixing bowl, combine the plumped raisins, spinach, parsley, eggs, bread crumbs, candied citron, chocolate, lemon zest, sugar, cinnamon, nutmeg, salt, and pepper.

SERVES 6

For the dough:

3 cups unbleached all-purpose flour, plus extra for the counter

1/2 teaspoon salt

3 extra-large eggs

1/4 cup whole milk, plus extra if needed

For the filling:

3 tablespoons raisins

1 1/2 pounds spinach leaves, washed thoroughly

1 bunch Italian parsley, leaves only

2 extra-large eggs

1 2/3 cups fresh bread crumbs (preferably from rye bread)

2 tablespoons finely diced candied citron

1 ounce bittersweet chocolate, grated

Grated zest of 1/2 lemon

1 teaspoon sugar

Pinch ground cinnamon

Pinch freshly grated nutmeg

1 teaspoon salt

1/8 teaspoon freshly ground black pepper

To cook and serve:

2 tablespoons salt

8 tablespoons (1 stick) unsalted butter

1 tablespoon sugar

1 cup freshly grated smoked Ricotta

Cut the dough into 2 pieces. Working with 1 piece at a time and keeping the other covered, roll out each piece on a lightly floured counter into an 18 × 24-inch rectangle. Cut into 2-inch disks with a round cookie cutter. Spoon a dollop of filling on each disk and brush the inside edges lightly with water. Fold in half and seal the edges, forming half-circles. Spread out in a single layer on a floured tray and cover with a towel. These are the cjalzons.

To cook, bring 5 quarts of water to a boil. Add the cjalzons and salt and cook until al dente, about 3 minutes. Remove with a slotted spoon to a platter.

Meanwhile, melt the butter in a 6-inch skillet over medium heat. Pour the butter over the cjalzons, sprinkle with the sugar and smoked Ricotta, and serve hot.

PREPARATION TIPS: Shape the cjalzons up to 4 hours ahead, spread out in a single layer on a floured tray, and refrigerate, covered with a towel.

THE POLENTA SONG

Polenta is so central to life in Friuli–Venezia Giulia that a song even describes the ritual of cooking it: *"La polenta clociava soto vose 'po la s'gonfiava fofa e per i busi la sbufava fis'ciando come un vulcan rabià. Nona la la voltava e rivoltava. . . . Tonda alegra dorada e profumada la risplendeva come 'l sol nassente grande bel e possente tra i vapori d'està."* ("The polenta gurgled softly then it swelled and from the holes it sighed, whistling like an angry volcano. *Nonna* stirred it and stirred it. . . . Round, happy, golden, and perfumed, it shone like the rising sun, big and beautiful and mighty among the vapors of summer.")

FRIULI–VENEZIA GIULIA'S WINES

INEMAKING HAS BEEN AN INTEGRAL PART of life in Friuli–Venezia Giulia since vines were first planted in the thirteenth century B.C. In the Middle Ages, viticulture flourished, and much of the local wine was exported, first to the Republic of Venice, and later to Austria and Germany. Today, Friuli–Venezia Giulia is responsible for some of the cleanest, freshest fruity whites coming out of Italy, as well as an increasing number of reliable, top-quality reds. After Trentino–Alto Adige and Piedmont, the region produces Italy's highest percentage of DOC wines: over half of its wine production meets DOC regulations. Much of Friuli–Venezia Giulia's strength lies in its deft approach to single-varietal wines, and indigenous grapes (Tocai Friulano or Friulano, Ribolla, Malvasia di Istria, Verduzzo, Picolit, Refosco, Schiopettino, Pignolo, and Tazzelanghe) remain the forerunners of its wine industry. Other significant varietals (Riesling, Riesling Italico, Traminer, Müller-Thurgau, and Franconia) arrived from Austria, and still others were introduced in the nineteenth century under Hapsburg rule (Pinot Grigio, Bianco, and Nero, as well as Chardonnay, Merlot, Cabernet, and Sauvignon).

Most vineyards are located in hilly, windy areas south of Udine: growing vines farther north is nearly impossible given the cold climate. The two areas known as Colli Orientali and Collio (or Collio Goriziano), which are subdivided into five DOC zones (Lison-Pramaggiore, Latisana, Grave del Friuli, Aquileia, and Isonzo), are home to most of Friuli–Venezia Giulia's winemaking activity. In general, Collio wines have more bouquet and greater delicacy than Colli Orientali wines.

White wines first earned Friuli–Venezia Giulia international recognition, chief among them Ribolla (or Ribolla Gialla); light-bodied, floral, delicate, fresh, lively, and high in acidity, it has been known since at least 1289 and ages very well. Tocai, obtained from the most widely planted white grape varietal in Friuli–Venezia Giulia, is unrelated to the Tokay of Alsace or the Tokaji of Hungary, and is now called simply Friulano to differentiate it from these other wines. Light in color and body, slightly bitter, with a floral aroma and hint of almonds, it is best young. Verduzzo is vinified both dry and sweet; sweet Verduzzo is at its most expressive in the Ramandolo area north of Udine, and offers a delicate honey aroma.

Among notable reds, there is Pignolo ("fussy"), named after a difficult grape varietal; this intensely hued, fruity wine ages marvelously in *barriques*. The Refosco grape yields deeply colored reds characterized by a plum flavor and almond notes, medium to full body, and rather high acidity; look for Refosco del Peduncolo Rosso from Aquileia, the best of the bunch. Schiopettino (also called Ribolla Nera), known since at least 1282, when it was cited in a marriage contract, is a medium-bodied, velvety, warm, full, elegant, aromatically rich red with hints of violets and pepper. The most renowned dessert wine is Picolit: made from Picolit grapes that may be left to raisin for months on mats before pressing, it offers noticeable hints of peaches and apricots and a light sweetness best appreciated on its own.

Gnocchi con il Cacao

Potato Gnocchi with Cocoa, Golden Raisins, and Cinnamon

The bitterness of cocoa plays off the sweetness of sugar, raisins, cinnamon, and candied citron, resulting in a dish far less cloying than you might think. See Sources (page 372) to buy smoked Ricotta, or substitute equal parts smoked Mozzarella and Ricotta Salata (salted, dry Ricotta).

SERVES 8

1½ pounds potatoes, peeled
2 tablespoons plus ½ teaspoon salt
2 extra-large eggs
2¼ cups unbleached all-purpose flour, plus extra for the counter
½ cup golden raisins
3 tablespoons finely diced candied citron
1 teaspoon sugar
¼ teaspoon ground cinnamon
1 tablespoon unsweetened cocoa
¼ pound freshly grated smoked Ricotta

Place the potatoes in a 4-quart pot and add cold water to cover by 2 inches. Bring to a boil, reduce the heat to medium, and cook until tender when pierced with a knife, about 30 minutes. Drain, pass through a ricer onto a counter, and cool.

Add ½ teaspoon of the salt, the eggs, and enough of the flour to form a dough; you may not need all of the flour. (Test the dough at this point: drop a ⅓-inch piece into a pot of boiling water and cook until it rises to the surface. If the dough falls apart, add more flour.) Knead until smooth, cut into 8 pieces, and roll each into a finger-thick log. Cut into ⅓-inch-long pieces; these are the gnocchi. Toss with flour to prevent sticking and spread out in a single layer on a floured tray, covered with a towel.

Meanwhile, soak the raisins in cool water to cover for 30 minutes; drain and blot dry. In a serving bowl, mix the raisins, candied citron, sugar, cinnamon, cocoa, and smoked Ricotta.

Bring 6 quarts of water to a boil. Add the gnocchi and the remaining 2 tablespoons of salt. When the gnocchi float to the surface, after about 2 minutes, remove with a slotted spoon to the serving bowl. Gently fold into the cocoa mixture with a rubber spatula and serve hot.

PREPARATION TIPS: Make the gnocchi up to 12 hours ahead, spread out in a single layer on a floured tray, cover, and refrigerate.

GNOCCHI-LOVER'S PARADISE

Friuli–Venezia Giulia is a gnocchi-lover's paradise. There are fruit-filled gnocchi, potato gnocchi, Ricotta gnocchi, Swiss chard or spinach gnocchi, and imposing bread gnocchi. *Gnocchi in brodo* are a robust variation on potato gnocchi: ground meat, liver, and brains are added to potato gnocchi dough, then the gnocchi are fried and served in a rich beef broth.

Bomba di Polenta al Ragù

Polenta Bombe with Beef Ragù

Corn thrives in Friuli–Venezia Giulia's flatlands, and polenta is the region's favored first course after bean soup. The most distinctive polenta is zuf, made with cornmeal, flour, and butter; but bisma, with beans, sauerkraut, and onions, is common too. Sweet polente are also prepared; one calls for poppy seeds, another for cinnamon. The polenta "bombe" offered here is a staple across Italy; the Friulian touch is the sprinkling of bread crumbs rather than grated cheese over the top.

SERVES 4

7 tablespoons unsalted butter, plus extra for greasing the mold
3 tablespoons extra-virgin olive oil
1 medium yellow onion, minced
¾ pound ground beef
½ teaspoon salt
⅛ teaspoon freshly ground black pepper
½ cup dry red wine
3 canned Italian plum tomatoes, chopped
1 garlic clove, crushed
1 clove
2 tablespoons unbleached all-purpose flour
½ recipe Polenta (page 371)
¼ cup fresh bread crumbs

Heat 3 tablespoons of the butter with the olive oil in an 8-inch sauté pan over a medium flame. Add the onion and cook 10 minutes, then add the beef, salt, and pepper. Cook until browned all over, about 10 minutes, stirring.

Deglaze with the wine. After 5 minutes, add the tomatoes, cover, and cook over medium-low heat 15 minutes. Tie the garlic and clove in a piece of cheesecloth and add to the beef; cover and cook 45 minutes. Stir in the flour, cover again, and cook another 45 minutes. Discard the cheesecloth bundle.

Make the polenta according to instructions on page 371. Brush the inside of a deep ovenproof 6-inch round mold with water. Pour in the hot polenta and smooth the top. Cool until set, about 2 hours, then unmold and cut into 4 horizontal layers. Dry the inside of the mold and butter it.

Preheat the oven to 375°F.

Place the bottom slice of polenta in the mold and top with one-third of the ragù. Continue layering the ingredients in this manner, finishing with a layer of polenta. Dot the top with the remaining 4 tablespoons of butter and sprinkle with the bread crumbs. Bake in the preheated oven 45 minutes and serve hot.

PREPARATION TIPS: Prepare the recipe through layering the polenta up to 2 days before baking, and refrigerate.

Jota

Cranberry Bean and Sauerkraut Soup

After polenta, bean soup is Friuli–Venezia Giulia's defining dish: Beans, greens, and vegetables are cooked into a porridge called polenta d'erbe; minestrone alla triestina combines beans, cabbage, potatoes, and bacon; tripe soup is laced with Pancetta, onions, and beans; and smoked ham, beans, potatoes, and corn form minestra di bobici. But no bean soup is as well known or as well loved as jota. Versions of this stick-to-your-ribs bean soup abound; one includes macerated turnips (page 109) and polenta, while another calls for barley. The rendition below features mashed potatoes and Pancetta and is from Mario Suban, owner of Trieste's Antica Trattoria Suban.

SERVES 6

1½ cups dried cranberry beans, soaked 12 hours in cool water to cover

5 bay leaves

½ pound Pancetta, ¼ pound in a single slice, ¼ pound cut into ⅛-inch dice

1 pound potatoes, peeled and cut into ¼-inch dice

½ cup extra-virgin olive oil

5 garlic cloves, peeled

3 tablespoons unbleached all-purpose flour

1 pound prepared sauerkraut, drained and rinsed

2 teaspoons caraway seeds

½ teaspoon salt

⅛ teaspoon freshly ground black pepper

1 medium yellow onion, minced

Drain the beans and place in a 4-quart pot with 3 of the bay leaves, the slice of Pancetta, and 10 cups (2½ quarts) of cool water. Bring to a boil, reduce the heat to medium, and cook, uncovered, until the beans are nearly cooked, about 1 hour and 15 minutes, adding water as needed to keep them covered by 1 inch. When the beans are tender but still hold their shape, add the potatoes and cover the pot. Cook 25 minutes, or until the beans and potatoes are fully cooked. Discard the slice of Pancetta and bay leaves. Transfer to a food processor and process until smooth. Return to the pot and keep warm.

Meanwhile, heat ¼ cup of the olive oil with the garlic in a 2-quart pot over a medium flame. After 1 minute, add the diced Pancetta, 1 tablespoon of the flour, and the sauerkraut; cook 10 minutes, stirring. Add the remaining 2 bay leaves, the caraway seeds, salt, pepper, and 2 cups of water and bring to a boil. Cook over medium-low heat 45 minutes, uncovered, then discard the bay leaves.

When you are ready to serve, heat the remaining ¼ cup of olive oil in an 8-inch skillet over a medium flame and add the onion; cook 5 minutes. Add the remaining 2 tablespoons of flour and cook 5 minutes, stirring.

Stir the onion and sauerkraut mixtures into the bean and potato purée, dilute with as much water as needed (about ½ to 1 cup) to obtain a thick, soupy consistency, and return to a boil; cook 5 minutes and serve hot.

Capesante alla Triestina

Broiled Scallops and Oysters with Watercress

This is an unusual and elegant specialty of Trieste. Scallops and oysters are blanched and minced, then combined with watercress, onion, parsley, bread crumbs, and melted butter, and finally stuffed into shells and broiled. In Trieste, the mixture is stuffed into scallop shells and served as a main course; since scallop shells can be hard to find, I use oyster shells.

FISH AND SEAFOOD THE FRIULIAN WAY

Dill, tarragon, horseradish, apples, sour cream, cinnamon, cloves, and ginger all find their way into the Friulian fish pot (not all at once, of course). Seafood specialties range from humble fish like salt cod baked with potatoes, olives, and raisins to luxurious offerings like Prosciutto-wrapped scampi braised with tomatoes and wine, or cuttlefish stuffed with crab.

SERVES 2 AS A MAIN COURSE OR 4 AS AN ANTIPASTO

12 blue point or other large oysters, shucked, shells reserved
12 sea scallops
2½ cups watercress leaves, washed and dried
1 medium yellow onion, minced
1 tablespoon minced Italian parsley
½ cup fresh bread crumbs
3 tablespoons unsalted butter, melted
½ teaspoon salt
⅛ teaspoon freshly ground black pepper
⅓ cup extra-virgin olive oil

Preheat the broiler.

Bring 1 quart of water to a boil and add the oysters and scallops. Cook 1 minute, drain, cool, and mince. Mince ½ cup of the watercress and add it to the oysters and scallops in a medium mixing bowl; stir in the onion, parsley, bread crumbs, butter, ¼ teaspoon of the salt, and a pinch of the pepper. Divide the mixture among the oyster half-shells, using the 12 smooth half-shells only. Pile the mixture high and compact it with your hand to ensure that it holds its shape. Place on an 11 × 17-inch baking sheet 10 inches from the heating element and broil in the preheated oven 7 to 10 minutes, or until browned on top.

Meanwhile, toss the remaining 2 cups of watercress with the remaining ¼ teaspoon of salt and pinch of pepper in a bowl. Drizzle with the olive oil and divide among 2 or 4 plates, depending on whether you are serving the dish as a main course or antipasto. Top the watercress with the oyster half-shells and serve immediately.

PREPARATION TIPS: Fill and refrigerate the oyster half-shells on the baking sheet up to 12 hours before broiling.

Rambasicci

Pork-Stuffed Savoy Cabbage Bundles

In Trieste, this dish is known as uccelletti scappati nella verza ("*runaway birds in cabbage*"). Like most of Friuli–Venezia Giulia's stuffed vegetables, rambasicci are Slavic in origin, and their filling often contains beef as well as pork. In Trieste, the sides of the cabbage leaves are not folded over the stuffing before rolling, so the stuffing peeks out; if you prefer this unfinished look, spear each bundle with a toothpick to prevent unrolling. To purchase smoked Ricotta, see Sources (page 372) or substitute equal amounts of smoked Mozzarella and dry, salted Ricotta (Ricotta Salata).

An Ode to the Pig

Friulians love pork. In the Carnic Alps, families still raise pigs, and the yearly slaughter yields delicious home-cured sausages and hams. Among Friuli–Venezia Giulia's pork offerings, there is Musetto, a rich sausage best boiled; pork loin with fresh raspberries or gooseberry sauce, a typical Austrian pairing; pork liver wrapped in caul fat with bay and sage leaves; and *toc de purcit,* a stew scented with cloves and cinnamon.

SERVES 4

2 extra-large eggs
24 Savoy cabbage leaves (2 medium heads)
1¼ pounds fatty ground pork
3 garlic cloves, minced
2 tablespoons minced Italian parsley
¼ pound thinly sliced mild salami, such as Genoa, minced
1 teaspoon sweet paprika
2 teaspoons salt
2 tablespoons (¼ stick) unsalted butter
2 tablespoons extra-virgin olive oil
1 medium yellow onion, coarsely chopped
1½ cups Chicken Broth or Beef Broth (page 368), plus extra if needed
¼ cup freshly grated smoked Ricotta
¼ cup fresh bread crumbs

Bring 6 quarts of water to a boil in a 10-quart pot. Gently drop in the eggs and cook 12 minutes; remove with a slotted spoon, cool, shell, mince, and set aside, keeping the water boiling. Add the cabbage to the boiling water and cook 8 minutes. Drain, rinse in cool water, blot dry, and cut out the rib from each leaf. Lay the leaves on a counter.

In a medium bowl, mix the pork, garlic, parsley, minced hard-boiled eggs, salami, paprika, and 1½ teaspoons of the salt. Divide among the cabbage leaves. Roll up each leaf once from the bottom to enclose the stuffing, fold in the sides, and roll into a bundle.

Heat the butter and olive oil in a 14-inch sauté pan over a medium flame. Add the onion and cook 5 minutes, or until wilted. Place the bundles in a single layer in the pan, seam side down, and cook 5 minutes. Add the broth and the remaining ½ teaspoon of salt, reduce the heat to medium-low, and cover. Cook for 1 hour, turning the bundles after 30 minutes and adding broth as needed to keep them moist.

Transfer to a platter, sprinkle with the smoked Ricotta and bread crumbs, and serve hot.

Frittata alle Erbe

Spinach, Leek, and Basil Frittata

The Friulians stud frittate with mussels, shrimp, or, as in the recipe below, a medley of vegetables and herbs, to be served as appetizers or main courses. I sometimes add sliced scallions and minced fresh tarragon, or some grated Montasio to the egg base.

SERVES 4

¼ pound arugula leaves, washed and chopped
½ pound spinach leaves, washed and chopped
1 leek, white part only, thinly sliced
1 medium yellow onion, thinly sliced
¼ cup plus 2 tablespoons extra-virgin olive oil
1 cup packed basil leaves, washed and torn
4 sage leaves, minced
6 extra-large eggs
½ teaspoon salt
⅛ teaspoon freshly ground black pepper

Bring 3 quarts of water to a boil and cook the arugula, spinach, leek, and onion 5 minutes. Drain, rinse under cold water, and squeeze dry.

Heat 2 tablespoons of the olive oil in a 10-inch skillet. Add the arugula mixture and cook 3 minutes over medium-high heat, stirring. Add the basil and sage and cook 5 minutes. Remove from the heat and allow to cool slightly.

In a large bowl, beat the eggs with the salt and pepper; stir in the arugula mixture. Dribble 2 tablespoons of the olive oil into the skillet, heat 1 minute over a medium flame, add the egg-arugula mixture, and cook 10 minutes, or until set and golden on the bottom.

Place a large plate over the skillet, flip the skillet upside down to invert the frittata onto the plate, and add the remaining 2 tablespoons of olive oil to the skillet. Return the frittata to the skillet, uncooked side down, and cook until set and golden on the bottom, about 5 minutes. Serve hot, warm, or at room temperature.

A MOST UNIQUE VEGETABLE

Perhaps the most unique vegetable specialty of Friuli–Venezia Giulia is *brovada*, an unpromising-looking but flavorful accompaniment to pork dishes. To make brovada, young turnips are macerated with fresh grape skins in wooden barrels for two to three months, where they ferment and become pungent. The fermented turnips are then cut into strips or grated and cooked with garlic, lard, and parsley until they become brown and tender. Brovada lends its potent tang to a number of soups, including some versions of *jota* (page 106).

Torta di Mandorle e Cannella

Cinnamon-Almond Pie

Most desserts in Friuli–Venezia Giulia are rich, stuffed with nuts and fresh or dried fruit, flavored with spices like nutmeg and cinnamon, and sweetened with honey. In Friulian style, this dense pie features a cinnamon-scented almond filling sandwiched between two layers of crisp, cookie-like almond crust.

SERVES 8

2⅔ cups blanched almonds
¾ cup plus ⅓ cup sugar
1¾ cups unbleached all-purpose flour,
    plus extra for the counter
Grated zest of 1 lemon
3 extra-large egg whites
3 extra-large egg yolks
2 extra-large eggs
⅓ teaspoon ground cinnamon
Unsalted butter for greasing the pie pan

In a food processor, grind 1⅓ cups of the almonds with ⅓ cup of the sugar until powdery. Transfer to a bowl; stir in the flour, zest, and 3 egg whites. Turn out onto a counter; add 1 tablespoon of water if needed to form a dough. Cut into 2 pieces and roll out on a floured counter into two 11-inch disks. Set aside.

Preheat the oven to 400°F.

In a food processor, grind the remaining 1⅓ cups of almonds and ¾ cup of sugar until powdery. In a bowl, whisk the 3 egg yolks, 1 of the whole eggs, and the cinnamon, then stir in the ground almond mixture; this is the filling.

Butter a 10-inch springform pie pan and line it with 1 dough disk. Spoon in the filling, spreading until it almost reaches the edges. Top with the second dough disk. Seal the edges and cut off excess dough. Prick the top with a fork. Beat the remaining whole egg and brush it over the dough. Bake in the preheated oven 30 minutes, or until the crust is golden and lightly crisp. Cool on a rack, unmold, and serve at room temperature.

A SHOT OF GRAPPA

Distilled from the skins and seeds left over from winemaking, grappa has been produced in Friuli–Venezia Giulia since the time of the ancient Romans. Legend has it that when the Burgundians came down from Austria in 511 B.C., they showed locals how to distill a liquid from grape skins and seeds. Friulians often add grappa to their morning espresso for a double shot of energy and warmth, yielding what they call a *caffè corretto* ("corrected coffee"). It takes about 220 pounds of grape skins to yield 10 quarts of grappa whose alcoholic content ranges from 40 to 50 percent. Grappa is typically matured for a minimum of one year in oak casks, but it is a true revelation when aged longer. Friuli–Venezia Giulia also offers delightful fruit-based grappas, as well as "therapeutic" grappas featuring medicinal herbs.

Strucolo di Ricotta

Ricotta Strudel

Years under Hapsburg rule have left Friuli–Venezia Giulia with an impressive repertoire of strudels and strudel-like sweets, which range from the strucolo below (strucolo means strudel in Furlan, the Friulian language) to the more complex putizza and presnitz and gubana displayed in pastry shops like so many horseshoe-shaped jewels. Strucolo can be filled with Ricotta, apples, pears, jam, or crushed poppy seeds; the latter (like savory pasta sprinkled with poppy seeds) is a Hungarian legacy.

SERVES 8

1 cup plus 1 tablespoon unbleached all-purpose
　flour, plus extra for the counter
¼ teaspoon salt
1 extra-large egg
3 tablespoons unsalted butter, melted and cooled,
　plus extra for greasing the baking sheet
¼ cup golden raisins
¾ pound fresh Ricotta
¾ cup sugar
Grated zest of 1 lemon
2 tablespoons fresh bread crumbs

Mix the flour and salt in a bowl. Work in the egg and 1 tablespoon of the butter until a dry dough forms, then add ¼ cup of room-temperature water. Turn out onto a counter and knead into a supple dough, adding flour as needed to prevent sticking, about 5 minutes, slamming the dough onto the counter a few times. Dust with flour, shape into a ball, wrap, and let rest 30 minutes.

Meanwhile, soak the raisins in cool water to cover for 30 minutes; drain and blot dry. In a food processor, mix the Ricotta, ½ cup plus 2 tablespoons of the sugar, and the lemon zest until smooth. Transfer to a bowl and stir in the bread crumbs and raisins; this is the filling.

Preheat the oven to 375°F.

Roll out the dough on a lightly floured counter into a 10 × 14-inch rectangle. Draping the dough over the knuckles of your two hands, stretch it until it is almost transparent into a 17 × 25-inch rectangle. Don't panic if you make a hole, since the dough will be rolled over itself.

Place the dough on a clean, dry towel. Spoon on the filling, leaving a 1-inch border all around. Pull the edge of the towel up to roll the dough over the filling, forming a log. Gently transfer to an oiled 11 × 17-inch baking sheet, using the towel to help. Remove the towel and rotate the log so the seam faces down. Curve into a horseshoe shape.

Brush the top of the log with the remaining 2 tablespoons of butter and sprinkle with the remaining 2 tablespoons of sugar. Make 3 very shallow diagonal slashes with a sharp knife and bake in the preheated oven 35 minutes, or until the crust is golden and crisp. Serve warm or at room temperature.

PREPARATION TIPS: Bake up to 6 hours ahead and hold at room temperature.

The Veneto

Sarde in Saor
Sardines in Sweet-and-Sour Sauce

Bacalà Mantecato
Garlic Cod over White Polenta

Bigoli in Salsa
Whole Wheat Spaghetti in Wilted Onion–Anchovy Sauce

Cassunziei Ampezzani
Beet-Filled Ravioli with Poppy Seeds

Risi e Bisi
Rice with Fresh Spring Peas

Risotto de Scampi
Scampi Risotto

Pasta e Fasoi al Radicchio
Pasta and Bean Soup over Slivered Radicchio

Paeta Rosta al Malgarano
Roasted Turkey with Pomegranate Sauce

Zaleti
Crumbly Cornmeal Cookies

Torta de Paparele
Lemony Tagliatelle Cake

*I*t *was a cold, drizzly autumn evening,* our first in Venice. We had been driving much of the day, hadn't yet had a chance to meander through the streets, and needed a quiet, restorative meal before bed. We had heard so many bad things about dining in Venice—phrases like "tourist trap" and "too commercial" popped up in every conversation—that our expectations were low. When the waiter arrived, we ordered desultorily: *bacalà mantecato, bigoli in salsa,* and the house white.

I'll always remember that night—if not the name of the trattoria where we ate—because it was then that I learned something all travelers should know: eat first, judge later. The food was flavorful and honest—the perfect antidote to the chill in the air and the ache in our bones.

The Veneto takes its name from the Veneti, an ancient people famous for horsebreeding who were conquered by the Romans in the second century B.C. The city of Venice was founded when barbarians, invading northeastern Italy in the fifth century, forced the Veneti to flee to the islands and mudflats of a lagoon at the tip of the Adriatic. Ruled in turn by the Ostrogoths, Longobards, and Carolingians, the Veneti eventually transformed Venice into an independent city-state, developing important towns and, later, free communes in the area.

Over the centuries, this lonely colony of Veneti grew into the Venetian Republic. Known as La Serenissima, the Venetian Republic was one of the greatest commercial and maritime powers of the late Middle Ages and Renaissance. Its influence extended across the Mediterranean into the Byzantine world, bringing in exotic goods and spices that spawned a flavorful, Eastern-inspired cuisine. In the fourteenth century, Venice's virtual monopoly over the grain trade in the eastern Mediterranean ensured even greater wealth; her only serious rival was the Republic of Genoa, which Venice defeated in 1380. But beginning in the sixteenth century, Venice's power declined, partly due to the increased importance of Dutch and British trade and partly due to the decreasing demand for spices. She was invaded by France in 1797; then the city and its territories fell to the Austrians; and finally, Venice joined the Kingdom of Italy in 1866.

The Veneto borders Austria to the north, and includes three zones with three distinct cuisines: a mountainous area linked to agriculture and sheepherding; a hilly interior where farming and livestock are key; and a coastal area with an abundance of seafood. Yet despite differences in primary ingredients, climate, and local preference, all three areas share a love of polenta and rice, versatile staples that form the basis of the diet. The spices most commonly used—cinnamon and cloves—are a legacy of the Venetian spice trade. And the presence of sweet ingredients like raisins and pomegranates in savory dishes is a reminder of La Serenissima's centuries-long contact with the Eastern world.

Favorite Restaurants, Shops, and Places

- ALIANI, Ruga Rialto San Polo 654, Venice, 041.5224913. Gastronomy shop with excellent *sarde in saor*.
- ANTICO PIGNOLO, San Marco, Calle dei Specchieri 438, Venice, 041.5228123. Memorable *risotto di scampi e rucola*.
- ANTICO RISTORANTE BECCHERIE, Piazza Ancilotto, Treviso, 0422.540871. Old-fashioned, elegant cuisine; try the *pasta e fagioli* and *baccalà mantecato*.
- BOTTEGA DEL VINO, Via Scudo di Francia 3, Verona, 045.8004535. Great wines and *risotto all'Amarone*.
- DODICI APOSTOLI, Vicolo Corticella S. Marco 3, Verona, 045.596999. Traditional Veronese cuisine at its best.
- DOLADA, Frazione Dolada Plois, Pieve d'Alpago (10 miles from Belluno), 0437.479141. Try the *cape-sante allo zenzero*.
- HARRY'S BAR, San Marco, Calle Valaresso 1323, Venice, 041.528777. The birthplace of carpaccio.
- PIAZZA DELLE ERBE, off Via Mazzini (near Juliet's home), Verona. The city's best outdoor market.
- SALUMERIA VALDOBBIADENSE, Via Madean 5, Località Guia, Valdobbiadene, 0423.901065. Excellent Soppressa and salami rubbed with Prosecco.

Telephone country code: 011.39

Sarde in Saor

Sardines in Sweet-and-Sour Sauce

In Venetian—a sing-songy dialect that was for centuries the official language of the Venetian Republic—the word saor means sapore, or "flavor," and typically refers to sweet-and-savory sauces. Sarde in saor dates back to the sixteenth century and was made differently depending on the season: topped only with fried onions and vinegar in the summer, and in the winter embellished with sugar, pine nuts, and raisins.

SERVES 4

⅓ cup golden raisins
1 pound fresh sardines, scaled, gutted, boned, heads and fins removed, and butterflied
½ cup unbleached all-purpose flour
1½ cups extra-virgin olive oil
2 large yellow onions, thinly sliced
½ teaspoon salt
⅛ teaspoon freshly ground black pepper
⅔ cup white wine vinegar
⅓ cup pine nuts

Soak the raisins in water to cover for 30 minutes; drain and blot dry.

Meanwhile, rinse the sardines and blot them dry. Dredge them in the flour, shaking off the excess. Heat 1 cup of the olive oil until it is smoking in a 12-inch skillet. Fry half of the sardines over medium-high heat until golden on both sides and lightly crispy, about 3 minutes per side, turning once; remove with a slotted spoon to a plate lined with paper towels and blot dry. Fry the remaining sardines in the same manner in the oil that is left in the skillet. Place all the fried sardines on a platter.

Heat the remaining ½ cup of olive oil over a medium flame in a clean 12-inch skillet. Cook the onions until soft and translucent, about 20 minutes, stirring often. Add the salt, pepper, and vinegar and bring to a boil. Cook over medium heat 10 minutes, or until the vinegar reduces by half. Scatter the pine nuts and raisins over the sardines, pour on the warm vinegar mixture, and cool to room temperature. Refrigerate 2 to 4 days before serving.

THE BEST SALAMI . . . MAYBE

There are many incredible salamis in Italy: the sheep's meat salami of Sulmona in Abruzzo, the fennel-laced pork salami of Florence, the spicy, chili-packed Soppressata of Basilicata. So I am hesitant to admit that there is one I crave most often: the delicate pork salami of the Veneto. Called Soppressa (from the words *sotto pressa,* or "under a weight," because of how it's shaped), it owes its particular flavor to garlic that is steeped in red wine. Soppressa is made in Pasubio from the meat of free-roaming pigs fed mostly on chestnuts and potatoes, and is aged one year to acquire depth and character; it is most often served alongside grilled polenta. Unfortunately, there is no North American equivalent, so I know what I'll be eating every day on my next visit to the Veneto.

Bacalà Mantecato
Garlic Cod over White Polenta

*I*n most of Italy, salt cod is called baccalà *and dried cod is* stoccafisso, *or stockfish. But in the Veneto,* bacalà *is dried cod, and* stoccafisso *is salt cod. There are two famous* bacalà *dishes:* Bacalà alla vicentina *is an onion-and-anchovy-laced specialty of Vicenza, whose leftovers have inspired the saying, "Bacalà alla vicentina, buono di sera e di mattina" ("Bacalà alla vicentina, good in the evening and in the morning"). The second is* bacalà mantecato, *with garlic and parsley, served with white polenta for bulk. (To buy white cornmeal, see Sources, page 372.)*

SERVES 6

1 pound dried cod (substitute salt cod)
2 cups whole milk
1 cup extra-virgin olive oil
$\frac{1}{2}$ teaspoon salt
$\frac{1}{8}$ teaspoon freshly ground black pepper
2 tablespoons minced Italian parsley
2 small garlic cloves, minced extremely fine
1 recipe Polenta (page 371) made with
    white cornmeal

Soak the cod in cool water to cover for 2 days, changing the water every 8 hours. Drain, place in a 3-quart pot with the milk and 2 cups of cool water, and bring to a gentle boil. Simmer 40 minutes, uncovered, then drain. Peel off any skin and pick out any bones from the cod. Tear into chunks and place in a large bowl. Pour in the olive oil in a thin stream as you beat with a whisk; continue beating, always in the same direction, until creamy, fluffy, and pale, about 10 minutes. (Some cooks pound the cod in a mortar; others use a wooden spoon.) Add the salt, pepper, parsley, and garlic and cool 15 minutes.

Meanwhile, make the polenta according to instructions on page 371. Spoon the hot polenta onto 6 plates, top with the cod, and serve immediately.

PREPARATION TIPS: Make the cod up to 3 hours ahead and hold at room temperature.

COD'S STRANGE JOURNEY

How did cod—a fish that loves the cold waters off the coast of Iceland, Norway, and Newfoundland—become a staple in Venice? It started with a merchant named Piero Querini, whose ship left the Island of Candia (today's Crete) in 1431 for Bruges and Antwerp. Disaster struck, and Querini was rescued off the coast of Norway by cod fishermen. Querini described his travels and sang the praises of cod in two manuscripts. A century later, when the Catholic Church drew up a liturgical calendar that specified forty days of Lent, fifty-two meatless Fridays, and other Fast Days, the need to secure large quantities of nonperishable fish made cod and stockfish central to the Venetian economy and the Italian table.

Bigoli in Salsa

Whole Wheat Spaghetti in Wilted Onion–Anchovy Sauce

In the Veneto, rustic whole wheat spaghetti called bigoli are extruded using a machine that looks uncannily like a meat grinder. The pasta is tossed with a variety of condiments: a garlicky walnut sauce, a chicken giblet ragù, an anchovy-and-onion sauce, or a brothy duck sauce. Since bigoli cutters are unavailable in North America, the recipe below calls for rolling out the dough and cutting it with the spaghetti attachment of a pasta machine.

SERVES 4

For the sauce and to cook:
½ cup extra-virgin olive oil
2 large yellow onions, thinly sliced
10 salted anchovies, boned, gutted, and rinsed
2 tablespoons salt
¼ teaspoon freshly ground black pepper

For the bigoli:
3 cups whole wheat flour, plus extra for the counter
½ teaspoon salt

Make the sauce: Heat ¼ cup of the olive oil in a 12-inch sauté pan over a medium flame. Add the onions and cook 15 minutes. Add ½ cup of water, cover, and simmer 1 hour. Uncover, add the anchovies, and cook 3 more minutes, crushing the anchovies with a fork.

Meanwhile, make the bigoli according to instructions on page 370 using the ingredients listed above, adding 1 cup of water. Knead 5 minutes, or until smooth, adding a little water if the dough is dry or a little flour if it is sticky. Shape into a ball, wrap, and let rest 30 minutes.

Cut the dough into 4 pieces. Working with 1 piece at a time and keeping the others covered, roll out each piece using a pasta machine into a 14-inch-long sheet (the sheets should be slightly thicker than most pastas; the third-to-last setting on most pasta machines is ideal). Cut each sheet into two 7-inch-long rectangles. Let dry 15 minutes. Cut with a spaghetti attachment and toss with flour to prevent sticking. Spread out in a single layer on a floured tray.

To cook the bigoli, bring 5 quarts of water to a boil. Add the bigoli and the 2 tablespoons of salt and cook until al dente; drain, reserving ½ cup of the pasta cooking water. Fold the bigoli and the reserved cooking water into the onion-anchovy sauce. Season with the pepper, stir in the remaining ¼ cup of olive oil, and serve hot.

Cassunziei Ampezzani
Beet-Filled Ravioli with Poppy Seeds

In Ampezzo, a striking beet-filled pasta called *cassunziei* shows its Austro-Hungarian roots and wears a sumptuous topping of butter, poppy seeds, and smoked Ricotta. See Sources (page 373) to buy smoked Ricotta or substitute a combination of smoked Mozzarella and Ricotta Salata (salted, dry Ricotta) in equal parts.

Make the filling: Place the beets in a 3-quart pot. Add water to cover by 3 inches and bring to a boil. Cook over medium heat 45 minutes, or until tender. Drain, peel while still hot, slice, and purée in a food processor.

Melt the butter in an 8-inch skillet. Add the beet purée and cook 10 minutes over medium-high heat, stirring. Transfer to a bowl, cool, and fold in the Ricotta, eggs, salt, and bread crumbs.

Meanwhile, make the dough according to instructions on page 000 using the ingredients listed

SERVES 4

For the filling:
1 pound beets
3 tablespoons unsalted butter
¼ pound fresh Ricotta
2 extra-large eggs
½ teaspoon salt
¾ cup fresh bread crumbs

For the dough:
3 cups unbleached all-purpose flour,
    plus extra for the counter
¼ teaspoon salt
2 extra-large eggs
½ cup plus 1 tablespoon whole milk,
    plus extra if needed

To cook and serve:
2 tablespoons salt
6 tablespoons (¾ stick) unsalted butter
2 tablespoons poppy seeds
½ cup freshly grated smoked Ricotta

above, adding a little milk if the dough is dry or a little flour if it is sticky. Knead 5 minutes, or until smooth, shape into a ball, wrap, and let rest 30 minutes.

Cut the dough into 4 pieces. Working with 1 piece at a time and keeping the others covered, roll out each piece into a nearly transparent sheet using a pasta machine. Cut each sheet into 2-inch disks with a round cookie cutter. Spoon a dollop of filling onto each disk; moisten the inside edges with water, fold in half, and seal the edges. These are the cassunziei; spread out in a single layer on a floured tray and cover with a towel.

To cook, bring 5 quarts of water to a boil. Add the cassunziei and 2 tablespoons of salt and cook until al dente, about 3 minutes. Remove with a slotted spoon to a serving platter.

Melt the butter in a 6-inch skillet over medium heat until foaming, then add the poppy seeds and stir. Pour over the cassunziei, sprinkle with the smoked Ricotta, and serve hot.

MEDIEVAL CHEESES

THE VENETO'S MOST WIDELY DISTRIBUTED CHEESES—Asiago, Monte Veronese, and Piave—are all made of cow's milk. Asiago, produced since the eleventh century in the provinces of Vicenza and Treviso, is marketed in two versions: Pressato, made from whole milk and pressed in metal or plastic molds, then aged a maximum of forty days, and d'Allevo, made from partly skim milk and aged up to two years. The latter is undoubtedly the most complex of the two, with a sharp, salty flavor and firm texture that lends itself to grating. Monte Veronese, like Asiago, is made in two versions: a young one from whole milk with a delicate flavor, and an aged one from partly skim milk. Cylindrical in shape, it has a smooth, yellowish-red rind and elastic flesh marked by visible holes. Piave, produced in the vineyard-rich Vallata del Piave, is reminiscent of Friuli–Venezia Giulia's Montasio; straw-yellow in color and cured in a salt brine, it is considered Fresco after two months of aging, Mezzano after six months, and Stravecchio after ten months, yet retains its milky, subtly delicate flavor even when it has been aged. All of these cheeses can be purchased in North America (see Sources, page 372).

Risi e Bisi

Rice with Fresh Spring Peas

Most modern versions of this recipe call for chicken broth, but the best is made with a broth sweetened by fresh pea pods. If the craving for this rice strikes when pea season is over, substitute 2 cups of frozen sweet peas, thawing them first, and use a simple chicken broth to cook the rice. Cooks in the Veneto use Vialone Nano (page 122) instead of Arborio or other short-grain rice varieties.

SERVES 4

8 cups (2 quarts) Chicken Broth (page 368)
2 pounds fresh peas, shelled, pods reserved
2 tablespoons extra-virgin olive oil
5 tablespoons unsalted butter, cubed, at room temperature
1 scallion, white and green parts, thinly sliced
One 2-ounce slice Prosciutto di Parma, minced
2 tablespoons minced Italian parsley
½ teaspoon salt
¼ teaspoon freshly ground black pepper
1 cup Vialone Nano rice
¼ cup freshly grated Grana Padano, plus extra for passing at the table

Place the broth and reserved pea pods in a 4-quart pot. Bring to a boil and simmer 2 hours, uncovered. Strain. Reserve the broth and discard the pea pods. Measure 5 cups of the broth, adding water to make up the quantity if needed, and heat to just below the boiling point in a clean 2-quart pot.

Heat the olive oil and 2 tablespoons of the butter in a 10-inch sauté pan over a medium flame. Add the scallion, Prosciutto, and parsley and cook 5 minutes. Stir in the peas and 1 cup of the measured broth, season with the salt and pepper, and cook 10 minutes, uncovered. Add the rice and cook 2 minutes, stirring with a wooden spoon.

Begin adding the measured broth by the ½ cup, stirring all the while; add more broth only when the previous portion has been absorbed. Cook until the rice is al dente, about 18 minutes, adding broth and stirring all the while. Fold in any remaining broth, the remaining 3 tablespoons of butter, and the Grana; the rice will be soupy. Serve hot, passing additional Grana at the table.

FOREIGN FOODS IN VENETIAN CUISINE

Consider the ingredients on which the Veneto's cooking is built: polenta, beans, rice, and cod. Now consider where these ingredients came from: polenta and beans from America, rice from the Far East, and cod from the northern seas. The Veneto's reliance on foreign foods is not surprising, considering Venice's strategic position at the mouth of the Adriatic and her far-reaching influence in the Middle Ages and Renaissance.

Risotto de Scampi

Scampi Risotto

The Veneti grow an immense quantity of short-grain rice, the most prized of which is Vialone Nano, a costly hybrid of the Vialone and Nano varieties that thrives on the shores of Lago di Garda. This elegant risotto from the capital city of Venice can be made with head-on shrimp if scampi, small members of the lobster family with long claws, are hard to find.

SERVES 4

1½ pounds scampi, heads on
3 tablespoons unsalted butter, cubed,
    at room temperature
1 medium yellow onion, sliced
2 garlic cloves, crushed
1 bay leaf
8 Italian parsley sprigs
3 tablespoons extra-virgin olive oil
4 scallions, white parts only, thinly sliced
2 plum tomatoes, halved, seeded, and diced
2 cups Vialone Nano rice
½ cup dry white wine
½ teaspoon salt
⅛ teaspoon freshly ground black pepper

THE ART OF RISOTTO

Risotto is more than a rice dish: it's a technique for cooking typical of northern Italy. There are three fundamental steps that differentiate risotto from other rice dishes. The first is the toasting of the raw rice in hot fat before liquid is added; this seals in the starch and coats each rice grain so that it remains distinct from its neighbor after cooking. The second is the gradual addition of hot liquid (water, broth, or wine) to the rice as it cooks. The third is the folding in of butter (or, less often, olive oil), usually along with grated cheese, to result in a rich, creamy texture. In the Veneto, risotto is served brothy, a preference that goes by the name of *all'onda* ("with a wave").

Separate the scampi tails from the heads and bodies; reserve the heads and bodies. Shell the tails and chop each into 4 pieces. Place the reserved heads and bodies in a large mortar and crush with a pestle into a coarse paste.

Melt 1 tablespoon of the butter in a 3-quart pot over medium heat. Add the onion and garlic and cook 5 minutes. Stir in the scampi paste and cook 5 minutes. Pour in 8 cups (2 quarts) of water, add the bay leaf and parsley, and bring to a boil. Reduce the heat to medium-low and cook 1 hour, uncovered. Strain and discard the solids. Measure the broth; you should have 6 cups. If needed, add water to make up the quantity. In a clean 2-quart pot, return the broth to just below the boiling point.

Heat the olive oil in a 12-inch sauté pan over a medium flame. Add the scallions and cook 3 minutes, stirring. Add the tomatoes and cook 2 minutes. Add the rice and cook, stirring with a wooden spoon, 3 minutes. Deglaze with the wine. When the wine evaporates, after about 2 minutes, begin adding the measured scampi broth by the ½ cup. Add more broth only when the preceding portion has been absorbed. Cook in this manner, adding broth by the ½ cup and stirring, for 15 minutes. Fold in the scampi tails and cook, adding broth as needed, until the rice is al dente and a little brothy, about 5 minutes; you may not need all of the broth. Fold in the remaining 2 tablespoons of butter, the salt, and the pepper, and serve hot.

THE CATCH OF THE DAY

Fish and seafood are the pinnacles of Venetian cuisine. At Venice's central fish market, locals choose among mullet, sole, monkfish, eel, sea bass, red mullet, sardines, trout, cuttlefish, squid, scampi, shrimp, octopus, and more under a sign that stipulates the precise size and weight of fish that can be sold. In the old days, Mantis shrimp could be found along Venice's canals, but today these succulent shellfish have become as costly as scampi, the creature they most closely resemble in flavor. Venetian seafood dishes include cuttlefish cooked in its own ink, tiny fried fish called *gò,* and soft-shell crabs (*moleche* in Venetian) fried to a crispy, golden brown.

Pasta e Fasoi al Radicchio

Pasta and Bean Soup over Slivered Radicchio

There is not a single region in Italy that doesn't offer some sort of pasta and bean soup. In Campania, pasta e fagioli *includes garlic and tomatoes; in Liguria, it is often laced with pesto; in Tuscany, cannellini are the beans of choice. In the Veneto, pasta e fagioli—called* pasta e fasoi *in dialect—is made with the beans grown in Lamon at an altitude of 2,000 feet. This rendition is from Beccherie, my favorite restaurant in Treviso, and includes radicchio— a vegetable indigenous to the Veneto—for crunch and a pleasantly bitter note. The variety of radicchio used is native to Treviso: sleek and elongated, it is equally lovely slivered into soups, grilled, dipped in batter and fried, or sautéed with bacon and onions. Other radicchio varieties from the Veneto are the round radicchio most commonly available in North America, which hails from the city of Chioggia, and the mild, variegated ivory and purple radicchio from the town of Castelfranco. To buy Lamon beans, see Sources (page 372). The homemade tagliatelle can be replaced with* 1/2 *pound of store-bought fresh tagliatelle, but the cooking time will increase.*

SERVES 4

For the soup:

1⅓ cups dried Lamon beans, soaked 12 hours in cool water to cover

½ medium yellow onion, minced

⅓ cup plus 2 tablespoons extra-virgin olive oil

¾ teaspoon salt

½ teaspoon freshly ground black pepper

1 head radicchio di Treviso, cut into ½-inch-wide strips

1 tablespoon white wine vinegar

For the tagliatelle:

¾ cup unbleached all-purpose flour, plus extra for the counter

¼ teaspoon salt

1 extra-large egg

Make the soup: Drain and rinse the beans. Place in a 4-quart pot, add 5 cups of water, and bring to a gentle boil. Cook, covered, over medium-low heat for 2½ hours, or until tender. Using a slotted spoon, transfer half of the beans with 1 cup of their cooking liquid to a food processor. Process until smooth, return to the pot, and keep warm.

Meanwhile, make the tagliatelle according to instructions on page 370 using the ingredients listed above, adding a little water if the dough is dry or a little flour if it is sticky. Knead 5 minutes, or until smooth, shape into a ball, wrap, and let rest 30 minutes.

Roll out the dough on a floured counter into a 10 × 18-inch rectangle. Cut into three 6 × 10-inch strips. Sprinkle each strip with flour and roll lengthwise; cut into ⅙-inch-wide pieces. Toss with flour to prevent sticking, spread out in a single layer on a floured tray, and cover with a towel.

Add the onion, ⅓ cup of the olive oil, the salt, and ¼ teaspoon of the pepper to the bean purée and cook 5 minutes. Return to a boil, fold in the tagliatelle, and cook until al dente, about 2 minutes.

Mound the radicchio in 4 bowls. Spoon on the soup, drizzle with the remaining 2 tablespoons of olive oil and the vinegar, season with the remaining ¼ teaspoon of pepper, and serve hot.

PREPARATION TIPS: The bean purée can be made up to 2 days ahead, refrigerated, and reheated before adding the onion, olive oil, and tagliatelle.

VERONA'S GNOCCHI DADDY

In Verona, the Venetian capital of potato gnocchi, a celebration called Venerdì Gnoccolar is held on the last Friday of Carnevale. Ever since 1500, when a wealthy doctor in the neighborhood of San Zeno distributed flour, cheese, and wine during a famine, locals have joined forces to prepare massive amounts of gnocchi. Everyone feasts on gnocchi after the King of Carnevale, Papà Gnoc, leads a procession dressed in a red cloak (to symbolize tomato sauce), carrying an oversized fork on which a huge gnocco is speared. A long-simmered beef or horse stew called *pastizada* is standard fare alongside the gnocchi.

Paeta Rosta al Malgarano
Roasted Turkey with Pomegranate Sauce

It is in the meat and game dishes of the Veneto that the region's luxurious flavors and Byzantine touches are most evident. In Montecchio, near Vicenza, young turkey (paeta in Venetian) is paired with a fruit that is rarely seen in modern Italian cooking: the pomegranate, bestower of a sweet and astringent flavor like no other. Indigenous to Iran, pomegranates reached the ancient Romans via Carthage (modern-day Tunisia); their Latin name, malum punicum, means "Carthaginian apple."

SERVES 8

3 pomegranates
1 small turkey (about 8 pounds), giblets minced and set aside
2 teaspoons salt
1 teaspoon freshly ground black pepper
4 tablespoons (½ stick) unsalted butter
½ pound thinly sliced Pancetta
2 tablespoons extra-virgin olive oil

A TASTE FOR FOWL

The Veneti cook duck, geese, capon, guinea hen, squab, and songbirds such as lark and thrush, favorites at Renaissance banquets, with sweet spices like cinnamon and cloves or fragrant herbs like rosemary and bay leaves. Family celebrations are likely to bring roasted guinea hen with *salsa peverada,* a peppery chicken-liver sauce; squab (*toresani* in local parlance) spit-roasted and served over polenta; and capon accompanied by *peverà,* a sauce made with toasted bread crumbs, butter, and marrow.

Preheat the oven to 450°F.

Cut the pomegranates in half; scoop out the seeds from 1 pomegranate and set aside. Squeeze the juice from the 2 remaining pomegranates and reserve.

Season the turkey inside and out with 1½ teaspoons of the salt and ¾ teaspoon of the pepper, and place the butter inside its cavity. Wrap the Pancetta around the turkey, then truss with butcher's string. Place in a roasting pan and roast in the preheated oven for 1½ hours, basting every 15 minutes with the cooking juices. Pour all but ¼ cup of the pomegranate juice over the turkey and roast 30 more minutes, basting every 10 minutes with the cooking juices. Cover with aluminum foil to prevent excess browning; roast 30 more minutes.

Remove the turkey from the oven, discard the string, cut into serving pieces, and arrange on a platter. Strain the cooking juices into a bowl.

Meanwhile, heat the olive oil in an 8-inch skillet. Add the turkey giblets and cook 5 minutes over medium heat. Add the strained cooking juices, the remaining ¼ cup of pomegranate juice, the remaining ½ teaspoon of salt and ¼ teaspoon of pepper, and the reserved pomegranate seeds. Cook 10 minutes. Pour the pomegranate sauce over the turkey and serve hot.

Zaleti

Crumbly Cornmeal Cookies

A few desserts in the Veneto incorporate sweet spices as a fragrant reminder of the spice trade, yet most are uncomplicated combinations of butter, flour, dried fruit, eggs, and cornmeal. Every cornmeal-rich region bakes polenta-based desserts: In Lombardy, there is a bread dubbed pan de mei *and a cake named* sbrisolona; *in Piedmont, serpentine cookies known as* crumiri; *in Val d'Aosta, doughnut-shaped cookies called* ciambelle; *and in the Veneto (as well as Friuli–Venezia Giulia), cornmeal cookies affectionately nicknamed* zaleti *(from* giallo, *meaning "yellow"). In true Venetian fashion, white cornmeal is combined with yellow for a more delicate flavor and lighter color. This recipe was offered by Francesca and Carlo Campeol, owners of Beccherie, an elegant restaurant in Treviso.*

MAKES 30 COOKIES

¼ cup raisins

¼ cup grappa

8 tablespoons (1 stick) unsalted butter, cubed, at room temperature, plus extra for greasing the baking sheets

¼ cup plus 1 teaspoon whole milk

½ cup sugar

½ cup plus 2 tablespoons white cornmeal

½ cup plus 2 tablespoons yellow cornmeal

In a medium bowl, macerate the raisins in the grappa for 3 hours. Drain and blot dry, discarding the grappa.

Preheat the oven to 300°F.

Butter two 11 × 17-inch baking sheets. In a small saucepan, heat the milk until just warm to the touch. Keep warm over the lowest possible flame.

In an electric mixer with the paddle attachment, beat the butter and sugar until pale and fluffy, about 2 minutes. Add the white and yellow cornmeal and beat 1 minute. Add the warm milk and beat until incorporated, about 1 minute, then beat in the raisins. The batter should be soft.

Spoon into a pastry bag fitted with a flat tip and pipe by the tablespoon onto the baking sheets, about 2 inches apart. Bake in the preheated oven for 30 minutes, or until golden around the edges and just set; do not overbake or the cookies will be dry. Cool on a rack.

PREPARATION TIPS: The cookies keep in airtight tins up to 1 week.

THE VENETO'S WINES

THE VENETO, Italy's third most prolific producer of wine after Apulia and Sicily, bottles nearly 200 million gallons every year. The most distinctive wines hail from the hills east of Lago di Garda, as well as areas known as the Colli Berici, Colli Euganei, Piave, and Breganze. Indigenous grape varietals like the white Garganega, Tocai, and Verduzzo and the red Corvina (also known as Cruina), Molinara, and Rondinella provide the basis for the region's better-known local wines, but international varietals like Merlot and Cabernet have also shown potential.

Soave, a dry Garganega-based white laced with Chardonnay, Pinot Bianco, or Trebbiano di Soave, is the best known of the Veneto's wines. The same grapes are shriveled into raisins to make Recioto di Soave, a sweet, complex, amber-hued dessert wine. Also made from raisined grapes, but far from sweet, is Amarone: vinified from a blend of Corvina, Rondinella, and Molinara grapes, its robustness is the result of how little must is obtained from the shriveled grapes after pressing. Recioto della Valpolicella, Amarone's sweet cousin, is a sumptuous red dessert wine with a slightly oxidized character.

Corvina, Rondinella, and Molinara grapes also form the basis for Bardolino, a light red or rosé that has been famous since the time of the Barbarian invasions, and Valpolicella, a straightforward red. Valpolicella con Ripasso is strengthened over the unpressed skins of grapes from which Amarone or other dried grape wines have been vinified, thereby acquiring complexity and intensity.

Garganega, a medium-bodied, straw-yellow white with a characteristic perfume of lemons and almonds, is dry, with a slight bitterness; like Garganega, the crisp, lightly aromatic Bianco di Custoza is obtained from Garganega grapes. The prolific Prosecco varietal, on the other hand, is used to produce one of Italy's most famous sparkling wines: fizzy or fully sparkling Prosecco di Conegliano Valdobbiadene, made using the Charmat method whereby a second fermentation occurs in the bottle rather than in the tank; in the cooler Cartizze subzone, Prosecco is vinified medium-dry.

Torta de Paparele

Lemony Tagliatelle Cake

This almond and noodle cake hails from Verona, a city better known for its pan-doro, *a high, star-shaped, airy Christmas cake. It has cousins in Emilia-Romagna and Lombardy, but what makes this version so interesting is its texture: crumbly, crunchy, yet not dry. It is delicious hot from the oven.*

SERVES 8

For the tagliatelle:

2¼ cups unbleached all-purpose flour, plus extra for the counter

¼ teaspoon salt

3 tablespoons plus 1 teaspoon unsalted butter, melted

3 extra-large eggs

¼ cup whole milk, plus extra if needed

For the cake:

12 tablespoons (1½ sticks) unsalted butter, cubed, plus extra for greasing the cake pan and parchment paper

Unbleached all-purpose flour for the cake pan

1 cup almonds (preferably with the skin on)

1 cup sugar

Grated zest of 1 lemon

¼ cup sweet Marsala

Make the tagliatelle according to instructions on page 370 using the ingredients listed above, adding a little milk if the dough is dry or a little flour if it is sticky; the dough should be suppler and softer than for ordinary pasta. Knead 5 minutes, or until smooth, shape into a ball, and cut into 2 pieces.

Working with 1 piece at a time and keeping the other covered, roll out each piece into a very thin (but not nearly transparent) sheet with a pasta machine; the third-to-last setting on most machines is ideal. Cut each sheet into 4 rectangles, sprinkle both sides with flour, and spread out on a counter, uncovered, for 15 minutes. Cut into tagliatelle with a tagliatelle attachment; do not toss with flour, but spread out in a single layer on a large tray.

Preheat the oven to 350°F.

Make the cake: Butter and flour a 10-inch springform cake pan. Grind the almonds with the sugar in a food processor until finely chopped but not powdery. Fold in the lemon zest. Arrange one-third of the tagliatelle in the cake pan, sprinkle with half of the almond-sugar mixture, top with 6 tablespoons of the butter, and splash with 2 tablespoons of the Marsala; repeat until all of the ingredients have been used. The final layer should be tagliatelle.

Cut a sheet of parchment paper into a 10-inch disk, butter it, and arrange it over the tagliatelle to prevent excess browning. Bake the cake for 1 hour. Remove the parchment paper and bake 15 more minutes, or until the top is golden and lightly crisp. Unmold onto a platter and serve hot, warm, or at room temperature.

Emilia-Romagna

Gelato di Parmigiano
Parmigiano "Ice Cream"

Cassoni Fritti
Greens-Stuffed Pastry Half-Moons

Piadina Romagnola
Griddle Bread from Romagna

Garganelli al Ragù
Garganelli with Creamy Ragù

Orecchioni di Ricotta al Pomodoro
Ricotta-Filled "Ears" in Tomato Sauce

Pisarei e Fasò
Tiny Gnocchi with Beans

Storione in Umido alla Ferrarese
Braised Sturgeon from Ferrara

Scaloppine di Vitello alla Bolognese
Veal Scaloppine alla Bolognese

Arrosto Ripieno
Veal Roast Stuffed with Spinach, Pancetta, and Frittata

Torta Bonissima
Honey and Nut Pie

A sk Italians where the best food in Italy is found, and when they don't name their own city, they will likely say Bologna. The capital of Emilia-Romagna, Bologna is a culinary mecca. Italy's first university was founded there in 1080, attracting young aristocrats from near and far who brought in money, foreign foods, and exotic dining preferences that shaped the city's rich cuisine.

And Bologna is only part of Emilia-Romagna's story. There is also Parma, with its rosy ham and stuffed pastas; Modena, with its regal desserts and nectarlike vinegar; Cesenatico, with its tranquil port and splendid seafood; and Ferrara, with its sweet-and-savory dishes that bespeak a golden past and a rich Jewish legacy. I have been to Emilia-Romagna countless times, visited its mountain villages in search of an herbed flatbread and its quiet seaside towns for a taste of their seafood soup. Every time I leave, I feel I have only begun to uncover what makes the region unique.

Dubbed "Italy's Food Basket" thanks to its thriving agriculture, Emilia-Romagna is home to many of Italy's best-known foods: Prosciutto di Parma, Mortadella, Parmigiano-Reggiano, balsamic vinegar, and a vast array of fresh and stuffed pastas. Everything here is produced on a large scale—annual production reaches 2.5 billion pounds of wheat, 220 million pounds of durum wheat, and 1.5 billion pounds of corn—yet with the utmost artisanal care, resulting in some of the tastiest, most honest food imaginable.

Administratively a single unit, Emilia-Romagna is really made up of two very distinct places: the fertile, never-ending plains and gentle hills of Emilia and the rugged mountains and coastline of Romagna. The name Emilia is derived from the Roman road built in 187 B.C., the Via Aemilia, which crossed the region from Ariminium (today's Rimini) in the southeast to Placentia (today's Piacenza) in the northwest, connecting Emilia-Romagna with Venice and Genoa and beyond to central and northern Europe. Today, one of Italy's main highways coasts this ancient Roman thruway.

Regal Emilia, a land of sprawling golden plains, contrasts with mountainous, sea-hugging Romagna both geographically and gastronomically. Emilia—nicknamed La Grassa ("The Fat")—is northern Italian through and through: butter, cream, and meat have free reign, poaching and braising are favorite techniques, and Renaissance flavors are alive and well. In Romagna, the cuisine is more austere, closer in character to that of central Italy: herbs are used generously, olive oil is the building block of most dishes, and spit-roasting and griddle-baking are everyday affairs.

Aside from their geographic differences, Emilia and Romagna have also been shaped by different political forces. The Emilian cities of Ferrara, Modena, Reggio Emilia, Parma, and Piacenza were dominated by the Este and Farnese duchies, who defined political and economic life in the Renaissance and, in some cases, through the nineteenth century, spawning a sophisticated court cuisine. Romagna, on the other hand, was under Byzantine rule after the Roman Empire fell—one of its main ports, Ravenna, was the western capital of the Byzantine Empire in the sixth century. After Lombard and Frank rule, it became part of the Papal States. Yet as different as the cuisines of Emilia and Romagna are, they are united by a love of fresh egg pastas, rich cheeses, and salty cured meats, staples that are turned into an array of beguiling specialties.

Favorite Restaurants, Shops, and Places

- AL CAVALLINO BIANCO, Via Sbrisi 2, Polesine Parmense, 0524.96136. Exceptional cuisine and artisanally produced Culatello.
- AL PAPPAGALLO, Piazza della Mercanzia 3, Bologna, 051.231200. Sample the *lasagne alla bolognese* and *tortellini in brodo*.
- AL SORRISO, Viale delle Nazioni 12, Località Marina di Ravenna, Ravenna, 0544.530462. Typical seafood cuisine.
- ANGIOL D'OR, Vicolo Scutellari 1/A, Parma, 0521.282632. Sample the *tortelli di erbette*.
- CAFFÈ ARTE E MESTIERI, Via Emilia San Pietro 16, Reggio Emilia, 0522.432202. Excellent *gnocco fritto* and *gamberi in padella con asparagi*.
- FOSSE VENTURI DI ROSARIA COLICCHIO, Via Roma 67, Sogliano al Rubicone, 0541.948521. The place to buy the pit-ripened cheese of Romagna.
- LA ROMANTICA, Via Ripagrande 36, Ferrara, 0533.765975. Don't miss out on the *cappellacci di zucca*.
- MALPIGHI ERMES, Via Pica 310, Modena, 059.280893. Aged balsamic vinegars for sale; schedule a visit of the *acetaia* by appointment.
- PIADINA DI MELANIA, Via Comunale Paderno 2309, San Vittore di Cesena, 0547.660308. One of the best *piadine*, by an award-winning *piadina*-maker.
- TAMBURINI ANTICA SALSAMENTERIA, Via Caprarie 1, Bologna, 051.234726. The ultimate gastronomy shop in Bologna.

Telephone country code: 011.39

Gelato di Parmigiano

Parmigiano "Ice Cream"

In Boccaccio's Decameron, *Maso describes the marvelous land of Bengodi: there was a "mountain of grated Parmigiano on which people did nothing but make maccheroni and ravioli." In this centuries-old recipe from Emilia, Parmigiano and cream are heated until smooth, then refrigerated, yielding a gelato-like treat best served as an appetizer.*

SERVES 8

2 cups heavy cream
10 ounces freshly grated Parmigiano-Reggiano
⅛ teaspoon cayenne pepper
1 cup aged balsamic vinegar
¼ cup honey

Combine the cream, Parmigiano, and cayenne in a large stainless-steel bowl over a pot of simmering water. Whisk until the Parmigiano melts and a smooth cream forms, about 5 minutes, then strain through a fine sieve into a deep 4 × 8½-inch container. Refrigerate 12 hours, or until set.

When you are ready to serve, reduce the vinegar to ¼ cup in a 1-quart pot, about 15 minutes over medium heat, then whisk in the honey. Using an ice cream scoop, mound the gelato in 8 ice cream bowls. Drizzle with the warm vinegar-honey glaze and serve.

PREPARATION TIPS: The gelato keeps in the refrigerator up to 1 week.

THE KING OF GRATING CHEESES

Parmigiano-Reggiano, a nutty cow's milk cheese produced on an artisanal level in nearly seven hundred dairies across Emilia-Romagna, is Italy's most famous grating cheese. To make Parmigiano-Reggiano, the milk obtained from cows in the evening is set out overnight; in the morning, the cream that has risen to the top is skimmed off and morning milk is added. Calf's rennet is stirred in, the resulting curds are broken up and gathered in large cloths, and the whey is drained off. After a few days, the cheese —which has already acquired its shape—is salted, then aged for eighteen to thirty-six months. Each wheel is verified by an expert from the governing *consorzio*; those that pass the test are stamped with a seal guaranteeing their quality and origin.

Cassoni Fritti

Greens-Stuffed Pastry Half-Moons

Vegetables in Romagna often turn into fillings for shortcrust pastry and *pasta matta* ("crazy dough," so called because it is made with very little fat), yielding delicacies like erbazzone, a hearty Swiss chard pie, and these delicious fritters. The dough for cassoni fries up tender because of the milk and eggs it contains, and the filling varies from house to house: Some people omit onion and Pancetta but add raisins; others use spinach instead of Swiss chard; and still others include sausage.

SERVES 10

2¼ cups unbleached all-purpose flour, plus extra for the counter

1 teaspoon salt

3 extra-large eggs

¼ cup whole milk, plus extra if needed

1½ pounds Swiss chard leaves, washed and chopped

3¼ cups extra-virgin olive oil, or ¼ cup extra-virgin olive oil and 3 cups peanut oil

1 medium yellow onion, minced

One ¼-pound slice Pancetta, cut into ⅛-inch dice

1 cup freshly grated Parmigiano-Reggiano

¼ teaspoon freshly ground black pepper

Mix the flour and ½ teaspoon of the salt in a bowl. Stir in the eggs and milk until a dough forms, adding a little milk if the dough is dry or a little flour if it is sticky. Transfer to a counter and knead until smooth, about 5 minutes, then wrap and let rest 30 minutes.

Meanwhile, place the Swiss chard and 1 cup of water in a 12-inch sauté pan over medium-high heat. Cook, covered, 10 minutes, then drain, rinse, and squeeze dry.

Heat ¼ cup of the olive oil in the same pan over a medium flame. Add the onion and Pancetta and cook 5 minutes. Transfer to a bowl and stir in the reserved Swiss chard, the Parmigiano, ¼ teaspoon of the salt, and the pepper. Cool to room temperature.

Roll out the dough on a lightly floured counter into a 20-inch circle. Cut into 3½-inch circles with a cookie cutter. Top with heaping teaspoons of the filling and fold in half, then seal the edges with a fork. These are the cassoni. Gather scraps of dough and roll out again. Make more cassoni in the same manner.

Heat the remaining 3 cups of oil in a deep 10-inch pan until it registers 350°F or is hot enough to brown a cube of bread in 1 minute. Fry a few cassoni at a time until they are golden on both sides, turning once, 2 minutes per side. Remove with a slotted spoon to a plate lined with paper towels and blot dry. Continue in the same manner with the remaining cassoni, maintaining the temperature of the oil by regulating the heat, and serve hot, sprinkled with the remaining ¼ teaspoon of salt.

EMILIA-ROMAGNA'S WINES

THE FERTILE ALLUVIAL FLATLANDS OF EMILIA and long coastline and hills of Romagna offer a diversity of microclimates in which vines have thrived since at least 1700 B.C. The bulk of wine production takes place in the wide plains of the Pò River, but the best vineyards are located in the drier foothills of the Apennines.

Trebbiano, Albana, Sangiovese, and Lambrusco grapes are the most prolific varietals. The latter yields sparkling red and rosé wines that became wildly popular in North America in the 1980s in their slightly sweet incarnation, Lambrusco Reggiano. Yet the Lambruscos the Emilians and Romagnols enjoy—Lambrusco Grasparossa di Castelvetro, Lambrusco di Sorbara, and Lambrusco Salamino di Santa Croce—are dry or off-dry, with a pronounced acidity. Trebbiano, a golden-hued wine based on the eponymous grape, is Emilia-Romagna's most widespread white; harmonious, with a dry flavor and grapey aroma, it is made both still and sparkling in Ravenna, Forlì, and Bologna. Albana, vinified in a dry, medium-dry, sweet, and raisined version from the Albana grape, was awarded DOCG status in 1986. Legend has it that the Roman empress Galla Placidia, upon drinking a glass of Albana in A.D. 435, uttered, *"Vorrei berti in tazza d'oro"* ("I would like to drink you in a golden cup"), giving rise to the name of the township where the best Albana is produced, Bertinoro. Albana is straw-yellow when young, tending toward gold as it ages; slightly tannic and warm, it is especially promising in its sweet and raisined versions.

Sangiovese, the most heavily cultivated varietal in Romagna, shows its greatest potential in the eastern hills of the province of Bologna and the Apennine areas of the provinces of Forlì and Ravenna thanks to a combination of hot summer temperatures and rich clay and sandstone in the soil. Lighter than Tuscany's Sangiovese, Romagna's Sangiovese gains complexity as it ages, resulting in smooth and velvety reds. Gutturnio, a dry red made from Barbera and Croatina grapes in the Colli Piacentini, offers tobacco and fruit notes and shows good potential for wood aging.

French grape varietals have also met with success in Emilia-Romagna; the Colli Bolognesi produce very good Sauvignon Blanc, Merlot, and Cabernet Sauvignon, and in the Riverargo-Vigolzone, a subzone of the Colli Piacentini, excellent Chardonnay, Cabernet Sauvignon, and Pinot Nero are vinified.

Piadina Romagnola
Griddle Bread from Romagna

Romagna's piadina accompanies Prosciutto and other salty cured meats and is devoured at the start of a meal or as a snack throughout the day. When it is split horizontally, it can be stuffed with all manner of goodies: creamy cheese, salami, Prosciutto Cotto, and more. This recipe for piadine—*if not for the topping—is from Melania Facciani, owner of Piadina di Melania in San Vittore di Cesena, who has won numerous piadina contests in Romagna.*

SERVES 6

3½ cups unbleached all-purpose flour, plus extra for the counter
1½ teaspoons salt
2 scant ounces lard
2½ teaspoons baking soda
2 tablespoons minced rosemary
1 small garlic clove, minced
1 cup freshly grated Parmigiano-Reggiano
1 teaspoon freshly ground black pepper
¾ cup extra-virgin olive oil
24 thin slices Prosciutto di Parma

Mix the flour, salt, and lard in a bowl and stir in 1 cup of warm water. Turn out onto a counter and knead 2 minutes, then sprinkle with the baking soda and 1 tablespoon of water. Knead 8 minutes, or until a soft, smooth dough forms, sprinkling in additional water if the dough is dry or additional flour if it is sticky. Shape into a flat disk, wrap, and let rest 30 minutes.

Roll out the dough on a lightly floured counter into a ⅛-inch-thick circle. Using a 5-inch round cookie cutter, cut into disks. These are the piadine. Gather scraps and roll out again, then cut into more disks. Prick each piadina 3 times with a fork; this prevents ballooning as they cook. You should have 12 piadine.

Heat a grill pan 5 minutes over a high flame. Add as many piadine as will fit in a single layer and cook until speckled on the bottom, about 2 minutes. Turn and cook until speckled on the other side, about 2 minutes, then remove to a towel and wrap to keep warm. Continue in the same manner with the remaining piadine.

To serve, mix the rosemary, garlic, Parmigiano, and pepper in a bowl. Drizzle each of the warm piadine with 1 tablespoon of the olive oil, sprinkle with 1½ tablespoons of the rosemary mixture, and top with 2 slices of Prosciutto. Serve immediately.

Garganelli al Ragù

Garganelli with Creamy Ragù

This quill-shaped pasta from Lugo di Romagna pairs perfectly with a Romagnol ragù featuring veal, besciamella, tomatoes, and a touch of cinnamon and nutmeg. To buy garganelli, see Sources (page 372).

ROMAGNA'S PIT-RIPENED CHEESE

Romagna's most interesting cheese is Formaggio di Fossa, a sheep's milk cheese ripened in tufaceous pits. The first reference to it dates to 1497, when cheese was set to ripen in pits used to hide wheat from soldiers' raids. In August, the cheese is stacked inside the pits; the pits are hermetically sealed and the cheese ferments in anaerobic conditions until the pits are opened on November 25, the Feast of Saint Catherine. Formaggio di Fossa is lovely in savory pies and pasta fillings, draped over salads, stirred into polenta, or drizzled with honey and served with a dried-grape wine for dessert. See Sources (page 372) to purchase.

SERVES 4

For the ragù:

5 tablespoons unsalted butter

1 medium yellow onion, minced

1 carrot, minced

1 celery stalk, minced

2 tablespoons minced Italian parsley

½ pound boneless veal shoulder, trimmed of fat and sinew, cut into ⅛ × ⅛ × ¼-inch strips

¼ cup dry Marsala

6 plum tomatoes, peeled (see page 369), seeded, and diced

¾ cup Besciamella (page 370)

½ cup Beef Broth (page 368), plus extra if needed

⅛ teaspoon ground cinnamon

Pinch freshly grated nutmeg

¼ teaspoon salt

¼ teaspoon freshly ground black pepper

One ¼-pound slice Prosciutto di Parma, cut into ⅛ × ⅛ × ¼-inch strips

For the garganelli:

3 cups unbleached all-purpose flour, plus extra for the counter

¼ teaspoon salt

⅛ teaspoon freshly grated nutmeg

½ cup freshly grated Parmigiano-Reggiano

4 extra-large eggs

To cook and serve:

2 tablespoons salt

1 cup freshly grated Parmigiano-Reggiano

Make the ragù: Melt 4 tablespoons of the butter in a 12-inch sauté pan. Add the onion, carrot, celery, and parsley and cook over medium-high heat 10 minutes. Add the veal and cook until browned all over, about 15 minutes, stirring often. Deglaze with 1 tablespoon of the Marsala, let it evaporate, and repeat, adding the Marsala in this way until it is all used; it will take about 5 minutes. Lower the heat to medium, add the tomatoes, and cook 10 minutes. Fold in the besciamella, broth, cinnamon, nutmeg, salt, and pepper. Cook 45 minutes, covered, adding broth if needed.

Melt the remaining tablespoon of butter in an 8-inch skillet. Add the Prosciutto and cook 5 minutes over medium heat, then fold into the ragù. Keep warm.

Meanwhile, make the garganelli according to instructions on page 370 using the ingredients listed opposite, adding a little water if the dough is dry or a little flour if it is sticky. Knead 5 minutes, or until smooth, shape into a ball, wrap, and let rest 30 minutes.

Cut the dough into 2 pieces. Working with 1 piece at a time and keeping the other covered, roll out each piece into a 20-inch square on a lightly floured counter. Cut into 1½-inch-wide strips, then into 1½-inch squares.

Place a ridged gnocchi paddle on the counter in front of you (or use a fine-tooth comb with long teeth, placing the comb so the teeth are farther from you). Place 1 square of the dough on the gnocchi paddle with one corner closer to you; the square now looks like a diamond. Place a pencil just above the midpoint of the diamond as though it were a miniature rolling pin. Using your fingers, wrap the top corner of the diamond around the pencil. Roll the pencil toward you, pressing firmly. The diamond will wrap around the pencil and form a ridged, quill-shaped piece of pasta. (If you like, roll the pencil back and forth to make the ridges more pronounced.) Slip the pasta off the pencil onto a floured tray. Continue with the remaining dough in the same manner. These are the garganelli. Spread out in a single layer on a floured tray and cover with a towel.

To cook, bring 6 quarts of water to a boil. Add the garganelli and salt and cook until al dente, about 2 minutes. Drain, reserving ½ cup of the pasta cooking water. Toss the garganelli, ragù, and the reserved cooking water in a bowl and serve hot, passing the Parmigiano at the table.

PREPARATION TIPS: Make the ragù up to 2 days ahead and refrigerate; reheat as you boil the garganelli.

From Bakers' Guilds to Borlengo

Y THE MIDDLE AGES, bakers' guilds had been formed in Emilia-Romagna, and with the guilds came legislation of that most primal food: bread. In 1287, the Statuti di Ferrara in Emilia stipulated that bakers who sold underweight or poorly baked bread would be severely fined.

Ferrara's bread, the *coppietta* ("the couple"), has been baked since at least 1536, when it was offered at each place setting at a Carnevale banquet presided over by Cristoforo di Messisbugo for the Cardinal Ippolito d'Este. Shaped like a hand or, some say, like a man and a woman, the coppietta is made of soft wheat flour, water, yeast, oil or lard, and salt, and its crumbly yet tender texture makes it the perfect partner for the rich, buttery *salumi* and cheeses of its region.

Another favorite Emilian bread—really more of a focaccia—is *gnocco* studded with cracklings. In Romagna, many breads are baked on a griddle; aside from *piadina,* there is *borlengo,* a very thin, parchment paper–like pancake that is rubbed with rosemary and lard while still hot, and *tigelle,* yeasted, round breads whose dough is enriched with eggs.

Orecchioni di Ricotta al Pomodoro

Ricotta-Filled "Ears" in Tomato Sauce

Romagna's pastas are generally simpler than those of Emilia. The Romagnols are fond of strozzapreti ("priest stranglers"), dough shaped into twisting strands, and cheese-stuffed cappelletti ("little hats"), which they serve in shortcrust pastry for celebrations. In the old days, when cappelletti were served in broth, a large cappelletto was hidden in the tureen; it was believed that whoever found it in his or her bowl would be lucky in the year to come. Orecchioni are a specialty of Ravenna, akin to the tortelli of Tuscany. While tomato sauce is a lovely topping, melted butter infused with sage is just as nice.

SERVES 6

1 recipe Pasta Dough (page 370)
1½ pounds fresh Ricotta
1¼ cups freshly grated Parmigiano-Reggiano, plus extra for passing at the table
¼ cup minced Italian parsley
1 extra-large egg
¼ teaspoon freshly grated nutmeg
2 tablespoons plus ¼ teaspoon salt
Unbleached all-purpose flour for the counter
1 recipe Tomato Sauce (page 369)

Make the dough and let it rest according to instructions on page 370.

Meanwhile, in a large mixing bowl, combine the Ricotta, 1 cup of the Parmigiano, the parsley, egg, nutmeg, and ¼ teaspoon of the salt, and mix until smooth; this is the filling.

Cut the dough into 4 pieces. Working with 1 piece at a time and keeping the others covered, roll out each into a nearly transparent sheet using a pasta machine. Cut into disks with a 3-inch round cookie cutter. Place 1 generous teaspoon of filling on each disk; brush the inner edges with water, fold in half, and seal the edges with a fork. These are the orecchioni. Spread out in a single layer on a lightly floured tray and cover with a towel.

Bring 6 quarts of water to a boil. Add the orecchioni and the remaining 2 tablespoons of salt and cook until al dente, about 3 minutes. Remove to a bowl with a slotted spoon.

Meanwhile, heat the tomato sauce.

Fold the tomato sauce into the orecchioni, sprinkle with the remaining ¼ cup of Parmigiano, and serve hot, passing additional Parmigiano at the table.

PREPARATION TIPS: Make the tomato sauce up to 4 days ahead and refrigerate; reheat it as you cook the orecchioni. Shape the orecchioni up to 4 hours ahead, spread out in a single layer on a floured tray, and refrigerate, covered with a towel.

Pisarei e Fasò

Tiny Gnocchi with Beans

Pisarei is Piacenza's most glorious dish. In the old days, when a young man's mother wanted to be sure of her potential daughter-in-law's skills and suitability as a wife, she would check the girl's right thumb: if it was callused, then she made pisarei on a regular basis, and the marriage was in good order.

EMILIA'S GOLDEN TAGLIATELLE

If Emilia-Romagna had to have a symbol, it would be a golden sheet of pasta. More than any other region, Emilia-Romagna (and Emilia more than Romagna) is the home of egg pasta, none more renowned than tagliatelle. Legend has it that tagliatelle were created in Bologna in 1487 for the wedding of Lucrezia Borgia to the Duke of Ferrara, when Mastro Zafirano, inspired by the bride's golden tresses, cut egg pasta into long strips. The Bolognese sauce for tagliatelle is a three-meat ragù; in Parma, Prosciutto and cream or chicken-liver sauce are common; and in Piacenza, a nut sauce is favored.

SERVES 6

1 cup dried cranberry beans, soaked 12 hours in
    cool water to cover
2 medium yellow onions, 1 peeled and 1 minced
2 tablespoons extra-virgin olive oil
3 tablespoons unsalted butter
One 2-ounce slice Pancetta, cut into ¼-inch cubes
3 tablespoons minced Italian parsley
2 garlic cloves, minced
2 cups canned chopped Italian plum tomatoes
12 basil leaves
⅛ teaspoon freshly ground black pepper
2 tablespoons plus ½ teaspoon salt
3¼ cups unbleached all-purpose flour,
    plus extra for the counter
½ cup fresh bread crumbs
1 cup freshly grated Parmigiano-Reggiano

Drain the beans and place them in a 2-quart pot with the peeled onion and the olive oil. Add 4 cups of cool water and bring to a boil. Reduce the heat to medium-low, cover, and cook for 1 hour, or until half cooked, then remove from the heat. Drain, reserving the cooking liquid; discard the peeled onion.

Melt the butter in a 2-quart pot over medium-high heat. Add the Pancetta, parsley, garlic, and minced onion and cook 5 minutes. Add the drained beans, tomatoes, basil, pepper, and 1 cup of the reserved bean cooking liquid, then bring to a boil. Reduce the heat to medium, cover, and cook for 1 hour, or until the beans are done and the sauce is thick; add a little of the reserved bean cooking liquid if needed. Season with ½ teaspoon of the salt.

Meanwhile, pour the flour on a counter. Place the bread crumbs in a bowl, add ½ cup of hot water, and set aside 5 minutes. Work the moistened bread crumbs into the flour, adding as much additional hot water as needed (about 1 cup) to form a soft, smooth dough. Knead 5 minutes, cut into 8 pieces, and roll out each piece into a pencil-thick log on an unfloured surface.

Working with 1 log at a time and keeping the others covered, cut into pea-sized pieces; press and roll each piece onto a floured counter with your thumb so that it rolls over itself, forming a shell. These are the pisarei. Continue with the remaining dough. Toss with flour to prevent sticking, spread out in a single layer on a floured tray, and cover with a towel if not cooking immediately.

Bring 6 quarts of water to a boil and add the pisarei and the remaining 2 tablespoons of salt. Cook 15 minutes, or until al dente. Remove to a tureen with a slotted spoon, stir in the beans, and serve hot, sprinkled with the Parmigiano.

PREPARATION TIPS: Make the beans up to 2 days ahead and refrigerate; reheat as you boil the pisarei.

THE BIRTH OF TORTELLINI

The most famous stuffed Emilian pasta is tortellini—savory nuggets that are a must for Christmas dinner, floating in capon broth. Mentioned in culinary texts as early as the fourteenth century, recipes for tortellini's stuffing (veal, pork, Mortadella, Prosciutto, and Parmigiano) and sauce (ragù) have since undergone changes. But the Confraternità del Tortellino, founded in Bologna in 1965, decreed that the dough must be made mostly of soft wheat flour with a whisper of semolina flour. Eight to twelve eggs are needed per kilo (2¼ pounds) of flour, and the dough must be rolled out until it is nearly transparent with a wooden rolling pin. Giuseppe Ceri, a Tuscan engineer and amateur poet who adopted Bologna as his homeland, wrote a poem about the creation of tortellini to calm a raging dispute between the Bolognesi and Modenesi, who both claimed they invented the pasta. In Ceri's poem, the owner of an inn in Castelfranco Emilia (a town in the diocese of Bologna that also belonged to the province of Modena) spied a sleeping Venus. Struck by her beauty, the man ran into the kitchen and re-created a likeness of her navel out of pasta dough. However or wherever tortellini were born, they deserve to be savored on any visit to Emilia.

Storione in Umido alla Ferrarese
Braised Sturgeon from Ferrara

When it comes to seafood, sea-hugging Romagna beats Emilia hands down. Emilia's specialties, on the other hand, rely on sweetwater fish like eel and farm-raised sturgeon. One of northern Italy's favorite banquet fish, sturgeon is especially well loved in Emilia, where the Este and Farnese dukes feasted on it, and in Tuscany, where it was fished in the Arno River.

JEWISH CUISINE IN FERRARA

The Jewish community of Ferrara was one of Renaissance Italy's most sizeable thanks to the Dukes of Este, who offered Jews protection even as anti-Semitism broke out all over Europe. In the sixteenth century, a large number of Jews settled in this Emilian city; some had come from Germany, others were fleeing the Spanish Inquisition. As a result, Ferrara's cuisine includes a number of Jewish dishes like preserved goose breast, savory pumpkin recipes, and *buricche,* chicken-filled fried pastry crescents; the name has its roots in Turkey's *borekas,* half-moon pastries that evolved from Spain's empanadas, a specialty of Jews of Spanish origin.

SERVES 6

1 medium yellow onion, minced

1 celery stalk, minced

2 garlic cloves, 1 sliced and 1 minced

1 bay leaf, crumbled

1½ pounds boneless and skinless sturgeon fillet, cut into ½-inch-thick steaks

1½ cups dry white wine

½ teaspoon salt

¼ teaspoon freshly ground black pepper

¼ cup extra-virgin olive oil

3 anchovy fillets, minced

2 tablespoons minced Italian parsley

2 teaspoons tomato paste

In a large bowl, combine the onion, celery, sliced garlic, and bay leaf. Scatter half of this mixture in a 12-inch container, top with the sturgeon, and cover with the remaining onion mixture. Pour in the wine, ¼ teaspoon of the salt, and ⅛ teaspoon of the pepper. Cover and refrigerate for 2 to 24 hours.

Remove the sturgeon from its marinade and blot dry. Strain and reserve ½ cup of wine from the marinade; discard the solids and remaining wine.

Heat the olive oil in a 12-inch sauté pan over a medium-high flame. Add the anchovies and cook for 1 minute; add the minced garlic and parsley and cook 1 minute. Add the sturgeon in a single layer; season with the remaining ¼ teaspoon of salt and ⅛ teaspoon of pepper. Cook 3 minutes, turn, and cook 3 minutes. Add the reserved ½ cup of wine from the marinade; and bring to a boil. Stir in the tomato paste, reduce the heat to medium-low, cover, and cook 10 minutes.

Transfer the sturgeon to a serving platter. Cook the sauce until it is reduced by half and almost syrupy, about 2 minutes over medium-high heat, then pour it over the sturgeon. Serve hot, warm, or at room temperature.

Scaloppine di Vitello alla Bolognese
Veal Scaloppine alla Bolognese

Bolognese cooks sometimes substitute sliced melting cheese such as Gruyère for the Parmigiano and opt for dry Marsala instead of white wine and balsamic vinegar.

SERVES 4

8 veal scaloppine (3 ounces each), pounded thin with a mallet
1 cup unbleached all-purpose flour
¼ cup extra-virgin olive oil
4 tablespoons (½ stick) unsalted butter
⅛ teaspoon freshly ground black pepper
8 thin slices Prosciutto di Parma
½ cup freshly grated Parmigiano-Reggiano
½ cup dry white wine
¼ cup aged balsamic vinegar

Preheat the oven to 500°F.

Dredge the scaloppine in the flour, shaking off the excess. Heat 2 tablespoons each of the olive oil and butter in a 12-inch skillet over a high flame until foaming. Brown 4 of the scaloppine on both sides, turning once, about 2 minutes per side. Remove with a slotted spatula to an 11 × 17-inch baking sheet. Repeat with the remaining 2 tablespoons of olive oil, 2 tablespoons of butter, and 4 scaloppine. Top each of the browned scaloppine on the baking sheet with the pepper, 1 slice of Prosciutto, and 1 tablespoon of Parmigiano.

Deglaze the skillet with the wine and vinegar and cook until syrupy, about 2 minutes over medium-high heat. Pour over the scaloppine on the baking sheet, then bake in the preheated oven 3 minutes. Serve immediately.

THE REAL BALSAMIC VINEGAR

Already hailed as salutary in 1046 by a Benedictine monk, Modena's balsamic vinegar was sipped by Lucrezia Borgia to fight childbirth pains, by Francesco IV, Duke of Modena, to soothe his ulcer, and by composer Gioacchino Rossini to calm his nerves. This prized nectar is made from the reduced must of Trebbiano and other grapes, which matures in oak barrels over the winter. Every spring, the vinegar is poured into smaller and smaller casks made of various kinds of wood, each of which bestows a specific aroma and color on the final product as it ages. It takes 770 pounds of grapes to produce 15 quarts of vinegar, which explains the high cost of genuine balsamic vinegar. The longer it ages, the more complex and expensive the vinegar becomes: twelve years of aging is the minimum, yet one hundred years or longer is not unheard of. Rich, thick, and aromatic, its acidity balanced by its sweetness, balsamic vinegar is delicious on salads and vegetables, in sauces for meat or fish, over strawberries and vanilla gelato, or whisked into *zabaione*. To be sure you are buying the real thing, look for the words *Consorzio Produttori Aceto Balsamico Tradizionale di Modena* on the bottle.

Arrosto Ripieno

Veal Roast Stuffed with Spinach, Pancetta, and Frittata

Emilia's meats are just as likely to be stuffed as its pastas. Capon is filled with ground veal, pork, Mortadella, Prosciutto, chicken livers, pistachios, and Parmigiano; Cotechino sausage is wrapped in beef and Prosciutto; and veal loin in Reggio Emilia is butterflied and rolled around spinach, Pancetta, and frittata, as below. If you prefer, you can substitute Prosciutto di Parma for the Pancetta and Swiss chard for the spinach. While the veal is not roasted—it is cooked in a covered pan—the result is a browned, moist loin.

SERVES 6

1½ pounds spinach leaves, washed thoroughly
6 tablespoons (¾ stick) unsalted butter
⅔ cup freshly grated Parmigiano-Reggiano
2 extra-large eggs
2 pounds boneless veal loin, butterflied and
    pounded thin with a mallet
¼ pound thinly sliced Pancetta
¼ cup extra-virgin olive oil
1 cup dry white wine
2 cups Chicken Broth (page 368), plus extra if
    needed
¼ teaspoon salt
⅛ teaspoon freshly ground black pepper

Cook the spinach in a covered 12-inch sauté pan over high heat for 5 minutes. Remove from the pan, rinse, chop, and squeeze dry. Melt 2 tablespoons of the butter in the same pan over medium heat and add the spinach and ⅓ cup of the Parmigiano; cook 5 minutes. Cool and drain off any liquid.

In a medium bowl, beat the eggs with the remaining ⅓ cup of Parmigiano. Heat a 10-inch nonstick skillet over a medium flame, add the eggs, and cook until set on both sides, about 2 minutes per side, turning once. Remove this frittata to a plate.

Place the veal on a cutting board, smooth side down. Top with the Pancetta, then with the frittata, cutting the frittata as needed to cover it, and finally with the sautéed spinach. Roll lengthwise into a bundle and tie with butcher's string.

Heat the olive oil and the remaining 4 tablespoons of butter in a 12-inch sauté pan over a medium-high flame. Add the veal and sear until browned on all sides, about 10 minutes, turning to cook evenly. Add the wine and cook 5 minutes. Add the broth, salt, and pepper. Reduce the heat to medium-low, cover, and cook for 1 hour, or until the veal is firm but not dry and lets out a clear juice when pierced, adding broth as needed. Discard the string, slice thinly, and serve hot, with the pan juices.

PREPARATION TIPS: Stuff the veal up to 12 hours ahead and refrigerate.

CHEESE AND PIGS, A NATURAL BALANCE

THROUGHOUT ITALY, cheese production is complementary to the curing of meats: wherever there is cheese, there is excess whey, which, when combined with bran and corn, becomes perfect feed for pigs. In Emilia-Romagna, where whey from cheesemaking is plentiful, *salumi* are abundant. There are over two million pigs in the region; archaeological data shows that they have been raised since at least 1000 B.C. near Piacenza, where some of the best Pancetta, salami, and Coppa (a forcemeat from the top of the pig's neck) are produced.

The two most famous Emilian cured meats are Mortadella di Bologna and Prosciutto di Parma. Mortadella is the original "baloney," made from ground pork threaded with wide strips of lard since the Middle Ages; pistachios, garlic, or truffles are sometimes added. Prosciutto di Parma, cured in and around the town of Langhirano, relies on top-choice thighs from meaty, heavy pigs. The thighs are trimmed of fat and rind and hung for one day; then massaged with salt and laid on salt-covered tables for one month; then rinsed, brushed, hung to dry, coated with a mixture of lard, flour, water, and pepper; and finally aged for ten to twelve months. Fortunately, both Mortadella and Prosciutto di Parma are exported to North America (see Sources, page 372).

Zampone is pork meat, head, and rind stuffed into the skin of the pig's hoof, a long-standing partner for lentils on holiday tables. It is made domestically, since the Emilian version does not yet meet FDA regulations.

Torta Bonissima

Honey and Nut Pie

Emilian desserts can be comfort foods like baked rice pudding or sophisticated creations like creamy liqueur-soaked trifles. A handful of medieval desserts have survived the centuries: Bologna's *certosino*, laced with anise and cinnamon; Ferrara's peppery *panpepato*; and Modena's *torta bonissima*. Dense and moist, *bonissima* is best fresh out of the oven, accompanied by a sweet wine such as Albana di Romagna.

SERVES 8

3 cups unbleached all-purpose flour, plus extra for the counter and pie pan

1⅓ cups sugar

¼ teaspoon salt

Grated zest of 1 lemon

3 sticks unsalted butter, cubed, at room temperature, plus extra for greasing the pie pan

6 extra-large egg yolks

3 cups walnut halves

¼ cup rum

1 cup honey

Place the flour, sugar, salt, and lemon zest in a powerful 11-cup food processor and pulse to mix. Add the butter and pulse until the mixture resembles coarse meal. Add 5 of the egg yolks and pulse until the dough begins to gather around the blade. Turn out onto a floured counter, gather into a ball, cut into 2 pieces, 1 slightly larger than the other, and pat into 2 flat disks. Wrap and refrigerate 1 hour.

Meanwhile, in a medium bowl, mix the walnut halves, rum, and honey.

Preheat the oven to 350°F.

Butter and flour an 11-inch springform pie pan. Roll out the larger dough disk on a lightly floured counter into a 13-inch circle and line the pan with it. (Don't panic if the dough tears: simply patch it once it is inside the pan.) Spoon in the walnut mixture. Roll out the smaller dough disk on a lightly floured counter into a 12-inch circle and place it over the filling, sealing the edges. Cut off excess dough.

Beat the remaining egg yolk and brush the top of the pie with it. Bake in the preheated oven 40 minutes, or until the crust is golden and lightly crisp. Serve the pie hot, warm, or at room temperature.

PREPARATION TIPS: Make the dough up to 24 hours ahead and refrigerate.

Giuseppe Verdi's Favorite Cake

Composer Giuseppe Verdi, born in Roncole, a small town in the province of Parma,
loved pasta—rumor has it that he ate it every day of his life. But he was also an ardent
fan of a cake called *spongata,* made by sandwiching honey, crushed cookies, almonds,
hazelnuts, walnuts, orange and citron zests, pine nuts, and raisins between two sheer
disks of dough. Spongata is among Italy's oldest sweets, cited in recipe books and texts
dating back to the fifteenth century; it remains a favorite for Christmas and New Year's
in Busseto (where Verdi moved at the age of ten to study music), Brescello, and Reggio
Emilia. Some versions call for a rich chocolate glaze, but most are simply dusted
with confectioner's sugar after baking.

Tuscany

Foglie di Salvia Fritte
Deep-Fried Sage Leaves

Panzanella
Summer Bread and Tomato Salad

Insalata di Fagioli e Tonno
Cannellini Beans and Tuna

Pappardelle sull'Anatra
Wide Pasta Ribbons in Duck Sauce

Polenta Ficca
Chestnut-Flour Polenta with Sausage and Scallions

Ignudi
"Nude" Ravioli

Calamari all'Inzimino
Braised Squid with Chili, Greens, and Tomatoes

Braciole di Maiale con le Olive
Pork Chops with Olives and Fennel Seeds

Schiacciata con l'Uva
Florentine Flatbread with Grapes

La Crostata di Bietole di Giulio
Giulio's Sweet Swiss Chard Tart

If *there's one region most Italophiles know and love,* it's Tuscany: the golden home of Michelangelo and Da Vinci, a mythic countryside that brings us world-famous wine and olive oil. Travelers who go to Italy for the first time flock to Florence. Those who have been time and again head to San Gimignano, the city of a hundred towers, or Montalcino, to visit its noble vineyards.

The Tuscans have promoted themselves and their region so skillfully and for so long that convincing someone to go to Tuscany is not a difficult task. I've been to Tuscany every year for twenty years. Each time I go, I discover something new: Last year it was a thick handmade spaghetti called *pici* topped with a garlicky bread crumb sauce in Montepulciano; the year before it was wild boar braised with bitter chocolate and pine nuts in Florence. I'm already wondering what this year will bring.

The Tuscan landscape alternates between hills and mountains, dotted with olive groves and punctuated by cypress trees that frame ancient estates and solitary homes. Tuscany was home to the Etruscans, a mysterious people who, scholars believe, hailed from Asia Minor and arrived around 1000 B.C. The Etruscans called their land Etruria. In the fourth century B.C., Romans conquered the area and changed its name to Tuscia; Tuscia eventually evolved into Tuscania and, finally, into Toscana. After the fall of the Roman Empire, the Lombards ruled Tuscany, followed by the Franks.

By the eleventh century, a number of cities in Tuscany had become free communes; Pisa, Lucca, Siena, and Florence soon developed into competing republics. In the fourteenth century, Florence—the city where much of the great thinking and artistry of the Renaissance took place—superseded all other Tuscan cities. From 1434, when Cosimo de' Medici became the Signore of Florence, to 1737, when the Hapsburg-Lorraine family took over after the death of the last Medici, the region's fate was determined by the ruling Medici family.

Tuscany played a pivotal role in the fight for Italy's unification; Baron Bettino Ricasoli, an enlightened man who also produced fine wines on his family's centuries-old estate in the heart of the Chianti zone, became prime minister in 1861 and again in 1866. Four years after Italy's unification, Florence was named the new Italian capital, an honor it held for six years; it remains Tuscany's capital to this day.

As simple and sober as its landscape, as judicious and refined as its artists, the cuisine of Tuscany is founded on the holy trinity of saltless bread, vegetables, and olive oil. Yes, there are impressive, complicated feast dishes, heavily spiced recipes harking back to the Middle Ages and the Renaissance. But most Tuscan specialties are straightforward, and the skill of the cook lies precisely in his or her restraint: never add something when you can just as well do without, always let the individual ingredients speak for themselves. No more, no less.

Favorite Restaurants, Shops, and Places

- CEREALI SEMENTI MARCUCCI, Via Santa Lucia 13, Lucca, 0583.343747. Dried beans, lentils, farro, and pastas.
- CIBREO, Via Andrea del Verocchio 8/R, Florence, 055.2341100. One of Florence's top tables.
- COCO LEZZONE, Via del Parioncino 26/R, Florence, 055.287178. Excellent soups, including *pappa col pomodoro*.
- DA GIULIO IN PELLERIA, Via delle Conce 45, Lucca, 0583.55948. Paolo Sari offers tasty trattoria food and a sweet Swiss chard pie.
- ENOTECA PINCHIORRI, Via Ghibellina 87, Florence, 055.242777. To many, Florence's best restaurant; don't miss out on *gamberoni allo spiedo con gran farro*.
- FATTORIA DEI BARBI E DEL CASATO, Località Podernovi, Montalcino, 0577.848277. Wine and olive oil for sale; visit the wine museum.
- IL CAMINETTO DEL CHIANTI, Via della Montagnola 52, Greve in Chianti, 055.8588909. Try the *pici al sugo d'anatra*.
- LA BUCA DI SANT'ANTONIO, Via della Cervia 1/3, Lucca, 0583.55881. Divine cuisine; order the *capretto allo spiedo*.
- PASTICCERIA NANNINI, Via F. Tozzi 2, Siena, 0577.41301. *Cantuccini*, *ricciarelli*, and *panforte*.
- THE GIOVANNI F. MARIANI MUSEUM OF GLASS AND WINE, Castello Banfi (20 minutes west of Montalcino), 0577.840111. Guided tours by appointment.

Telephone country code: 011.39

Foglie di Salvia Fritte

Deep-Fried Sage Leaves

Florentines love frying so much that they have a saying: "Fritta è buona anche una ciabatta" ("*Even a slipper is good fried*"). Many of their favorite antipasti are fritters: salt cod nuggets, stuffed zucchini blossoms, yeasted dough puffs called coccoli, *diamond-shaped* crescentine, *and these deep-fried sage leaves wrapped around anchovies and dipped in beaten egg. Select the freshest, most fragrant, largest sage leaves possible for this unusual finger food.*

SERVES 4

1 cup extra-virgin olive oil
2 extra-large eggs
½ teaspoon salt
48 sage leaves, stems removed, rinsed and blotted dry
4 anchovy fillets, cut into 6 pieces each
½ cup unbleached all-purpose flour

Heat the olive oil in a deep 10-inch pan until it registers 350°F, or until it is hot enough to brown a cube of bread in 1 minute.

Meanwhile, beat the eggs and salt in a plate. Dip in the sage leaves, coating both sides. Place 1 piece of anchovy over each of 24 sage leaves, top with the remaining 24 sage leaves, and dredge each sandwich in the flour, shaking off the excess.

Fry in 3 batches until golden on both sides, turning once, about 3 minutes, maintaining the temperature of the oil by regulating the heat. Remove with a slotted spoon to a plate lined with paper towels, blot dry, and serve hot.

THE BLIND EEL OF PISA

In Pisa, the city of the leaning tower, tiny newborn eel (or elvers) are considered a delicacy: known as *cee* or *cieche* ("blind ones," because of their poor sight), they are sautéed with garlic and sage in olive oil, then finished in the oven under a cloak of beaten eggs, lemon juice, and grated Parmigiano.

DINING WITH THE DE' MEDICIS

MENTION THE NAME DE' MEDICI and images of Renaissance Florence spring to mind. The Medicis ruled Tuscany from the mid-fifteenth to the mid-eighteenth century almost without interruption, and their court was known for its high level of culture and justice, its liberal ideals, its aesthetics, and its appreciation of good food. Lorenzo the Magnificent, who reigned from 1469 to 1492, was so fond of the pleasures of the table that he compared his lady love, Nencia da Barberino, to his favorite foods: she was "fairer than flour, sweeter than Malvasia, and as tasty as cheese."

Some forty years later, Caterina de' Medici married the future King of France, Henri II, and moved to Paris, where she introduced her court to many new dishes and to the practice of eating with a fork. Seventy years later, Bernardo Buontalenti, a Florentine architect who perfected the art of sherbet-making in Florence's underground ice rooms, organized a spectacular banquet for the wedding of Maria de' Medici to King Henri IV. Songbirds fluttered out of napkins and guests were served twenty-four cold dishes (salads, veal and boar pies, squab, beef's tongue, and more), followed by eighteen hot dishes (quail, pheasant, and capon among them), ten more hot dishes (roasted thrush, suckling pig, and so on), and a selection of sweets, sherbets, cheeses, vegetables, and poached peaches.

The Medicis' cuisine lives on in the roasted goose, stuffed pheasant, spit-roasted squab, monumental savory pies, and sweet-and-sour meat braises still prepared in Tuscan homes and trattorie today.

Panzanella

Summer Bread and Tomato Salad

One of Tuscany's great salads, panzanella marries day-old bread, tomatoes, basil, and olive oil. You can add cucumbers, anchovies, and capers if you like; I prefer the unembellished version below. Similar salads exist in Liguria, Campania, and Sicily—the common origin was the need to use up leftover bread.

SERVES 4

60 cherry tomatoes, quartered

1 large purple onion, quartered and thinly sliced

½ pound crustless day-old Tuscan bread, cut into ½-inch cubes

¼ cup red wine vinegar

¾ cup extra-virgin olive oil

¾ teaspoon salt

⅛ teaspoon freshly ground black pepper

60 basil leaves, torn (about 1 bunch)

Toss all the ingredients except the basil in a large bowl. Let rest 30 minutes at room temperature, then fold in the basil and serve.

If you prefer more of a porridge-like consistency, crush all the ingredients together with your hands rather than tossing with a spoon.

BREAD AND WHAT GOES WITH BREAD

In Italy, people say *pane e companatico* ("bread and what goes with bread") to describe a way of cooking and eating, a philosophy of the table that places bread at the center and offers tasty tidbits as garnish: pungent sheep's milk cheese, rosy slices of ham, roasted vegetables. Some say Tuscany's bread is saltless to better accompany the intensely savory Tuscan fare. Others maintain that it was first baked without salt because salt used to be costly. Still others propose the longer shelf life of saltless bread as the motivation. Whatever the reason for Tuscany's saltless bread, the end result is that it not only marries beautifully with Tuscan food, but that it is the perfect base for many Tuscan appetizers, salads, soups, and sauces. The hamlet of Vinca in the Apuan Alps is especially renowned for its bread—a bread whose ultimate *companatico* is said to be the creamy lard from Colonnata, a town on the other side of the mountain.

Insalata di Fagioli e Tonno

Cannellini Beans and Tuna

Called mangiafagioli (*"bean eaters"*) by other Italians, Tuscans have had a love affair with beans since these versatile legumes first arrived from the New World in the early sixteenth century. Cannellini beans are the hands-down favorite: They are cooked in a flask; braised with sage, garlic, and tomatoes in a style known as all'uccelletto (*"in the manner of small birds,"* because the flavorings are the same as those used for fowl); or combined with canned tuna, as below, for a main-course salad. The variety of beans grown in the town of Sorana has a particularly thin skin and is highly prized.

SERVES 6

Two 16-ounce cans cannellini beans, drained and rinsed
Two 6-ounce cans tuna packed in olive oil, drained and crumbled
1 purple onion, sliced paper-thin
1/3 cup fresh lemon juice (from 2 lemons)
1/2 cup extra-virgin olive oil
1/2 teaspoon salt
1/4 teaspoon freshly ground black pepper
16 celery leaves, minced
16 pitted oil-cured black olives, such as Taggiasche
8 cherry tomatoes, halved

Spoon the beans onto a plate. Top with the tuna and onion.

In a small bowl, whisk together the lemon juice, olive oil, salt, pepper, and minced celery leaves. Pour over the bean mixture. Top with the olives, garnish with the tomatoes, and serve within 30 minutes.

Pappardelle sull'Anatra

Wide Pasta Ribbons in Duck Sauce

Fresh Tuscan pastas include tortelli alla mugellana *stuffed with mashed potatoes, eggs, Pancetta, and rosemary, served in meat sauce; cannelloni filled with meat, chicken livers, truffles, eggs, and bread crumbs; and wide noodles called* pappardelle, *tossed with hare or duck as below. Duck, geese, boar, and hare figure among Tuscany's favorite meats for braising and roasting, thanks to a countryside where wild animals still roam free. The homemade pappardelle can be replaced with 1 1/2 pounds of store-bought fresh or dried pappardelle, but the cooking time will likely increase.*

SERVES 4

1 recipe Pasta Dough (page 370)
Unbleached all-purpose flour for the counter
1/3 cup extra-virgin olive oil
1 medium yellow onion, minced
1 carrot, minced
1 celery stalk, minced
One 2-ounce slice Pancetta, cut into 1/8-inch dice
1 bay leaf
2 tablespoons minced Italian parsley
2 duck thighs, bone in and skinned (ask the butcher for the heart and liver as well if possible)
1 cup dry white wine
1 1/2 cups canned chopped Italian plum tomatoes
2 tablespoons plus 1/2 teaspoon salt
1/4 teaspoon freshly ground black pepper
1/4 teaspoon fennel seeds, crushed (optional)
1 cup freshly grated Parmigiano-Reggiano

Make the dough and let it rest according to instructions on page 370.

Cut the dough into 4 pieces. Working with 1 piece at a time and keeping the others covered, roll out each piece into a nearly transparent sheet using a pasta machine. Cut into 1 × 4-inch strips. These are the pappardelle. Toss with flour to prevent sticking, spread out in a single layer on a floured tray, and cover with a towel.

Heat the olive oil in a 2-quart pot over a medium flame. Add the onion, carrot, celery, Pancetta, bay leaf, and parsley and cook 5 minutes, stirring. Add the duck and cook until golden on both sides, about 10 minutes, turning once. Deglaze with the wine and cook until it evaporates, about 15 minutes. Stir in the tomatoes, 1/2 teaspoon of the salt, and the 1/4 teaspoon of pepper. Reduce the heat to medium-low, cover, and cook for 1 hour.

Remove the duck from the pot, cool 5 minutes, then bone and cut the meat into 1/2-inch cubes; return to the pot. Stir in the fennel seeds and cook over medium-low heat 10 minutes; this is the sauce.

Bring 6 quarts of water to a boil. Add the pappardelle and the remaining 2 tablespoons of salt and cook until al dente, about 2 minutes. Drain, reserving 1/2 cup of the pasta cooking water. Transfer the pappardelle to a bowl, fold in the sauce, and dilute with as much of the reserved cooking water as needed to give the sauce a slippery texture. Serve hot, passing the Parmigiano at the table.

PREPARATION TIPS: The pappardelle can be made up to 12 hours ahead, spread out in a single layer on a floured tray, and refrigerated, covered with a towel; the sauce can be made up to 2 days ahead, refrigerated, and reheated as you boil the pappardelle.

THREE TUSCAN SHEEP'S MILK CHEESES

TUSCANS ARE AVID EATERS—and prolific producers—of sheep's milk cheese. Pecorino Toscano, best from Pienza (labeled *di Pienza*) and Siena (labeled *Senese*), is the most important of the region's sheep's milk cheeses. When it is aged twenty to forty days, it is mild and milky; as it ages up to four months, it acquires a pungent aroma and becomes ideal for grating. Less renowned than Pecorino Toscano is Marzolino; produced in March (*marzo* in Italian), it is aged very briefly before it is marketed and has a soft consistency, ivory to rose flesh, and reddish rind thanks to a rub of sheep's blood or tomato. Rossellino, a young Pecorino whose rind is rubbed with olive oil, owes its name to the lovely red color (*rosso* in Italian) it develops as it ages; its flavor is mildly nutty and fairly salty, its flesh firm and compact. See Sources (page 372) to purchase these cheeses in North America.

Polenta Ficca

Chestnut-Flour Polenta with Sausage and Scallions

*V*ariously called pattona, polenta di necci, and polenta dolce, *chestnut-flour polenta is common to the Lunigiana area that straddles Tuscany and Liguria. Tuscany has more woodland than any other Italian region, and chestnuts grow prolifically in its woods. Chestnut trees were so important to Tuscany's economy that they were once called "bread trees." In the recipe below, chestnut-flour polenta is cooled, sliced, and fried in hot olive oil, then topped with an irresistible sausage and scallion sauce.*

SERVES 2 AS A FIRST COURSE OR
4 AS AN ANTIPASTO

1 tablespoon plus ½ teaspoon salt

1¼ cups chestnut flour, sifted

½ cup plus 3 tablespoons extra-virgin olive oil, plus extra for greasing the plate

½ pound string beans, ends trimmed and very thinly sliced

6 ounces Italian sausage, casings removed and crumbled

12 scallions, white parts only, very thinly sliced

½ cup Chicken Broth (page 368)

¼ teaspoon freshly ground black pepper

Bring 2 cups of water to a boil in a 2-quart pot. Add ¼ teaspoon of the salt. Very slowly add the chestnut flour by the tablespoon, beating constantly with a whisk to avoid lumps. (It will take about 5 minutes to work in all the chestnut flour; it is best if one person adds the chestnut flour and another whisks.)

Cook the polenta over medium-low heat 15 minutes, stirring constantly with a wooden spoon. Add 1 tablespoon of the olive oil and cook 15 more minutes, stirring constantly. Pour the hot polenta onto a lightly oiled 8-inch plate. Cool to room temperature and cut into 1 × 3-inch strips.

Bring 1 quart of water to a boil. Add the string beans and 1 tablespoon of the salt; cook 2 minutes, then drain.

Heat 2 tablespoons of the olive oil in a 12-inch skillet over a medium flame. Add the sausage and cook 8 minutes, stirring often. Add the scallions and cook 5 minutes, stirring often. Fold in the blanched string beans and cook 2 minutes. Add the broth, the remaining ¼ teaspoon of salt, and the ¼ teaspoon of pepper. Cook 5 minutes, or until the liquid reduces by half. Keep this sauce warm.

Meanwhile, in a 12-inch skillet, heat the remaining ½ cup of olive oil over a medium-high flame until it is nearly smoking. Fry 6 polenta strips at a time until crisp and browned lightly on both sides, turning once, about 3 minutes per side; be sure the polenta is browned on the bottom before turning it, or it might fall apart. With a slotted spatula, remove to a plate lined with paper towels and blot dry. Fry the remaining polenta in the same manner. Arrange the polenta on a serving platter, top with the sauce, and serve hot.

PREPARATION TIPS: The polenta can be cooked and cut up to 2 days ahead, then refrigerated until needed.

SMUGGLED SALAMI

There are those among us who will risk anything for a sausage: paying steep fees at customs, having one's suitcase confiscated, being subjected to a strip search, and other such travel indignities. I don't belong to this group of traveling culinary renegades. But luckily I have friends who do, so I often find myself with sausages, salami, and cheeses smuggled in from Italy. I still remember the Florentine Finocchiona that a chef friend from Milan presented me with upon his return from Tuscany: as wide as a skillet, this imposing pork salami had been generously spiced with wild fennel and black pepper. My husband and I devoured it within days in great, thick slices, the cubes of fat threaded throughout melting on our tongues, reminding us of days in Florence. Finocchiona is produced in North America, since the Tuscan version does not meet FDA regulations; for the same reason, Salame Toscano, a flavorful pork salami studded with peppercorns and scented with garlic, is made on North American soil.

Ignudi

"Nude" Ravioli

Tuscans affectionately refer to potato gnocchi as topini ("little mice," because of their shape) and to gnocchi made of Swiss chard or spinach and Ricotta as ignudi: "nude ones," because they are, in fact, the stuffing for ravioli without the enveloping pasta dough. These light spinach ignudi are baked rather than boiled; since water does not dilute their taste, they are more intensely flavored.

THE ANNUAL SOUP PILGRIMAGE

My husband and I are inveterate lovers of soup, a passion that keeps us coming back to the same trattoria in Lucca every summer. Our annual pilgrimage results in a succession of unabashedly rustic, thick soups: A bread and tomato porridge called *pappa col pomodoro;* a hearty lentil concoction; a creamy farro and cranberry bean soup; and the crowning glory, *ribollita,* featuring a dozen vegetables, cannellini beans, and day-old bread. Each soup arrives at the table in a white bowl and the owner of the trattoria watches over us to make sure we drizzle the top with a little (read: a lot) of Lucca's celebrated olive oil and a copious dose of freshly ground black pepper.

SERVES 4

1½ pounds spinach leaves, washed thoroughly
½ pound fresh Ricotta
1¼ cups freshly grated Parmigiano-Reggiano
¼ teaspoon salt
¼ teaspoon freshly ground black pepper
⅛ teaspoon freshly grated nutmeg
5 tablespoons unsalted butter, 2 tablespoons melted and 3 tablespoons cubed
8 sage leaves

Preheat the oven to 400°F.

Cook the spinach in a covered 12-inch sauté pan over medium-high heat for 5 minutes. Remove from the pan, drain, cool, and squeeze dry. Mince the spinach, place it in a medium mixing bowl, and stir in the Ricotta, ¾ cup of the Parmigiano, the salt, pepper, and nutmeg.

With moistened hands, shape the mixture into walnut-sized balls and arrange on an 11 × 17-inch baking sheet lined with parchment paper, about ½ inch apart. These are the ignudi. Pour on the 2 tablespoons of melted butter and sprinkle with ¼ cup of the Parmigiano. Bake in the preheated oven for 15 minutes.

Meanwhile, melt the 3 tablespoons of cubed butter with the sage in a 6-inch skillet over medium heat. Transfer the ignudi to a serving platter, pour on the sage butter, and sprinkle with the remaining ¼ cup of Parmigiano. Serve hot.

PREPARATION TIPS: Shape the ignudi up to 24 hours ahead, spread out in a single layer on the baking sheet, and refrigerate until you are ready to bake.

Calamari all'Inzimino

Braised Squid with Chili, Greens, and Tomatoes

Livorno is Tuscany's major fishing center, a busy port famous for its seafood preparations: red mullet with tomatoes, garlic, parsley, and celery; salt cod with pine nuts and raisins or leeks; and couscous with fish, a legacy of Livornese Jews whose contacts with Tunisian Jews spawned an altogether unusual Sabbath dish. Inzimino, one of Livorno's most beloved fish and seafood preparations, can feature salt cod, cuttlefish, or squid, and is a staple in both Tuscany and Liguria; the common point to all inzimino preparations is the inclusion of greens.

THE MOST COMPLEX FISH AND MEAT STEWS

Despite Tuscans' preference for simple flavors, they are big on combining many kinds of fish or meat in a single dish. When they are made with fish, these stews are called *cacciucco*; for a really good version, say the residents of Viareggio, drop a stone from the bottom of the sea into the pot as the fish cooks. When they are made with meat, as in the towns of Arezzo and Grosseto, these stews go by the name of *scottiglia*. Most versions combine veal, chicken, rabbit, pork, guinea hen, and lamb, with the possible addition of squab, venison, or duck.

SERVES 4

¾ cup extra-virgin olive oil
1 medium yellow onion, minced
1 celery stalk, minced
1 carrot, minced
2 garlic cloves, minced
1 tablespoon minced Italian parsley
¼ teaspoon chili flakes
1 pound cleaned squid, bodies cut into ¼-inch rings and tentacles halved
½ cup dry white wine
1 cup canned chopped Italian plum tomatoes
1 pound Swiss chard leaves, washed thoroughly
1 pound spinach leaves, washed thoroughly
½ teaspoon salt

Heat ¼ cup of the olive oil over a medium flame in a 2-quart pot. Add the onion, celery, carrot, half of the garlic, the parsley, and chili; cook for 10 minutes. Stir in the squid and cook for 3 minutes. Add the wine and tomatoes and cook 35 minutes, uncovered, adding a little water if needed.

Meanwhile, place the Swiss chard and spinach in a 12-inch sauté pan over medium heat; cover and cook for 5 minutes. Remove from the pan, rinse under cold water, chop, and squeeze dry.

Heat ¼ cup of the olive oil over a medium flame in the same sauté pan. Add the remaining half of the garlic and cook 1 minute. Add the chopped Swiss chard and spinach and cook 10 minutes. Fold into the squid, cover, and cook 15 more minutes. Season with the salt and serve hot, drizzled with the remaining ¼ cup of olive oil.

Tuscany's Wines

THE ETRUSCANS WHO SETTLED IN TUSCANY more than three thousand years ago planted vines across the region, laying the foundations for an oenological tradition that remains one of Italy's most advanced to this day. A wine sellers' guild had been formed in Florence by the fourteenth century, and the personal records of bankers and tradesmen—chief among them a wealthy merchant from the town of Prato, Francesco di Marco Datini—offered insights as to which grape varietals were predominant, which wines were most prized, and what the market prices were for various wines.

Tuscany's famously hilly terrain is ideal for growing the region's signature grape, Sangiovese, which benefits from significant temperature shifts between day and night, ample sunlight, and calcium-rich soil. Canaiolo, Malvasia, and Trebbiano also thrive, and are often blended with Sangiovese in the region's traditional wines. Tuscany's flagship red wine, Chianti, was first mentioned in one of Datini's letters in 1398 as a white wine. Dry, tangy, with hints of violets, its best incarnation is Chianti Classico, vinified between Florence and Siena. If Chianti is Tuscany's most famous red, Brunello di Montalcino is its most prestigious: Heady, with dried fruit, tobacco, and plum notes, it is full-bodied, intense, and long-lasting, aged two years in casks; by contrast, Rosso di Montalcino, Brunello's younger brother, is aged one year in casks. Vino Nobile di Montepulciano, a noble red vinified from Sangiovese with or without the addition of Trebbiano, Malvasia, and Canaiolo in Montepulciano, is full-bodied, less aromatic, and more robust than Chianti, a result of its warmer production zone. When the same wine is aged less long, it yields the lighter Rosso di Montepulciano.

The long strip of Tuscan coastline below Livorno, known as the Maremma, was once a swampy marshland plagued by malaria; high-quality wine production in the area is a recent phenomenon, with Morellino di Scansano, a dry, austere, age-worthy red, leading the way. Carmignano, a Sangiovese-based red with low acidity, firm tannins, and hints of chocolate, is vinified in the province of Prato, and is the only Tuscan DOC to require the addition of Cabernet Sauvignon. French varieties such as Cabernet and Merlot have been used on their own or blended with the local Sangiovese, spawning a class of international wines dubbed "super-Tuscans" that includes big, expensive names like Sassicaia and Tignanello, two of the world's most prestigious wines.

In this sea of exceptional, imposing red wines, there is one Tuscan white that has long been prized: Vernaccia di San Gimignano, vinified from the Vernaccia grape in San Gimignano. Smooth, nutty, with hints of fruit, almonds, and honey, it offers a mineral backbone, crisp acidity, and slightly bitter finish. Vin Santo, an amber-hued dessert wine made mostly from Trebbiano and Malvasia grapes that have been dried on straw mats under rafters in well-ventilated rooms, is vinified dry, semi-sweet, or sweet; aged a minimum of three years in small barrels before being released, it is a symbol of Tuscan hospitality, offered to guests and poured at every important occasion.

Braciole di Maiale con le Olive

Pork Chops with Olives and Fennel Seeds

Olives, queen on the Tuscan table, are cooked with tomatoes to create a quick sauce for pork chops; fennel seeds supply the aromatic undercurrent. A similar recipe substitutes black cabbage for the olives, making for a warming winter main course.

Heat the olive oil in a 12-inch skillet over a medium-high flame. Add the garlic and fennel seeds and cook 30 seconds. Add the pork and cook until browned on both sides, turning once, about 3 minutes per side.

SERVES 4

¼ cup extra-virgin olive oil

4 garlic cloves, chopped

1 tablespoon fennel seeds, crushed

4 pork chops, bone in (½ pound each)

½ cup dry white wine

4 plum tomatoes, peeled (see page 369), seeded, and diced

⅔ cup pitted black olives, such as Gaeta

½ teaspoon salt

⅛ teaspoon freshly ground black pepper

Deglaze with the wine and cook until it nearly evaporates, about 3 minutes. Add the tomatoes, olives, salt, and pepper; cook 10 more minutes, covered, turning twice. Serve hot.

THREE TOWNS, THREE UNUSUAL MEATS

Every Tuscan village, town, and city has its special dish. In Impruneta, a town famous for its terra-cotta tiles, a peppery veal casserole called *peposo* is baked overnight in the dying heat of the kiln. Campi, in the province of Prato, offers sheep many ways: steaks are marinated with wine vinegar, olive oil, garlic, and parsley before hitting the grill, and humble cuts are diced and braised into a ragù for pasta. And in Prato, celery stalks are blanched, stuffed with veal, chicken livers, and Parmigiano, tied in bundles, battered and fried, then served over meat sauce.

THE TRIPE TRUCK

Tripe is a way of life in Florence. Sandwiches piled high with the slithering stuff are proffered from trucks near Florence's central market and doused with a savory parsley and hard-boiled egg sauce called *salsa verde,* and great big pots of tripe braised with tomatoes and dusted with Parmigiano are cooked in the city's osterie.

Schiacciata con l'Uva

Florentine Flatbread with Grapes

This sweet focaccia studded with grapes can be found in most Florentine bakeries and pastry shops. Its Etruscan ancestor, baked three thousand years ago, was unleavened and sweetened with honey rather than with sugar. Some Florentine bakers add a handful of fennel or anise seeds along with the grapes and sugar.

SERVES 8

4 cups unbleached all-purpose flour, plus extra for the counter
1 tablespoon instant yeast
½ teaspoon salt
1 cup granulated sugar
¾ cup extra-virgin olive oil, plus extra for greasing the bowl and baking sheet
2½ pounds seedless red grapes, stemmed
¼ cup confectioner's sugar

Place the flour, yeast, salt, and ½ cup of the granulated sugar in a large bowl. Stir in enough warm (110°F) water—about 1 cup plus 2 tablespoons—to make a soft dough; add ¼ cup of the olive oil and turn out onto a lightly floured counter. Knead 10 minutes, or until smooth and silky, adding flour as needed to prevent sticking. Place the dough in an oiled bowl, cover, and let rise at room temperature until doubled, about 2 hours.

Preheat the oven to 375°F.

Oil an 11 × 17-inch baking sheet. Roll out the dough on a lightly floured counter with a rolling pin into a 10 × 30-inch rectangle. Line the baking sheet with half of the dough; the other half will hang over lengthwise. Spread half of the grapes over it, drizzle with ¼ cup of the olive oil, and sprinkle with ¼ cup of the granulated sugar.

Bring the overhanging dough up over the grapes, covering them and pressing to seal. Scatter the remaining half of the grapes over the dough, pressing them down so they won't roll off later (this also encourages the grapes to burst as the schiacciata bakes). Spread the dough to the edges of the baking sheet with your fingers. Drizzle with the remaining ¼ cup of olive oil and sprinkle with the remaining ¼ cup of granulated sugar. Let rest 45 minutes. Dimple vigorously with your fingers to prevent the dough from rising too crazily in the oven.

Bake in the preheated oven until the crust is golden brown and the grapes are soft and syrupy, about 45 minutes. Serve hot, warm, or at room temperature, dusted with the confectioner's sugar.

PREPARATION TIPS: Make the dough up to 24 hours ahead and refrigerate it; return to room temperature before proceeding.

La Crostata di Bietole di Giulio
Giulio's Sweet Swiss Chard Tart

Paolo Sari is the proprietor of Lucca's Da Giulio in Pelleria, where this unusual—yet typically Lucchese—tart is a staple. In Lucca, a sweet spice-based cordial called alchermes is used to plump the raisins for the filling. Alchermes initially drew its color and name from a dye-producing insect known as al qirmiz in Arabic, alquermes in Spanish, and coccus ilicis in Latin. Alchermes is illegal in North America because of the cochineal insect, or Dactylopius coccus, which is used in Italy to lend it a rosy hue. I substitute rum or anisette, an anise-flavored liqueur. Paolo Sari sometimes uses Tuscan bread soaked in milk (try about 3 slices) instead of the rice below in the filling.

SERVES 8

⅓ cup **Arborio rice**
1⅓ cups **whole milk**
¾ cup **sugar**
½ teaspoon **salt**
¼ cup **raisins**
½ cup **rum or anisette**
1 pound **Swiss chard leaves, washed thoroughly**
6 extra-large **egg yolks**
¼ cup **freshly grated Parmigiano-Reggiano**
¼ cup **pine nuts**
1½ teaspoons **grated lemon zest**
Pinch **freshly grated nutmeg or ground cinnamon**
⅛ teaspoon **freshly ground black pepper**
1⅓ cups **unbleached all-purpose flour, plus extra for the counter**
1 teaspoon **vanilla extract**
8 tablespoons (1 stick) **unsalted butter, chilled and cubed, plus extra for greasing the pie pan**
1 extra-large **egg**

Place the rice, milk, 2 tablespoons of the sugar, and ⅛ teaspoon of the salt in a 1-quart pot and bring to a boil. Reduce the heat to medium-low and cook uncovered until the rice is soft and has absorbed the milk, about 30 minutes. Cool.

Meanwhile, in a small bowl, soak the raisins in the rum for 30 minutes.

Bring 4 quarts of water to a boil. Drop in the Swiss chard and cook 10 minutes. Drain, rinse under cold water, squeeze dry, and chop coarsely. In a large mixing bowl, combine the Swiss chard and the rice, the raisins with their soaking liquid, the egg yolks, Parmigiano, pine nuts, 1 teaspoon of the lemon zest, the nutmeg, the pepper, ¼ cup plus 2 tablespoons of the sugar, and ⅛ teaspoon of the salt; this is the filling. Cover and refrigerate 2 to 24 hours; chilling the filling helps it to firm up and prevents it from making the dough soggy as it bakes.

In a food processor, combine the flour and the remaining ¼ cup of sugar, ¼ teaspoon of salt, and ½ teaspoon of lemon zest with the vanilla and butter. Using quick pulses, process until the ingredients resemble coarse meal. Add the whole egg and process again, using quick pulses, until a dough forms. Turn out onto a counter, gather into a ball, and shape into a flat disk. Wrap and refrigerate 30 minutes to 24 hours.

Preheat the oven to 375°F.

Roll out the dough on a lightly floured counter into a ⅛-inch-thick circle. Line a buttered 9-inch fluted springform pie pan with it, cut off excess dough, and spoon in the filling. Level the filling with a spatula.

Bake in the preheated oven for 40 minutes, or until the crust is golden and the filling is set. Cool on a rack, unmold onto a platter, and serve at room temperature.

COOKIES AND THE WINE OF FRIENDSHIP

Most meals in Tuscany culminate in a glass of amber-hued Vin Santo, a dessert wine made for centuries on Tuscan soil, and a handful of almond-studded biscotti called *cantuccini*. Ritual suggests offering Vin Santo and cantuccini to surprise guests as a sign of friendship and hospitality; the cookies are dipped into the wine as the evening winds down.

Umbria

La Fojata del Panciolle
Greens and Sausage Bundle from Panciolle

Strangozze con Asparagi, Erbe e Pomodorini
Pasta with Asparagus, Herbs, and Cherry Tomatoes

Blo Blo
Tagliatelle in Bubbling Tomato Broth

Zuppa di Lenticchie di Castelluccio
Castelluccio Lentil Soup

Il Tegamaccio di Pesce del Lago Trasimeno
A Medley of Sweetwater Fish with Rosemary
over Garlic-Rubbed Bread

Trota ai Tartufi Neri
Trout Bathed in Black Truffle Sauce

Pollo alla Cacciatora
Hunter-Style Chicken

Salsiccia all'Uva
Pan-Fried Sausages and Juicy Grapes

Scaloppine di Maiale con Capperi e Vino Rosso
Pork Scaloppine in Caper and Red Wine Glaze

Serpentone delle Monache di Perugia
Nut-and-Fruit "Snake" of the Capuchin Nuns

It's one of those perfect moments: the sky is deep blue with whispery white clouds, the road empty, the radio playing a favorite song. We're driving to Orvieto, whizzing past vineyards where people are plucking fat grapes. Just when I think it can't get any better, I spot a three-wheeler around a bend. An old man stands by the truck, arranging straw bags under a handwritten sign: LENTICCHIE DI CASTELLUCCIO.

I throw the car into reverse, back up, and hop out: what better place to stock up on Umbria's most famous lentils? The man who sells the lentils offers me a toothless smile, his eyes as warm as the sun. When he tells me his recipe for lentil soup—he adds a touch of rosemary, he whispers—I suddenly wish I could stop time.

Dubbed the "Green Heart of Italy," Umbria takes its name from the Umbri who settled in the area before the Etruscans; conquered by the Romans in the third century B.C., it fell to the Goths when the Roman Empire crumbled, then was divided between the Lombards and Byzantines. Perugia, the region's capital, was an important city-state until the sixteenth century, when it became part of the papal states. Succumbing to the French in 1808, Umbria was returned to the pope six years later, annexed to the Kingdom of Sardinia in 1860, and incorporated into the newly formed Kingdom of Italy in 1861.

Umbria is the only central Italian region entirely tucked away from the sea: land-locked, nestled between Tuscany and Latium, it is a continuous unfolding of dulcet hills and undulating green valleys, gentle mountains and glittering lakes. Sanctuaries dot the roads, hilltop villages reign over the vast countryside, medieval castles and churches beckon behind silvery olive groves.

Less rich and more isolated from the rest of Europe than neighboring Tuscany, Umbria uses the foods her land offers ingeniously, without pretense. The Umbrians will be the first to tell you that theirs is a peasant cuisine, one that remains tied to its pastoral roots, and they keep things simple more out of necessity than out of rigor or philosophy. Olive oil, golden and delicate, laces almost every dish. Bread is baked without salt, as in Tuscany and parts of the Marches. Pork, king of the Umbrian table, is at its best in Norcia, a town so renowned for its butchers that the Italian word for pork butcher is *norcino*. Sheep's milk cheese, both fresh and aged, delivers pungent flavor to soups, pastas, and breads. And the precious black truffles of Spoleto and Norcia—nubby, warty, and deeply aromatic—are incorporated in some of the region's most glorious preparations.

Favorite Restaurants, Shops, and Places

- AZIENDA AGRICOLA IL COLLACCIO, Preci (10 miles from Norcia). They will teach you to make hams and more in intensive two-day courses. Call their offices in Milan at 02.315755.
- HOTEL RISTORANTE LA BASTIGLIA, Piazza Valle Gloria 7, Spello, 0742.651277. Unbeatable cuisine, including a raw pork Ciauscolo wrapped in cucumbers.
- IL PANCIOLLE, Vicolo degli Eroi 1, Spoleto, 0743.45598. Unbelievable view and homemade *strangozze ai tartufi*.
- IL TARTUFO, Piazza Garibaldi 24, Spoleto, 0743.40236. Umbrian specialties, including *strangozze con asparagi ed erbe*.
- LE TRE VASELLE, Via Giuseppe Garibaldi 48, Torgiano, 075.9880447. One of Italy's top cooking schools and restaurants; spearheaded by the Lungarottis. To visit their wine museum, call 075.9880348.
- RISTORANTE I SETTE CONSOLI, Piazza Sant'Angelo 1/A, Orvieto, 0763.343911. Outstanding soups, pastas, and meats.
- RISTORANTE SAN FRANCESCO, Via di San Francesco 52, Assisi, 075.813302 or 075.812329. Pure Umbrian flavors and impeccable quality.
- SPEZIERIA BAVICCHI, Piazza Matteotti 32, Perugia, 0755.731752. Castelluccio lentils, farro, beans from the shores of Lago Trasimeno, and more for sale.
- VISSANI, Strada Statale 448, Civitella del Lago, 0744.950396. The playground of Giancarlo Vissani, grand master of creative Italian cuisine.

Telephone country code: 011.39

La Fojata del Panciolle

Greens and Sausage Bundle from Panciolle

Among Umbria's savory pies and focacce, there are an onion-topped, sage-scented focaccia; a griddle-cooked bread called *torta al testo* similar to Romagna's *piadina (page 137)*; a cheese-laced *pizza campagnola* akin to one baked in the Marches *(page 205)*; and a number of bundles stuffed with greens. The recipe for the bundle below hails from the Gualdo Tadino and Nocera Umbra area and was offered by Sandro Argilli, owner of Ristorante Il Panciolle in Spoleto. The classic fojata is stuffed with wild chicory, but because wild chicory is only available in the spring, a mixture of greens and herbs is substituted in summer, fall, and winter; a combination of spinach and escarole makes a wonderful alternative.

SERVES 4 AS AN ANTIPASTO OR
2 AS A FIRST COURSE

½ pound escarole, washed thoroughly
1 tablespoon plus ½ teaspoon salt
½ pound spinach leaves, washed thoroughly
¼ cup plus 3 tablespoons extra-virgin olive oil
2 garlic cloves, crushed
⅛ teaspoon chili flakes
½ pound spicy Italian sausage, casings removed and crumbled
½ cup freshly grated Pecorino Romano
1 cup unbleached all-purpose flour, plus extra for the counter

Bring 3 quarts of water to a boil. Drop in the escarole and 1 tablespoon of the salt and cook 2 minutes. Add the spinach and cook 2 more minutes. Drain, rinse under cold water, squeeze dry, and chop.

Heat ¼ cup of the olive oil with the garlic and chili in a 12-inch skillet over a medium-high flame. After 1 minute, discard the garlic; add the sausage and cook 3 minutes. Add the chopped escarole and spinach with ¼ teaspoon of the salt and cook 7 minutes, or until the sausage is cooked through and lightly browned, stirring often. Turn out into a bowl, fold in the Pecorino, and cool to room temperature; this is the filling.

Preheat the oven to 425°F.

Pour the flour, 2 tablespoons of the olive oil, and the remaining ¼ teaspoon of salt into a food processor. With the motor running, add enough cool water (about ¼ to ⅓ cup) to form a dough that rides the blade, and process 30 seconds. Turn the dough out onto a counter and cut it into 2 equal pieces; you will need only 1 piece for this recipe (freeze the other piece for up to 1 month).

Roll out into a 12 × 18-inch rectangle on a lightly floured counter; if the dough tears, patch it with your fingers. Gently lift the rectangle onto a floured kitchen towel and arrange the filling over it, leaving a 1-inch border all around. Roll it into a tight bundle, lifting the towel to help. Seal the seam and ends with your fingers.

Place the bundle on an 11 × 17-inch baking sheet, seam side down, and stretch into a curved 18-inch log. Brush the top with the remaining tablespoon of olive oil, then with 1 tablespoon of water. Bake in the preheated oven 35 minutes, or until the crust is golden brown and crisp. Serve hot or warm.

PREPARATION TIPS: The dough and filling can be prepared up to 24 hours ahead and refrigerated until needed; bring to room temperature before shaping.

AN UNEXPECTED TASTE OF RAW PORK

Umbrians, and their neighbors in the Marches, make a spreadable pork salami called Ciauscolo. The first time I tasted Ciauscolo was at La Bastiglia, an elegant restaurant in the Umbrian town of Spello, where young chef Marco Gabbiotti experiments with local ingredients in often surprising ways. Marco's Ciauscolo was wonderful: creamy, garlicky, slightly peppery, wrapped in paper-thin slices of cucumber and accompanied by a refreshing julienne of vegetables. When I asked for the recipe, I discovered that he marinates raw pork with salt, pepper, lemon, and garlic for hours—no cooking, no aging, no lengthy curing. Marco buys organically raised pork from a nearby farm and swears it can safely be eaten raw. His raw pork Ciauscolo, while not exactly traditional, was delectable. Unfortunately there is currently no domestic version of Ciauscolo available in North America, so if you want a taste of the real Ciauscolo, or if you are concerned about eating uncooked pork, head to any Umbrian *salumeria* for an unforgettable experience.

Strangozze con Asparagi, Erbe e Pomodorini

Pasta with Asparagus, Herbs, and Cherry Tomatoes

*S*trangozze, a specialty of the towns of Terni and Spoleto, are traditionally made with only flour and water, since eggs were once too costly to "waste" in pasta. Legend has it that their name is derived from the cord, or stran-gozza, used by medieval peasants to strangle the tax collector when they were not inclined to pay up. Despite the bloody connotations of this pasta, rest assured that its texture and flavor are nothing if not absolutely good. Strangozze are usually topped with garlicky olive oil, or with grated black truffles when in season. Some cooks, including myself, prefer herb-laced tomato sauces such as this one from the Di Marco family, owners of Spoleto's Il Tartufo.

THE POOREST GNOCCHI

Umbria's most unusual gnocchi are also its poorest: called *frascarelli,* they are made from the dough that sticks to the counter when preparing fresh pasta. The clinging bits of dough are scraped off the counter and passed through a metal screen to create pea-sized gnocchi. In the summer, fras-carelli are boiled and sauced with tomatoes; in the winter, they are cooked directly in broths of bean, wild chickpea, or lentil.

SERVES 4

For the strangozze:
2¼ cups semolina flour, plus extra for the counter
½ teaspoon salt

For the sauce and to cook:
20 thin asparagus spears, woody ends trimmed
2 tablespoons plus ½ teaspoon salt
½ cup extra-virgin olive oil
2 garlic cloves, minced
20 cherry tomatoes, quartered
3 tablespoons minced Italian parsley
3 tablespoons minced basil
3 tablespoons snipped chives
1 tablespoon minced thyme
1 tablespoon minced mint
1 teaspoon minced marjoram
1 teaspoon minced oregano
1 teaspoon minced tarragon
⅛ teaspoon chili flakes

Make the strangozze according to instructions on page 370 using the ingredients listed above, adding enough water (about ⅔ cup) to form a firm dough. Knead 5 minutes, or until smooth, adding a little water if the dough is dry or a little semolina flour if it is sticky. Shape into a ball, wrap, and let rest 30 minutes.

Cut the dough into 2 pieces. Working with 1 piece at a time and keeping the other covered, roll out each piece on a semolina-dusted counter into a 14-inch square. Cut each square into two 7 × 14-inch rectangles. Dust the rectangles on both sides with semolina flour to prevent sticking. Fold each rectangle over itself, rolling it up jelly roll–style, and cut into ¼-inch-wide strips. Toss with semolina flour to prevent sticking. Spread out in a single layer on a semolina-dusted tray and cover with a towel.

Make the sauce: Bring 4 quarts of water to a boil. Add the asparagus and 2 tablespoons of the salt and cook 3 minutes; remove with a slotted spoon or tongs to a bowl of ice water, drain, and cut into ½-inch pieces, keeping the water boiling.

Heat the olive oil in a 12-inch skillet over a medium-high flame. Add the garlic and cook 30 seconds. Fold in the asparagus and tomatoes and cook until the tomatoes break down slightly, about 3 minutes. Add the parsley, basil, chives, thyme, mint, marjoram, oregano, tarragon, chili, and the remaining ½ teaspoon of salt. Cook 1 minute, then reduce the heat to very low and keep warm.

Meanwhile, add the strangozze to the reserved boiling water; cook until al dente, about 1 minute. Drain, reserving ½ cup of the pasta cooking water. Fold the strangozze into the sauce, increase the heat to high, and sauté for 1 minute, diluting with some of the reserved cooking water if needed. Serve hot.

PREPARATION TIPS: The strangozze can be made up to 12 hours ahead, spread out in a single layer on a semolina-dusted tray, and refrigerated, covered with a towel.

Blo Blo

Tagliatelle in Bubbling Tomato Broth

The name of this summer soup is ono-matopoeic for the sound the broth makes as it sputters away on the stove. Blo blo is one of many Umbrian soups based on little more than fragrant herbs, good olive oil, fresh tomatoes, bread or pasta for bulk, and water. The same soup, made with day-old bread instead of pasta, becomes the acquacotta ("cooked water") savored in both Umbria and neighboring Tuscany. The homemade tagliatelle can be replaced with ³/₄ pound of store-bought fresh tagliatelle, but the cooking time will likely increase.

SERVES 4

For the tagliatelle:
2¼ cups semolina flour, plus extra for the counter
½ teaspoon salt

For the soup:
½ cup extra-virgin olive oil
4 garlic cloves, chopped
1 tablespoon minced marjoram
5 plum tomatoes, peeled (see page 369), seeded, and diced
½ teaspoon salt
¼ teaspoon freshly ground black pepper
½ cup freshly grated Pecorino Romano

Make the tagliatelle according to instructions on page 370 using the ingredients listed above, adding enough water (about ⅔ cup) to form a firm dough. Knead 5 minutes, or until smooth, adding a little water if the dough is dry or a little semolina flour if it is sticky. Shape into a ball, wrap, and let rest 30 minutes.

Cut the dough into 2 pieces. Working with 1 piece at a time and keeping the other covered, roll out each piece on a semolina-dusted counter into a 14 × 18-inch rectangle. Cut each rectangle into three 6 × 14-inch strips. Sprinkle with semolina flour. Fold each strip over itself lengthwise, jelly roll–style, and cut into ⅙-inch-wide pieces with a sharp knife. Toss with semolina flour to prevent sticking and spread out in a single layer on a semolina-dusted tray; cover with a towel.

Meanwhile, make the soup: Heat ¼ cup of the olive oil in a 2-quart pot over a medium-high flame. Add the garlic and marjoram and cook 1 minute. Stir in the tomatoes and cook 5 minutes. Add 5 cups of water and bring to a boil. Reduce the heat to medium-low and cook, uncovered, for 30 minutes. Season with the salt and pepper.

Return the soup to a boil. Add the tagliatelle and cook 2 minutes, or until al dente, stirring often. Serve hot, drizzled with the remaining ¼ cup of olive oil, passing the Pecorino at the table.

PREPARATION TIPS: The tagliatelle can be made up to 12 hours ahead, spread out in a single layer on a semolina-dusted tray, and refrigerated, covered with a towel.

Zuppa di Lenticchie di Castelluccio

Castelluccio Lentil Soup

In Italy, lentils are standard offerings on New Year's tables as a symbol of luck and prosperity—their round shape is thought reminiscent of coins. They also serve as the building block for soups. The one below features tiny lentils from the town of Castelluccio. Their thin, delicate skin and nutty flavor (not to mention propensity for cooking up firm) make them one of Italy's most prized legumes. This soup, which is more like a stew, is poured over toasted bread for a sustaining one-dish meal. See Sources (page 372) to buy Castelluccio lentils.

SIMPLE, SAVORY SOUPS

In the old days, every Umbrian family had a stone mill for crushing farro into a coarse meal called *farricello,* which was cooked with a ham bone into a robust soup. Today Umbrians buy their farro crushed but continue to make farro soup the way their grandparents did. Just as hearty as farro soup are *'mbrecciata,* a thick bean soup; *cipollata,* made with onions, tomatoes, eggs, and bread; and *pan cotto,* a humble concoction of bread, onions, and tomatoes.

SERVES 4

2 cups Castelluccio lentils
6 cups (1½ quarts) Chicken Broth (page 368), plus extra if needed
½ cup extra-virgin olive oil
1 medium yellow onion, minced
1 rosemary sprig
1 tablespoon tomato paste
½ cup dry red wine
½ teaspoon salt
¼ teaspoon freshly ground black pepper
Four ¼-inch-thick × 6-inch-wide slices Tuscan bread
½ cup freshly grated Pecorino Romano

Rinse the lentils, pick them over, and place in a 2-quart pot with the broth. Bring to a boil, reduce the heat to medium, and cook for 30 minutes, or until almost tender. Remove from the heat.

Meanwhile, heat ¼ cup of the olive oil in a 2-quart pot over a medium-high flame. Add the onion and rosemary and cook 10 minutes. Add the tomato paste and wine, bring to a boil, and cook 10 minutes, stirring. Pour in the lentils and their broth, bring to a boil, reduce the heat to low, and cook, covered, for 30 minutes, or until the lentils are done; add a little broth if needed. Season with the salt and pepper; discard the rosemary. Keep warm.

Heat a grill pan over a high flame for 5 minutes; toast the bread until browned on both sides, turning once, about 2 minutes per side. Divide the bread among 4 bowls. Pour on the soup; drizzle with the remaining ¼ cup of olive oil. Serve hot, passing the Pecorino.

PREPARATION TIPS: The soup can be made up to 4 days ahead and refrigerated; reheat, then pour over the bread and garnish as above.

Umbria's Wines

DESPITE A TERRAIN AND CLIMATE similar to neighboring Tuscany, Umbria is far less distinguished for its wines. But verdant hills, hot, dry summers, warm autumns, and limestone, clay, and gravel outcrops in the soil make Umbria an ideal location for growing vines.

Umbrian viticulture has ancient roots: Orvieto, a faintly nutty, honeyed white wine, has been vinified in the area since Etruscan times. Dry, medium-dry, or sweet, Orvieto is one of Umbria's many Trebbiano-based wines; sweet Orvieto, described by poet Gabriele d'Annunzio as "the sun of Italy in a bottle," is quite rare nowadays, but worth seeking out. Trebbiano and Sangiovese are the region's main grape varietals, but recent experiments with Chardonnay, Merlot, Cabernet Sauvignon, and Pinot Nero have proved fruitful.

The most important vinegrowing areas are the Colli Altotiberini (responsible for a round red, well-balanced white, and slightly fruity rosé), Torgiano, Colli del Trasimeno, Colli Perugini, Colli Martani, and Colli Amerini. Torgiano is a fine, slightly oaky, well-structured red packed with plummy, gentle fruit obtained from a blend of Sangiovese and Canaiolo and ages well. Sangiovese is sometimes added to Sagrantino di Montefalco, a dry, full-bodied red with a blackberry bouquet; the raisined version is medium-dry and can be mated with desserts. Also vinified in Montefalco are a red and white wine; Montefalco is harmonious, dry, and velvety when red, lightly fruity and dry when white.

Il Tegamaccio di Pesce dal Lago Trasimeno

*A Medley of Sweetwater Fish with Rosemary
over Garlic-Rubbed Bread*

Most of Umbria's fishermen made their living from the waters of Lago Trasimeno. *Certain varieties of fish and seafood remained something of a luxury: eel was costly, and salt cod brought in from afar was traded for precious foods like squab and appeared on most Christmas tables. This tegamaccio (from tegame, meaning "pot") combines a number of fish varieties typical of Lago Trasimeno and falls somewhere between a stew and a soup in consistency. For the most complex flavor, select at least three fish varieties.*

SWEETWATER FISH UMBRIAN-STYLE

The only central Italian region without a coastline, Umbria finds an abundance of fish in its lakes, streams, and rivers. The waters of Lago Trasimeno, Italy's fourth-largest lake, are teeming with eel, carp, trout, salmon trout, pike, and sweetwater shrimp, and Lago di Corbara offers plenty of catfish. Sweetwater specialties from Umbria include large carp stuffed with garlic and wild fennel roasted in a style known as *porchetta,* usually reserved for pork and other meats; trout stuffed with herbs, then roasted; eel braised with tomatoes, garlic, onions, white wine, and parsley; and catfish purged in an acidic marinade before baking to rid it of its muddy taste.

SERVES 4

¼ cup plus 2 tablespoons extra-virgin olive oil
3 shallots, minced
4 garlic cloves, 3 minced and 1 peeled
2 bay leaves
3 rosemary sprigs
2 tablespoons minced Italian parsley
1½ pounds assorted skinless and boneless sweetwater fish fillets (pike, perch, carp, striped bass, or salmon trout), cut into 3-inch pieces
½ cup dry white wine
4 plum tomatoes, peeled (see page 369), seeded, and diced
½ teaspoon salt
¼ teaspoon freshly ground black pepper
Eight ¼-inch-thick × 6-inch-wide slices country bread

Heat ¼ cup of the olive oil in a 14-inch terra-cotta or nonstick pot over a medium flame. Add the shallots, minced garlic, bay leaves, rosemary, and parsley; cook 3 minutes. Add the fish in a single layer; cook 10 minutes, shaking the pot every minute. Deglaze with the wine and cook 5 minutes. Add the tomatoes, salt, and pepper; cook 10 minutes, shaking the pot every minute. Never stir the fish or it will fall apart.

Heat a grill pan over a high flame for 5 minutes; toast the bread until browned on both sides, about 2 minutes per side. Rub the bread with the peeled garlic. Place 2 slices in each of 4 bowls. Spoon on the fish and its cooking liquid, drizzle with the remaining 2 tablespoons of olive oil, and serve hot.

Trota ai Tartufi Neri

Trout Bathed in Black Truffle Sauce

There are Umbrians who maintain that dressing trout with a truffle sauce is masking a humble fish in a noble cloak. Others scoff at the snobbery, countering that trout is a lovely fish indeed and that its delicate flesh is the ideal foil for the richness of truffles. For the ultimate Umbrian antipasto, double the truffle sauce, refrigerate half, and warm it as a topping for toasted bread.

BLACK TRUFFLE PARADISE

If you're lucky enough to be in Umbria when winter truffles are available—from December through March in a good year—you might also be lucky enough to feast on a cheese-laced flatbread topped with shavings of black truffles. Other truffled Umbrian offerings are a creamy frittata; polenta enriched with Parmigiano and eggs; and crostini, pasta, and meat napped in a warm truffle sauce. If truffle season rolls around and you're not in Umbria, you can enjoy truffles all year long—even in North America—thanks to Caciotta al Tartufo, a black truffle-laced cheese from Norcia that is shipped all over the world (see Sources, page 372).

SERVES 4

¼ pound black truffles (winter truffles are best)
⅓ cup plus 3 tablespoons extra-virgin olive oil
1 small garlic clove, minced
1 small salted anchovy, boned, gutted, and rinsed
¾ teaspoon salt
4 rainbow trout fillets, skin on, scaled (6 ounces each)
¾ cup dry white wine
1 bay leaf
1½ tablespoons fresh lemon juice (from ½ lemon)
⅛ teaspoon freshly ground black pepper

Brush the truffles to dislodge dirt, grate, and pound in a mortar with a pestle until a chunky paste forms. Heat ⅓ cup of the olive oil over a medium-low flame in a 1-quart pot for 1 minute. Add the truffle paste, garlic, anchovy, and ¼ teaspoon of the salt; heat very gently, stirring often, until an aromatic sauce forms, about 10 minutes.

Meanwhile, rinse the trout and blot it dry. In a 12-inch sauté pan, bring the wine, bay leaf, and 1½ cups of water to a boil. Arrange the trout in a single layer in the pan and cook over medium heat 8 minutes, or until cooked, spooning the cooking liquid over the trout constantly; when it is done, the trout will be firm when pressed with a finger. Remove to 4 plates with a fish spatula, leaving the cooking liquid in the pan.

Drizzle the trout with the lemon juice and the remaining 3 tablespoons of olive oil, season with the remaining ½ teaspoon of salt and the pepper, and top with the warm truffle sauce. Serve hot.

Pollo alla Cacciatora
Hunter-Style Chicken

There are almost as many versions of this chicken as there are cooks in Italy. What changes from region to region, and town to town, is the flavors that go into the pot: most cacciatora dishes (from cacciatore, meaning "hunter") in northern Italy include tomatoes, while those of central and southern Italy call for anchovies, garlic, and a hint of acidity provided by lemon juice or vinegar. In Umbria, capers, anchovies, garlic, rosemary, and lemon juice are added to the chicken, making for a vivaciously flavored main course. Other meats cooked cacciatora style are lamb, hare, and rabbit; when hare is cooked alla cacciatora in Umbria, it is marinated for days in red wine before braising.

SERVES 4

1 chicken, cut into 8 pieces and skinned
3 tablespoons fresh lemon juice (from 1 lemon)
¼ teaspoon freshly ground black pepper
4 garlic cloves, chopped
2 rosemary sprigs, leaves only, minced
⅓ cup extra-virgin olive oil
1 cup Tomato Sauce (page 369)
¼ cup capers, drained
2 salted anchovies, boned, gutted, rinsed, and minced
1½ cups Chicken Broth (page 368)
½ teaspoon salt

Rinse the chicken, rub it with 2 tablespoons of the lemon juice, rinse again, and blot dry with paper towels. (Rinsing with lemon juice cuts down on the potential gaminess of chicken.) In a shallow container, toss with the pepper, garlic, and rosemary and refrigerate at least overnight and up to 3 days.

Heat the olive oil in a 12-inch sauté pan over a medium-high flame. Brown the chicken on both sides, about 5 minutes per side, turning once. Add the tomato sauce, capers, anchovies, broth, salt, and the remaining tablespoon of lemon juice. Cook over medium-low heat, covered, for 1 hour, or until tender. Serve hot.

BASTING A BIRD WITH ITS OWN FEATHERS

When Umbrians roast fowl *alla leccarda* (or *alla ghiotta*), they place a whole bird—usually a dove, squab, or guinea hen—on a spit over a terra-cotta pot called a *leccarda* that contains onions, carrots, garlic, olive oil, juniper berries, and giblets. As the bird roasts, its fat trickles into the pot, creating a luscious sauce. In the old days, one of the bird's feathers was used to baste the meat with the cooking juices; today cooks rely on barbecue brushes. But the end result is still a succulent, crisp bird with moist flesh. Slices of toasted bread are dipped in the cooking juices and wine, then used as a base for the quartered spit-roasted bird.

Salsiccia all'Uva

Pan-Fried Sausages and Juicy Grapes

The marriage of grapes and sausages is classically Umbrian, although a similar recipe exists in Friuli–Venezia Giulia. As the grapes cook with the sausages, they absorb the flavor of the meat and let out their own sweet juices, resulting in a memorable combination. The same dish can be prepared with pork chops instead of sausages; in that case, deglaze the pan with dry Vin Santo before adding the grapes.

SERVES 4

2 tablespoons extra-virgin olive oil
4 Italian sausages with fennel seeds
   (6 ounces each)
¾ pound seedless white grapes, stemmed
½ teaspoon salt
¼ teaspoon freshly ground black pepper

Heat the olive oil in a 12-inch skillet over a medium flame. Add the sausages, pierce with a fork to prevent bursting, and cook for 20 minutes, or until almost done, turning often to cook evenly.

Discard the fat from the pan, add the grapes, and raise the heat to medium-high. Season with the salt and pepper and cook, stirring often, for 10 more minutes. Serve hot.

SUGAR AND SPICE

In the Middle Ages and Renaissance, sugar and spices were costly, lavished on food by the wealthy as a sign of status for important guests and festive banquets. Sweet and salty dishes were mingled throughout the meal, rather than separated in distinct courses like today. Over the centuries, sugar and spices became more affordable, yet their aura of luxury never altogether disappeared. Special occasions in Italy continue to be marked by sugar- and spice-scented savory dishes, especially pastas; while some of these pastas now fall into the dessert category, others are still served as first courses. One example is the *gnocchi dolci* prepared for Christmas in Umbria: boiled pasta squares are layered with grated chocolate, sugar, pounded walnuts, cinnamon, lemon juice, and liqueur, then offered before the main course. A number of sweet-and-savory meats—most featuring game like wild boar and hare—are also favorites.

Scaloppine di Maiale con Capperi e Vino Rosso
Pork Scaloppine in Caper and Red Wine Glaze

Umbrians are a carnivorous people. They grill their meat, season it with wild herbs, and roast it over a spit. They make smart use of every last part of the pig, their favored animal. This home-style main course is best prepared with pork scaloppine from the butt, which are the most tender; avoid scaloppine from the loin, which tend to be tough.

EASTER LAMB WITH A TWIST

In Umbria, as elsewhere in Italy, roasted lamb is a mainstay for Easter. But Umbrians cook their lamb with a twist. To achieve a crisp yet tender texture, a technique known as *pilotto* is used: a piece of lard is wrapped in butcher paper and attached to a skewer above the lamb, then the paper is set on fire, causing the lard to melt and drip onto the meat as it roasts. The same technique is used to baste skewered lamb's intestines in Apulia (page 288).

SERVES 4

⅓ cup unbleached all-purpose flour

8 pork scaloppine (¼ pound each), pounded thin with a mallet

⅓ cup extra-virgin olive oil

2 rosemary sprigs

½ cup dry red wine

¼ cup fresh lemon juice (from 1 large lemon)

½ teaspoon salt

¼ teaspoon freshly ground black pepper

3 tablespoons capers, drained

4 tablespoons (½ stick) unsalted butter, cubed

Pour the flour on a plate and dredge the scaloppine in it, shaking off the excess. Heat the olive oil and rosemary in a 12-inch skillet over a high flame until the oil is smoking. Add 4 of the scaloppine and cook 2 minutes, or until the scaloppine are browned on the bottom; turn with tongs and cook 30 seconds, then remove to a plate. Repeat with the remaining 4 scaloppine. When done, return the first 4 scaloppine to the skillet.

Deglaze with the wine and lemon juice, season with the salt and pepper, and cook 1 minute. Sprinkle with the capers and cook 1 more minute.

Remove all the scaloppine to a platter with clean tongs.

Add the butter to the skillet and cook until the sauce reduces and becomes shiny, about 2 minutes. Pour over the scaloppine and serve hot.

Serpentone delle Monache di Perugia

Nut-and-Fruit "Snake" of the Capuchin Nuns

Nuts and dried fruit are used extensively in Umbrian desserts: There is a pine-nut brittle called pinoccata; zuccherini di Bettona, spirals studded with raisins, anise seeds, pine nuts, and candied citron; pine-nut balls called birbanti; marzipan and candied fruit pastries called strichetti; and tozzetti, almond cookies dipped in sweet wine to close a meal. Perugia's serpentone pastry is filled with an abundance of nuts and dried fruit. Some say it is coiled like a snake to resemble the eel of Lago Trasimeno. Others bestow religious symbolism on the serpent form (after all, it is the nuns of Perugia who are known for this sweet creation) and maintain that the snake represents renewal (snakes shed their skin) and continuity (the pastry is coiled into a semicircle). Umbrians bake it for the New Year as a token of luck; here the attribution might be derived from the serpentone's phallic shape, a symbol of fertility, strength, and vigor.

SERVES 8

2 cups unbleached all-purpose flour, plus extra for the counter

⅔ cup plus 2 tablespoons sugar

⅛ teaspoon salt

½ cup extra-virgin olive oil, plus extra for greasing the baking sheet

⅓ cup currants

⅓ cup golden raisins

¼ cup walnut halves, chopped

½ cup blanched almonds, chopped, plus 1 whole blanched almond

5 dried figs, chopped

5 pitted prunes, chopped

2 Golden Delicious apples, peeled, cored, and chopped

2 tablespoons Vin Santo or Marsala

2 whole coffee beans

In a large bowl, combine the flour, ⅓ cup of the sugar, the salt, ¼ cup of the olive oil, and enough water (about ⅓ cup) to make a firm dough. Turn out onto a counter and knead until smooth, about 5 minutes, adding a little water if the dough is dry or a little flour if it is sticky. Wrap and let rest 30 minutes.

Meanwhile, in a medium bowl, soak the currants and raisins in warm water to cover for 30 minutes; drain and blot dry. In a large bowl, combine the plumped currants and raisins with the walnuts, chopped almonds, figs, prunes, apples, ⅓ cup of the sugar, the remaining ¼ cup of the olive oil, and the Vin Santo.

Preheat the oven to 325°F.

Roll out the dough into a 14 × 18-inch rectangle on a lightly floured counter. Spread the filling over it, leaving a ½-inch border all around. Roll lengthwise into a log, enclosing the filling. Place seam side down on an oiled 11 × 17-inch baking sheet. Shape into a slightly coiled snake; the head of the snake should be a little wider than the body.

Sprinkle with the remaining 2 tablespoons of sugar, place the coffee beans where the eyes should be and the whole almond where the tongue should be, and bake in the preheated oven for 45 minutes.

Raise the oven temperature to 375°F.

Bake 30 minutes more, or until the crust is golden and lightly crisp. Serve hot, warm, or at room temperature.

PREPARATION TIPS: The pastry can be shaped up to 2 hours ahead, covered with plastic wrap, and set aside at room temperature until you are ready to bake.

DESSERTS AND OLIVE OIL, A HAPPY PAIR

Every region of Italy that produces olive oil has a long-standing tradition of making pastries with it. In Umbria, many desserts call for olive oil rather than butter or lard: in addition to serpentone, there is *pizza dolce,* a lemon-scented cake; peppery *pan pepato* from Spoleto and Foligno, baked by farmers after the wheat threshing; *pan nociato,* a bread with walnuts, red wine, and Pecorino from Todi; and a pudding-like Carnevale sweet called *crescionda* made with milk, amaretti, eggs, and flour in Spoleto. If you have never made desserts with olive oil before, try the serpentone or one of the other olive oil–based sweets in this book: Schiacciata con l'Uva (page 167), Taralli all'Anice (page 223), and Calciuni del Molise (page 258). The taste can be quite delicate, provided you use fresh extra-virgin olive oil with good flavor, mild enough to allow the character of other ingredients to shine through.

The Marches

Olive all'Ascolana
Stuffed and Fried Olives from Ascoli Piceno

Crescia Sfogliata con Verdure
Flaky Griddle Bread with Greens

Vincisgrassi
Truffled Lasagna

Muscioli Arrosto Ripieni di Prosciutto e Prezzemolo
Baked Mussels Topped with Prosciutto and Parsley

Brodetto allo Zafferano di Porto Recanati
Seafood Stew from Porto Recanati

Triglie all'Anconetana
Baked Red Mullet Wrapped in Prosciutto

Coniglio in Porchetta
Roasted Rabbit Stuffed with Pancetta and Fennel

Cavolfiore Fritto
Deep-Fried Cauliflower in White Wine Batter

Pizza al Formaggio di Pasqua
Easter Cheese Bread

Crostata di Ricotta
Ricotta Tart

My *first taste of the Marches* came in the form of plump green olives stuffed with braised meat, rolled in eggs and bread crumbs, and deep-fried to a golden brown. It was the first summer my husband and I were together, and his father prepared these memorable stuffed olives from his birthplace of Ascoli Piceno in the Marches. I took one bite and knew I was on to something: I had to make my way to the Marches for a taste of those olives on their native soil.

The Marchigiani, as the people of the Marches are called, have patience, the sort of patience required to pit olives, stuff them, batter them, and fry them; the sort of patience necessary to make a fish stew with no fewer than thirteen varieties of fish and shellfish. The Marches is a tranquil interweaving of blue coastline, green hills, and dense forests, and its cuisine is as varied as its dialects. Yet whether they live on the coast, in the hills, or in the mountains, the Marchigiani love pasta and bread of all kinds. In fact, pasta and grains are so important that in the 1950s, Professor Ancel Keys of the University of Minnesota started the research that would form the basis of the "Mediterranean diet" in Montegiorgio, a town in the province of Ascoli Piceno.

Among the earliest settlers in the Marches were the Piceni, who occupied the seaboard and earned a living from its bountiful waters. The capital of the region is Ancona, a port city of Greek origin whose name is derived from *ancon,* meaning "elbow" in Greek (a reference to its shape); it is the region's only cosmopolitan center, home to more than one hundred thousand people. Like the rest of the area, Ancona fell to the Romans in the third century B.C. and flourished. Even Hannibal stopped there, ordering his army to massage the horses with the local wine for strength, and feasting on hams and cheeses made in the mountains of Montefeltro. After the fall of the Roman Empire, the Byzantines, Lombards, Goths, and Franks all invaded. But it was the church that ultimately dominated life in the Marches for centuries. Much of the cuisine developed in monasteries and convents, as well as in the court of Duke Federico of Montefeltro, and a sharecropping system defined the region's economy well into the postwar years.

Today, nearly 150 years after Italy's unification, every town and city in the Marches still offers its own specialty: there is Campofilone, where golden *maccheroncini* are twirled into nests and filled with ragù, and Fabriano, where the salami is especially tasty. The city of Acqualagna is the site of one of the most important truffle markets in the world; one-third of Italy's truffles are sold there (some to buyers who will later sell them as Piedmontese truffles at Alba's famous truffle market), and both white and black truffles impart a haunting flavor to many local dishes.

Favorite Restaurants, Shops, and Places

- AL MOLO DA ULIASSI, Via Bianchini di Levante 6, Senigallia, 071.65463. Incredible *brodetto* and seafood creations.
- ASSOCIAZIONE PRO LOCO MONDAVIO, Piazza Matteotti 11, Mondavio, 0721.97102. The local tourism office will reserve you a spot at the Tavola del Duca, an annual Renaissance feast.
- GASTRONOMIA ENOTECA MIGLIORI, Piazza Arringo 2, Ascoli Piceno, 0736.250042. Homemade food to go, including *vincisgrassi* and *crema fritta,* plus wines and distillates.
- NENÈ, Via Crocicchia 30, Urbino, 0722.2996. Superb *strozzapreti* and *coniglio in porchetta.*
- PASTIFICIO AZIENDA AGRARIA LATINI, Via Pastore 8, Osimo, 0717.819768. One of Italy's top producers of pasta.

- RISTORANTE LA CAPINERA, Via Passo Cantoniera, Carpegna, 0722.77458. Wonderful homemade pastas and *coniglio ripieno.*
- RISTORANTE LA PALOMBA, Via A. Gramsci 13, Mondavio, 0721.97105. Try the *crescia* and *tacconi.*
- RISTORANTE VECCHIA URBINO, Via dei Vasari 3/5, Urbino, 0722.4447. Amazing *vincisgrassi* and *crescia sfogliata.*
- TARTUFI TOFANI, Via Bellaria 37, Acqualagna, 0721.798918. Everything truffled your heart desires.

Telephone country code: 011.39

Olive all'Ascolana

Stuffed and Fried Olives from Ascoli Piceno

The olives of Ascoli Piceno are prized for their sweet taste and large size, which makes them easier to pit and stuff. Reputedly born in the home of a noble family in the eighteenth century, these stuffed olives are perfect appetizers or finger food.

FEASTING IN THE MARCHES

When the Marchigiani plan a feast, they invariably offer tasty tidbits to start the meal: a platter of rosy ham from Carpegna (page 198), the famous Ciauscolo (page 175) of Visso, some sheep's milk Casciotta, and a few meaty olives are always on hand. If it's Easter, a cheese focaccia will be brought to the table; and if someone particularly skilled is in the kitchen, savory Pecorino-filled pastry half-moons might just emerge.

MAKES 40

40 very large green olives, such as Spanish colossal
4¼ cups extra-virgin olive oil, or ¼ cup extra-virgin olive oil and 4 cups peanut oil
½ pound boneless pork loin, cut into 2 equal pieces
1 tablespoon tomato paste
1 ounce crustless white country bread
1 cup whole milk
¼ cup freshly grated Parmigiano-Reggiano
3 extra-large eggs
½ teaspoon salt
¼ teaspoon freshly ground black pepper
⅛ teaspoon freshly grated nutmeg
Pinch ground cinnamon
1 cup unbleached all-purpose flour
2 cups fresh bread crumbs

Pit each of the olives carefully, removing the flesh in a single unbroken piece by running a paring knife from the top to the bottom of each olive in a wide circular motion, following the shape of the pit with the blade of the knife. (Alternately, buy very large pitted green olives, but you won't be able to accommodate as much stuffing in the olives.) Place the olives in a bowl of cool water to cover and set aside for 1 hour, then rinse and thoroughly blot dry.

Meanwhile, heat ¼ cup of the olive oil in an 8-inch skillet over a medium-high flame. Add the pork and cook until browned on both sides, about 10 minutes, turning once. Dissolve the tomato paste in ¼ cup of water and add to the pork; cover and simmer 30 minutes. Transfer the pork to a food processor, reserving the cooking juices, and purée until a coarse paste forms.

Soak the bread in the milk for 5 minutes, squeeze dry, and add to the pork in the food processor. Add the reserved cooking juices, the Parmigiano, 1 of the eggs, the salt, pepper, nutmeg, and cinnamon, and purée. Cool to room temperature.

Tuck a teaspoon of the pork mixture where the pit of each olive used to be, wrapping the olive around the stuffing so it takes on its original shape, only a little plumper; the filling can peek out here and there. You might have leftover filling depending on the size of the olives.

Beat the remaining 2 eggs in one plate, pour the flour in a second plate, and the bread crumbs in a third. Heat the remaining 4 cups of oil in a deep pan to 350°F, or until it is hot enough to brown a cube of bread in 1 minute. Roll the olives in the flour, shaking off the excess, dip them in the eggs to coat on all sides, and finally roll them in the bread crumbs. Fry the olives in 4 batches until golden, turning once, about 3 minutes, maintaining the temperature of the oil by regulating the heat. Remove with a slotted spoon to a plate lined with paper towels and blot dry. Serve hot or warm.

PREPARATION TIPS: Stuff the olives up to 24 hours in advance and refrigerate before battering and frying.

Crescia Sfogliata con Verdure

Flaky Griddle Bread with Greens

The Marches are home to an array of griddle-baked flatbreads that are the ideal foil for its salty *salumi* and cheeses. Gabriele Monti, owner of Ristorante Vecchia Urbino in Urbino, supplied me with this recipe when I fell in love with these flaky flatbreads on my last visit to his city.

NATURALLY SALTY LAMB

The most prized lamb in the Marches is raised on the marshy lands near the coast, where the grass confers a subtle yet distinctly salty taste to the meat thanks to the blowing sea breeze. Locals braise the lamb with tomatoes and herbs or batter and fry it as part of a *fritto misto*.

SERVES 8

3½ cups unbleached all-purpose flour, plus extra for the counter

1 tablespoon plus 1 teaspoon salt

¼ teaspoon freshly ground black pepper

3½ ounces lard, at room temperature

1½ pounds spinach, stems on, washed thoroughly and chopped

2 pounds Swiss chard leaves, washed thoroughly and chopped

3 pounds escarole, washed thoroughly and chopped

½ cup extra-virgin olive oil

1 cup freshly grated Pecorino Romano

In a medium bowl, mix the flour, ¼ teaspoon of the salt, and ⅛ teaspoon of the pepper. Add 2 ounces of the lard; work it in with your fingertips until the mixture resembles coarse meal. Work in 1¼ cups of cool water; add more if needed to form a supple dough. Transfer to a counter and knead 5 minutes, or until almost smooth. Wrap and let rest 30 minutes.

Meanwhile, bring 6 quarts of water to a boil. Add the spinach and 1 tablespoon of the salt and cook 10 minutes. Remove to a bowl of cool water with a slotted spoon and add the Swiss chard to the boiling water; cook 10 minutes, then remove to the same bowl with the slotted spoon. Add the escarole to the boiling water and cook 10 minutes, then drain and add to the same bowl. Squeeze the greens dry.

Heat the olive oil in a 12-inch skillet over a medium flame, add the greens, and cook for 15 minutes, stirring often. Season with the remaining ¾ teaspoon of salt and ⅛ teaspoon of pepper and keep warm.

Roll out the dough on a lightly floured counter into a 20-inch circle. Rub the top with the remaining 1½ ounces of lard and roll into a loose bundle. Cut into 8 equal pieces. Flour the counter lightly and flatten each piece into a disk, then roll out each into a 10-inch circle. Roll each circle into a loose bundle again; roll each bundle into a coil, tuck the outer end under, and press gently so it sits beneath the coil. Spread out in a single layer on a floured counter, cover with a towel, and let rest 15 minutes.

Roll out each coil on a lightly floured counter into an 11-inch disk. Heat a griddle or 12-inch skillet for 5 minutes over a medium-high flame. Cook each disk of dough until golden, speckled with brown spots, and puffed on both sides, about 2 minutes per side, turning once; these are the *crescie*. Wrap the crescie in a folded towel to keep warm.

Spoon one-eighth of the warm greens over each warm crescia, sprinkle each with 2 tablespoons of the Pecorino, fold in half, and serve.

PREPARATION TIPS: The filling can be made up to 2 days ahead and refrigerated, then heated while you cook the crescie.

ROSSINI'S APPETITES

Few artists have had as many dishes named after them as the Marches' prodigal son, Gioacchino Rossini. Born in Pesaro in 1792, Rossini was unabashedly fond of good food and devoted much of his free time to the pleasures of the table. He hosted lavish dinners, creating such elaborate dishes as guinea hen in a salt pyramid (prepared on November 20, 1842, in Bologna, on the eve of the premiere of *Moses in Egypt*) and pâté–stuffed rigatoni layered with chicken giblets and cockscombs, butter, Mortadella, Prosciutto, and truffles (invented for Bellentani, the Maestro's favorite *salumiere* in Bologna). Other dishes that bear Rossini's name are tournedos alla Rossini (browned beef medallions topped with cheese and Prosciutto, served with foie gras and truffles) and risotto alla Rossini (with tomatoes, mushrooms, and eggs), luxurious dishes that reflect Rossini's epicurean philosophy: "After doing nothing, I know of no other activity as delicious as eating. Appetite is to the stomach as love is to the heart . . . Eating and loving, singing and digesting: these are in truth the four acts of this funny opera we call life, which fades like the bubbles from a bottle of champagne. Anyone who lets it escape without partaking in the pleasure is crazy."

Vincisgrassi

Truffled Lasagna

Every region has its defining dish, the one people rhapsodize about and legends are woven around. In the Marches, the honor goes to vincisgrassi, a lasagna featuring meat, porcini mushrooms, and white truffles. The anecdote goes that vincisgrassi was named after the Austrian prince Windisch-Graetz, who reached the Marches in 1799 to wrest Ancona from Napoleon. But the tale, romantic as it sounds, skirts the fact that a similar dish called prigsgras *was described in* Il Cuoco Maceratese, *a cookbook written in the eighteenth century by Antonio Nebbia. I have substituted ground pork and beef for the chicken giblets traditionally used, for a more delicate flavor.*

A LOVE OF ALL THINGS STUFFED

The Marchigiani have a love affair with all things stuffed, and pasta is no exception. There are maccheroni stuffed with turkey, liver, truffles, and cream, sauced with a veal ragù, and *cappelletti* filled with pork and chicken. In Ancona, *lasagne incassettate* are layered with ragù and cheese and topped with white truffles; in San Leo, greens-stuffed *tortelli* are tossed with ragù; and in Pesaro, Ricotta ravioli are served with tomato sauce and fried sole in a hybrid of coastal and mountain cookery.

SERVES 8

For the sauce:

½ cup dried porcini mushrooms
4 tablespoons (½ stick) unsalted butter
1 medium yellow onion, minced
1 carrot, minced
½ pound ground pork
½ pound ground beef
½ cup dry white wine
1 tablespoon tomato paste
½ cup Beef Broth (page 368)
½ teaspoon salt
⅛ teaspoon freshly ground black pepper
Pinch ground cinnamon
½ cup whole milk

For the lasagne:

1 cup unbleached all-purpose flour, plus extra for the counter
½ cup semolina flour
¼ teaspoon salt
2 extra-large eggs
2 tablespoons Vin Santo or dry Marsala, plus extra if needed

To layer:

2 tablespoons salt
2 tablespoons (¼ stick) unsalted butter, cubed, plus extra for greasing the baking dish
1 recipe Besciamella (page 370)
1 cup freshly grated Parmigiano-Reggiano
1 white truffle, shaved paper-thin with a truffle slicer (optional)

Make the sauce: Soak the porcini in water to cover for 30 minutes. Drain (reserve the water for risotti, straining it through a cheesecloth-lined sieve), rinse, and mince. Melt the butter in a 10-inch sauté pan over medium heat and add the onion and carrot; cook 10 minutes. Add the pork and beef, increase the heat to medium-high, and cook until browned all over, about 15 minutes, stirring often. Fold in the minced porcini and wine and cook 5 minutes. Add the tomato paste, broth, salt, pepper, and cinnamon. Reduce the heat to medium-low, cover, and cook for 1½ hours. Add the milk and cook 30 more minutes, covered.

Meanwhile, make the lasagne according to instructions on page 370 using the ingredients listed opposite, adding a little Vin Santo if the dough is dry or a little all-purpose flour if it is sticky. Knead 5 minutes, or until smooth, shape into a ball, wrap, and let rest 30 minutes.

Cut the dough into 3 pieces. Working with 1 piece at a time and keeping the others covered, roll out each piece using a pasta machine into a nearly transparent sheet. Cut into 14-inch-long rectangles. These are the lasagne.

To layer the lasagne, bring 4 quarts of water to a boil. Add the salt and drop in 4 lasagne, stirring immediately to prevent sticking. Cook until al dente, about 1 minute, then remove to a bowl of cool water with a slotted spoon, spread out in a single layer on kitchen towels, and blot dry. Continue in the same manner with the remaining lasagne.

Preheat the oven to 400°F.

Butter a deep 10 × 14-inch baking dish. Spoon ½ cup of sauce over the surface of the dish. Line with enough lasagne to cover, cutting them as needed to fit. Spoon on a thin layer of besciamella, top with some sauce, sprinkle with some Parmigiano, and top with a few truffle slivers. Layer the ingredients in the same sequence until they are used up, making 5 layers in all; you may not need all of the lasagne. Finish with a layer of besciamella, Parmigiano, and truffles. Dot the top with the butter.

Bake in the preheated oven 40 minutes. Remove from the oven and increase the heat to broil. Return to the broiler 6 inches from the heating element and broil 3 minutes, or until lightly browned on top. Serve hot.

PREPARATION TIPS: Layer the lasagne up to 2 days ahead and refrigerate until you are ready to bake.

Muscioli Arrosto Ripieni di Prosciutto e Prezzemolo

Baked Mussels Topped with Prosciutto and Parsley

Mussels go by many different names in Italy: cozze, mitili, muscoli, *and, in the Marches,* muscioli. *When the Marchigiani make this recipe, they pry the mussels open while still alive, then stuff them. I find it easier to steam the mussels open before stuffing them, but you are welcome to go the supertraditional route.*

CARPEGNA'S ROSY HAM

Prosciutto has been cured in the town of Carpegna since the days of ancient Rome; deep pink, with a delicate flavor, it is salted and aged fourteen months. Luckily, you need not travel so far for a taste of this prized ham: a number of well-stocked Italian markets now carry it. See Sources (page 372) to purchase it by mail.

SERVES 4

3 pounds mussels, rinsed, beards removed
1 tablespoon plus ¼ teaspoon salt
3 plum tomatoes, peeled (see page 369), seeded, and minced
One 2-ounce slice Prosciutto di Carpegna, minced (substitute Prosciutto di Parma or San Daniele)
2 tablespoons minced Italian parsley
1 garlic clove, minced
½ cup fresh bread crumbs
¼ teaspoon freshly ground black pepper
¼ cup extra-virgin olive oil

Soak the mussels in cool water to cover with 1 tablespoon of the salt for 30 minutes. Drain and rinse. Place in a 12-inch sauté pan over medium-high heat, cover, and steam for 3 minutes. Remove with a slotted spoon to a plate. Strain the pan juices through a cheesecloth-lined sieve and reserve. Scoop out the mussel from each shell and reserve one-quarter of the half-shells. Place 2 mussels in each half-shell and spread out in a single layer in a 10 × 14-inch roasting pan.

Preheat the oven to 400°F.

In a medium bowl, mix the tomatoes, Prosciutto, parsley, garlic, bread crumbs, the remaining ¼ teaspoon of salt, and the pepper. Press onto the mussels in the half-shells, drizzle with the olive oil and the reserved pan juices from the mussels, and bake in the preheated oven for 15 minutes. Serve hot.

Brodetto allo Zafferano di Porto Recanati

Seafood Stew from Porto Recanati

The Marches is responsible for more than 10 percent of Italy's fish and seafood, and coastal towns like San Benedetto del Tronto are among Italy's leading fishing centers. Local cooks offer more versions of brodetto, a chunky fish and seafood stew, than any other Italian region. In Ancona, tomatoes are added for sweetness and acidity; in Porto Recanati, the fish and seafood are floured before going in the pot, and the broth is infused with wild saffron. The Marchigiani are so serious about their brodetto that they founded the Accademia Marchigiana del Brodetto to stipulate what an authentic brodetto contains and how it should be prepared. As the Accademia will tell you, the more varieties of fish you use, the better your brodetto will be. Scampi, also called Dublin Bay prawns or langoustines, are a small species of lobster; they can be replaced with additional head-on shrimp.

SERVES 4

1 teaspoon saffron pistils
⅓ cup extra-virgin olive oil
1 medium yellow onion, minced
¾ pound cleaned baby cuttlefish or cleaned
    small squid, bodies cut into rings
    and tentacles halved
4 cups (1 quart) Fish Broth (page 369)
½ teaspoon salt
⅛ teaspoon freshly ground black pepper
4 jumbo head-on shrimp
4 head-on scampi
1 pound assorted skinless and boneless saltwater
    fish fillets (hake, cod, monkfish, red mullet,
    mullet, red snapper), cut into 3-inch pieces
½ cup unbleached all-purpose flour
1 cup dry white wine
1 tablespoon white wine vinegar
Eight ¼-inch-thick × 6-inch-wide slices
    country bread

Dissolve the saffron in 1 tablespoon of hot water and set aside 10 minutes. Meanwhile, heat the olive oil in a 3-quart pot over a medium flame. Add the onion and cook for 5 minutes. Add the cuttlefish and cook 5 minutes. Add the saffron water, broth, ¼ teaspoon of the salt, and a pinch of the pepper. Bring to a boil and cook, uncovered, 30 minutes. Remove the cuttlefish to a plate with a slotted spoon; reserve the cooking liquid.

Dredge the shrimp, scampi, and fish in the flour, shaking off the excess. Layer the shrimp, scampi, fish, and poached cuttlefish in a heavy-bottomed 10-inch sauté pan; pour in the reserved cuttlefish cooking liquid, the wine, and the vinegar. Season with the remaining ¼ teaspoon of salt and pinch of pepper. Bring to a gentle boil and cook for 15 minutes over medium heat, uncovered, shaking the pot every few minutes. Do not stir or the fish will fall apart.

Meanwhile, heat a grill pan over a high flame for 5 minutes. Grill the bread until golden brown on both sides, about 2 minutes per side, turning once.

Serve the brodetto hot, accompanied by the bread.

Triglie all'Anconetana

Baked Red Mullet Wrapped in Prosciutto

Among the Mediterranean's most beloved fish, red mullet has yet to catch on in North America, largely because of its many bones. If you are averse to bony fish, use boned red mullet fillets rather than the whole fish. Mediterranean red mullet is often sold under its French name, rouget.

SERVES 4

4 small Mediterranean red mullet (6 ounces each), heads on, scaled, gutted, rinsed, and blotted dry
3 tablespoons fresh lemon juice (from 1 lemon)
4 garlic cloves, crushed
4 rosemary sprigs
½ teaspoon freshly ground black pepper
½ cup fresh bread crumbs
2 tablespoons minced Italian parsley
4 thin slices Prosciutto di Carpegna (substitute Prosciutto di Parma or San Daniele)
¼ cup extra-virgin olive oil

Place the red mullet in a 12-inch roasting pan. Add the lemon juice, garlic, rosemary, and pepper; refrigerate 1 hour. Stuff the cavity of each mullet with 1 garlic clove and 1 rosemary sprig from the marinade.

Preheat the oven to 375°F.

Combine the bread crumbs and parsley on a plate. Roll the mullet in the bread-crumb mixture, pressing with your hands so the mixture adheres on all sides. Wrap each mullet in 1 slice of Prosciutto. Return to the roasting pan, drizzle with the olive oil, and bake in the preheated oven for 20 minutes. Serve hot.

THE CAPITAL OF BLUE FISH AND BEYOND

The picturesque town of Fano is Italy's capital of *pesce azzurro* ("blue fish," known as oily fish in North America), so sardines, anchovies, mackerel, and the like are treated with reverence in the Marchigiano kitchen. Yet of all fish, none is more emblematic of the Marches than stockfish: after soaking in water or milk to plump up, it is cooked with rosemary, chili, garlic, and tomatoes, or with potatoes, tomatoes, and anchovies.

Coniglio in Porchetta

Roasted Rabbit Stuffed with Pancetta and Fennel

Potacchio *and porchetta are the Marches'*
most common cooking techniques for meat
(and, to a lesser extent, for fish). The word
potacchio *shares a root with the French* potage,
meaning "soup"; but in reality it refers to a stew,
more often than not of chicken or rabbit, fla-
vored with garlic and rosemary. Porchetta is
roasted whole suckling pig, chicken, or rabbit
stuffed with garlic, wild fennel, and the animal's
own innards; the name is derived from porco,
meaning "pig," because suckling pig is most
often cooked in this manner. Cooks in Umbria
and Latium insist they "invented" porchetta, but
the Marchigiani can really lay claim to this dish.
In the absence of wild fennel, use a combination
of minced fennel tops (the tender celerylike
stalks and feathery leaves that resemble dill at
the top of each bulb) and crushed fennel seeds.

SERVES 4

1 rabbit (about 3 pounds)
¼ cup white wine vinegar
½ teaspoon salt
½ teaspoon freshly ground black pepper
¾ pound fennel tops
3 garlic cloves, 2 crushed and 1 minced
¼ cup extra-virgin olive oil
1 tablespoon fennel seeds, crushed
One 2-ounce slice Prosciutto di Carpegna,
   minced (substitute Prosciutto di Parma
   or San Daniele)
One 2-ounce slice mild salami, such as Genoa,
   minced
One 2-ounce slice Pancetta, minced

Preheat the oven to 375°F.

Cut the belly of the rabbit open, remove and discard the innards, reserve the liver, and
mince it. Rinse the rabbit, rub it with the vinegar, rinse again, and blot dry. Season it inside
and out with the salt and pepper.

Place the fennel tops and the 2 cloves of crushed garlic in a pot, add 4 cups of cool water,
and bring to a boil; cook 10 minutes over high heat. Drain the fennel tops, reserving 2 cups
of their cooking liquid but discarding the garlic, and mince.

Heat 2 tablespoons of the olive oil in a 12-inch skillet over a medium flame. Add the
minced fennel tops, fennel seeds, the minced clove of garlic, Prosciutto, salami, Pancetta,
and rabbit liver, and sauté for 5 minutes. Cool to room temperature.

Stuff the rabbit with the fennel-Pancetta mixture. Tie with butcher's string and place in
a 10 × 14-inch roasting pan, lying on one side. Drizzle with the remaining 2 tablespoons of
olive oil and roast in the preheated oven 30 minutes.

Raise the oven temperature to 475°F.

Pour the reserved 2 cups of fennel cooking liquid over the rabbit and roast 15 minutes.
Turn the rabbit so it is lying on its other side. Roast 35 more minutes, or until golden
brown, basting with the cooking juices every 10 minutes. Remove from the oven, discard
the string, and serve hot.

Cavolfiore Fritto

Deep-Fried Cauliflower in White Wine Batter

Cauliflower, cardoons, peas, and zucchini are four of the Marches' main crops. These deep-fried cauliflower florets enrobed in wine batter are favorites among the Marchigiani. If you have mistrà, an anise liqueur made in the region, add a tablespoon of it to the batter.

SERVES 4

⅔ cup unbleached all-purpose flour
1 tablespoon plus ½ teaspoon salt
¼ teaspoon freshly ground black pepper
1 extra-large egg
½ cup dry white wine, plus extra if needed
1 head cauliflower, cut into small florets
3 cups extra-virgin olive oil or peanut oil

Combine the flour, ¼ teaspoon of the salt, and the pepper in a large bowl. Whisk in the egg and enough of the wine to obtain a smooth, creamy mixture with a consistency similar to pancake batter; you may not need all of the wine. Cover and let rest 30 minutes.

Meanwhile, bring 4 quarts of water to a boil. Add the cauliflower and 1 tablespoon of the salt. Cook 5 minutes, drain, rinse in cold water, and blot dry.

Heat the oil in a deep 10-inch pan until it registers 350°F, or until it is hot enough to brown a cube of bread in 1 minute. Dredge the cauliflower in the batter and fry in batches until it is golden all over, about 3 minutes, turning to cook evenly and maintaining the temperature of the oil by regulating the heat. Remove with a slotted spoon to a platter lined with paper towels and blot dry. Serve hot, sprinkled with the remaining ¼ teaspoon of salt.

THE MARCHES' WINES

ALTHOUGH THE WILD ANCESTOR OF THE GRAPE may have thrived on the slopes of Monte Conero as long as one hundred thousand years ago, it was likely the Greeks settling in Ancona around 1000 B.C. who actively started cultivating vines in the area and shipping local wines to Greece. Years later, Hannibal stopped in the Marches, reinvigorating his horses by rubbing their legs with wine from Piceno. A temperate Mediterranean climate with hot, dry summers and cool winters, calcareous soil, ample plantings of Sangiovese, Verdicchio, Montepulciano, and Trebbiano, and hillside vineyards make the Marches a prime location for viticulture.

Despite the area's great oenological potential, only one Marchigiano wine has become renowned outside its boundaries: Verdicchio dei Castelli di Jesi, a refreshing, crisp white vinified near Jesi with delicate apple notes, a honeyed quality, and hints of nut. It first became an international star in 1953, when Fazi-Battaglia packaged it in an amphora-shaped bottle. Less renowned but perhaps more distinctive is Verdicchio di Matelica, a white vinified in a still, sparkling, or raisined version around Matelica, near the Umbrian border. Because of the higher altitude of its vineyards, the Matelica wine has more character and is fuller-bodied than the Jesi wine. Falerio dei Colli Ascolani, a lightly scented, dry, somewhat bitter, Trebbiano-based white, is also popular.

The slopes of Monte Conero are a happy home for Montepulciano and Sangiovese grapes, which are used to vinify Rosso Conero, one of the Marches' flagship wines; it offers rich, complex notes of under-ripe plums, dried fruit, spice, and herbs, and its vinous bouquet softens as it ages. Somewhat less imposing than Rosso Conero is Rosso Piceno, a firm, fruity red with good acidity that becomes flowery as it ages. Lacrima di Morro d'Alba, a red with scents of red fruit and underwood, is vinified in a dry and raisined version, and Vernaccia di Serrapetrona, a sparkling red obtained from slightly raisined grapes, is medium dry, with an aroma of ripe fruit, jam, flowers, and spices.

COOKING WITH GRAPE MUST

Before World War II, when wine production in the Marches was mostly carried out on small farms according to the sharecropping system, a portion of the grape must was transformed into *vino cotto* ("cooked wine"), *sapa,* and *vino di visciole.* To make vino cotto, grape must was reduced over a slow fire to one-fifth of its original volume, then aged in barrels for years; in the old days, babies' arms were rubbed with vino cotto to make them strong. Sapa, obtained by reducing grape must by two-thirds, was poured over polenta and used in pastries. Vino di visciole, made by fermenting sour cherries (*visciole*) in the must of Sangiovese and Montepulciano grapes, was offered as a dessert wine. Today it is difficult to find vino di visciole or sapa and nearly impossible to find artisanal vino cotto, but many of the Marches' older desserts still call for a spoonful or two of vino cotto or sapa. Three sweets made with these wine derivatives are logs of sun-dried figs, a sweet polenta from Ancona called *frustenga,* and ring-shaped yeasted breads baked during the grape harvest. To buy vino cotto, see Sources (page 372).

Pizza al Formaggio di Pasqua

Easter Cheese Bread

This cheesy bread owes its brioche-like texture to a generous dose of eggs and olive oil, and is baked in a small cake pan so it puffs up to resemble a golden dome. It is an Easter staple both in the Marches and Umbria, served with Prosciutto, sheep's milk cheeses, and hard-boiled eggs as an appetizer.

SERVES 6

3 cups unbleached all-purpose flour, plus extra
    for the bowl and counter
1 tablespoon instant yeast
1/2 teaspoon salt
4 extra-large eggs
3 tablespoons extra-virgin olive oil, plus extra for
    greasing the cake pan
1 cup freshly grated Grana Padano
2 tablespoons freshly grated Pecorino Romano
1/4 pound mild, young sheep's milk cheese, such
    as Marzolino, Fiore Sardo, or other, cut into
    1/4-inch dice
1 teaspoon freshly ground black pepper

Place 1 cup of the flour and the yeast in a food processor. With the motor running, add as much warm (110°F) water as needed to form a dough that rides the blade (about 1/3 to 1/2 cup); process 45 seconds. Turn out into a floured bowl, shape into a ball, and cover. Let rise at room temperature 1 hour, or until doubled.

Process the remaining 2 cups of flour, the salt, 3 of the eggs, and the olive oil with the risen dough in the food processor until a dough forms, about 30 seconds, adding as much room-temperature water (about 1/4 to 1/3 cup) as needed to make a dough that rides the blade. Turn out onto the counter. Knead in the Grana, Pecorino, sheep's milk cheese, and pepper until the dough is smooth, about 3 minutes.

Shape the dough into a ball and place it, seam side down, in a generously oiled 6-inch round springform cake pan with 4-inch-high sides. Cover and let rise at room temperature until doubled, about 1 hour.

Preheat the oven to 400°F.

Slash the top of the dough with a sharp knife, making a shallow cross. Beat the remaining egg and brush the dough with it (you will not need all of it). Bake in the preheated oven 35 minutes, or until the crust is golden and crisp and the bottom sounds hollow when thumped. Unmold onto a rack and serve hot or warm.

PREPARATION TIPS: The dough can be shaped and allowed to rise in the cake pan in the refrigerator overnight; return to room temperature before baking.

Crostata di Ricotta

Ricotta Tart

This tart descended from the salty-sweet cheese-filled pastries of medieval and Renaissance feasts, when the savory and the sweet mingled from first course through dessert. It is made across Italy with minor and major variations; the Marchigiano touch here is the lemon zest, cinnamon, and rum in the filling. In the town of Macerata, the same ingredients are used to make bite-sized crescent pastries called *piconi.* Since the sheep's milk Ricotta used in the Marches is hard to find in North America, I approximate its flavor by adding a touch of Pecorino to cow's milk Ricotta.

SERVES 8

2½ cups unbleached all-purpose flour, plus extra for the counter

¼ teaspoon salt

1½ teaspoons grated lemon zest

2 cups plus 2 tablespoons sugar

8 tablespoons (1 stick) unsalted butter, cubed, at room temperature, plus extra for greasing the tart pan

7 extra-large egg yolks

¼ cup whole milk

1 pound fresh Ricotta

¼ cup freshly grated Pecorino Romano

2 tablespoons rum

⅛ teaspoon ground cinnamon

In a large bowl, mix 2 cups of the flour, the salt, 1 teaspoon of the lemon zest, and ½ cup plus 2 tablespoons of the sugar. Work in the butter with your fingertips until the mixture resembles coarse meal. Add 3 of the egg yolks and the milk; knead quickly until a dough forms, adding flour by the tablespoon as needed if the dough is sticky. Turn out onto a counter, gather into a ball, flatten into a disk, wrap, and refrigerate 45 minutes.

Meanwhile, in another large bowl, use a spatula to combine the Ricotta, Pecorino, rum, cinnamon, the remaining ½ teaspoon of lemon zest, ½ cup of flour, 1½ cups of sugar, and 4 egg yolks; do not overmix or the Ricotta will liquefy. Refrigerate for 45 minutes.

SWEETS IN THE LAND OF HONEY—AND OLIVE OIL

The Marchigiani have a penchant for sweetening with honey rather than sugar, a holdover from days when sugar was an expensive commodity and honey was easily found on farms. And like any region with a plentiful supply of olive oil, the Marches offers a profusion of sweet fritters: chestnut-shaped *castagnole* scented with anise seeds, staples for Carnevale (also made in Emilia-Romagna); *caciunitti,* half-moons stuffed with a chickpea purée, similar to the *calciuni* stuffed with boiled chestnuts in Molise (page 258); and *cicerchiata,* chickpea-sized fritters doused with honey and shaped into a wreath as in nearby Umbria and Abruzzo.

Preheat the oven to 325°F.

Butter a 10-inch springform tart pan. Knead the dough 15 seconds. Roll out on a lightly floured counter into a 12-inch circle and line the prepared pan with it. Spoon in the Ricotta mixture and cut off excess dough.

Bake in the preheated oven 35 to 40 minutes, or until the crust is golden around the edges and the filling is set. Cool on a rack and enjoy at room temperature.

PREPARATION TIPS: Make the dough up to 24 hours ahead and refrigerate.

MICHELANGELO'S FAVORITE CHEESE

MICHELANGELO BOUGHT LAND IN URBINO just to have a steady supply of the local Casciotta: this firm cheese, made from 70 to 80 percent sheep's milk with the addition of cow's milk, has a thin yellow to gray rind, compact flesh with minute holes, and fresh flavor, and has been produced in the area since the thirteenth century. But Casciotta is by no means the only outstanding sheep's milk cheese from the Marches. There is also Erborinato di Pecora, a tangy, spreadable, blue-veined cheese; Formaggio di Fossa, essentially a Casciotta aged for months in the stone pits of Talamello, as in Emilia-Romagna (page 138); and Pecorino Sotto le Foglie di Noci, a specialty of Carpegna, swathed in walnut leaves to acquire aroma and complexity. See Sources (page 372) to buy these cheeses in North America.

Latium

Pizzacce Viterbesi
Folded and Stuffed Flour-and-Water Pancakes

Bucatini all'Amatriciana
Bucatini in Chili-Pancetta Sauce

Gnocchi di Semolino
Baked Semolina Gnocchi

La Minestra di Farro degli Antichi Rivista
The Roman Legionnaire's Farro Soup Revisited

Luccio Brodettato alla Romana
Pike in Velvety Egg-Lemon Sauce

Coda alla Vaccinara
The Cowmen's Braised Oxtail with Celery

Uova in Trippa alla Romana
Egg Ribbons in Tomato Sauce with Pecorino and
Fresh Mint

Piselli al Prosciutto
Spring Peas with Diced Prosciutto

Taralli all'Anice
Anise Taralli

Pizza di Polenta e Ricotta
Sweet Polenta and Ricotta Cake

I'm standing in the Campo dei Fiori, Rome's most famous open-air market. It's seven in the morning and the vendors are setting up, creating glorious displays of auburn mushrooms, ruby radicchio, emerald asparagus, scarlet tomatoes. An old man carefully spreads ferns on a wooden table, then arranges his offerings over the leaves like a still life of the sea: head-on shrimp the size of my hand, silvery-blue sardines with bright eyes, translucent squid with delicate tentacles and purplish flaps.

The bakery around the corner has opened its doors. I down a slice of warm focaccia as I watch two little girls at a nearby stall sort flowers under their mother's attentive gaze. I am back in Rome, a city I have visited dozens of times, a city that never fails to surprise me with its noise, its brilliant colors, its indefatigable energy.

When Rome was founded by a group of shepherds on the banks of the Tevere River in 753 B.C. (the year its first king, Romulus, was crowned), the surrounding countryside was already home to the Latins, an Italic tribe of Indo-European origin. The area, dubbed Latium Vetus by the Romans, was under Etruscan rule for centuries. In the fourth century B.C., this enterprising tribe of shepherds managed to subjugate the Etruscans, Latins, and other neighboring groups, giving rise to the Roman Republic and, later, to the Roman Empire. The influence and holdings of Rome quickly spread throughout the western world, reaching as far north as modern-day Britain and as far south as Africa. The entire Italian peninsula was under Roman rule, where it remained as a single entity until the fall of the empire in A.D. 476. It would be another fourteen centuries until the country was whole again, unified under its first king, Vittorio Emanuele, in 1861.

When the empire crumbled, the barbarians settled in. Rome and its countryside were overrun by Goths and Visigoths, and power passed from Roman emperors to barbarian chieftains. Despite these invasions, the fate of Rome and Latium after the fifth century was largely determined by the papacy, which owned huge tracts of land in the area and wielded considerable power over matters both sacred and secular. In 1870, Rome once again became the capital of Italy, an honor it holds to this day.

It's almost impossible to speak of Latium without immediately thinking of Rome, and not only because of its glorious past: 55 percent of the region's population, ringing in at three million inhabitants, is concentrated in the capital. The second-largest center in Latium is Latina, home to just over one hundred thousand people. Many Italians will tell you that there is no such thing as a regional cuisine of Latium, and that in Rome the cooking is "continental"; but the truth is that Latium's cooks have kept an ancient pastoral cuisine alive. These traditions are best preserved in Latium's hilly rural areas, where sheepherding remains fundamental. Second only to Sardinia for its sheep's milk cheese production, Latium flavors many of its dishes with Pecorino; and its favorite meat, aside from the pork adored in central Italy, is lamb.

Within Rome itself, two groups have had a lasting impact on the cuisine. The Jews who lived in the city for two thousand years have contributed a wealth of dishes, including marinated fish with raisins and pine nuts and sweet Ricotta fritters, staples in the old Jewish ghetto of Trastevere. And the *vaccinari* ("cowmen") who worked in the city's slaughterhouse developed a number of rustic recipes using tripe, oxtail, intestines, and other innards, making for a flavorful, if peasant, urban cuisine.

Favorite Restaurants, Shops, and Places

- ANTICA NORCINERIA, Campo dei Fiori 43, Rome. Pork shop that cures hams and salami.
- CAMPO DEI FIORI, Rome. The Eternal City's outdoor market; don't miss it for the world.
- CHECCHINO DAL 1887, Via di Monte Testaccio 30, Rome, 06.5746318. The cuisine of the *quinto quarto*; try the *rigatoni con pajata* and *coda alla vaccinara*.
- DA CHECCO AL CALICE D'ORO, Via Marchetti 10, Rieti, 0746.204271. Try the *fregnacce alla sabinese*.
- DA GIGGETTO, Via del Portico d'Ottavia 21/A, Rome, 06.6861105. Jewish-Roman dishes like *carciofi alla giudea*, fried cod, and fried zucchini blossoms.
- LAOOCONTE DA ROCCO, Via Cristoforo Colombo 4, Sperlonga, 0771.548122. Not to be missed: *bruschetta alla Laooconte*.

- LA VERANDA, Hotel Maga Circe, Via Ammiraglio Bergamini 7, San Felice Circeo, 0773.547821. First courses are excellent; try the *tarallucci* for dessert.
- LE COLLINE CIOCIARE, Via Prenestina 27, Acuto, 0775.56049. Traditional foods including *fini fini con fave, piselli e menta*.
- LEONE LIMENTANI, Via Portico d'Ottavia 47, Rome, 06.68806686. Amazing selection of kitchenware.
- MUSEO NAZIONALE DELLE PASTE ALIMENTARI, Piazza Scandeberg 114-120, Rome. Museum devoted entirely to pasta.

Telephone country code: 011.39

Pizzacce Viterbesi

Folded and Stuffed Flour-and-Water Pancakes

These soft, thin pancakes are similar to the borlenghi of Emilia-Romagna. They sometimes go by the name fregnacce *("silly things") or* Diomeneguardi *("God forbid," perhaps because they are made only of flour and water and are considered "poor" food). Standard fare in Viterbo, they are folded around grated Pecorino as an appetizer or snack, or dusted with a veil of sugar and cinnamon for dessert. When lamb ragù is the filling, the pizzacce are baked before serving, just as in Abruzzo.*

EATING IN THE FRY SHOPS

The Romans have two telling proverbs: *"Acqua e pane, vita da cane"* ("Water and bread, a dog's life") and *"Non si vive di solo pane"* ("One does not live by bread alone"). And certainly in Latium, one does not live by bread and water alone. The Romans are notorious for their love of fried food, and the city is dotted with *friggitorie,* informal eateries that specialize in frying. Favorite fried antipasti include skewered bread and buffalo's milk cheese served in a warm anchovy sauce; slices of bread enclosing Prosciutto and Mozzarella; half-moons of pizza dough stuffed with cheese and Prosciutto or Ricotta and vegetables; and cinnamon-scented dumplings dusted with Parmigiano.

SERVES 4

2 cups plus 3 tablespoons unbleached all-purpose flour

½ teaspoon salt

1 slab Prosciutto rind or pork rind (substitute 1 tablespoon extra-virgin olive oil)

1 cup freshly grated Pecorino Romano

4 teaspoons minced Italian parsley (optional)

Sift the flour and salt into a medium bowl. Whisking all the while, beat in enough warm water (about 3 cups) to make a smooth, fluid, fairly thin batter that flows like heavy cream. Strain through a fine sieve into a clean bowl.

Heat a 12-inch cast-iron or nonstick pan over a high flame for 5 minutes. Rub the surface with the Prosciutto rind, pork rind, or a kitchen towel imbibed with the olive oil. Pour in ⅓ cup plus 1 tablespoon of the batter (measure first, but use a ladle to spoon it into the pan), tilting the pan immediately to spread it to the edges. (If the batter does not spread easily, dilute it with water.)

Cook 3 minutes, or until the pancake is crisp around the edges and speckled with brown spots on the bottom. Turn and cook the other side for 1 minute, or until speckled with brown spots. Remove to a towel. Continue with the remaining batter, making 8 pancakes in all.

To serve, heat the pancakes, one by one, in a hot skillet over a medium flame for 3 minutes; sprinkle each with 2 tablespoons of the Pecorino and ½ teaspoon of the parsley. Fold in quarters and serve hot.

Bucatini all'Amatriciana

Bucatini in Chili-Pancetta Sauce

Latium's most famous pastas, including egg-laced *spaghetti alla carbonara* and spicy *bucatini all'amatriciana*, feature bits of cured meat: Pancetta (unsmoked pork belly), Guanciale (salted and spiced pig's cheek), or Prosciutto (raw ham). Amatriciana sauce hails from the town of Amatrice, which once belonged to Abruzzo, and was originally made without tomatoes; today this white-sauce version goes by the name of *gricia*. To try your hand at bucatini alla gricia, omit the tomatoes from the recipe below and substitute ¹/₂ teaspoon of freshly ground black pepper for the chili.

SERVES 4

5 tablespoons extra-virgin olive oil
One 5-ounce slice Pancetta, cut into
    ¹/₄ × ¹/₄- to ¹/₂-inch strips
1 large yellow onion, thinly sliced
¹/₄ teaspoon chili flakes
3 cups canned chopped Italian plum tomatoes
2 tablespoons plus ¹/₄ teaspoon salt
1 pound bucatini
1 cup freshly grated Pecorino Romano

Heat 3 tablespoons of the olive oil in a heavy 2-quart pot over a medium-high flame. Add the Pancetta and cook 5 minutes. Fold in the onion and chili and cook 5 minutes. Add the tomatoes, bring to a boil, reduce the heat to medium, cover, and cook for 10 minutes. Season with ¹/₄ teaspoon of the salt; keep the sauce warm.

Meanwhile, bring 5 quarts of water to a boil. Add the bucatini and the remaining 2 tablespoons of salt and cook until al dente, about 8 minutes. Drain, reserving ¹/₂ cup of the pasta cooking water. Return the bucatini to the pot and fold in the sauce, ¹/₂ cup of the Pecorino, and the remaining 2 tablespoons of olive oil. Add as much of the reserved cooking water as needed to coat the bucatini. Serve hot, sprinkled with the remaining ¹/₂ cup of Pecorino.

PREPARATION TIPS: The sauce can be made up to 3 days ahead, refrigerated, and reheated while you cook the bucatini.

FOUR HANDMADE PASTAS

In rural areas of Latium like the Ciociaria (between Frosinone and Cassino), fresh fettuccine are tossed in a long-simmered chicken-giblet sauce; across the region, *quadrucci* ("little squares") of pasta are boiled in a creamy pea broth. *Lombrichelli*—stout spaghetti from Viterbo—are made with nothing more than flour and water, then topped with tomato sauce. But the most unusual handmade pasta is *frigulozzi,* made from flour, yeast, and salt, shaped into sticks, boiled, and served with tomato or meat sauce.

Gnocchi di Semolino

Baked Semolina Gnocchi

Romans claim that they invented potato gnocchi—likely untrue, since the earliest recipes for the dish seem to hail from Liguria, where potatoes were adopted faster than elsewhere in Italy upon their arrival from the New World. Yet as much as they love potato gnocchi, Romans are even more partial to semolina gnocchi baked until golden under a dusting of Parmigiano and pats of sweet butter.

SEMOLINA VERSUS DURUM FLOUR

Durum flour and semolina flour are both derived from durum wheat, a particularly hard strain of wheat. Durum flour is powdery, just like other wheat flours, and is used for bread, especially in southern Italy, Sicily, and Sardinia. Semolina flour is ground much more coarsely, although the precise texture of the grind depends on its intended use in the kitchen: fine for desserts, pasta, or semolina gnocchi (above) and coarse for *fregola* (page 359) or couscous. Even fine semolina flour is much coarser than durum flour, so never substitute one for the other when cooking or baking. See Sources (page 372) to purchase both.

SERVES 6

4 cups (1 quart) whole milk
1⅔ cups semolina flour
¼ teaspoon salt
6 tablespoons (¾ stick) unsalted butter, plus
    extra for greasing the baking dish
2 extra-large egg yolks
¾ cup freshly grated Parmigiano-Reggiano

Bring the milk to a gentle boil in a heavy 2-quart pot. Pour in the semolina flour in a thin stream, whisking all the while to avoid lumps. Reduce the heat to low and cook for 30 minutes, stirring almost constantly with a wooden spoon.

Remove the pot from the heat. Stir in the salt, 3 tablespoons of the butter, the egg yolks, and ¼ cup of the Parmigiano. Moisten a 12 × 14-inch tray with a wet towel. Spread the hot semolina porridge onto the damp tray; level the top with a spatula. Cool to room temperature.

Preheat the oven to 375°F.

Butter a 12-inch round baking dish. Using a 3-inch round cookie cutter, cut the cooled porridge into disks. These are the gnocchi. Line the buttered dish with the trimmings and top with 2 layers of gnocchi, dotting each layer with the remaining 3 tablespoons of butter and sprinkling with the remaining ½ cup of Parmigiano. Bake in the preheated oven 30 minutes, or until golden on top, and serve hot.

PREPARATION TIPS: The gnocchi can be layered in the baking dish up to 2 days ahead and refrigerated before baking.

La Minestra di Farro degli Antichi Rivista

The Roman Legionnaire's Farro Soup Revisited

Farro (Triticum dicoccum *in Latin, emmer wheat in English) is the oldest strain of wheat grown in Italy, cooked whole or cracked in soups and ground into flour for bread and polenta. This two-spiked grain is often confused with spelt (*Triticum spelta*), which has only one spike. Farro was a staple in the days of the Roman legionnaires, given by the bagful to soldiers and cooked into sustaining soups; it was so important to the ancient Roman diet, in fact, that it formed the root of the Italian word for flour,* farina. *In Latium, as in Umbria, soups are usually made from cracked farro, but that is hard to come by in North America; in any case, I prefer the texture of whole farro, which is what I suggest you use for the soup below. If you would like to crack whole farro, crush the grains in a flour mill or a mortar with a sturdy pestle before soaking them in water.*

SERVES 4

¼ cup extra-virgin olive oil

¼ pound Pancetta, minced

2 garlic cloves, minced

1 medium yellow onion, minced

2 tablespoons minced Italian parsley

12 basil leaves, torn

1 teaspoon minced marjoram

4 plum tomatoes, peeled (see page 369), seeded, and diced

6 cups (1½ quarts) Chicken Broth (page 368), plus extra if needed

½ teaspoon salt

¼ teaspoon freshly ground black pepper

2 cups farro, soaked 24 hours in cool water to cover

½ cup freshly grated Pecorino Romano

Heat 2 tablespoons of the olive oil in a heavy 2-quart pot over a medium flame. Add the Pancetta, garlic, and onion and cook 5 minutes. Stir in the parsley, basil, and marjoram and cook 2 minutes. Fold in the tomatoes and cook 5 minutes. Add the broth, bring to a boil, and season with the salt and ⅛ teaspoon of the pepper.

Drain the farro and stir it into the pot. Return the liquid to a boil, then reduce the heat to medium, cover, and cook for 45 minutes, or until the farro is al dente, adding more broth if needed.

Ladle into 4 bowls, drizzle equally with the remaining 2 tablespoons of olive oil, sprinkle with the Pecorino and the remaining ⅛ teaspoon of pepper, and serve hot.

THE ROMAN CHEESE BOARD

IF LOVERS OF COW'S MILK CHEESE should visit northern regions like Val d'Aosta, Piedmont, and Lombardy, lovers of sheep's milk cheese should head to Latium. The Roman shepherds refined the art of making cheese from ewe's milk thousands of years ago. Latium's most widespread sheep's milk cheese is Pecorino Romano, made from pasteurized milk, salted, rubbed with olive oil, and aged eight to twelve months. Despite its appellation, however, much of it is produced in Sardinia. Also misleading in name is Pecorino Toscano, a firm, grainy, pungent cheese made in Latium as well as Tuscany. Caciotta Romana, a pale, semi-soft cheese with a thin rind, is flavored with saffron; it is round, flat, and milky when aged two weeks and cylindrical and sharp when aged a few months. Ricotta Romana is tangy and creamy, sold fresh for use in desserts and pastries or salted and dried until firm for grating. All of these cheeses are exported to North America; see Sources (page 372).

A SOUP MADE OF RAGS

Like all pastoral cuisines, that of Latium offers a spectacular number of soups: after all, soups are cheap and nourishing, managing to stretch a bit of vegetables, grains, or meat trimmings into a satisfying first course. The prized thin-skinned lentils of the towns of Onano, Grotte di Castro, and San Lorenzo Nuovo are perfect for soups. But other legumes and beans are transformed into soups too: *scafata* features fava beans and pork rind, and a dense pea soup is studded with artichokes and Guanciale. One soup calls for cooking pasta and broccoli in a broth made from skate (the skate is then served as a second course) and another, known as *stracciatella* (from *stracci,* meaning "rags"), is thickened with beaten eggs and grated Parmigiano.

Luccio Brodettato alla Romana

Pike in Velvety Egg-Lemon Sauce

As in the days of the Roman Empire, when they were rare and costly, fish and seafood still play a minor role in Latium's kitchen, except near the coast. Standard dishes include hake braised with tomatoes and fresh peas; strips of salt cod dredged in a wine-scented batter and deep-fried; baby squid or cuttlefish stewed with vinegar or lemon juice; tiny eel called ciriole, fished in the Tevere River, sautéed with garlic and parsley; and pike from Latium's many lakes, poached until tender and topped with a warm egg-lemon sauce, as below. Cooks in central Italy are fond of creamy egg-lemon sauces, reminiscent of the avgolemono of Greece, which they use to thicken Easter lamb soups and to nap lamb, goat, turkey, chicken giblets, or sweetwater fish. This love of egg-lemon sauces may have its roots in Constantinople, the seat of the Byzantine Empire and the eastern part of the Roman Empire, founded in A.D. 330.

SERVES 4

1 pike (2 pounds), head on, scaled, gutted, and rinsed (substitute trout)

1½ cups dry white wine

1 carrot, chopped

1 celery stalk, chopped

1 bay leaf

4 Italian parsley sprigs

¾ teaspoon salt

2 tablespoons (¼ stick) unsalted butter

2 tablespoons unbleached all-purpose flour

3 tablespoons plus 1 teaspoon fresh lemon juice (from 1 large lemon)

1 tablespoon extra-virgin olive oil

2 extra-large egg yolks

Place the pike in a shallow, long, and wide pan (a fish poacher is ideal). Add the wine, carrot, celery, bay leaf, parsley, ½ teaspoon of the salt, and enough cool water to cover the fish by ½ inch.

Bring to a gentle boil, then reduce the heat to medium-low and cook, uncovered, for 15 minutes, or until the pike is done, spooning the cooking liquid over the fish continuously with a spoon. Cool the pike in the broth, then skin and fillet it, remove the pin bones, and place on a platter. Measure 1 cup of the broth (reserve the remaining broth for soup or risotto).

Melt the butter in a 1-quart pot over medium heat. Whisk in the flour and cook, whisking all the while, for 5 minutes, never allowing the mixture to brown. Add the measured cup of broth and bring to a boil, still whisking. Cook 10 minutes, or until thick, then remove from the heat. Whisk in the lemon juice, olive oil, egg yolks, and the remaining ¼ teaspoon of salt, and pour over the pike. Serve immediately.

Coda alla Vaccinara

The Cowmen's Braised Oxtail with Celery

The old slaughterhouse in Rome stood in a neighborhood called Testaccio. Its workers, the vaccinari, or "cowmen," were often paid with the humbler parts of the animals they butchered. Ingenious and frugal—or married to ingenious and frugal women—they turned these scraps into tasty dishes that have become symbols of their city's cuisine. The delicate braised oxtail below is one of the vaccinari's offerings; other specialties are rigatoni con la pajata, sauced with calf's intestines, and tripe stewed with carrots, celery, and tomatoes. These dishes belong to a tradition known as the quinto quarto ("fifth quarter"), because they are made from a primary ingredient that is not even considered part of the animal.

SERVES 4

2 pounds oxtail, cut into 4-inch pieces
⅓ cup extra-virgin olive oil
2 medium yellow onions, minced
2 carrots, minced
2 garlic cloves, minced
¼ cup minced Italian parsley
½ teaspoon salt
¼ teaspoon freshly ground black pepper
1 cup dry white wine
2 tablespoons canned strained Italian plum tomatoes
2 cups Beef Broth (page 368)
8 celery stalks, leaves on, stalks thinly sliced and leaves chopped

Rinse the oxtail. Bring 4 quarts of water to a boil and drop in the oxtail. Cook 5 minutes, drain, and blot dry.

Heat the olive oil in a heavy 3-quart pot over a medium-high flame. Add the oxtail and cook until browned all over, stirring often, about 10 minutes. Fold in the onions, carrots, garlic, and parsley and cook 5 minutes. Season with the salt and pepper.

DINING WITH THE SHEPHERDS

The hills and plains of Latium are home to a centuries-old sheepherding tradition and to a host of dishes featuring *abbacchio,* milk-fed lamb slaughtered when it is barely twenty days old. Lamb is prepared *alla cacciatora* ("hunter's style") with lard, garlic, sage, rosemary, vinegar, and anchovies; chops are cooked *a scottadito* ("burn the fingers"), to be eaten by hand at outdoor feasts; Easter calls for roasted leg of lamb; and the ultimate harbinger of spring is lamb *braciole* braised with artichokes. Goat too is well loved, prepared much like lamb. And since every part of the animal is put to good use in Latium's kitchens, innards are a staple: calf's innards are cooked with wine, and humble cuts of beef and pork are cooked slowly in a hermetically sealed pot with potatoes and vegetables until deliciously tender.

Add 1 tablespoon of the wine at a time, scraping the bottom of the pot, adding more wine only when the previous addition has evaporated; it will take about 15 minutes. Add the tomatoes and broth, bring the liquid to a boil, reduce the heat to medium-low, cover, and cook for 4 hours, stirring every 30 minutes.

Fold in the celery and cook 30 more minutes, covered. Serve hot.

PREPARATION TIPS: Cook the oxtail up to 2 days ahead and refrigerate; reheat gently over a medium flame, covered, before serving.

Uova in Trippa alla Romana

Egg Ribbons in Tomato Sauce with Pecorino and Fresh Mint

In this recipe, frittate are cut into strips that resemble tripe (hence the Italian name, uova in trippa, or "eggs in the style of tripe") and sauced with tomato, Pecorino, and mint, much like tripe would be. A variation calls for a clove-scented beef and tomato ragù called garofalato instead of tomato sauce, but I am partial to this lighter vegetarian version.

SERVES 4

6 extra-large eggs
2 tablespoons minced Italian parsley
¼ teaspoon salt
⅛ teaspoon freshly ground black pepper
2 tablespoons extra-virgin olive oil, plus extra for greasing the baking dish
2 cups Tomato Sauce (page 369)
½ cup mint leaves, julienned
½ cup plus 1 tablespoon freshly grated Pecorino Romano, plus extra for passing at the table

Preheat the oven to 400°F.

In a medium bowl, beat the eggs with the parsley, salt, and pepper. Heat an 8-inch skillet over a high flame for 2 minutes. Grease with ½ tablespoon of the olive oil and pour in one-quarter of the egg mixture, tilting the pan to spread the eggs. Cook until set on the bottom, about 1 minute, then turn and cook until the other side is also set, about 1 minute. This is the frittata. Remove to a plate. Make 3 more frittate in the same manner, greasing the skillet each time with ½ tablespoon of the olive oil.

Roll each frittata over itself jelly roll–style and cut into ¼-inch-wide strips with a sharp knife. Toss with the tomato sauce, mint, and all but 1 tablespoon of the Pecorino in an oiled 12-inch baking dish. Sprinkle with the remaining tablespoon of Pecorino and bake in the preheated oven 15 minutes. Serve hot, passing additional Pecorino at the table.

FAVORITE FRITTATE

Frittata is the ultimate comfort food to many Italians. Similar to an omelet but simpler to make since it is turned rather than folded, frittata can include any manner of vegetable, cheese, meat, or fish. Certain regions, especially Trentino–Alto Adige, even make sweet *frittate* filled with fruit or jam. In Latium, frittata easily becomes a main course thanks to the addition of a rich sauce and a generous sprinkling of Pecorino.

Piselli al Prosciutto

Spring Peas with Diced Prosciutto

In the spring, cooks in Latium pair fava beans or peas with Prosciutto, creating a simple stew that tastes as delicious on its own as it does over pasta with a dusting of Pecorino. While this dish is best made with just-shelled peas fresh from the garden (their sugars convert to starch very quickly once plucked from the plant), I'm unable to hold off until peas are ready in April, and make it year-round with frozen peas.

SERVES 4

One 3-ounce slice **Prosciutto di Parma, fat attached**
4 tablespoons (½ stick) **unsalted butter**
1 medium **yellow onion, minced**
2 cups **shelled fresh peas or thawed frozen peas**
¼ teaspoon **freshly ground black pepper**
Four ¼-inch-thick × 6-inch-wide slices **country bread, halved**

Cut the fat from the Prosciutto and mince it. Dice the meaty part of the Prosciutto and set aside.

In a heavy 1-quart pot over medium heat, melt the Prosciutto fat and 2 tablespoons of the butter. Add the onion and cook 5 minutes. Fold in the peas and pepper and cook, covered, 15 minutes. Fold in the diced Prosciutto and cook 2 minutes.

Meanwhile, melt 1 tablespoon of the butter in a 12-inch skillet over medium-high heat. Cook 2 slices of the bread until golden on both sides, about 3 minutes per side, turning once. Repeat with the remaining tablespoon of butter and 2 slices of the bread. Serve the peas hot, accompanied by the bread.

ARTICHOKES AND PUNTARELLE

Latium's volcanic soil is full of mineral deposits that lend an exalted flavor to the local produce. Of all vegetables, most prized are artichokes and a variety of chicory known as *puntarelle*. Baked or sautéed, stuffed with anchovies, garlic, and bread crumbs, or simply with mint and garlic, artichokes are one of spring's most anxiously awaited offerings. And no artichoke dish compares to *carciofi alla giudea*, a Jewish specialty made by frying upside-down artichokes in hot olive oil with a few droplets of water until they resemble open chrysanthemums. To make the puntarelle salad that Romans are so fond of, *Cichorium intybus*, an elongated variety of chicory, is cut into long strips, soaked in cool water until it curls, and sauced with a fragrant anchovy-and-garlic dressing.

LATIUM'S WINES

Like Campania and Sicily, Latium has a rich volcanic soil. Viticulture has long flourished in the Castelli Romani, the volcanic hills surrounding Rome. Malvasia and Trebbiano, as well as the more obscure indigenous Cesanese grown in the province of Frosinone, are the most prominent varietals. The Castelli Romani wine area comprises the following six appellations: Colli Albani; Colli Lanuvini; Frascati; Marino; Montecompatri Colonna; and Velletri. Frascati, the best known of these, is a white wine vinified from Malvasia and Trebbiano and offers soft, refreshing citrus notes. The memorably named Est! Est!! Est!!! is a delicately aromatic white with a dry, persistent, balanced flavor, and has been made in Montefiascone, in the province of Viterbo, since the thirteenth century. Legend has it that a prelate's servant was sent ahead of his master to taste wine in local taverns and write *"Est"* on the tavern door if the wine was good. When he reached Montefiascone, he loved the wine so much that he wrote *"Est! Est!! Est!!!"* While Latium has traditionally emphasized white wines rather than reds, recent efforts at vinifying reds, especially blends of Merlot and Cabernet, have been promising.

Taralli all'Anice

Anise Taralli

These crunchy cookies are made in every southern Italian region, but the best I've tasted were at Ristorante La Veranda in San Felice Circeo, a pretty little town facing the Isole Pontine (where Ulysses is said to have fallen in love with the sorceress Circe). They can be savored with sweet wine at the end of a meal or munched on as a snack throughout the day.

MAKES ABOUT 10 DOZEN
2-INCH COOKIES

2½ cups unbleached all-purpose flour,
    plus extra for the counter
1⅔ cups sugar
¼ teaspoon salt
1½ teaspoons anise seeds
½ cup extra-virgin olive oil
⅓ cup plus 1 tablespoon dry white wine,
    plus extra if needed

Preheat the oven to 375°F.

In a large bowl, mix the flour, ⅔ cup of the sugar, the salt, and the anise seeds. Stir in the olive oil and wine; turn out onto a counter. Knead until a smooth and supple dough forms, about 5 minutes, adding a little wine if the dough is dry or a little flour if it is sticky. Snip off hazelnut-sized pieces of dough, roll each into a 4-inch-long log, and join the two ends to create a sphere with a large hole in the middle and slightly overlapping ends. These are taralli.

Arrange the taralli at least 1 inch apart on two 11 × 17-inch baking sheets. Bake in the preheated oven for 22 minutes, or until still pale on top but golden on the bottom and around the edges. Dredge while still hot in the remaining cup of sugar, pressing to help the sugar adhere on both sides. Serve at room temperature.

PREPARATION TIPS: The taralli can be stored in airtight tins for up to 2 weeks.

Pizza di Polenta e Ricotta

Sweet Polenta and Ricotta Cake

A golden cake redolent of cinnamon, sprinkled with pine nuts, studded with raisins: such is this homey polenta cake whose secret weapon is a good dose of sheep's milk Ricotta. Today this decidedly rustic dessert is usually made without the Ricotta and cinnamon, but I like the older version for its creaminess and tang. Be sure to serve it piping hot for the most tender texture. Since finding sheep's milk Ricotta can be a challenge in North America (see Sources, page 372), you can approximate the flavor of it by whisking 1 tablespoon of freshly grated Pecorino Romano into every pound of fresh cow's milk Ricotta.

OTHER RICOTTA-BASED SWEETS

Given the prominence of sheep in Latium, many of the region's desserts call for sheep's milk Ricotta. There is Ricotta beaten with sugar, drowned in espresso or sambuca (an anise-based liqueur); a semolina and Ricotta pudding; Ricotta fritters; a Ricotta tart bedecked with a lattice crust; a Ricotta cake enriched with lard; a sweet focaccia filled with Ricotta; and a yeasted Easter bread reminiscent of one baked in Umbria and the Marches, made with Ricotta rather than Pecorino.

SERVES 8

¼ cup raisins

½ pound fresh sheep's milk Ricotta

½ cup plus 2 tablespoons sugar

1½ cups coarse cornmeal

⅛ teaspoon ground cinnamon

3 tablespoons unsalted butter, cut into 8 cubes, plus extra for greasing the cake pan

¼ cup pine nuts

In a small bowl, soak the raisins in warm water to cover for 15 minutes. Drain and blot dry.

Meanwhile, preheat the oven to 300°F.

In a large bowl, beat the Ricotta and 2 cups of water with a whisk until smooth. Whisk in the sugar, then the cornmeal in a thin stream. Fold in the cinnamon and plumped raisins.

Generously butter an 8-inch springform cake pan. Pour in the cornmeal batter and sprinkle with the pine nuts. Top with the 3 tablespoons of cubed butter and bake in the preheated oven for 1 hour.

Carefully unmold the sides of the cake pan; place the cake, with the bottom of the cake pan still attached, on a platter. Cut the cake into wedges and serve hot.

CLOCKWISE FROM ABOVE: *Roasted Peppers in Bagna Caôda (Piedmont)* • *Greens-Stuffed Pastry Half-Moons (Emilia-Romagna)* • *Towering Seafood Salad (Liguria)*

ABOVE: *Flaky Griddle Bread with Greens (Marches)* • LEFT: *Marinated Olives (Sicily)*

ABOVE: *Tomato-and-Cheese-Topped Potato Pie (Apulia)* • LEFT: *Soaked Bread with Sweet Onion, Tomato, and Basil (Basilicata)*

CLOCKWISE FROM ABOVE: *The Roman Legionnaire's Farro Soup Revisited (Latium)* • *"Thirsty" Pizza (Molise)* • *Fregola Soup with Cockles (Sardinia)*

LEFT: *Orecchiette with Wilted Arugula and Tomatoes (Apulia)* •
BELOW: *Beet-Filled Ravioli with Poppy Seeds (Veneto)*

CLOCKWISE FROM ABOVE: *Rice with Fresh Spring Peas (Veneto)* •
Butternut Squash Gnocchi in Rosemary Butter (Lombardy) • *"Guitar
Pasta" in Lamb and Sweet Pepper Ragù (Abruzzo)*

CLOCKWISE FROM ABOVE: *Baked Potatoes, Onions, and Tomatoes with Oregano and Bread Crumbs (Basilicata) • Asparagus in Egg-Horseradish Sauce (Trentino–Alto Adige) • Garganelli with Creamy Ragù (Emilia-Romagna)*

ABOVE: *Stuffed Escarole Bundles (Campania)* •
LEFT: *Luciano's Focaccia (Liguria)*

A Taste of Ancient Rome

T's a familiar image: the citizens of ancient Rome, resting on bent elbows on a triclinium, gorging on grapes, cheeses, sweetmeats, roasts, exotic seafood, and staggering amounts of wine. But is this what life was really like in Rome two thousand years ago? Certainly not for the majority of people. As in all societies, what the ancient Romans ate—and how often—was a function of how well-off they were. Slaves, peasants, and ordinary plebeians ate bread, fruit, watery vegetable soups, and grain porridges (the ancestors of today's polenta); their bread was dark, made from coarse, whole-grain, mixed flours. The rich mostly ate bread obtained from *siligo* (a flour so white it was used to powder the face), olives and olive oil, legumes cooked into thick soups, and hearty grain porridges, rounding out their meals with dried, smoked, or fresh meat, sheep's milk cheese, and wine.

On special occasions, the wealthy threw banquets and noble guests did indeed indulge in gustatory orgies. They started with antipasti (*gustum* in Latin), which might have included fried anchovies and a nettle or greens pie. Next came the first course (*mensa prima*), perhaps stuffed squab, pork with garlic and spices, or braised lamb with coriander. A dessert (*mensa secunda*) would then arrive, possibly a sheep's milk cheesecake or fried bread slathered with honey. As for the flavor of these foods, there were three factors that gave them their "ancient Roman" character: the tendency to mingle the sweet and savory within a dish; a generous hand with herbs and spices such as rosemary, cumin, rue, coriander, celery seed, and cinnamon, added together in varying combinations; and the use of a fermented fish paste called *garum,* the ancestor of Worcestershire sauce and a close relative of Southeast Asia's fish sauce, which provided a salty, fishy, ripe flavor.

Abruzzo

Pizza Rustica
Cinnamon-Scented Pie Stuffed with Prosciutto, Cheese, and Eggs

Maccheroni alla Chitarra con Ragù d'Agnello e Peperoni
"Guitar Pasta" in Lamb and Sweet Pepper Ragù

Ravioli di Scamorza allo Zafferano
Scamorza Ravioli in Saffron Cream Sauce

Polenta sulla Spianatoia
Polenta Topped with Sausages in Spicy Tomato Sauce

Scrippelle Imbusse
Delicate Cheese-Filled Crêpes in Broth

Scapece di Razza alla Vastese
Fried Skate in Aromatic Vinegar Marinade

Pollo all'Abruzzese
Chicken with Roasted Peppers and Onions

Agnello con le Olive
Lamb Scaloppine with Black Olives and Lemon

Carciofi Ripieni di Tonno
Tuna-Filled Artichokes

Parrozzo
Chocolate-Covered Almond Cake

D*usk is gathering above the mountain tops,* softening contours, blurring edges. The car noses around a bend, comes face to face with a herd of cows, an ancient man following with a stick and a dog. Soon the path clears. We have a good hour before nightfall, an hour to get to Sulmona, where dinner awaits.

But the cowbells and the mountains silhouetted against the twilight colors are more than we can pass up: it's time to stop, stretch, take in the moment. In Abruzzo, the silence is majestic, broken only by the occasional sound, like the still, glittering lakes that punctuate the countryside. We park at a lookout—every spot along this road is a lookout—and sit, watching night claim the valley below and peaks above.

Initially called Aprutium, perhaps after the Praetutii, an Italic tribe who lived here, Abruzzo was conquered by the Romans and dominated by the Goths and Byzantines after the fall of the empire. During the early Middle Ages, the Lombards gained control, followed by the Normans, Angevins, Spanish, and Bourbons under the Kingdom of Naples. In 1861, Abruzzi (the plural form, given its division under the Bourbons) and Molise joined the newly formed Kingdom of Italy, remaining a single entity until 1963, when Molise became a distinct region. Not surprisingly, overlap between Abruzzo's and Molise's cuisines is strong, although Abruzzo's is less austere, thanks to the region's more generous coastline and gentler winter climate.

One of the least populated regions in Italy, in great part because of its rugged terrain, Abruzzo is both a land of mountains and a land of sea, and has developed two diverse cuisines as a result. High in the mountains, where even fewer people make their home, cooks knead flour and water into toothsome gnocchi, cure their own hams, make wise use of every part of the pig or calf. Near the coast, fish is a way of life: cooked into thick *brodetti*, battered and fried, or marinated in a vinegary brine for days. Abruzzo's political capital is L'Aquila, but its culinary capital is indisputably Villa Santa Maria: this small village in the province of Chieti has spawned some of Italy's finest chefs, including a man named Palumbo, who moved to Japan and cooked at the emperor's court, and another named Turco, who became head chef of the White House under President Eisenhower.

Aside from the wealth of raw ingredients that make up the Abruzzese cook's palette —sheep's milk cheese, hand-hewn pasta, rosy hams, cured pork belly, lamb, fish and seafood, green olive oil—there are two indigenous ingredients that add fiery color and haunting flavor to local specialties: saffron, grown in the province of L'Aquila and used judiciously in a handful of dishes, and chili pepper, aptly called *diavolicchio* (from *diavolo,* meaning "devil") and tossed into nearly everything that reaches the table.

Favorite Restaurants, Shops, and Places

- COOPERATIVA ALTOPIANO DI NAVELLI, Via Umberto I 17, Civitaretenga, 0862.959163. Buy saffron, the black lentils of Santo Stefano, and more.
- IL CAMINETTO, Via Antica Arischia, Località Cansatessa, L'Aquila, 0862.311410. Must-trys include *pasta e fagioli, Pecorino ai ferri,* and *gnocchi allo zafferano.*
- IL CARPACCIO DELL'HOTEL SPORTING, Via de Gasperi 41, Teramo, 0861.412661. Order the *scrippelle imbusse* and *maccheroni alla chitarra.*
- IULIA, Località Ceppo, Rocca Santa Maria, 0861.63100. Unforgettable *timballo di scrippelle ai porcini.*
- L'ANGOLO DELL'ABRUZZO, Piazza Aldo Moro 8, Carsoli, 0863.997429. Great *minestra di farro ai porcini* and *maccheronacci con fagioli.*

- NORCINERIA PEPPONE, Via Patini 45, L'Aquila, 0862.26147. A wide array of cured meats.
- NURZIA, Piazza Duomo 74-75, L'Aquila, 0862.21002. Historical café; buy the moist chocolate torrone the city is famous for.
- RISTORANTE RIGOLETTO, Via Stazione Introdacqua 46, Sulmona, 0864.55529. Celestino Le Donne's *ravioli di Scamorza con zafferano* are amazing.
- TRE MARIE, Via Tre Marie 3, L'Aquila, 0862.413191. Don't miss out on the *scrigno alle Tre Marie.*
- VILLA MAIELLA, Via Sette Dolori 30, Guardiagrele, 0871.809319. Sample the *chitarrine alle erbe* and *farricello.*

Telephone country code: 011.39

Pizza Rustica

Cinnamon-Scented Pie Stuffed with Prosciutto, Cheese, and Eggs

Variations on this pie are served at holiday meals, especially Easter, across central and southern Italy. Some Abruzzese cooks prefer a short-crust dough rather than a yeasted one; the dough for the pie below resembles brioche.

SERVES 8 AS AN ANTIPASTO OR 4 AS A MAIN COURSE

3 cups unbleached all-purpose flour

1 tablespoon instant yeast

$^{1}/_{2}$ teaspoon salt

1 tablespoon sugar

8 extra-large eggs

$^{1}/_{3}$ cup plus 2 teaspoons extra-virgin olive oil, plus extra for greasing the bowl and pizza pan

$^{1}/_{4}$ pound thinly sliced mildly spicy salami

$^{1}/_{2}$ pound Scamorza, thinly sliced

$^{1}/_{4}$ cup freshly grated aged Pecorino Romano

Pinch ground cinnamon

$^{1}/_{4}$ teaspoon freshly ground black pepper

$^{1}/_{4}$ pound thinly sliced Prosciutto di Parma, Carpegna, or San Daniele

$^{1}/_{4}$ pound young sheep's milk cheese, such as Marzolino or Fiore Sardo, thinly sliced

In a food processor, mix the flour, yeast, salt, and sugar. With the motor running, add $^{1}/_{2}$ cup of warm (110°F) water. Add 3 of the eggs and the olive oil. Process 45 seconds, adding warm water as needed until a ball forms around the blade. Add a little water if the dough is dry or a little flour if it is sticky. Turn out into an oiled bowl, cover, and let rise at room temperature until doubled, about 1 hour.

Place 2 of the eggs in a 1-quart pot, add cool water to cover by 2 inches, and bring to a boil over medium heat; cook 12 minutes. Drain, cool, shell, and slice.

Preheat the oven to 450°F.

Oil a deep 10-inch pizza pan. Cut the dough into 2 pieces, 1 twice as large as the other. Roll out the larger piece on a floured counter into a 16-inch circle. Line the pan with it. Top with the salami, Scamorza, sliced eggs, Pecorino, cinnamon, pepper, Prosciutto, and sliced sheep's milk cheese. Beat the 3 remaining eggs; pour all but 1 tablespoon of the beaten eggs over the filling.

Roll out the second piece of dough into an 11-inch circle. Place over the filling, press the edges to seal, and cut off the excess. Seal the edges. Brush with the reserved tablespoon of beaten egg and let rest 15 minutes (this allows the gluten in the dough to relax). Bake 30 minutes in the oven, or until the crust is golden and lightly crisp. Serve hot or warm.

PREPARATION TIPS: Prepare the dough and let it rise in the refrigerator up to 24 hours; bring to room temperature before proceeding.

Maccheroni alla Chitarra con Ragù d'Agnello e Peperoni

"Guitar Pasta" in Lamb and Sweet Pepper Ragù

Maccheroni alla chitarra, the region's proudest pasta, derive their name from the instrument used to cut the pasta: a wooden frame on which parallel strings are mounted. If you don't have a chitarra ("guitar"), use 1 pound of dried maccheroni alla chitarra instead. See Sources (page 372) to buy a chitarra.

SERVES 6

1 pound boneless lamb shoulder, trimmed of fat and sinew, cut into 1/8-inch dice
2 tablespoons plus 1/2 teaspoon salt
1/4 teaspoon freshly ground black pepper
1/2 cup extra-virgin olive oil
4 garlic cloves, sliced
4 bay leaves
1 cup dry white wine
4 plum tomatoes, peeled (see page 369), seeded, and diced
2 red bell peppers, cut into long, thin strips
2 yellow bell peppers, cut into long, thin strips
1 recipe Pasta Dough (page 370)
Unbleached all-purpose flour for the counter
1 cup freshly grated Pecorino Romano

In a medium bowl, toss the lamb with 1/2 teaspoon of the salt and the pepper; cover and refrigerate for 2 to 24 hours.

Heat the olive oil in a 4-quart sauté pan over a high flame. Add the garlic and bay leaves and cook 1 minute. Add the lamb and cook until browned all over, stirring often, about 10 minutes. Deglaze with the wine; when it evaporates, after about 10 minutes, add the tomatoes and red and yellow peppers. Cover and simmer 2 hours, stirring once in a while and adding a little water if needed. Discard the bay leaves.

Meanwhile, make the dough and let it rest according to instructions on page 370. Cut the dough into 4 pieces. Working with 1 piece at a time and keeping the others covered, roll out each piece on a lightly floured counter into a nearly transparent rectangle. Cut into rectangles of the same size as the stringed part of the "guitar." Lay 1 rectangle over the strings and press down with the rolling pin to cut. These are the maccheroni alla chitarra. Toss with flour, spread out in a single layer on a floured tray, and cover with a towel.

Bring 6 quarts of water to a boil. Add the maccheroni and the remaining 2 tablespoons of salt and cook until al dente, about 3 minutes. Drain, reserving 1/2 cup of the pasta cooking water. Toss the maccheroni with the ragù and the reserved cooking water in a bowl. Serve hot, passing the Pecorino at the table.

PREPARATION TIPS: Prepare the maccheroni up to 12 hours ahead, spread out in a single layer on a floured tray, and refrigerate, covered with a towel. Make the ragù up to 3 days ahead and refrigerate; reheat as you boil the maccheroni.

Ravioli di Scamorza allo Zafferano

Scamorza Ravioli in Saffron Cream Sauce

Filled pastas in Abruzzo are luxuriant. Some, like lasagne, resemble those of Naples, a reflection of years the two regions spent under Bourbon rule: fillings include ragù, meatballs, hard-boiled eggs, and Scamorza and Pecorino cheeses. The ravioli below make the most of two Abruzzese products: Scamorza and saffron. They are a specialty of Celestino Le Donne at Ristorante Rigoletto in Sulmona. Celestino is a maestro della panarda (page 240) who re-creates the Lucullan feast every two years, cooking over fifty dishes for the lucky souls in attendance. Some cooks opt for Ricotta rather than Scamorza in the filling; the Ricotta ravioli are fried for feasts.

A GRILLED ANTIPASTO

There is no better way to start—or end—a meal in Abruzzo than with Scamorza cheese grilled over glowing embers. The best Scamorza is made from the milk of cows that graze at an altitude of 4,500 feet: the cows munch on mountain flowers, herbs, and wild grasses that imbue their milk and cheese with powerful aromas.

SERVES 6

For the dough:
3½ cups unbleached all-purpose flour, plus extra
    for the counter
⅓ teaspoon salt
4 extra-large eggs

For the filling:
¾ pound Scamorza, finely grated
¼ pound fresh Ricotta
1 extra-large egg
¼ teaspoon salt
¼ teaspoon sugar
¼ teaspoon freshly grated nutmeg
⅛ teaspoon ground cinnamon

For the sauce:
½ cup Chicken Broth (page 368)
½ teaspoon saffron pistils
4 tablespoons (½ stick) unsalted butter
1 cup heavy cream
¼ teaspoon salt
⅛ teaspoon freshly ground black pepper

To cook and serve:
2 tablespoons salt
¼ cup freshly grated Pecorino Romano
10 basil leaves, julienned
2 ounces Prosciutto di Parma, julienned

Make the dough according to instructions on page 370 using the ingredients listed above, adding enough cold water (about ¼ cup) to form a firm dough. Knead 5 minutes, or until smooth, adding a little water if the dough is dry or a little flour if it is sticky. Shape into a ball, wrap, and let rest 30 minutes.

Prepare the filling by beating all the ingredients in a large bowl.

Cut the dough into 4 pieces. Working with 1 piece at a time and keeping the others covered, roll out into a nearly transparent sheet using a pasta machine. On the bottom half of each sheet, spoon dollops of the filling about ¾ inch apart. Use a pastry brush dipped in water to moisten around the mounds of filling, to help seal the ravioli later. Flip the top half of the sheet over to cover the mounds of filling, lining up the two edges; press around the filling with your hand to squeeze out any air pockets. Cut into squares with a fluted pastry wheel. These are the ravioli. Spread out in a single layer on a floured tray, cover with a towel, and refrigerate until needed.

Make the sauce: Bring ¼ cup of the broth to a boil in a 1-quart pot over medium heat; transfer to a small bowl and dissolve the saffron in it; set aside 5 minutes.

In the same pot, heat the butter, cream, and remaining ¼ cup of broth. Bring to a boil, reduce the heat to medium-high, and cook 5 minutes, or until reduced by two-thirds. Add the reserved saffron broth, salt, and pepper; cook 2 minutes.

To cook, bring 6 quarts of water to a boil. Add the ravioli and the 2 tablespoons of salt and cook until al dente, about 3 minutes. Remove to a bowl with a slotted spoon. Fold in the sauce and sprinkle with the Pecorino, basil, and Prosciutto. Serve hot.

PREPARATION TIPS: Shape the ravioli up to 12 hours ahead, spread out in a single layer on a floured tray, and refrigerate, covered with a towel.

THE GOLDEN SAFFRON OF L'AQUILA

Saffron, at a cost of $7,000 a pound, is the world's costliest spice, added with an alchemist's touch to broths and rices and pastas, stirred into simmering stews, dissolved in bubbling sauces. Obtained from the stigmas (the end part of the pistils) of *Crocus sativus* that are hand-picked and dried in a painstakingly precise procedure, saffron has long been used as a dye and to add a golden hue to stained glass. The Abruzzesi have been growing saffron for five hundred years, ever since a Dominican father named Santucci returned from Spain with some bulbs and planted them in his native town of Navelli. Today Abruzzo is Italy's largest saffron producer and sells most of its cherished spice to other Italian regions and European countries. The Abruzzesi add saffron to artisanal cheeses, stir it into a creamy zucchini-blossom sauce for pasta, and dissolve it in a vinegar marinade for fish (page 237).

Polenta sulla Spianatoia

Polenta Topped with Sausages in Spicy Tomato Sauce

This dish is meant to be shared—literally. *Abruzzese custom dictates that hot polenta be poured onto a marble or wooden table called a* spianatoia, *leveled with a spoon, and topped with sausage ragù. Everyone digs in with forks, starting from the outside in, until the forks meet in the middle. The host sometimes places a whole sausage in the center, and the only way to get it is to eat faster than everyone else. Less customary than* polenta sulla spianatoia, *but equally beguiling, is a savory polenta pie dotted with raisins and salami.*

GARLIC WORTHY OF A CELEBRATION

A few miles from the town of Sulmona, in the hills that surround the villages of Torre di Nolfi and Campo di Fano, the Abruzzesi grow a unique variety of garlic whose papery inner skin is a deep red. The garlic is planted in November and harvested in July, when it becomes the star of town-wide fests: growers sell wreaths and braids of the garlic, local restaurants cook garlic-laced specialties, and everyone indulges in a taste of this aromatic member of the lily family.

SERVES 4

¼ cup extra-virgin olive oil
1 medium yellow onion, minced
2 garlic cloves, minced
1 celery stalk, minced
5 basil leaves, torn
¼ to ½ teaspoon chili flakes
1 pound spicy Italian sausage, casings removed and crumbled, plus 1 whole spicy Italian sausage (¼ pound), casings on and pierced
¼ cup tomato paste
½ teaspoon salt
⅛ teaspoon freshly ground black pepper
1 recipe Polenta (page 371)
½ cup freshly grated Pecorino Romano

Heat the olive oil in a 12-inch sauté pan over a medium-high flame. Add the onion, garlic, celery, basil, and chili, and cook 8 minutes, stirring often. Add the crumbled sausage and cook, stirring, until browned, about 10 minutes. Stir in the tomato paste and 1 cup of water; bring the liquid to a gentle boil. Add the whole sausage, reduce the heat to medium-low, and cook for 1 hour, covered, adding water if needed. Season the sauce with salt and pepper and keep warm.

Meanwhile, make the polenta according to instructions on page 371.

To serve, place a very large, clean wooden or marble board on the dining table. Pour the polenta onto it and smooth the top. Pour on the sauce, dust with the Pecorino, arrange the whole sausage in the center, and dig in.

PREPARATION TIPS: Prepare the sauce up to 2 days ahead and refrigerate; reheat gently over a medium flame as the polenta cooks.

ABRUZZO'S WINES

ABRUZZO NOW RANKS FIFTH among Italy's wine producers thanks to its mountainous terrain, solar radiation from the Adriatic, and summer heat. Hillside vineyards are planted mostly in Montepulciano d'Abruzzo and Trebbiano d'Abruzzo grapes, and more than one-sixth of total production falls under DOC classification. Montepulciano d'Abruzzo is the region's most important red; plummy, velvety, and dry, it has firm tannins and low acidity. Suitable for aging, it is vinified from 85 percent Montepulciano d'Abruzzo grapes, and should not be confused with Tuscany's Vino Nobile di Montepulciano, which is mostly Sangiovese-based. Cerasuolo d'Abruzzo, a fruity, intense, dry wine with a deep cherry color and light almond aftertaste, is also vinified from Montepulciano d'Abruzzo and is the region's second most important red. Trebbiano d'Abruzzo, a delicate, dry, velvety white, was praised by Cervantes in his *Novelas Ejemplares*. Despite its name, it is vinified not from Trebbiano but from Bombino Bianco grapes; in its best vintages, it has outstanding aging potential.

Scrippelle Imbusse

Delicate Cheese-Filled Crêpes in Broth

Second to Abruzzo's love of pasta is its love of crêpes. But not just any crêpes: golden, cheese-laced crêpes dropped into broth or layered with spinach, artichokes, Mozzarella, and meat. There are many legends concerning the crêpe specialty below, which hails from Teramo. The story most people tell is that it was born when a cheese-filled crêpe meant for a high-ranking officer slipped into a bowl of broth destined for a soldier. The whole was greater than the sum of its parts, and a new dish was inscribed in the annals of Abruzzese cuisine.

A VIRTUOUS SOUP

The best-known Abruzzese soup is Teramo's *virtù* ("the virtue"), a springtime favorite featuring seven types of grains, legumes, herbs, vegetables, and the meat from seven parts of the pig. Tales surround virtù's birth: One holds that seven virtuous women created it, each adding something to the pot; another maintains that it is a virtuous cook's soup, made at winter's end to clean the pantry.

SERVES 6

4 extra-large eggs
1 cup plus 1 tablespoon unbleached
   all-purpose flour
1 cup whole milk, plus extra if needed
1/3 cup plus 2 tablespoons freshly grated
   Parmigiano-Reggiano
3/4 teaspoon salt
2 tablespoons minced Italian parsley
Pinch freshly grated nutmeg
1 tablespoon extra-virgin olive oil
6 cups (1 1/2 quarts) Chicken Broth (page 368)
1/3 cup freshly grated Pecorino Romano

In a medium bowl, beat the eggs and flour with a whisk. Whisk in the milk. Pass through a sieve into a clean bowl. Whisk in 2 tablespoons of the Parmigiano, 1/4 teaspoon of the salt, the parsley, and the nutmeg. The batter should be fluid, like heavy cream; add a little more milk if needed to thin it out.

Heat a 6-inch nonstick pan over a medium-high flame 2 minutes. Rub the pan with the olive oil using kitchen paper. Pour in 3 tablespoons of the batter and tilt the pan immediately to spread the batter. Cook until golden on the bottom, about 2 minutes; flip and cook until the other side is also golden, about 1 minute. Remove to a plate; continue with the remaining batter. Do not grease the pan again. You will need 12 crêpes (freeze extras up to 1 month).

Heat the broth to just below boiling. Season with the remaining 1/2 teaspoon of salt.

Sprinkle the crêpes evenly with the remaining 1/3 cup of Parmigiano and the Pecorino; roll into tight scrolls. Arrange 2 crêpes in each of 6 bowls. Ladle on the broth and serve.

PREPARATION TIPS: The crêpes can be cooked, stuffed, and rolled up to 12 hours ahead and held at room temperature, covered with plastic wrap.

Scapece di Razza alla Vastese

Fried Skate in Aromatic Vinegar Marinade

Many of Abruzzo's most populated centers are port cities like Pescara, and every seaside town offers its specialty. Vasto is renowned for its scapece, a dish whose roots are shared with ceviche and escabeche, *perhaps a result of Spanish dominion. In the old days, cooks prepared massive quantities of fish in* scapece *and let it rest for months in earthenware containers; today the fish is served after it marinates for a day or two. The bed of lettuce is not traditional, but it attenuates the intensity of the vinegar and turns scapece into an elegant antipasto or main course.*

SERVES 4 AS A MAIN COURSE OR 8 AS AN ANTIPASTO

1½ pounds trimmed skate fillets, central
    cartilage removed, cut into 12 pieces
⅓ cup unbleached all-purpose flour
1⅓ cups extra-virgin olive oil
¾ teaspoon salt
½ teaspoon saffron pistils
4 cups (1 quart) white wine vinegar
1 head frisée lettuce, washed and dried
⅛ teaspoon freshly ground black pepper

Rinse the skate and blot it dry. Dredge it in the flour, shaking off the excess.

    Heat 1 cup of the olive oil in a 12-inch skillet over a medium-high flame. Add as many pieces of skate as will fit in a single layer and fry until golden on both sides, turning once, about 3 minutes per side. Remove with a slotted spoon to a platter lined with paper towels and blot dry. Fry the remaining skate in the same manner in the olive oil left in the skillet. Sprinkle all the fried skate with ½ teaspoon of the salt.

    Dissolve the saffron in ¼ cup of the vinegar, and let sit 5 minutes. Heat the remaining 3¾ cups of the vinegar in a medium saucepan over a medium-high flame. Add the saffron vinegar to the hot vinegar and bring to a boil. Arrange the fried skate in a platter and pour on the hot vinegar. Cool, cover, and refrigerate 24 hours.

RAW SQUID AND MORE

The very best fish and seafood in Abruzzo are found in Vasto, Ortona, and Pescara. Each of these coastal cities is famous for its rendition of *brodetto,* a fish and seafood stew, and for a heavenly *guazzetto alla marinara,* a medley of scampi, shrimp, and cod. Other Abruzzese seafood specialties include raw baby squid with olive oil, vinegar, onion, and abundant chili; monkfish *alla cacciatora* ("hunter's style"), with garlic, rosemary, and anchovies; and grilled or parchment paper–baked red mullet.

To serve, drain the skate. Pile the lettuce on a platter and top with the skate. Drizzle with the remaining ⅓ cup of olive oil and season with the remaining ¼ teaspoon of salt and the pepper. Serve immediately.

Pollo all'Abruzzese

Chicken with Roasted Peppers and Onions

This family-style dish is an Abruzzese variation on the chicken stews laced with tomato that grace many Italian tables. Most recipes do not call for roasting the peppers, nor do they suggest skinning the chicken. But I find roasted peppers sweeter and more complex in flavor, and skinless chicken more digestible.

SERVES 4

1 chicken, cut into 8 pieces and skinned,
   or 4 chicken legs, halved and skinned
1 lemon, halved
½ cup extra-virgin olive oil
1 medium yellow onion, minced
2 garlic cloves, minced
¼ to ½ teaspoon chili flakes (optional)
2 tablespoons minced Italian parsley
2 bay leaves
½ teaspoon salt
⅛ teaspoon freshly ground black pepper
5 plum tomatoes, peeled (see page 369), seeded,
   and diced
4 yellow bell peppers, halved lengthwise and
   seeded
16 basil leaves, torn

ASH-COOKED POTATOES

Burying food under the smoldering ashes of a dying fire is a time-honored way of cooking meat, fish, and vegetables in Italy. In Abruzzo, this frugal technique is applied to potatoes with delectable results: the potatoes emerge from the hearth tender and imbued with a smoky scent, ready to be drizzled with a touch of olive oil and wine vinegar as a simple side dish or salad.

Rinse the chicken under cool water, rub with the lemon halves, and blot dry. Heat the olive oil in a 12-inch sauté pan over a medium-high flame. Add the chicken and cook until browned on both sides, turning once, about 5 minutes per side. Add the onion, garlic, chili, parsley, and bay leaves, and cook 5 minutes. Add the salt, pepper, and tomatoes, reduce the heat to medium-low, and cook, covered, for 30 minutes.

Meanwhile, preheat the broiler.

Place the pepper halves, cut side down, on an aluminum foil–lined baking sheet. Broil until the skin is blackened and blistered, about 15 minutes. Wrap in the foil; cool 15 minutes, unwrap, peel, and cut into strips. Stir the roasted peppers into the chicken and simmer 15 more minutes. Remove from the heat, fold in the basil, discard the bay leaves, and serve hot.

PREPARATION TIPS: Braise the chicken up to 2 days ahead, refrigerate, and reheat before serving; fold in the basil at the last moment.

Agnello con le Olive

Lamb Scaloppine with Black Olives and Lemon

Lamb is Abruzzo's favorite meat. One ingenious recipe calls for braising it in a hermetically sealed pot until tender with a whole onion and butter so that it bastes itself in its own fat as it cooks. In the town of Scanno, lamb is stewed over a wood fire with white wine, garlic, olive oil, and rosemary. Across the region, lamb innards are wrapped in Swiss chard or endive leaves, then braised in wine; mutton, a staple among shepherds, is stewed with herbs, tomatoes, and Pancetta. In this more refined recipe, lamb scaloppine are briefly cooked with olives, oregano, and chili, then doused with lemon juice for a vibrant, easy main course.

SERVES 4

12 lamb scaloppine from the loin (2 ounces each), double-cut (1 inch thick), butterflied, and pounded thin with a mallet
½ cup unbleached all-purpose flour
¼ cup extra-virgin olive oil
3 garlic cloves, slivered
2 tablespoons minced fresh oregano or 1 teaspoon dried oregano
¼ to ½ teaspoon chili flakes
½ cup pitted black olives, such as Gaeta, minced
¼ cup fresh lemon juice (from 2 small lemons)
¼ teaspoon salt

MUTTON AND MOUNTAIN PIGS

In the Abruzzese mountains, lamb, kid, sheep, mutton, and goat are transformed into satisfying main courses. Sheep is skewered and grilled, or ground and stuffed into casings, then aged before reaching the table as a full-flavored salami. Free-roaming mountain pigs offer lean, flavorful meat, which the Abruzzesi proudly turn into 'ndocca 'ndocca ("large pieces"): humble parts of the pig (snout, skin, ears, and so on) are boiled with herbs and chili, then served hot in tomato sauce or cold as a rich, quivering gelatin.

Dredge the lamb in the flour, shaking off the excess. Heat 2 tablespoons of the olive oil in a 12-inch skillet over a medium-high flame. Add 6 of the lamb scaloppine and half of the garlic and cook for 2 minutes, or until the lamb is browned on the bottom. Turn and cook 2 more minutes, or until the other side is also browned, then remove to a plate. Repeat with the remaining 2 tablespoons of olive oil, the remaining 6 lamb scaloppine, and the remaining half of the garlic.

Return all the browned lamb to the skillet over medium-high heat. Add the oregano, chili, olives, and lemon juice, and cook for 30 seconds. Turn the lamb once, season with the salt, transfer to a platter, and serve hot.

Carciofi Ripieni di Tonno

Tuna-Filled Artichokes

Essential to the success of this dish is tuna packed in olive oil. If you only have water-packed tuna, drain it, then toss with 2 tablespoons of olive oil before filling the artichokes.

SERVES 4 AS A MAIN COURSE OR 8 AS AN ANTIPASTO

16 baby globe artichokes
1 lemon, halved
One 6-ounce can tuna packed in olive oil, drained and crumbled
5 salted anchovies, boned, gutted, rinsed, and minced
¼ cup capers, drained and minced
2 garlic cloves, minced
2 tablespoons minced Italian parsley
½ teaspoon freshly ground black pepper or ¼ teaspoon chili flakes
⅓ cup extra-virgin olive oil

Trim each artichoke, removing the tough outer leaves and cutting away the hard leaves at the top. Scoop out the hairy inner choke with a small spoon and discard. Rub the trimmed artichokes with the lemon halves; drop into a bowl of cool water and squeeze the lemon halves into the water.

In a small bowl, mix the tuna, anchovies, capers, garlic, parsley, and pepper. Drain the artichokes and stuff them with the tuna mixture. Place, cut side down, in an 8-inch skillet. Pour in the olive oil and ¼ cup of water. Cover and cook over medium heat 1 hour, adding a little water if needed. Serve hot, warm, or at room temperature.

AN INVITATION TO A PANARDA

If you are invited to a panarda in Abruzzo, make sure you are very hungry and drop all notions of moderation before you sit at the convivial table. A typical panarda goes something like this: Friends and family members gather, usually outdoors, and as many as forty dishes are served. First come savory nibbles and *salumi,* then soups, followed by boiled meats and pastas. Roasted meats, vegetables, and savory pies come next, then cheeses and desserts. Such outrageous feasting makes sense in Abruzzo: Excess is a reaction to deprivation, and since the local economy was underdeveloped until a few decades ago, the Abruzzesi celebrated with a vengeance when an occasion arose. Given the region's much-improved economy, the panarda is increasingly rare. But the old rules still apply, and everyone must partake of each dish or risk offending the host. In the nineteenth century, journalist Edoardo Scarfoglio was unable to eat after the thirtieth dish; satisfied, he stood up, only to be threatened with a rifle by the host.

Parrozzo

Chocolate-Covered Almond Cake

If Abruzzo's savory cuisine is a balancing act of the fiery and the delicate, its sweet dishes are less sophisticated. Except for a few layered or filled cakes, like a chocolate and nougat cassata or a triple-domed sponge cake with pastry cream, most desserts are modest. This moist almond cake was born as a shepherd's bread (pane rozzo, or "rough bread") and was transformed into a lush sweet in 1911 by Pescara baker Luigi d'Amico, who added sugar and chocolate to the original recipe. D'Amico was a good friend of Abruzzese poet and man of letters Gabriele d'Annunzio; so enamored of the cake was d'Annunzio that he even devoted a few verses to it. Some versions of parrozzo resemble the rudimentary semispherical shepherd's bread in appearance, while others, like the one below, do not.

SERVES 8

2 tablespoons (¼ stick) unsalted butter, plus extra for greasing the cake pan
⅓ cup plus 1 tablespoon unbleached all-purpose flour, plus extra for the cake pan
1 cup plus 1 tablespoon blanched almonds
¾ cup sugar
¼ teaspoon salt
Pinch ground cinnamon
6 extra-large eggs, separated
1 teaspoon vanilla extract
5 ounces bittersweet chocolate, chopped

Preheat the oven to 375°F.

Butter and flour a 10-inch springform cake pan.

Spread out the almonds on an 11 × 17-inch baking sheet and bake in the preheated oven 15 minutes. Cool, then grind with ¼ cup of the sugar in a food processor until powdery.

In a small bowl, sift together the flour, salt, and cinnamon. In a large bowl, whisk the egg yolks with the remaining ½ cup of sugar and the vanilla for 2 minutes, or until thick and pale. Fold in the ground-almond mixture with a rubber spatula, then fold in the flour mixture a little at a time.

In an electric mixer, beat the egg whites until stiff peaks form. Gently fold one-quarter of the egg whites into the egg yolk–almond mixture without deflating, using a rubber spatula, then fold in the remaining egg whites. Spoon it into the prepared cake pan and bake in the preheated oven for 25 minutes, or until a tester inserted in the middle comes out clean. Cool on a rack, then unmold onto a platter.

Meanwhile, melt the chocolate, butter, and 1 tablespoon of water in a bowl set over simmering water until smooth, stirring often. Cool to room temperature.

Using a long metal spatula, glaze the cake with the melted chocolate-butter mixture. Serve at room temperature.

Molise

Calciuni di Ricotta Rustici
Ricotta, Provolone, and Prosciutto Fritters

Pizza Assetata
"Thirsty" Pizza

Taccozze alla Crema d'Asparagi
Hand-Cut Pasta Squares in Asparagus Cream

Laianelle al Ragù di Chiavarre
Ricotta Ravioli in Country Ragù

Mappatelle Unto e Cacio
Pasta-Stuffed Crêpes

Fruffella
Bean, Cabbage, and Potato Soup with
Garlic-Pancetta-Chili Oil

Zuppa di Pesce alla Termolese
Seafood Pot from Termoli

Coniglio alla Molisana
Grilled Rabbit and Sausage Skewers

La Pezzata
The Shepherd's Celebratory Meat

Calciuni del Molise
Sweet Chestnut Fritters

Consider a land so tiny it fits almost three times inside of Rhode Island, a land whose people still herd sheep the old way and raise their own pigs, a land where sharp mountain peaks are covered in snow half the year and silence reigns in the valleys all year long.

This is Molise, a region many Italians forget to put on a map, including it in the more considerable sprawl of neighboring Abruzzo. In Molise, foodways and customs have skirted the modern penchant for speed and mass culture for the very reasons that made life within its bounds such a challenge: isolation, harsh terrain, and poverty. If Molise is one of Italy's most forgotten regions, it is also one of its most untarnished, a place where the cuisine pays homage to a humble past and speaks of ancient ties to the land.

The history and fate of Molise, Italy's smallest region after Val d'Aosta, was tied to that of neighboring Abruzzo until 1963, when the two were divided into distinct regions. Molise occupies a narrow strip of terrain that spans less than 550 square miles. Its soil is difficult, less yielding than that of Abruzzo to the north or Apulia to the south. As a result, the Molisani were plagued by poverty until the 1960s, and many migrated to other Italian regions or took a boat to America. Only 10 percent of Molise's terrain is neither hilly nor mountainous, and it is in this short strip of lowlands along the Adriatic Coast and in the capital city of Campobasso that most Molisani live; the hulking, silent mountains, by contrast, are almost uninhabited.

Archaeologists have speculated that Molise might be the site of the oldest human settlement in Italy: a gigantic ossuary containing thousands of bones, perhaps a butchering post, was unearthed near Iscania and dated to the Lower Paleolithic Age. The Samnites, an Italic tribe, settled the area, followed by the Romans in the third century B.C. After the Roman Empire fell, Molise was invaded by the Goths, Byzantines, Lombards, and Saracens; like Abruzzo, it belonged to the Kingdom of Sicily (later of Naples and of the Two Sicilies) after the eleventh century.

Mountain centers like Capracotta, Pescopennataro, Frosolone, and Campitello Matese are havens of pristine nature, ideal for skiing. In this area, known as Alto Molise ("High Molise"), handmade pasta and meat—usually lamb, sheep, mutton, and kid—prevail. The wide sandy beaches along the coast resemble those of Abruzzo and the Marches; cooks in the tiny fishing towns and the main port city of Termoli transform every sea creature imaginable into a succulent, if modest, feast. The cooking of Molise is really two cuisines in one: that of the hills and mountains, with its shepherd's favorites, and that of the coast, with its fisherman's favorites. But the region is unified by two things: a love of pasta paired with vegetables, and a devilish hand with chili pepper.

Favorite Restaurants, Shops, and Places

- CASEIFICIO PALLOTTA, Via Santa Maria di Loreto 68, Capracotta, 0865.949022. Buy Caciocavallo, Scamorza, Burrino, Ricotta, and more in a mountain setting.
- FRATELLI DI RIENZO, Piazza Vittoria 263, Agnone, 0865.78572. A town known for its bell-making is also home to wonderful cheeses.
- HOTEL CAPRACOTTA, Capracotta, 0865.945368. Hotel and restaurant. Molisano mountain cuisine in a pristine setting.
- MASSERIA DI MAJO NORANTE, Contrada Ramitello 4, Campomarino, 0875.57208. Buy the best wine coming out of Molise, as well as preserved vegetables, olive oil, and honey; by appointment only.
- MUSEO RACCOLTA OGGETTI DELLA CIVILTÀ CONTADINA, Via Tratturo 63, San Pietro Avellana, 0865.940103. Museum devoted entirely to Molise's rural civilization.
- RIBO, Contrada Malecoste 7, Guglionesi, 0875.680655. Memorable seafood cuisine; try the *pasta e fagioli con le cozze*.
- VECCHIA TRATTORIA DA TONINO, Corso Vittorio Emanuele, Campobasso, 0874.415200. Savory pies, salt cod with raisins and pine nuts, stuffed veal on braised field vegetables.
- Z' BASS, Via Oberdan 8, Termoli, 0875.706703. Excellent seafood in every guise imaginable.

Telephone country code: 011.39

Calciuni di Ricotta Rustici

Ricotta, Provolone, and Prosciutto Fritters

In Molise, these delicate fritters are served as part of a fritto misto *that includes fried Scamorza slices, artichokes, cauliflower, and sweetbreads, and are sometimes shaped into larger rounds and offered as a main course. The unique Molisano touch is the lemon juice in the dough, which gives it a subtle acidity and makes it more tender.*

SERVES 8

4¼ cups unbleached all-purpose flour,
   plus extra for the counter

2 teaspoons salt

3 extra-large eggs

4½ cups plus 3 tablespoons extra-virgin olive oil,
   or ½ cup plus 3 tablespoons extra-virgin olive
   oil and 4 cups peanut oil

¼ cup fresh lemon juice (from 1 large lemon)

½ pound fresh Ricotta

¼ cup freshly grated Pecorino Romano

¼ pound Provolone, cut into ⅛-inch dice

One ¼-pound slice Prosciutto di Parma,
   Carpegna, or San Daniele, cut into ⅛-inch dice

2 extra-large egg yolks

¼ cup minced Italian parsley

½ teaspoon freshly ground black pepper

In a large bowl, mix the flour and 1 teaspoon of the salt. Stir in the eggs, ½ cup plus 3 tablespoons of the olive oil, the lemon juice, and ⅓ cup of room temperature water until a dough forms; add a little water if the dough is dry or a little flour if it is sticky. Knead for 5 minutes, or until perfectly smooth, then pat into a disk, wrap, and let rest 30 minutes.

Meanwhile, in a separate bowl, mix the Ricotta, Pecorino, Provolone, Prosciutto, egg yolks, parsley, ½ teaspoon of the salt, and the pepper; this is the filling.

Cut the dough into 3 pieces. Working with 1 piece at a time and keeping the others covered, roll out each piece on a lightly floured counter into an 8 × 22-inch rectangle. Spoon heaping tablespoons of the filling along the bottom half of the rectangle, about 3 inches apart. Moisten around the mounds of filling with a pastry brush dipped in water. Flip the top half of the rectangle over to cover. Press around the mounds of filling with your hands to squeeze out any air pockets, and cut around the mounds of filling with a round 3-inch cookie cutter. Seal the edges with the tines of a fork and spread out in a single layer on a floured tray. These are the calciuni. Continue in the same manner until you finish the filling and/or dough.

Heat the remaining 4 cups of oil in a deep 10-inch pan until it registers 350°F, or until it is hot enough to brown a cube of bread in 1 minute. Fry a few calciuni at a time until golden, turning once, about 3 minutes. Remove with a slotted spoon to a plate lined with paper towels and blot dry. Fry the remaining calciuni in the same manner, maintaining the temperature of the oil by regulating the heat. Sprinkle with the remaining ½ teaspoon of salt and serve hot.

PREPARATION TIPS: The calciuni can be stuffed up to 4 hours ahead, spread out in a single layer on a floured tray, and refrigerated, covered with a kitchen towel.

BRAIDED OR NOT, IT WAS DELICIOUS

One of the most memorable Mozzarella experiences I ever had was in Molise. I was a guest at someone's house for dinner; after the pasta bowls had been cleared from the table, out came a huge braided buffalo milk Mozzarella. We drizzled it with olive oil and ate it with just-picked asparagus, chasing both with a glass of Greco wine. Creamy, still oozing whey, the Mozzarella—whose official name is Bufalina del Matese—is produced in the Matese area, where the swampy land and wild grasses provide water buffaloes with an ideal environment for munching. See Sources (page 372) to purchase.

Pizza Assetata

"Thirsty" Pizza

The town of Sessano is best known for its pizza assetata, a simple flatbread enlivened by chili, fennel seeds, and olive oil. Local lore has it that pizza assetata is an adaptation of the matzo baked by Jews, since it contains no yeast and is baked immediately after kneading. The pizza is called assetata ("thirsty") because it is spiced with chili and topped with sea salt, which makes anyone who indulges in it thirsty.

ANTIPASTI AS A SYMBOL OF WEALTH

Constructing a meal along the lines of starter, first course, second course, and dessert is a luxury most Italians—and certainly most Molisani—couldn't afford until after World War II. Italy's historically impoverished regions—Molise, Calabria, Basilicata, Sicily, and Sardinia—put little emphasis on the frills, focusing instead on dishes that best delivered nourishing sustenance at little cost. And so Molise offers few "traditional" appetizers. Today the Molisani are much better off than their grandparents were, and meals frequently start with antipasti such as bruschetta and cheese-filled pastries called *casciatielle*.

SERVES 4

3½ cups unbleached all-purpose flour,
  plus extra for the counter
1 teaspoon fennel seeds
¼ to ½ teaspoon chili flakes
1 teaspoon fine sea salt
¾ cup extra-virgin olive oil, plus extra for
  greasing the bowl
2 teaspoons coarse sea salt

Place the flour, fennel seeds, chili, and fine sea salt in a food processor. Pulse twice. Add ½ cup of the olive oil. With the motor running, add as much room temperature water as needed to form a dough that rides the blade; you will need about 1¼ cups. Process 45 seconds, adding a little water if the dough is dry or a little flour if it is sticky; place in an oiled bowl, cover, and let rest 30 minutes. (The rest is not traditional, but makes rolling easier.)

Meanwhile, preheat the oven with a baking stone in it to 550°F.

Cut the dough into 4 pieces. Working with 1 piece at a time and keeping the others covered, roll out each piece on a lightly floured counter into a 14-inch circle. Sprinkle a baking peel generously with flour. Place 1 dough circle on it, brush with 1 tablespoon of the remaining olive oil, and sprinkle with ½ teaspoon of the coarse sea salt. Poke with a fork in 6 places.

Transfer to the baking stone and bake in the preheated oven 5 minutes, or until slightly crisp and browned in spots. Continue in the same manner with the remaining dough, olive oil, and coarse salt. Serve hot or warm, with sheep's milk cheese, salami, and olives.

PREPARATION TIPS: The dough can be made up to 24 hours ahead, wrapped, and refrigerated; return to room temperature before proceeding.

Taccozze alla Crema d'Asparagi
Hand-Cut Pasta Squares in Asparagus Cream

Taccozze, a toothsome semolina pasta, is common to Molise, the Marches, Umbria, Campania, and Sicily, although it has different names in each. At the home of Molise's foremost winemakers (Anna Maria, Luigi, and Alessio Di Majo Norante) I enjoyed taccozze in a sauce of puréed asparagus. Luigi's trick: cooking down the asparagus with water until it forms a purée, draining the pasta when it is half-cooked, and finishing it in the asparagus sauce.

SERVES 4

For the taccozze:
3 cups semolina flour, plus extra for the counter
1/2 teaspoon salt

For the sauce and to cook:
1/2 cup extra-virgin olive oil
1 medium yellow onion, minced
30 thin asparagus spears, woody ends trimmed,
    cut into 1/2-inch pieces
2 tablespoons plus 1/2 teaspoon salt
1/4 teaspoon freshly ground black pepper
1 cup freshly grated Pecorino Romano (optional)

Make the taccozze according to instructions on page 370 using the ingredients listed above, adding 3/4 cup of hot water to form a firm dough. Knead 5 minutes, or until smooth, adding a little hot water if the dough is dry or a little semolina flour if it is sticky. Shape into a ball, wrap, and let rest 30 minutes.

Cut the dough into 2 pieces. Working with 1 piece at a time and keeping the other covered, roll out each piece on a semolina-dusted counter into a 12 × 24-inch rectangle. Let rest 5 minutes. Sprinkle with semolina flour, roll up lengthwise, jelly roll–style, and cut into 1-inch-wide strips. Unravel the strips, sprinkle with semolina flour, and stack a few at a time; cut into 1-inch squares. Toss with semolina flour to prevent sticking and spread out in a single layer on a semolina-dusted tray.

Make the sauce: Heat 1/4 cup of the olive oil in a 12-inch sauté pan over a medium flame. Add the onion and cook for 5 minutes. Add the asparagus, 1/2 teaspoon of the salt, the pepper, and 2 cups of water. Cook, covered, for 30 minutes, crushing the asparagus against the pan every few minutes with a fork. The asparagus should form a chunky purée.

To cook, bring 6 quarts of water to a boil. Add the taccozze and the remaining 2 tablespoons of salt and cook until half-cooked, about 1 minute. Drain, reserving 1/2 cup of the pasta cooking water. Add the taccozze and the reserved cooking water to the sauce and cook, uncovered, for 5 minutes, or until the taccozze are al dente and the sauce has reduced to a coating consistency, stirring often. Transfer to a platter, drizzle with the remaining 1/4 cup of olive oil, and serve hot, passing the Pecorino.

PREPARATION TIPS: The taccozze can be made up to 12 hours ahead, spread out in a single layer on a semolina-dusted tray, and refrigerated, covered with a towel.

Laianelle al Ragù di Chiavarre

Ricotta Ravioli in Country Ragù

The shepherds who eke out their livings in the unforgiving mountains of Molise are geniuses at turning sheep and mutton into memorable ragùs, roasts, and braises. In Abruzzo and Molise, the word chiavarre *refers to a sheep that has not yet given birth; while you can't be expected to know whether the sheep you buy at the butcher's has had offspring or not, you should try this robust ragù nonetheless. Don't be put off by the idea of eating sheep: after all, it is but an adult female lamb, more tender and delicate than mutton (its male counterpart), if more strongly flavored than lamb. If you can't special-order sheep at your butcher, see Sources (page 372) or substitute lamb.*

SERVES 4

⅓ cup extra-virgin olive oil
3 garlic cloves, minced
2 rosemary sprigs, leaves only, minced
2 tablespoons minced Italian parsley
¼ to ½ teaspoon chili flakes
¾ pound boneless sheep's meat (preferably from the shoulder), cut into ¼-inch cubes
1½ cups dry white wine
1½ pounds plum tomatoes, peeled (see page 369), seeded, and diced
2 tablespoons plus ¾ teaspoon salt
1 recipe Pasta Dough (page 370)
½ pound fresh Ricotta (preferably sheep's milk)
1 extra-large egg
¼ teaspoon freshly grated nutmeg
¼ teaspoon freshly ground black pepper
Unbleached all-purpose flour for the counter
1 cup freshly grated Pecorino Romano

Heat the olive oil in a 2-quart pot over a medium flame. Add the garlic, rosemary, parsley, and chili and cook 2 minutes. Add the sheep and brown on all sides, stirring often, about 10 minutes.

Deglaze with ¼ cup of the wine; when it evaporates, after about 3 minutes, deglaze with another ¼ cup. Continue adding wine and letting it evaporate in this manner; it will take about 15 minutes. Fold in the tomatoes and ½ teaspoon of the salt, reduce the heat to medium-low, cover, and cook for 2 hours, or until the sheep is fork-tender. This is the ragù; keep warm.

Meanwhile, make the dough and let it rest according to instructions on page 370.

Mix the Ricotta, egg, nutmeg, ¼ teaspoon of the salt, and the pepper in a large bowl; this is the filling.

Cut the dough into 2 pieces. Working with 1 piece at a time and keeping the other covered, roll out each piece on a lightly floured counter into a 20-inch circle, sprinkling both sides often with flour to prevent sticking. Cut into 2½-inch disks with a round cookie cutter. Top each disk with 1 scant teaspoon of filling, fold in half, and seal the edges with your fingers. (If any filling leaks out, wipe it off and make sure the edges are sealed.) These are the laianelle. Spread out in a single layer on a floured tray; refrigerate until needed, covered with a towel.

Bring 6 quarts of water to a boil. Add the laianelle and the remaining 2 tablespoons of salt and cook until al dente, about 3 minutes. Remove to a serving platter with a slotted spoon, reserving ¼ cup of the pasta cooking water. Fold in the ragù and the reserved cooking water and serve hot, passing the Pecorino at the table.

PREPARATION TIPS: The ragù can be made up to 4 days ahead, refrigerated, and reheated as you cook the laianelle. The laianelle can be shaped up to 8 hours ahead, spread out in a single layer on a floured tray, and refrigerated, covered with a towel.

THE HIGHLIGHT OF A MOLISANO MEAL

The highlight of any Molisano meal is the first course, which more often that not mates pasta with beans, broccoli raab, bits of fried Pancetta, and chili, or with a ragù of lamb, mutton, sheep, or pork. Other than *taccozze* (page 249), the most typical pastas are *crejoli,* square spaghetti similar to the *maccheroni alla chitarra* of Abruzzo; *cavatelli,* concave gnocchi most often associated with Apulia; fusilli shaped around a knitting needle, like in Basilicata, Sicily, and Sardinia; *laganelle,* similar to tagliatelle; *sagne,* lasagna sheets shared with Calabria; and *recchietelle,* known as orecchiette in Apulia.

A CHEESE NOT FOR THE FAINT OF HEART

Called Cacio Punto ("stung cheese") in Molise, Cacio Marcetto ("rotten cheese") in Abruzzo, and Cacio Con i Vermi ("cheese with worms") in Sardinia, there is probably no Italian cheese that meets with less enthusiasm on the part of North Americans. To make this ancient, and now nearly extinct, cheese, a mold of sheep's milk cheese is injected with milk and vinegar to encourage the growth of larvae-like insects; after a few weeks, the cheese becomes moist, spreadable, and pungent. Likened in flavor to Gorgonzola by veterans, Cacio Punto can still be found—although more and more rarely—in Molise, Abruzzo, and Sardinia.

Mappatelle Unto e Cacio
Pasta-Stuffed Crêpes

Mappa *means "handkerchief" in Molisano;* mappatelle, *the diminutive form, means "little kerchiefs," which these dainty stuffed crêpes resemble. Quite unlike most Molisano dishes in terms of sophistication, mappatelle make their appearance on feast tables and are an ideal choice for formal dinners.*

In a large bowl, mix the flour and ½ teaspoon of the salt. Using a whisk, beat in the eggs and 1 tablespoon of the olive oil, then whisk in ½ cup plus 2 tablespoons of cool water. The batter should be fluid; add more water if needed. Strain through a fine sieve into a clean bowl.

SERVES 4

⅔ cup unbleached all-purpose flour

2 tablespoons plus ½ teaspoon salt

5 extra-large eggs

¼ cup extra-virgin olive oil, plus extra for greasing the baking dish

½ pound fresh or dried maccheroni alla chitarra (page 231) or spaghetti

One 6-ounce slice Pancetta, cut into ⅛ × ⅛ × 1-inch strips

¼ cup minced Italian parsley

½ teaspoon freshly ground black pepper

½ cup freshly grated Pecorino Romano

2 tablespoons (¼ stick) unsalted butter, melted

Heat a 6-inch nonstick pan over a medium-high flame for 2 minutes. Using a paper towel, rub the pan with 1 tablespoon of the olive oil. Pour in 3 tablespoons of the batter and tilt the pan quickly to spread it. Cook until set and golden on the bottom, about 2 minutes; flip and cook until the other side is also golden, about 1 minute. Remove to a plate. Continue in the same manner with the remaining batter; you do not need to oil the pan again. These are the crêpes; you will need 12 in all (freeze any leftover crêpes for up to 1 month).

Bring 3 quarts of water to a boil. Add the maccheroni alla chitarra and the remaining 2 tablespoons of salt and cook until firm, about 6 minutes, then drain.

Heat the remaining 2 tablespoons of olive oil in an 8-inch skillet. Add the Pancetta and cook over medium-high heat until golden, about 3 minutes. Add the parsley and pepper and cook 1 minute. In a large bowl, toss the maccheroni with the Pancetta mixture and fold in ¼ cup of the Pecorino; this is the filling.

Preheat the oven to 400°F.

Divide the filling among the 12 crêpes. Pull up the edges of each crêpe to enclose, forming a purse, and spear with 2 toothpicks, crisscrossing them to prevent opening. Arrange ½ inch apart in an oiled 10 × 14-inch baking dish. Drizzle with the melted butter and sprinkle with the remaining ¼ cup of Pecorino. Bake in the preheated oven for 15 minutes and serve hot, removing the toothpicks at the table.

Fruffella

Bean, Cabbage, and Potato Soup with Garlic-Pancetta-Chili Oil

Most of Molise's soups were born as a way of stretching a handful of vegetables or a hunk of meat to feed the family. The soups were cooked gently over slow embers, suspended in a cast-iron pot over the hearth until dinnertime. Today, the stove has replaced the fireplace, and cooks are more free with the vegetables, meat, and even cheese that they add to the pot. But Molisano soups remain hearty, stick-to-the-rib affairs. Although celery and potatoes, two of Campobasso's proudest crops, are often included, the vegetables used in the country soup below change with the seasons. So don't hesitate to add Swiss chard, cardoons, spinach, zucchini, or string beans if they beckon at the market.

SERVES 6

1 cup dried cannellini beans, soaked 12 hours in cool water to cover
1 pound boiling potatoes, peeled and cut into ¼-inch cubes
1 carrot, cut into ¼-inch cubes
1 celery stalk, cut into ¼-inch cubes
1 medium yellow onion, cut into ¼-inch cubes
8 Savoy cabbage leaves, cut into long, thin strips
2 tablespoons minced Italian parsley
1 tablespoon tomato paste
½ teaspoon salt
¼ teaspoon freshly ground black pepper
¼ pound sliced Pancetta, cut into long, thin strips
4 garlic cloves, minced
¼ teaspoon chili flakes

Drain the beans and place them in a 3-quart pot. Add 6 cups of cool water and bring to a gentle boil over medium-high heat. Reduce the heat to medium-low, cover, and cook for 1½ hours, or until almost tender. Add the potatoes, carrot, celery, onion, cabbage, parsley, and tomato paste; cover again and cook 1 more hour, or until the beans and vegetables are soft, adding a little water if needed. Season with the salt and pepper.

When the soup is ready, cook the Pancetta, garlic, and chili in an 8-inch skillet over medium heat for 10 minutes. Stir into the pot with the beans and serve hot.

A MEAT BY ANY OTHER NAME

Made pretty much across Italy, the square, generously seasoned forcemeat from the pig's neck and shoulder goes by different names and is cured differently in different places. In Emilia-Romagna it is called Coppa and is delicate in flavor; in Abruzzo it is nicknamed Lonza and is aged two months; in Apulia it is known as Capocollo and is flavored with wine, then smoked; in Basilicata and Calabria, it is also dubbed Capocollo, but it is coated with chili after aging; and in Molise, it is referred to as Mulette and is spiced with chili rather than black pepper.

Zuppa di Pesce alla Termolese
Seafood Pot from Termoli

The best Molisano fish specialties hail from the town of Termoli. Preparations span from marinated fish in a vinegary brine, like the scapece of Abruzzo (page 237), to succulent seafood and fish brodetti flavored with diced green pepper, like the one here. The trick to the success of this dish is the choice of fish: select ugly varieties like monkfish, which have the most intense flavor. And if you are not squeamish, opt for fish with their heads still on, as the bones impart depth and complexity (in this case, increase the quantity of fish to 3 pounds). Massimo Mastrangelo, owner of Z' Bass in Termoli, offered this recipe; he suggests serving the medley as a main course, or turning it into a first course by adding 1/2 pound of broken spaghetti along with the mussels and clams. Scampi, shellfish with long claws that resemble lobster, are typically used in this preparation; additional shrimp can be used instead.

SERVES 4

1 pound mussels, scrubbed, beards removed

1 pound littleneck clams or cockles

1 tablespoon plus 1 teaspoon salt

1/2 cup extra-virgin olive oil

4 garlic cloves, chopped

4 plum tomatoes, peeled (see page 369), seeded, and diced

1/2 green bell pepper, cut into 1/4-inch cubes

1/2 small jalapeño pepper, seeded and cut into 1/4-inch cubes

1/4 pound cleaned squid, bodies cut into rings and tentacles halved

1/4 pound cleaned cuttlefish, bodies cut into rings and tentacles halved

4 scampi, heads and shells on

4 jumbo shrimp, heads and shells on

2 pounds assorted skinless and boneless saltwater fish fillets (red mullet, monkfish, and sea bream), cut into 3-inch pieces

1 tablespoon minced Italian parsley

Soak the mussels and clams in cool water to cover with 1 tablespoon of the salt for 30 minutes, then drain and rinse.

Place the olive oil, garlic, tomatoes, green pepper, jalapeño, squid, and cuttlefish in a 12-inch terra-cotta or nonstick pot. Pour in 1 cup of warm water and season with the remaining teaspoon of salt. Cook over medium heat for 10 minutes. Raise the heat to medium-high, add the scampi, shrimp, and fish, and cook 5 minutes. Never stir or the fish might flake; instead, shake the pot back and forth once in a while to prevent sticking and to distribute the heat. Add the mussels and clams and cook, covered, until they open, about 10 more minutes. Sprinkle with the parsley and serve hot, in the pot.

Molise's Wines

LIKE NEIGHBORING ABRUZZO, Molise has vast plantings of Montepulciano d'Abruzzo and Trebbiano d'Abruzzo. These two grapes, along with Greco, Bombino Bianco, Aglianico, Sangiovese, and some lesser-known native varietals, lay the foundation for the region's viticulture. Produced in the hills above Campobasso, Biferno was named after the Biferno River and is by far Molise's most significant wine. The red and rosé versions are obtained from Montepulciano, Aglianico, and Trebbiano Toscano, while the white uses Malvasia instead of Aglianico. Pentro d'Isernia derives its name from an ancient Samnite tribe that valiantly resisted the Romans in the mountains of Isernia and is vinified in a red, white, and rosé version. Despite Biferno's and Pentro d'Isernia's prominence within Molise, neither wine is available in North America: for the time being, production is too small and interest in Molise's DOCs too scant. Luckily, outstanding wines from Molise's foremost winemakers, the Di Majo Norantes, are exported to North America (see Sources, page 373).

Coniglio alla Molisana
Grilled Rabbit and Sausage Skewers

Roasting and grilling over an open fire are favorite methods for cooking meat in rural areas of Molise. If you can find a butcher willing to debone a rabbit for you, these skewers take just minutes and are perfect for a summer barbecue. Accompany the skewers with toasted garlic-rubbed country bread and oven-roasted tomatoes for a real Molisano treat.

SERVES 4

1 rabbit (3 pounds), deboned and cut into twelve
    3-inch pieces
½ teaspoon salt
½ teaspoon freshly ground black pepper
2 rosemary sprigs, leaves only, minced
2 tablespoons minced Italian parsley
12 thin slices Prosciutto di Parma, Carpegna, or
    San Daniele
½ pound spicy Italian sausage, cut into 8 pieces
16 sage leaves
¼ cup extra-virgin olive oil

Heat an outdoor grill or preheat the oven to 375°F.

Sprinkle the rabbit with the salt, pepper, rosemary, and parsley. Roll each piece in 1 slice of Prosciutto. Distribute the rabbit bundles, sausage pieces, and sage leaves onto each of 4 short metal skewers. Place in a shallow container and drizzle with the olive oil.

Grill the skewers, or roast them in the preheated oven in a single layer in a 10 × 14-inch roasting pan, for 30 minutes. Every 5 minutes or so, baste with their olive oil and turn to cook evenly. Serve hot.

PREPARATION TIPS: Prepare the skewers up to 24 hours ahead and refrigerate.

COOKING WITH CRACKLINGS

Every part of Italy that raises pigs makes cracklings: crunchy, fatty bits of pork skin that are obtained by cooking down chopped pork rind until the fat melts and the skin takes on a deliciously crisp texture. The fat is strained out and reserved for baking or frying; the cracklings are eaten as a snack, kneaded into yeasted dough for breads, and stirred into sweet batters for dessert. Today, given rising concern over cholesterol, many crackling-studded recipes—including those from Molise, like *pizza con i cicoli* (Molisano for *ciccioli*, or "cracklings")—are disappearing from the Italian kitchen.

La Pezzata

The Shepherd's Celebratory Meat

The shepherds of Molise, forced by difficult soil and a harsh winter climate to move their flocks to Apulia for the fall and winter (page 259), cooked this rustic sheep dinner when they returned after a six-month absence from home. They cut up the sheep (the word pezzata is derived from pezzi, meaning "pieces"), then braised the meat with vegetables and herbs for hours in a hermetically sealed terra-cotta pot called 'u cutelloccia. Massimo Mastrangelo, who owns Z' Bass in Termoli, shared this recipe for pezzata, noting that the tomatoes and chili are a recent addition. See Sources (page 372) to buy sheep, or substitute lamb.

SERVES 6

2 pounds sheep (preferably from the shoulder), bone in, cut into 3-inch pieces

1 large yellow onion, thickly sliced

2 garlic cloves, chopped

½ cup extra-virgin olive oil

½ cup chopped Italian parsley

2 rosemary sprigs

¼ to ½ teaspoon chili flakes

4 plum tomatoes, peeled (see page 369), seeded, and diced

1 teaspoon salt

1 cup dry white wine

Combine all the ingredients in a deep 14-inch terra-cotta pot or Dutch oven, cover, and cook over medium-low heat for 5 hours. Do not stir the ingredients or open the pot; shake the pot from side to side once in a while to distribute heat.

Uncover and serve hot, in the pot.

POLENTA IN THE HIGHLANDS OF MOLISE

Polenta, called *macche* in Molise, is cooked firm rather than creamy, poured onto the table while still hot, and drizzled with reduced grape must, topped with sausages, or sauced with lamb ragù. In Pozzilli, near the mountain town of Isernia, it is prepared *a tordiglioni,* with vegetables that have been fried in garlicky olive oil.

Calciuni del Molise

Sweet Chestnut Fritters

Cooks in Molise and nearby regions offer countless versions of these fritters. The filling can include vino cotto *(page 204)* or chickpeas instead of chestnuts, and the dough often calls for wine in addition to eggs and oil, as in this recipe, for suppleness and flavor. See Sources *(page 372)* to buy boiled chestnuts and candied citron.

SWEET OCCASIONS

Most Molisano meals end with fruit, but for special occasions, various sweets are offered. Pastries range from *taralli* (page 223) to *pigna di Guardialfiera,* an egg and potato bread flavored with lemon zest and anise seeds. *Ceppellate di Trivento,* rich crescents stuffed with sour cherry jam, are similar to Apulia's *bocconotti.* Culinary overlap with Apulia is not surprising, considering that Molisano shepherds spent months every year in Apulia in search of better pastures for their animals.

MAKES SIXTEEN 3-INCH FRITTERS

1½ cups unbleached all-purpose flour, plus extra
    for the counter
2 extra-large egg yolks
4 cups plus 1 tablespoon extra-virgin olive oil or
    1 tablespoon extra-virgin olive oil plus 4 cups
    peanut oil
1 tablespoon dry white wine
1 tablespoon blanched almonds
¼ pound boiled chestnuts
1 teaspoon rum
2 tablespoons grated bittersweet chocolate
¼ cup honey
¼ teaspoon vanilla extract
1 teaspoon diced candied citron
½ teaspoon plus a pinch of ground cinnamon
½ cup confectioner's sugar

Pour the flour on a counter and work in the egg yolks, 1 tablespoon of the olive oil, the wine, and ¼ cup of cool water. Knead until a dough forms, adding a little water if the dough is dry or a little flour if it is sticky. Knead 5 minutes, or until smooth, then wrap and let rest 30 minutes.

Meanwhile, preheat the oven to 375°F.

Spread out the almonds on an 11 × 17-inch baking sheet; toast in the preheated oven for 12 minutes. Grind in a food processor until powdery but not pasty, then add the chestnuts and process until a paste forms. Transfer to a bowl. Stir in the rum, chocolate, honey, vanilla, candied citron, and a pinch of the cinnamon; this is the filling.

Roll out the dough on a lightly floured counter into a 16-inch circle. Cut into circles with a round 3-inch cookie cutter. Spoon a teaspoon of filling onto each circle, fold in half, and seal with your fingers, then press to decorate the edges with the tines of a fork. These are the calciuni. Spread out in a single layer on a floured tray.

To cook, heat the remaining 4 cups of oil in a deep 10-inch pan until it registers 350°F, or until it is hot enouth to brown a cube of bread in 1 minute. Fry a few calciuni at a time until golden all over, turning once, about 3 minutes. Remove with a slotted spoon to a plate lined with paper towels and blot dry. Fry the remaining calciuni in the same manner, maintaining the temperature of the oil by regulating the heat.

Mix the confectioner's sugar and the remaining ½ teaspoon of cinnamon in a sifter and dust over the fritters. Roll them to coat all sides. Serve hot, warm, or at room temperature.

PREPARATION TIPS: The calciuni can be shaped up to 12 hours ahead, spread out in a single layer on a floured tray, and refrigerated, covered with a towel.

THE SHEPHERD'S TWO-THOUSAND-YEAR-OLD HIGHWAY

AS LONG AS TWO THOUSAND YEARS AGO, the Samnites (who inhabited central Italy before the Romans took control) cleared footpaths so that shepherds and their flocks could travel from the snow-clad mountains of Abruzzo and Molise to the warmer plains of Apulia and back every year. On September 29, the Abruzzese and Molisano shepherds gathered their sheep, bid farewell to family, and trod—literally—to greener pastures. Spending half the year traveling back and forth, to and from Apulia, meant a dislocated life for these men and their families; it also meant that the three regions would be connected by more than proximity and roads, sharing much in terms of culture, language, and cuisine. Dozens of *tratturi,* as these ancient roads are called, can still be seen in Molise, and some—like the one linking Castel di Sangro in Abruzzo to Candela in Apulia—are still dotted with the taverns built to satisfy the needs of the traveling shepherds. The Taverna del Sangro (now dilapidated and closed) is one such place: it may just be the oldest "restaurant" in Italy, and there is talk of resurrecting it as a historical site. Today the tratturi, and the way of life they represent, are a thing of the past. But not such a distant past, for until the 1960s, shepherds were still making their way along Molise's silent highways, stopping along the way to kill a sheep, cook a *pezzata* over an open fire, and wonder what awaited them at the end of the road.

Campania

Insalata di Mare
Lemon-Soaked Seafood Salad

Pizza Margherita
Classic Pizza with Tomatoes and Mozzarella

Pizza di Melanzane
Layered Eggplant Pie

Spaghetti alla Caprese
Spaghetti with Tuna, Anchovies, and Olives from Capri

Scialatielli alle Vongole
Herb-Speckled Pasta with Clams, Garlic,
and Cherry Tomatoes

Cannelloni alla Sorrentina
Ricotta Cannelloni from Sorrento

Branzino all'Acqua Pazza
Sea Bass in "Crazy Water"

Braciole di Maiale alla Napoletana
Pork Braciole with Pine Nuts and Capers

Scarole Imbottite
Stuffed Escarole Bundles

Coviglie al Caffè
Coffee Custard over Ladyfingers

The salty seawater is running off my skin under the cool spray of the shower. It is early evening and my husband and I are in Sorrento, showering on a dreamlike terrace before dinner. We spent the day on a boat, dipping into the sea whenever the sun got too hot, exploring the coastline, building up an appetite.

I am ready for whatever the night will bring: a salad of buffalo milk Mozzarella and tomatoes, fresh pasta tossed with seafood, a glass of *limoncello* . . . I watch the silvery olive groves and plump evergreens grow less discernible against the darkening sky, and marvel over being in this corner of paradise, where my only thought is what I will taste next.

Campania was first settled by the Greeks and later dominated by the Etruscans, Samnites, and Romans. Like much of central and southern Italy, it fell to the Goths, Byzantines, and Lombards after the Roman Empire folded. In the eleventh century, the Normans conquered the area. One hundred years later, Campania was incorporated into the Kingdom of Sicily; to this day, Campania and Sicily share much in the kitchen. Both regions like to combine capers, anchovies, pine nuts, and raisins. And both offer a handful of aristocratic specialties and pies (including *gattò,* from the French *gâteau*) that hark back to the days of the Kingdom of the Two Sicilies, which comprised the Bourbon territory of Sicily and Naples. Split into various duchies and principalities in the Middle Ages and Renaissance, Campania reclaimed its original name when it joined the Kingdom of Italy in 1861.

More heavily populated along the coast and in the capital city of Naples, Campania is the region with the highest population density in the country. Its volcanic soil is both a curse and a blessing: while the threat of eruption is constant, the fertile lowlands are dotted with thriving farms. The area around the Bay of Naples, watched over by Mount Vesuvius, is especially prolific: eggplants, beans, fennel, tomatoes, cauliflower, figs, citrus, cherries, apricots, walnuts, grapes, and olives are the main crops, and they are transformed into a tantalizing array of dishes by local cooks. The sea too offers up its delicious catch, and the seafood cuisine is especially delectable near the town of Amalfi, a strip of land considered by many to be the most splendid coastline in the world.

Until a few decades ago, the Campani ate vegetables and pasta for the noon and evening meal, stretching a piece of meat into a long-simmered ragù and relying on "poor" fish like anchovies for a taste of the sea, so their vegetarian repertoire is extremely varied. Temperamental and fiery, imbued with the exuberant scent of herbs and redolent with garlic, Campania's cuisine takes after its people. Quick-cooking and frying are favorite techniques, and there is no such thing as too many herbs: in Campania, the food is all about sun-kissed flavor.

Favorite Restaurants, Shops, and Places

- ANTICA PIZZERIA BRANDI, Salita Santa Anna di Palazzo 1-2, Naples, 081.416928. The pizzeria where legendary *pizzaiolo* Raffaele Esposito baked pizza Margherita.
- DA CARMELO, Strada Statale 562, Località Isca, Palinuro, 0974.931138. Home cooking; try the *frittata di neonati* and *vermicelli con vongole*.
- DON ALFONSO 1890, Corso Sant'Agata 11, Frazione Sant'Agata sui Due Golfi, Massa Lubrense, 081.8780026. Don't miss out on the *astice marinato ai fiori di zucca*.
- GAMBRINUS, Via Chiaia 1/2, Naples, 081.417582. Sample the spumone at this legendary pastry shop.
- HOTEL SAN PIETRO, Via Laurito 2, Località Laurito, Positano, 089.875455. Unbeatable seafood, including *taglioni ai fiori di zucca con frutti di mare*.

- IL PRINCIPE, Piazza Bartolo Longo 8, Pompeii, 081.8505566. Ancient Roman dishes revisited.
- LA SCOGLIERA DELL'HOTEL PALATIUM, Via Marina Grande 225, Località Marina Grande, Capri, 081.8376144. Order the *ravioli al limone*.
- LA SPONDA DELL'ALBERGO LE SIRENUSE, Via C. Colombo 30, Positano, 089.875066. Try the elegant *sartù di riso*.
- LATTICINI STAIANO, Piazza Fontana 1, Ravello, 0898.57271. Artisanal buffalo milk Mozzarella production.
- TRATTORIA DA MARIA, near Piazza del Duomo, Amalfi, 089.871880. Informal atmosphere, excellent pizza, seafood, and *pasta con i ceci*.

Telephone country code: 011.39

Insalata di Mare

Lemon-Soaked Seafood Salad

Every Italian region with a coastline concocts a seafood salad, but the one from Campania ranks among the best: the trick is cooking the baby octopus, shrimp, and squid in the mussel and clam cooking juices. Don't overcook the shrimp and squid, or they will be rubbery; they are done as soon as they change color. If baby octopus is unavailable (see Sources, page 372), substitute additional shrimp and squid.

SERVES 6

3 pounds mussels, scrubbed, beards removed
1½ pounds clams or cockles
1 tablespoon plus ½ teaspoon salt
1 cup extra-virgin olive oil
1 pound baby octopus, beaks removed
1 pound large shrimp, shelled and deveined
1 pound cleaned squid, bodies cut into rings
    and tentacles halved
¼ cup plus 1 tablespoon fresh lemon juice
    (from 2 small lemons)
1 teaspoon Dijon mustard (optional)
⅛ teaspoon freshly ground black pepper
2 tablespoons minced Italian parsley

Soak the mussels and clams in cool water to cover with 1 tablespoon of the salt for 30 minutes. Drain and rinse. Place in a 4-quart sauté pan with 2 tablespoons of the olive oil and 1 cup of water and cover. Cook over medium-high heat for 12 minutes, or until open, then shell and place on a serving platter.

Strain the mussel and clam cooking juices through a cheesecloth-lined sieve into a 2-quart sauté pan. Add the octopus and cook over medium heat, uncovered, for 25 minutes, adding water if needed. Add the shrimp and squid and cook for 3 minutes, or until they change color. Using a slotted spoon, remove the octopus, shrimp, and squid to the serving platter with the mussels and clams.

In a bowl, mix the remaining ¾ cup plus 2 tablespoons of olive oil, the remaining ½ teaspoon of salt, the lemon juice, mustard, pepper, and parsley. Toss with the warm seafood and cool to room temperature, then refrigerate for 2 hours and serve.

PREPARATION TIPS: Marinate the salad up to 12 hours in the refrigerator.

FAVORITE ANTIPASTI

Campania's adoration of all things fried is evident in its antipasti: from Mozzarella sandwiched between slices of bread to *panzarotti* stuffed with Prosciutto, Mozzarella, and eggs, the Campani—and the Neapolitans above all—are masters at frying. They are also skilled bakers, and often start meals with delicate potato rounds topped with Mozzarella and tomatoes, or a handful of crisp bread rings called *taralli*. There are also *pizze* topped with clams, salami, eggplant, escarole, or anchovies. Other baked goods include cheese-stuffed *calzoni* (meaning "pants") and *tortani* (from *torta,* or "cake") enriched with cracklings.

Pizza Margherita

Classic Pizza with Tomatoes and Mozzarella

The success of this pizza depends on the perfection of its ingredients: fruity olive oil, fresh Mozzarella, plum tomatoes canned with nothing more than salt, and fragrant basil. To achieve the crisp crust characteristic of a wood-burning oven, use a baking stone; lacking that, heat an upside-down 11 × 17-inch baking sheet in the oven for 30 minutes before transferring the pizza onto it.

SERVES 4

3¼ cups unbleached all-purpose flour, plus extra for the counter

1 teaspoon instant yeast

1 tablespoon plus ½ teaspoon fine sea salt

¼ cup extra-virgin olive oil, plus extra for greasing the bowl

1⅓ cups canned chopped Italian plum tomatoes (preferably San Marzano)

1 pound fresh Mozzarella, thinly sliced, drained in a colander 30 minutes, and blotted dry

12 basil leaves, torn

Mix the flour, yeast, and 1 tablespoon of the salt in a food processor. With the motor running, add enough warm (110°F) water (about 1¼ cups) to make a soft dough that rides the blade. Process for 45 seconds. Add a little water if the dough is dry or a little flour if it is sticky. Lightly oil a bowl, place the dough in it, shape into a ball, and wrap. Let rise at room temperature until doubled, about 1 hour.

Preheat the oven with a baking stone in it to 550°F.

Cut the dough into 4 pieces. Shape into 4 balls on a lightly floured counter. Cover and let rest for 15 minutes (this allows the gluten to relax, making stretching easier). Using a rolling pin, or your hands for a lighter texture, roll into 10-inch circles; the edges should be slightly higher than the center.

Place 1 circle on a generously floured baking peel. Rub with 1 tablespoon of the olive oil. Spoon on ⅓ cup of the tomatoes and spread gently with the back of a spoon (pressing will make the dough stick to the peel). Season with ⅛ teaspoon of the remaining salt. Top with ¼ pound of the Mozzarella and stretch into an 11-inch circle.

Transfer directly to the baking stone and bake in the preheated oven for 5 minutes, or until the crust is crisp and the Mozzarella is bubbling. Continue in the same manner with the remaining ingredients and serve each pizza as it emerges from the oven, sprinkled with one-quarter of the basil.

PREPARATION TIPS: Make the dough up to 24 hours ahead and refrigerate; bring it to room temperature before proceeding.

Pizza di Melanzane

Layered Eggplant Pie

This eggplant pie is among Campania's most understated preparations; the beaten egg whites folded into the cheese filling lend airiness, and counterbalance the potential heaviness of the fried eggplants.

SERVES 8 AS AN ANTIPASTO OR 4 AS A MAIN COURSE

2½ cups unbleached all-purpose flour

1 tablespoon plus 1½ teaspoons salt

1 cup plus 1 tablespoon extra-virgin olive oil, plus extra for greasing the bowl and pizza pan

1½ pounds eggplant, peel on, cut into ⅓-inch-thick rounds

½ pound fresh Ricotta (preferably sheep's milk)

¾ pound Scamorza or young Caciocavallo, grated

¼ pound Provolone, grated

4 extra-large eggs, separated

¼ teaspoon freshly ground black pepper

Mix the flour, 1 teaspoon of the salt, and ⅓ cup of the olive oil in a food processor. With the motor running, add enough warm (110°F) water (about ¾ cup) to make a dough that forms a ball around the blade. Add a little water if the dough is dry or a little flour if it is sticky. Shape into a ball, place in an oiled bowl, cover, and let rest for 30 minutes.

Meanwhile, sprinkle the eggplant with 1 tablespoon of the salt and set in a colander over a plate for 30 minutes. Rinse and blot dry. Heat ⅓ cup of the olive oil in a 12-inch skillet over a medium-high flame. Add half of the eggplant in a single layer and fry until golden on both sides, turning once, about 4 minutes per side. Using a slotted spatula, remove to a plate lined with paper towels and blot dry. Repeat with ⅓ cup of the olive oil and the remaining eggplant. Set the fried eggplant aside.

In a medium bowl, mix the Ricotta, Scamorza, Provolone, egg yolks, ¼ teaspoon of the salt, and the pepper. In an electric mixer with the whisk attachment, beat the egg whites

---

WHEN EGGPLANTS MET CHOCOLATE

Eggplants in Campania are cooked in innumerable ways, but by far the most unusual recipe calls for baking fried eggplants with tomatoes, Mozzarella, and melted bittersweet chocolate; strange as the pairing sounds, the flavor is quite delicate. More common treatments for eggplants include baked eggplants with a stuffing of dried mushrooms, Mozzarella, and bread crumbs, and fried eggplants marinated with vinegar, oregano, chili, and garlic. Eggplants are also cooked into sumptuous sauces for pasta, deep-fried and stuffed with Mozzarella, and much more.

until stiff peaks form, then gently fold into the Ricotta mixture with a rubber spatula, being careful not to deflate them.

Preheat the oven to 400°F.

Generously oil a deep 10-inch pizza pan. Cut the dough into 2 pieces, 1 twice as large as the other. Roll out the larger piece on a lightly floured counter into a 16-inch circle and line the prepared pan with it. Layer with one-third of the eggplant and season with a pinch of the remaining salt. Top with half of the Ricotta mixture. Layer with half of the remaining eggplant and salt, and with the other half of the Ricotta mixture. Top with a final layer of eggplant.

Roll out the smaller piece of dough into an 11-inch circle. Place over the filling, seal the edges, and cut off excess dough by rolling a rolling pin over the top of the pie. Brush the top with the remaining tablespoon of olive oil and bake in the preheated oven for 45 minutes, or until the crust is golden and lightly crisp. Serve hot.

PREPARATION TIPS: Fry the eggplant and make the dough up to 2 days ahead and refrigerate; bring to room temperature before assembling.

SALAMI UNDER A WEIGHT

MANY ITALIAN REGIONS offer some form of Soppressata, a pork salami that derives its name from the fact that it is pressed under a weight (typically large stones), thereby acquiring a flattened oval shape. Campania, like nearby Abruzzo, Molise, Calabria, and Basilicata, makes a pleasing Soppressata, laced with garlic and sometimes smoked. Rounder in shape and more subtly flavored than Soppressata, Salame Napoli is made of ground pork and veal, flavored with orange zest, garlic, and wine, and smoked; some versions are conserved in olive oil or under ashes. Both Soppressata and Salame Napoli are produced in North America, since the Italian products don't meet FDA regulations.

THE BIRTH OF PIZZA

THE DAY WAS JUNE 15. The year was 1889. The place was the Royal Palace at Capodimonte, near Naples. On that fateful date, in that awesome setting, one of Italy's most symbolic dishes was born: a baker named Raffaele Esposito topped his pizza with Mozzarella, tomatoes, and basil in honor of the colors of the Italian flag and named his creation after Italy's Queen Margherita, to whom he presented his colorful creation. The queen loved Esposito's pizza, and soon Naples was buzzing in the throes of its *pizza Margherita* passion. But pizza had been made for millennia, if under different guises, before Esposito's stroke of genius. In the Neolithic Age, people cooked a porridge of flour and water on hot stones until it turned crisp. The ancient Romans topped flatbreads with anise seeds or onions and vinegar. Flavored flatbreads were baked throughout the centuries; when tomatoes became a staple on Naples' tables in the eighteenth century, they became a standard pizza topping. Today Naples remains the undisputed world capital of pizza; Neapolitans eat their favorite food folded in quarters (in a style known as *a libretto,* or "in the manner of a book") as they stroll along the narrow streets. They love their pizza so much, in fact, that they created a consortium to protect it: regulations stipulate that to be considered Neapolitan, a pizza must be made with local water, olive oil, tomatoes, and Mozzarella, and be baked in a burning hot wood-fired oven according to specific rising and baking times. Even if you can't aspire to such perfection, you can still make a delicious pizza at home (page 265).

Spaghetti alla Caprese

Spaghetti with Tuna, Anchovies, and Olives from Capri

Cooks in Campania, as in Sardinia and Sicily, have no qualms when it comes to combining fish and cheese—and why should they, when the two marry so well? Even if the combination sounds odd, try it: the savory tuna benefits from the creaminess of the Mozzarella.

Heat 2 tablespoons of the olive oil in a 1-quart pot over a medium flame. Add the tomatoes and ½ teaspoon of the salt and cook for 15 minutes. Keep warm.

In a food processor, process the anchovies, tuna, and olives until they form a coarse purée; place in a serving bowl.

Meanwhile, bring 5 quarts of water to a boil. Add the spaghetti and the remaining 2 tablespoons of salt; cook until al dente, about 8 minutes. Drain, reserving ½ cup of the pasta cooking water.

In the serving bowl, toss the spaghetti with the tuna purée. Stir in the tomatoes, reserved cooking water, the remaining 2 tablespoons of olive oil, and the pepper. Sprinkle with the Mozzarella and serve hot.

SERVES 4

¼ cup extra-virgin olive oil

6 plum tomatoes, peeled (see page 369), seeded, and diced

2 tablespoons plus ½ teaspoon salt

2 salted anchovies, boned, gutted, and rinsed

One 6-ounce can tuna packed in olive oil, drained and crumbled

¼ cup black olives, such as Gaeta, pitted

1 pound spaghetti

¼ teaspoon freshly ground black pepper

½ pound fresh Mozzarella, cut into ¼-inch dice

THE MANGIA-MACCHERONI

The art of drying pasta was perfected in Gragnano, near Naples, so it is no surprise that dried pasta is preferred to fresh in Campania. Until the late eighteenth century, Neapolitans bought pasta on the street, eating it with the fingers of the right hand, head tilted back to receive the squirming noodles. Nicknamed *mangia-maccheroni* ("maccheroni eaters"), they made an art of cooking and eating pasta. The Campani's favorite pastas are spaghetti, maccheroni, bucatini, and vermicelli, which they mate with quick-cooking sauces; slow-simmered ragùs are the exception. Most pasta sauces are tomato-based: There is *puttanesca* ("in the manner of the whore"), flavored with olives, anchovies, and capers; *vesuviana* ("in the style of Vesuvius"), whose Mozzarella topping is reminiscent of the lava that flowed from Vesuvius on more than one occasion; and *carrettiera*, sprinkled with bread crumbs rather than grated cheese.

Scialatielli alle Vongole

Herb-Speckled Pasta with Clams, Garlic, and Cherry Tomatoes

B asil and parsley color these delectable pasta ribbons from Amalfi.

Make the scialatielli according to instructions on page 000 using the ingredients listed above, adding a little milk if the dough is dry or a little semolina flour if it is sticky. Knead 5 minutes, or until smooth, shape into a ball, wrap, and let rest 30 minutes.

Soak the clams for the sauce for 30 minutes in cool water to cover with 1 tablespoon of the salt.

Cut the dough into 4 pieces. Working with 1 piece at a time and keeping the others covered, roll out each piece on a semolina-dusted counter into a 12 × 16-inch rectangle. Cut into 1/8 × 4-inch ribbons. Toss with semolina flour to prevent sticking and spread out in a single layer on a semolina-dusted tray, then cover with a towel. These are the scialatielli.

SERVES 4

For the scialatielli:

3 cups semolina flour, plus extra for the counter
2 extra-large eggs
2 tablespoons extra-virgin olive oil
1/2 cup whole milk, plus extra if needed
2 tablespoons minced Italian parsley
2 tablespoons minced basil
1 tablespoon freshly grated Pecorino Romano
1/4 teaspoon salt
1/4 teaspoon freshly ground black pepper

For the sauce and to cook:

3 pounds Manila clams or cockles
3 tablespoons plus 1/2 teaspoon salt
1/2 cup extra-virgin olive oil
6 garlic cloves, minced
1/4 teaspoon chili flakes
1 pound cherry tomatoes, quartered
1 bunch basil, leaves only, torn
2 tablespoons minced Italian parsley

Make the sauce: Drain and rinse the clams. Heat the olive oil in a 12-inch sauté pan over a medium-high flame. Add the garlic, chili, and clams, cover, and cook 5 minutes. Add the tomatoes, basil, and parsley, and cook 10 minutes, covered. Shell the clams, discarding unopened ones, and return to the pan. Add 1/2 teaspoon of the salt; keep warm.

To cook, bring 6 quarts of water to a boil. Add the scialatielli and the remaining 2 tablespoons of salt and cook until al dente, about 2 minutes. Drain, reserving 1/2 cup of the pasta cooking water. Sauté the scialatielli for 30 seconds with the sauce and enough of the reserved cooking water to coat well. Serve hot.

PREPARATION TIPS: Shape the scialatielli up to 12 hours ahead, spread out in a single layer on a semolina-dusted tray, and refrigerate, covered with a towel.

CAMPANIA'S WINES

CAMPANIA'S VOLCANIC SOIL, combined with an abundance of sunshine and sprawling hillside vineyards, made the region a cradle of Italian viticulture over three thousand years ago. In the classical world, Campania was home to some of the Mediterranean basin's most prized wines, including Falerno from Monte Massico; legend has it that in ancient Rome, Falerno was aged for one hundred years before being poured. Today, red Falerno has an intense aroma and dry, warm, robust flavor; white Falerno is light straw-yellow with greenish highlights; and all-Primitivo Falerno is an intense ruby red with a long, persistent finish.

Indigenous grape varietals such as Aglianico, Piedirosso, Fiano, and Falanghina yield wines ranging from rich and complex to supple and refreshing. The appellation Campi Flegrei encompasses a number of excellent wines, including a dry, harmonious, intense red called Piedirosso, and a still and sparkling white called Falanghina made from a grape that may have been the basis for the original Falerno. Red, rosé, and white wines from the province of Sorrento fall under the Costa d'Amalfi appellation.

Other than Falerno, Campania's three significant white wines are Fiano d'Avellino, Greco di Tufo, and Lacryma Cristi. Fiano d'Avellino, a spicy, dry, fruity wine with a delicate pear finish and hints of hazelnuts, can be aged a decade. Greco di Tufo is dry, fruity, with an almond and peach aftertaste, and is vinified both still and sparkling from a clone of the Greco grape. Lacryma Cristi is rich and complex thanks to the fertile soil near Monte Vesuvio.

As for reds, Taurasi, an Aglianico-based wine prized since antiquity for its full-bodied flavor and intense aroma, takes first place; reminiscent of chocolate and licorice, with herbal overtones, it is vinified northeast of Avellino and aged a minimum of three years before it is released.

Cannelloni alla Sorrentina

Ricotta Cannelloni from Sorrento

Sorrento, a town on the Amalfi Coast re-nowned for its citrus and walnuts, is home to this tasty version of cannelloni: the stuffing combines Ricotta, Prosciutto, Mozzarella, and eggs, and the topping is an herb-laced tomato sauce.

Make the lasagne according to instructions on page 370 using the ingredients listed above, adding a little water if the dough is dry or a little flour if it is sticky. Knead 5 minutes, or until smooth, shape into a ball, wrap, and let rest 30 minutes.

Meanwhile, mix all the ingredients for the filling in a bowl.

Cut the dough into 2 pieces. Working with 1 piece at a time and keeping the other covered, roll out each piece into a nearly transparent sheet using a pasta machine. Cut into 4-inch squares; you will need 16 squares (use trimmings for soups). These are the lasagne.

Preheat the oven to 400°F.

SERVES 4

For the lasagne:

¾ cup plus 1 tablespoon unbleached all-purpose flour, plus extra for the counter

¼ teaspoon salt

1 extra-large egg

For the filling:

One 6-ounce slice Prosciutto di Parma or San Daniele, cut into ¼-inch dice

¼ pound fresh Mozzarella, cut into ¼-inch dice

5 ounces fresh Ricotta (preferably sheep's milk)

2 tablespoons freshly grated Pecorino Romano

1 extra-large egg

⅛ teaspoon salt

⅛ teaspoon freshly ground black pepper

To cook:

2 tablespoons salt

1½ cups Tomato Sauce (page 369)

1 tablespoon minced Italian parsley

¼ cup freshly grated Pecorino Romano

To cook, bring 5 quarts of water to a boil and add the salt. Drop in a few lasagne and cook for 2 minutes, then remove to a bowl of cool water with a slotted spoon; blot dry on kitchen towels. Repeat with the remaining lasagne.

Mix the tomato sauce and parsley in a bowl and spread ½ cup of this sauce in a 10 × 14-inch baking dish.

Arrange the lasagne on a counter and divide the filling among them. Shape the filling into a log along one end of each; roll into tight bundles. These are the cannelloni. Arrange in a single layer, seam side down, in the baking dish. Top with the remaining cup of tomato sauce; sprinkle with the Pecorino. Bake for 30 minutes and serve hot.

PREPARATION TIPS: Shape the cannelloni up to 12 hours ahead; refrigerate until baking.

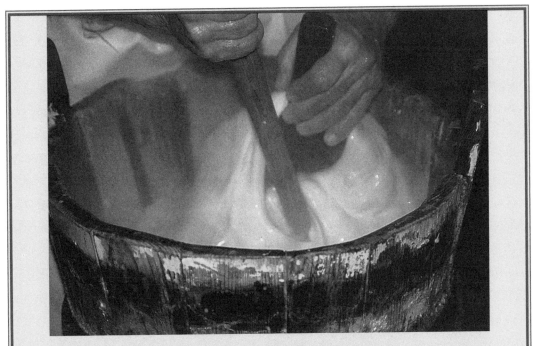

The Ultimate Mozzarella

BUFFALO MILK MOZZARELLA, like ripe summer tomatoes, aromatic basil and oregano, salty capers, plump anchovies, and oil-cured olives, is essential to Campania's cuisine. Made since at least the twelfth century, when water buffaloes were first raised in the region, it became a large-scale product in the seventeenth century. Today Campania is home to 80 percent of Italy's water buffaloes. Similar to cow's milk Mozzarella (called Fior di Latte in Italy, to distinguish it from buffalo milk Mozzarella), but tangier and fattier, buffalo milk Mozzarella has a thin, porcelain-white, shiny skin; a soft, delicate, yielding flesh that spills rivulets of whey when it is sliced; and a stringy, buttery texture.

The name *Mozzarella* is derived from *mozzare* ("to cut off"), a reference to the manner in which Mozzarella is formed by snipping off pieces from the mother loaf. Mozzarella is usually shaped as small ovals or spheres, but can appear in braids or cherry-sized balls. While Latium and other central and southern Italian regions produce excellent buffalo milk Mozzarella, the best is from the towns of Aversa and Battipaglia in Campania. Mozzarella producers say that the cheese should be eaten the day it is made, and suggest storing it in its packing water once opened.

Branzino all'Acqua Pazza

Sea Bass in "Crazy Water"

The "crazy water" in question is a flavorful cooking broth for poaching fish. Cooks on the Amalfi Coast are known for this dish, which calls for garlic, parsley, capers, and tomatoes. Instead of Mediterranean sea bass (known as branzino in Italian or loup de mer in French; see Sources, page 372, to order), you can use striped bass, monkfish, red snapper, or grouper, and even throw in a few shrimp or scampi for variety. This is a variation on the acqua pazza I enjoyed at the Hotel San Pietro in Positano.

GLORIOUS SEAFOOD SOUPS

Some seafood soups in Campania are so chunky and rich that they could fall into the category of main courses. The one most often prepared is clam or mussel soup *alla marinara* (from *mare,* meaning "sea"), flavored with tomatoes, garlic, and white wine and served over toasted bread rubbed with a whole garlic clove.

SERVES 4

⅓ cup extra-virgin olive oil

⅛ teaspoon chili flakes

6 garlic cloves, minced

3 tablespoons minced Italian parsley

20 basil leaves, torn

¼ cup salted capers, rinsed and chopped

20 cherry tomatoes, quartered

¼ teaspoon salt

1½ pounds Mediterranean sea bass fillets, skin on, scaled, boned, and cut into 3-inch pieces

⅛ teaspoon freshly ground black pepper

Heat the olive oil in a 12-inch sauté pan over a medium-high flame. Add the chili and garlic and cook until aromatic, about 1 minute. Add the parsley, basil, capers, cherry tomatoes, salt, and 1½ cups of water. Bring the liquid to a gentle boil, then add the sea bass in a single layer and reduce the heat to medium.

Cook for 8 minutes without allowing the liquid to return to a boil (the fish might flake if it does). Distribute the sea bass and its broth among 4 bowls and serve hot, sprinkled with the pepper.

Braciole di Maiale alla Napoletana

Pork Braciole with Pine Nuts and Capers

Braciole are quintessential Neapolitan food. The name refers to any cut of meat that is pounded thin and stuffed with various ingredients, then rolled up and braised until tender. But you can be sure that pork will be used more often than any other meat in Naples' kitchens. In this recipe, pork is wrapped around Prosciutto, capers, pine nuts, basil, and bread crumbs, then slow-cooked in a chili-enhanced tomato sauce.

A LOVE AFFAIR WITH TOMATOES

For all their importance in Campania's cuisine, tomatoes only became commonplace on the regional table in the eighteenth century. Today they are Campania's proudest crop, led by the pear-shaped San Marzano variety—ideal for canning. Tossed into salads, puréed into sauce, set atop pizza, roasted with fish, or married with fresh Mozzarella, tomatoes have become an essential ingredient in Campania's vibrant cuisine. Even the majority of the region's favorite meat dishes feature tomatoes: Beef is enjoyed *alla pizzaiola* ("in the manner of the pizza maker"), with tomatoes and oregano; lamb is roasted with tomatoes, potatoes, onions, and olives; poached turkey is baked with butter, Mozzarella, and tomatoes; and rabbit is braised with tomatoes and basil.

SERVES 4

8 slices boneless pork loin (¼ pound each), pounded thin with a mallet
One ¼-pound slice Prosciutto di Parma or San Daniele, minced
24 basil leaves, minced
¼ cup salted capers, rinsed and minced
¼ cup pine nuts, minced
2 tablespoons fresh bread crumbs
⅓ cup extra-virgin olive oil
2 tablespoons tomato paste
1 cup Chicken Broth (page 368), plus extra if needed
½ teaspoon salt
⅛ teaspoon freshly ground black pepper
¼ teaspoon chili flakes

Cut the pork slices into even rectangles and mince any trimmings. In a bowl, mix the pork trimmings with the Prosciutto, basil, capers, pine nuts, and bread crumbs.

Place the pork slices on a cutting board and divide the Prosciutto mixture evenly among them, then roll tightly to enclose. Spear each bundle with 2 toothpicks to prevent the filling from leaking out.

Heat the olive oil in a 12-inch sauté pan over a medium-high flame and add the bundles. Sear on all sides, about 10 minutes total, turning often. Dissolve the tomato paste in the broth and add to the pan along with the salt, pepper, and chili.

Bring the liquid to a boil, cover, and simmer for 2 hours, adding broth if needed. Discard the toothpicks and serve hot.

Scarole Imbottite
Stuffed Escarole Bundles

The combination of escarole, olives, pine nuts, and capers works so well that the same ingredients are often used as a pizza topping in Campania, Apulia, and Calabria. Serve these escarole bundles as a side dish or offer them as an appetizer.

SERVES 4

¼ cup raisins
4 heads escarole
1 tablespoon plus ¼ teaspoon salt
3 tablespoons salted capers, rinsed and minced
½ cup black olives, such as Gaeta, pitted
   and minced
¼ cup pine nuts
¼ cup plus 2 tablespoons extra-virgin olive oil
2 garlic cloves, crushed

In a small bowl, soak the raisins in warm water to cover for 15 minutes. Drain and blot dry.

Meanwhile, bring 6 quarts of water to a boil in a 10-quart pot. Wash the escarole, removing any bruised outer leaves and keeping the stem end intact. Lower the escarole into the water gently, add 1 tablespoon of the salt, and cook over medium heat for 8 minutes. Drain, cool under running water, and gently squeeze dry, being careful not to break the heads, then blot dry.

In a small bowl, mix the plumped raisins with the capers, olives, pine nuts, and 2 tablespoons of the olive oil. Open the escarole heads, being careful not to break them. Divide the caper mixture evenly among them and close into bundles, sealing in the filling by compacting the heads with your hands.

Heat the remaining ¼ cup of olive oil in a 12-inch sauté pan over a medium-high flame. Add the garlic and cook 1 minute, then add the bundles, seam side down. Cover and cook 8 minutes. Turn and cover again; cook 7 more minutes. Sprinkle with the remaining ¼ teaspoon of salt and serve hot, warm, or at room temperature.

VOLCANIC VEGETABLES

Every meal in Campania brings at least one vegetable dish. Tender, small heads of broccoli raab called *friarelli* are sautéed with garlic, olive oil, and chili pepper, and whole onions are stuck with cloves, then baked with Marsala. The local variant of Sicily's *caponata* (page 345 is *cianfotta,* a vegetable medley that includes potatoes, zucchini, and peppers. And for Christmas and Epiphany, regional cooks take whatever vegetable is on hand—usually cauliflower—and add anchovies, capers, olives, and gherkins to make a fortifying salad.

Coviglie al Caffè

Coffee Custard over Ladyfingers

Neapolitans are renowned for their sweet tooth. This decadent spoon dessert is one of their many specialties, and highlights the aromatic intensity of Neapolitan espresso. Another version of coviglie is flavored with chocolate and candied cherries rather than coffee, but I prefer the adult flavor and complexity of this one.

SWEET CREATIONS FROM NAPLES

Desserts abound in Naples, a city of excess and extravagance. Rum-soaked briochelike buns called *babà*—a staple in the city's pastry shops—were dreamt up by Polish king Stanislao Leszczynsky, who devoted himself to improving Austria's *kugelhopf*. *Pastiera napoletana,* a pie of wheat berries, Ricotta, and cream, is a must on Easter tables, and *sfogliatelle,* clam-shaped pastries stuffed with sweet Ricotta and candied fruit, have been cherished since the 1700s. And thanks to legendary Neapolitan baker Pintauro, Saint Joseph's Day always brings airy *zeppole.*

SERVES 6

1 cup whole milk
½ cup sugar
1 vanilla bean
3 extra-large egg yolks
¼ cup brewed espresso, at room temperature
⅓ cup unbleached all-purpose flour
1 cup whipping cream, whipped
⅓ cup coffee liqueur, such as Kahlúa
12 store-bought ladyfingers
6 whole coffee beans

In a 2-quart pot over a medium flame, heat the milk with the sugar and vanilla bean until almost boiling; scrape the vanilla bean into the milk, then discard it.

In a large bowl, whisk together the egg yolks and espresso; whisk in the flour, then, little by little, the hot milk. Strain through a fine sieve into the same pot. Cook over medium heat, whisking constantly, until thick, about 5 minutes; the mixture should mound slightly when dropped from the whisk. Pour into a large bowl and allow to cool to room temperature, whisking. Fold in two-thirds of the whipped cream.

Pour the liqueur into a shallow plate; very quickly dip the ladyfingers one by one in it (do not soak them or the flavor will be too strong). Arrange 2 ladyfingers, breaking them as needed to fit, in each of six 8-ounce glass goblets. Top with the espresso cream and refrigerate for 3 to 24 hours.

Spoon the remaining whipped cream into a pastry bag fitted with a star tip. Pipe it over the espresso cream, garnish each goblet with 1 coffee bean, and serve.

Apulia

Torta Tarantina di Patate
Tomato-and-Cheese-Topped Potato Pie

Sfogliata
Stuffed Focaccia Roses

Orecchiette con Rucola e Pomodoro
Orecchiette with Wilted Arugula and Tomatoes

Zuppa di Cavatelli con Fagioli e Cozze
Cavatelli and Bean Soup with Mussels

Pepata di Cozze al Limone
Peppery Mussels with Lemon

Agnello al Cartoccio
Lamb and Baby Onions Baked in Foil Packets

Frittata di Briciole e Menta
Bread Crumb and Mint Frittata

Zucchine alla Poverella
Fried Zucchini Coins in Garlic Marinade

Pane Pugliese
Apulian Bread

Frittelle di Ricotta
Ricotta Fritters

A *fter driving in the solitary silence* of neighboring Molise, with mountains looming over empty valleys, Apulia seems flat, golden, simple. The air is lighter, the sky wider. Yellow rectangles of wheat alternate with green stretches where olives and vines thrive under a blazing sun.

We drive past Alberobello, with its conical homes, through towns where women huddle, making pasta by hand, red cherry tomatoes hanging over door frames. The kaleidoscope of colors, the unmistakable sounds of families feasting and arguing, even the brilliant light are unabashedly Mediterranean. We have entered southern Italy.

Bari, Apulia's capital, was already a thriving center under the Greeks and Romans; also important in antiquity was Brindisi, a city that served as the Roman Empire's principal seaport for the East and remains an active harbor to this day. Ruled by the Goths, Byzantines, and Lombards in the early Middle Ages, Apulia then fell to the Spanish, French, Austrians, Neapolitans, and Bourbons. By the time it became part of the Kingdom of Italy in 1861, Apulia had accommodated various influences in its cuisine: the Greek preference for honey-drenched sweets; the Spanish affinity for rice; and the Neapolitan skill at drying pasta.

Modern-day Apulia includes part of what was ancient Calabria, and the two regions share much in the kitchen: both offer fish baked *in tortiera* (layered with bread crumbs, Pecorino, and herbs) and similar pasta and vegetable specialties. There is overlap with neighboring Basilicata too: some of the most characteristic semolina breads, vegetable soups, and lamb casseroles appear in both. But Apulia, with its wide, sandy beaches, rocky coves and grottoes, and prolific plains, is far luckier than Calabria or Basilicata: its soil is more generous, its pantry more diversified thanks to a gentler landscape.

In the Tavoliere Plain, much of Italy's wheat, as well as other cereals and grains, is grown; along the coast, sea urchin, baby cuttlefish, and octopus are plentiful; in the Murgia Plateau, olives, grape vines, and almonds dominate; and in the Gargano Peninsula and highlands, livestock happily graze. The result is a diet based largely on pasta and vegetables, especially broccoli raab, broccoli, cauliflower, cabbage, eggplants, fava beans, peppers, and tomatoes. The larder is rounded out with seafood, sheep's and cow's milk cheese, and meat, especially lamb, goat, mutton, and kid, since Apulia was the domain of shepherds until decades ago. And every dish is drizzled with the inimitable oil drawn from the region's olive trees.

Favorite Restaurants, Shops, and Places

- AZIENDA AGRITURISTICA MONTE SACRO, 5 miles above Mattinata, 0884.558941. Watch the farmers make cheese every morning at this charming *agriturismo*.
- BORGO ANTICO, Piazza Municipio 20, Molfetta, 080.6964236. Creative seafood; try the *soufflé di gnocchi con ragù di crostacei*.
- FORNO DEI FRATELLI DI GESÙ, Via E. Pimentel 15, Altamura, 0803.141213. A traditional bakery in one of Italy's foremost bread destinations.
- GROTTA DELLE RONDINI, Porto di Peschici, 0884.964007. If you eat on the terrace, venture inside for a glimpse of the swallows' grotto.
- HOSTERIA DEL SOLE, Piazza Curri 3, Alberobello, 080.4323904. Outstanding *branzino con olive*.
- IL BRIGANTINO UNO, Viale Regina Elena 30, Barletta, 0883.533345. The seafood antipasto is wonderful.
- IL GOLFO DEL GRAND HOTEL DELFINO, Viale Virgilio 66, Taranto, 099.339981. The cozze fritte are not to be missed.
- IL PASTAIO, Via Trani 153, Barletta, 0883.349014. Artisanal pasta manufacturer; pasta is sold vacuum-packed or in terra-cotta containers.
- IL POETA CONTADINO, Via Indipendenza 21, Alberobello, 080.4321917. Sample the *ravioli di pesce* and *spigola ai pomodorini*.
- TRATTORIA DA MIMMO, Via Cesare Battista 33/35, Vieste, 0884.707374. Try the *risotto ai frutti di mare, cavatelli con ceci e cozze,* and other seafood dishes.

Telephone country code: 011.39

Torta Tarantina di Patate

Tomato-and-Cheese-Topped Potato Pie

This potato torta illustrates three things about the Apulian kitchen: its love of intensely flavored vegetables; its skill at turning potatoes into succulent flatbreads, breads, and pizze; and its propensity for making peasant foods taste like a celebration of nature. If you enjoy crusty textures, place the pizza pan directly on a heated baking stone.

WHERE THE FAVA IS QUEEN

The Apulians are avowed vegetable addicts. They even have a saying: "*Di tutti i legumi la fava è regina, cotta la sera, scaldata la mattina*" ("Of all vegetables, the fava is queen, cooked in the evening, warmed in the morning"). Every year in Apulia, 33 million pounds of fava beans are harvested and transformed into antipasti, side dishes, and soups. The best-loved fava bean soup of all is *'ncapriata*: dried fava beans are boiled until tender, then puréed and served next to boiled wild chicory.

SERVES 6

½ pound boiling potatoes, peeled
¾ cup plus 2 tablespoons unbleached all-purpose flour, plus extra for the counter
½ teaspoon salt
¼ cup plus 2 tablespoons extra-virgin olive oil
20 cherry tomatoes, halved
1 teaspoon dried oregano
¼ teaspoon freshly ground black pepper
¼ pound fresh Mozzarella, cut into ¼-inch dice, drained in a colander 30 minutes, and blotted dry
¼ cup freshly grated Parmigiano-Reggiano

Place the potatoes in a 1-quart pot. Add cool water to cover by 2 inches and bring to a boil. Reduce the heat to medium and cook until tender when pierced with a knife, about 40 minutes. Drain, pass through a ricer, and cool.

Preheat the oven to 450°F.

Mix the potatoes, flour, and ¼ teaspoon of the salt on a counter until a smooth dough forms, adding a little water if needed to help the dough come together; if the dough is sticky, add a little flour. Roll out into a 12-inch circle on a floured counter.

Grease a 12-inch pizza pan with 3 tablespoons of the olive oil and line it with the dough. Drizzle with the remaining 3 tablespoons of olive oil; top with the tomatoes, cut side down. Season with the oregano, the remaining ¼ teaspoon of salt, and the pepper. Bake in the preheated oven 15 minutes, or until golden around the edges. Remove from the oven, top with the Mozzarella and Parmigiano, and return to the oven for 10 more minutes, or until golden brown around the edges. Serve hot.

PREPARATION TIPS: The pie can be shaped and topped up to 12 hours ahead and refrigerated until you are ready to bake.

Sfogliata

Stuffed Focaccia Roses

The Apulians are famous for their savory pies. They stuff *calzoni* with onions, olives, and anchovies, especially for Saint Joseph's Day, and bake an eggplant- or zucchini-filled pie called *cappello da gendarme* ("*the gendarme's hat,*" because of its shape). This focaccia makes a spectacular special-occasion dish because it resembles a crown of roses after baking. The filling varies from one Apulian town to the next; some cooks like onions, tomatoes, and anchovies, but I am partial to the Ricotta, Mozzarella, Scamorza, and Prosciutto Cotto filling below.

SERVES 6

½ recipe Yeasted Dough (page 371)
¼ cup plus 2 tablespoons extra-virgin olive oil,
    plus extra for greasing the pizza pan
One 5-ounce slice Prosciutto Cotto, cut into
    ⅛ × ⅛ × 1½-inch strips
½ pound fresh Ricotta
½ pound fresh Mozzarella, cut into ⅛-inch dice
5 ounces Scamorza or Caciocavallo, cut into
    ⅛-inch dice
2 extra-large eggs
¼ teaspoon salt
⅛ teaspoon freshly ground black pepper
Unbleached all-purpose flour for the counter

Make the dough and let it rise according to instructions on page 371.

Meanwhile, heat 2 tablespoons of the olive oil in an 8-inch skillet over a medium flame. Add the Prosciutto and cook 5 minutes. Set aside.

In a bowl, mix the Ricotta, Mozzarella, Scamorza, eggs, salt, and pepper. Stir in the Prosciutto. This is the filling.

Preheat the oven with a baking stone in it to 425°F.

Cut the dough into 12 pieces. Generously oil a 10-inch pizza pan with high sides. Working with 1 piece of dough at a time and keeping the others covered, roll out each piece on a lightly floured counter into a 6-inch disk. Top with one-twelfth of the filling; spread over the dough, leaving a ¾-inch border all around. Roll into an 8-inch-long log; seal the seam and edges. Coil the log around itself loosely and place in the middle of the prepared pan.

Continue with the remaining disks, arranging each coil around the preceding one in the pan; the coils should be snug in the pan. Brush the top with the remaining ¼ cup of olive oil and let rest 30 minutes (this allows the gluten to relax).

Place the pan directly on the baking stone in the preheated oven. Bake for 35 minutes, or until the crust is golden and lightly crisp. Serve hot or warm.

PREPARATION TIPS: The dough can rise in the refrigerator for up to 24 hours; return to room temperature before proceeding.

Cheese the Apulian Way

APULIAN SHEPHERDS AND FARMERS have a venerable tradition of making cheese. Every meal includes cheese in one form or another: grated over pasta, folded into stuffings for savory pies, whipped into a creamy mass for dessert, or served on its own, with a sliced tomato or a hunk of bread. Antipasto tables typically feature Burrata, a fresh cow's milk Mozzarella stuffed with cream; its name is derived from *burro,* meaning "butter." Equally luscious is Mozzarella Pugliese, made from cow's milk; like Burrata, it is highly perishable and is best eaten the day it is produced. Primo Sale, a soft, ivory-colored, rindless cow's milk cheese that oozes whey, is aged a day or two before reaching the market. Water buffaloes yield a protein-rich milk that is transformed into Provala di Bufala, essentially a fresh Provolone with a creamy, melting texture. At the pungent end of the cheese spectrum are Ricotta Forte, a sharp, spreadable, fermented Ricotta that can be flavored with pepper and vinegar, and Canestrato Pugliese, an almost spicy, salty, firm sheep's milk cheese shaped in molds called *canestri* and aged from two to ten months. All of the above cheeses are sold in North America; see Sources (page 372) to purchase.

Orecchiette con Rucola e Pomodoro

Orecchiette with Wilted Arugula and Tomatoes

Apulians adore bread and love pasta even more, especially when it is sauced with vegetables. Homemade tagliatelle are paired with chickpeas, mezze zite *are boiled with cauliflower, and* troccoli *(thick, chubby spaghetti similar to Tuscany's* pici *and Umbria's* strangozze) *are sauced with tomatoes and salted Ricotta. Ear-shaped orecchiette and tiny gnocchi called* cavatelli *are the region's proudest handmade pastas, best with broccoli raab, wild fennel, or arugula. Also called* strascinati, recchietedde, chiangarelle, *and* stacchiodde, *orecchiette are perfect with chunky vegetable sauces like the one below. This dish is also known as* recchie ai tre colori *("tricolor* recchie"), *given the green of the arugula, red of the tomatoes, and white of the orecchiette.*

SERVES 4

½ cup extra-virgin olive oil
2 garlic cloves, minced
1 tablespoon minced Italian parsley
6 plum tomatoes, peeled (see page 369), seeded, and diced
2 tablespoons plus ½ teaspoon salt
⅛ teaspoon freshly ground black pepper
1 pound orecchiette
6 bunches arugula, stems removed and washed
⅔ cup freshly grated Pecorino Romano, plus extra for passing at the table

Heat the olive oil in a 1-quart pot over a medium flame. Add the garlic and parsley and cook for 1 minute. Fold in the tomatoes. Bring to a boil and cook, uncovered, for 20 minutes. Season with ½ teaspoon of the salt and the pepper; keep the tomato sauce warm, covered, over the lowest possible flame.

Meanwhile, bring 6 quarts of water to a boil. Add the orecchiette and the remaining 2 tablespoons of salt; cook for 8 minutes. Add the arugula and cook until the orecchiette are al dente, about 6 more minutes, tasting often to determine doneness. Drain well; the arugula drinks in a lot of water. Return to the pot. Fold in the Pecorino and tomato sauce and serve hot, passing additional Pecorino at the table.

WHEN PASTA ISN'T ON THE MENU

When pasta isn't the first course in Apulia, polenta, rice, or soup are likely to be. Polenta is cooked into crisp fritters, whipped with toasted bread crumbs, onions, and Pecorino, or topped with ragù or melted lard and chili. Rice marries with everything the Apulians grow and pluck from the sea; *tiella,* Apulia's most remarkable rice dish, is made by layering rice and potatoes in a terra-cotta casserole (a tiella) with parsley, Pecorino, and vegetables or seafood. *Minestra maritata* marries a dozen vegetables and legumes with bread and Pecorino; the last Thursday of Carnevale brings cauliflower and pork soup; and Taranto is famous for its soup of baby squid, mussels, eel, hake, scorpion fish, and red mullet.

Zuppa di Cavatelli con Fagioli e Cozze
Cavatelli and Bean Soup with Mussels

Along the Apulian coast, seafood sauces for pasta reign: mussels with garlic and parsley, braised eel with tomatoes, or stuffed cuttlefish make luxuriant toppings. Soups featuring pasta, seafood, and vegetables are also prevalent, like this pasta e fagioli *from Mimmo Ciuffreda of Da Mimmo in Vieste.*

THE FISH THAT RAN AWAY

A curious seventeenth-century dish, invented by Apulians who had to make do with little when the craving for fish struck, has survived to this day: known as *vermicelli col sugo di pesce scappato* ("vermicelli with a sauce of runaway fish"), it is made by dropping sea shells and sea stones wrapped in seaweed in a vegetable broth, resulting in a seafood-flavored broth. Needless to say, the broth is strained before the pasta is added.

SERVES 4

1 cup dried cannellini beans, soaked 12 hours in cool water to cover
1 celery stalk, whole
1 medium yellow onion, whole
3 garlic cloves, 2 peeled and 1 chopped
2 bay leaves
3 tablespoons plus $\frac{1}{2}$ teaspoon salt
$\frac{1}{4}$ teaspoon freshly ground black pepper
1 pound mussels, scrubbed, beards removed
$\frac{1}{2}$ cup extra-virgin olive oil
1 tablespoon minced Italian parsley
$\frac{1}{2}$ cup dry white wine
$\frac{1}{2}$ pound cavatelli

Drain the beans. Bring to a boil in a 2-quart pot with the celery, onion, peeled garlic, bay leaves, and 8 cups of cool water. Reduce the heat to medium and cook, half-covered, for 2 hours, or until tender. Discard the celery, onion, garlic, and bay leaves; purée the beans and their cooking broth in a food processor. Add $\frac{1}{2}$ teaspoon of the salt and $\frac{1}{8}$ teaspoon of the pepper; return to the pot.

Meanwhile, soak the mussels in cool water to cover with 1 tablespoon of the salt for 30 minutes, then drain and rinse. Heat $\frac{1}{4}$ cup of the olive oil in a 12-inch sauté pan over a medium-high flame. Add the chopped garlic and parsley and cook for 1 minute. Add the mussels and cook for 2 minutes. Deglaze with the wine and cook until the mussels open, about 5 minutes. Remove to a plate; shell, discarding the cooking liquid and any unopened mussels. Add to the puréed beans in the pot and keep warm.

Bring 3 quarts of water to a boil. Add the cavatelli and the remaining 2 tablespoons of salt and cook until firm but not quite al dente, about 12 minutes. Drain.

Toss the cavatelli into the pot with the mussels and puréed beans. Cook over medium-high heat until the cavatelli are done, about 3 minutes, stirring often. Stir in the remaining $\frac{1}{8}$ teaspoon of pepper and serve hot, drizzled with the remaining $\frac{1}{4}$ cup of olive oil.

PREPARATION TIPS: The beans can be cooked up to 3 days ahead and refrigerated.

Pepata di Cozze al Limone

Peppery Mussels with Lemon

La pepata's *name hints that it contains a generous dose of black pepper. And that it does. But there's more than pepper to give pepata character: the fresh note of grated lemon zest, the delicate acidity of white wine, the aroma of garlic, and the fruitiness of olive oil each add a dimension of flavor. To truly savor mussels, clams, or any bivalves, set aside all notions of etiquette and eat with your hands: each of the half-shells is a perfect spoon and will bring the briny flavors of the cooking juices to your mouth much more effectively than any flat-ware. Dip each half-shell into the broth, bring it up to your mouth, and rejoice.*

SERVES 4

2 pounds mussels, scrubbed, beards removed
1 tablespoon plus ½ teaspoon salt
4 garlic cloves, chopped
Grated zest of 2 lemons
½ cup chopped Italian parsley
30 basil leaves, torn
1 tablespoon black peppercorns, cracked
⅓ cup extra-virgin olive oil
⅓ cup dry white wine

Soak the mussels in cool water to cover with 1 tablespoon of the salt for 30 minutes, then drain and rinse.

Place the garlic, lemon zest, parsley, basil, peppercorns and olive oil in a 4-quart pot over medium heat. Cook for 2 minutes, stirring constantly. Add the wine, mussels, and the remaining ½ teaspoon of salt. Cover and cook until the mussels open, about 8 minutes. Discard any mussels that remain closed and serve hot, in bowls, with the cooking juices.

RAW SEAFOOD ALONG THE APULIAN COAST

Despite government warnings that raw mussels are not the safest of treats, Apulians who live or vacation along the coast habitually feast on raw mussels. They also devour raw oysters, and in Bari, near the fishing boats, raw sea urchins are enjoyed, often accompanied by thick slices of tomato-topped focaccia. Taranto, the port city with the largest repertoire of seafood specialties, is the birthplace of *tarantello:* ground and spiced tuna belly, a delicacy on appetizer tables since the early sixteenth century. Yet the most singular offering is *schiuma di mare* ("sea foam"), featuring new-born raw fish in a lemony dressing.

Agnello al Cartoccio

Lamb and Baby Onions Baked in Foil Packets

Lamb in Apulia is roasted, grilled, baked, braised with peas or young cardoons, and stewed in a vinegar-laced tomato sauce. It is also baked in foil packets or in parchment paper, as below, intensifying aroma and sealing in moisture. In the town of Modugno, the baby onions in this recipe are often substituted with *lampasciuoli*, small bulbs that recall onions in shape. Their bitter flavor requires taming by blanching or by lengthy soaking in a salted water bath; after they are purged, *lampasciuoli* are sautéed with eggs, baked, fried, pickled, or tossed with lamb and roasted or braised.

HUMBLE INGENUITY

Offal is cooked ingeniously in Apulia, as in nearby Molise. *Gniummerieddi* (from *gnumiro,* dialect for *gomito,* or "elbow") are bundles of lamb's hearts, lungs, and intestines wrapped in caul fat; they are skewered and grilled, then eaten with celery or a twice-fermented sheep's milk cheese called Cacio Marcetto. *Torcinelli* are skewered bundles of lamb's intestines and lungs that owe their crisp texture to a peculiar cooking technique: a piece of paper is greased with lard, lit on fire, and placed above the skewers so the meat is basted with fat as it cooks. The same method, known as *pilotto,* is used with game birds in Umbria (page 185).

SERVES 4

1½ pounds boneless lamb shoulder, trimmed of fat and sinew, cut into 1-inch cubes
4 plum tomatoes, cut into 1-inch cubes
24 pitted black olives, such as Gaeta
24 baby onions, peeled
4 garlic cloves, quartered
8 rosemary sprigs
8 thyme sprigs
¼ teaspoon chili flakes
½ teaspoon freshly ground black pepper
¼ cup extra-virgin olive oil
1 teaspoon salt
1 pound baking potatoes, peeled and cut into ½-inch cubes

In a large bowl, toss all the ingredients except the salt and potatoes. Refrigerate for 2 days, tossing once in a while.

Preheat the oven to 375°F.

Add the salt and potatoes to the marinated ingredients and divide among four 12-inch squares of sturdy aluminum foil; close each foil packet tightly. Place the packets on an 11 × 17-inch baking sheet and bake in the preheated oven for 30 minutes. Place each packet on a plate and serve hot.

APULIA'S WINES

ALREADY ACTIVE IN VITICULTURE before the arrival of the Phoenicians and Romans, Apulia is Italy's most prolific producer of wine given its hot, dry climate, calcareous, iron-rich soil, and easy-to-cultivate, mostly flat or hilly terrain; only Sicily comes close to its staggering annual output of 340 million gallons. Since the majority of vineyards are located in the flatlands and yield grapes with a high alcohol content, Apulia has long sold the bulk of its grapes to northern Italian regions for blending into and adding body to local wines. The phylloxera (vine pest) epidemic that hit European vineyards in the nineteenth century gave additional impetus to viticulture in Apulia thanks to northern demand for Apulian grapes and wines.

Negroamaro, Malvasia Nera, Primitivo, Montepulciano, Bombino Bianco, and Uva di Troia are the most interesting native varietals. Brindisi, a red based on Negroamaro, is characterful, harmonious, and velvety, with a bitter aftertaste and deep tannins; when vinified as a rosé, it has a fruity aroma and dry taste and can age from two to three years. Primitivo di Manduria, a robust high-alcohol dry or sweet red, is made from the Primitivo grape, a varietal identical to California's Zinfandel.

The fertile, undulating plains of Salento are home to Salice Salentino, an appellation that includes six wines; the white offers a delicate, fruity scent, and the red is fruity, full-bodied, robust, aromatic. Gravina, a white with a zesty bouquet and delicate flavor, and Locorotondo, a dry white with a greenish hue best sipped within a year of vintage, are vinified both still and sparkling.

THE BREAD EATERS

Apulians are outright bread lovers, so it isn't surprising that most of their meals exalt bread in one form or another. Platters of tomato-topped bruschetta are passed around ceremoniously to friends and relatives at nearly every gathering and refreshing bread and vegetable salads abound: *cialledda,* a vegetable and bread medley, includes tomatoes, cucumbers, and onions. In the old days, farmers ate *frisedda,* a crisp doughnut-shaped bread, for the midday meal; today it is offered as a starter with tomatoes, basil, and Burrata cheese.

Frittata di Briciole e Menta

Bread Crumb and Mint Frittata

The procedure for making this dish is the same as the one used for making frittata, which explains the name. But the texture and flavor are different thanks to an abundance of bread crumbs and Pecorino. This frittata is dense and not the least bit eggy; tuck leftovers between slices of bread with slices of tomato.

SERVES 4

6 extra-large eggs
2 cups fresh bread crumbs
1 cup freshly grated Pecorino Romano
1/2 cup minced Italian parsley
1/2 cup minced mint
1/4 teaspoon freshly ground black pepper
1/4 cup plus 2 tablespoons extra-virgin olive oil

Combine all the ingredients except the olive oil in a bowl; the mixture will be quite firm. Heat a 12-inch skillet over a medium-high flame and add 3 tablespoons of the olive oil. After 1 minute, spoon in the egg mixture. Press with the back of a spatula until the mixture covers the entire surface of the skillet. Cook until golden on the bottom, about 5 minutes, then invert onto a 12-inch plate.

Heat the remaining 3 tablespoons of olive oil in the skillet for 1 minute. Return the frittata to the skillet, uncooked side down. Cook for 5 minutes, or until the bottom is also golden. Serve hot or warm.

THE WILD KITCHEN

The Apulians are experts at cooking wild greens. Their kitchens are filled with the aroma of wild arugula, chicory, and mustard. In lean times, this ability to turn a handful of field greens into a meal surely came in handy; today, it forms the basis for a unique cuisine. There are *frittate* laced with wild mint, penne with wild asparagus, and soups featuring corn poppy, olives, raisins, and walnuts. Apulian wild greens include *Rumex acetosella,* a sour-leafed garden sorrel; *Cicerbita alpina,* which belongs to the *asteraceae* family and sports mauve flowers in bloom; *Erysimum officinalis,* part of the cruciferous family, in season from spring through early fall; and *Cakile marittima,* a sea-loving member of the cruciferous family with fatty leaves and bluish flowers. Their pungent, earthy character often defines the region's most interesting and hard-to-reproduce soups, salads, rice dishes, and savory pies.

Zucchine alla Poverella

Fried Zucchini Coins in Garlic Marinade

The name of this boldly flavored vegetable dish—a staple in Apulia, Latium, and Sicily—denotes its poor roots (*povera* means "poor"). Eggplants are cooked the same way, but soak up more oil as they fry.

Heat ⅓ cup of the olive oil in a 12-inch skillet for 2 minutes over a medium-high flame. Add half of the zucchini coins in a single layer. Cook until golden brown on both sides, turning once, about 3 minutes per side. Remove with a slotted spatula to a plate lined with paper towels and blot dry, then transfer to a serving platter. Fry the remaining zucchini in the same manner in the olive oil that is left in the skillet.

Add the vinegar, garlic, mint, salt, pepper, and the remaining ⅓ cup of olive oil to the fried zucchini on the platter. Toss gently to avoid crushing the zucchini and cool to room temperature. Refrigerate for at least 4 hours, then serve at room temperature.

SERVES 4

⅔ cup extra-virgin olive oil
4 medium zucchini (6 ounces each), cut into ¼-inch-thick rounds
¼ cup red wine vinegar
2 garlic cloves, sliced
¼ cup chopped mint
½ teaspoon salt
⅛ teaspoon freshly ground black pepper

OLIVE OIL IN APULIA

Nearly every Italian region produces olive oil. But some, like Trentino–Alto Adige, Friuli–Venezia Giulia, Lombardy, and the Veneto, devote limited terrain to olive cultivation because of an unsuitably cold climate. Apulia, on the other hand, is responsible for roughly half of Italy's olive oil; many of its olives are sold to producers in other regions for blending into local olive oil (the same applies to Apulia's grapes, which are sold to winemakers in other regions for blending into their local wines). Apulia's mild weather and tractable soil make for generous trees: an Apulian tree yields twenty times as many olives as a similar tree in Tuscany. And while Apulian olive oil varies from mild or fruity to fruity-spicy (depending on the variety of olives used, the harvesting and processing methods, and the time of harvest), most of it is fruity, ideal with the region's full-flavored fare. Experts say it tastes vaguely like almonds, perhaps because of the numerous almond trees that grow in the area.

Pane Pugliese

Apulian Bread

The residents of Altamura in Apulia were already renowned for their bread two thousand years ago: the ancient Romans sent for Apulian bread daily, bringing in fat, burnished loaves to the capital of the empire. Until a few decades ago, Apulian families still used communal ovens to bake their weekly bread, and slashed their loaves with distinctive markings to differentiate them.

MAKES 2 LARGE LOAVES

1½ teaspoons instant yeast
8 cups bread flour, plus extra for the counter
  and bowl
1 tablespoon plus 1 teaspoon fine sea salt
¼ cup cornmeal

In a large bowl or in the bowl of an electric mixer, combine ¼ teaspoon of the yeast with 1 cup of the flour. Using a wooden spoon or the paddle attachment of the mixer, stir in ½ cup of warm (110°F) water; the ingredients should form a rough, soft dough, not a batter. Add a little more flour if needed. Stir with the spoon for 2 minutes, or with the paddle attachment for 1 minute. Cover and set aside to rise at room temperature for 24 hours. This is the *biga*.

Combine the remaining 1¼ teaspoons of yeast, 1 cup of the flour, and ½ cup of warm (110°F) water in a very large bowl or in the bowl of an electric mixer. Add 2¾ cups of room-temperature water, the salt, and the biga; beat with a wooden spoon for 2 minutes, or with the paddle attachment of the mixer for 1 minute. Work in the remaining 6 cups of flour by the ¼ cup until the dough pulls away from the sides (but not the bottom) of the bowl; it should be sticky. You may not need all the flour.

Knead by hand on a lightly floured counter 12 minutes, adding as little flour as possible, or beat with the dough hook of the electric mixer for 8 minutes; the dough should be soft and elastic. Place in a floured bowl, cover, and refrigerate for 24 hours.

Return the dough to room temperature. On a lightly floured counter, cut into 2 pieces, pat each into a rectangle, and roll into a log. Pat each log into a rectangle, roll into a log again, and shape into a taut ball with the palms of your hands. Place seam-side down on a cornmeal-sprinkled baking peel (or on the back of a cornmeal-sprinkled 11 × 17-inch baking sheet if you don't have a peel) about 3 inches apart, cover with a towel, and let rise at room temperature for 1 hour.

Meanwhile, preheat the oven with a baking stone in it to 450°F.

Uncover the loaves, dust with flour, and dimple gently with your fingers (this prevents the loaves from rising uncontrollably in the oven). Let rest 10 minutes. Transfer to the baking stone in the preheated oven. Bake 10 minutes, misting every 3 minutes with water from a spray bottle (this ensures a crisp crust), closing the oven door quickly each time. Bake 25 to 35 more minutes without misting again, or until the crust is golden brown and crisp. Cool on a rack.

Frittelle di Ricotta

Ricotta Fritters

Ricotta forms the basis of many Apulian sweets. The most sophisticated Ricotta dessert is a layered almond and Ricotta cake reminiscent of Sicily's cassata, while a pastry known as dita di apostoli ("the apostles' fingers") is the most peculiar: egg whites are beaten, fried into lacy pancakes, then rolled around a Ricotta-cocoa filling. The homey Ricotta fritters below are favorites in Apulian homes and are best made using firm Ricotta; if your Ricotta is too watery, drain it in a sieve set over a bowl for a few hours before mixing it with the other ingredients.

SERVES 6

¼ pound crustless white country bread, crumbled
½ cup whole milk
½ pound fresh Ricotta
⅔ cup sugar
2 extra-large egg yolks
Grated zest of 1 orange
4 cups extra-virgin olive oil or peanut oil
½ cup unbleached all-purpose flour
2 extra-large eggs

Soak the bread in the milk for 5 minutes, then squeeze dry and place in a large bowl. Stir in the Ricotta, ⅓ cup of the sugar, the egg yolks, and the orange zest.

Heat the oil in a deep 10-inch pan until it registers 350°F, or until it is hot enogh to brown a cube of bread in 1 minute. Pour the flour in one bowl; beat the eggs in another. Using a spoon, drop spoonfuls of the Ricotta mixture in the flour, then roll in the beaten eggs to coat all sides; transfer to the hot oil. Fry 8 or 10 Ricotta dumplings at a time until golden all over, turning once, about 2 minutes per side. Remove with a slotted spoon to a plate lined with paper towels and blot dry. Continue in the same manner with the remaining Ricotta mixture, maintaining the temperature of the oil by regulating the heat. Serve the fritters hot, rolled in the remaining ⅓ cup of sugar.

A SWEET FOR EVERY HOLIDAY

Every feast day in Apulia has its prescribed dessert. Christmas is the time for *cartellate,* strips of wine-and-flour dough shaped into knots, then fried and doused with *vino cotto* (page 204) or honey; when the same dough is shaped into dumplings, it goes by the name of *purciduzzi.* On Saint Joseph's Day, *zeppole* are fried twice—once in moderately hot oil, then a second time in viciously hot oil to attain a light texture—and stuffed with pastry cream or sour cherry jam; Easter brings *corrucolo,* a braided sweet bread nestling a whole egg.

PREPARATION TIPS: Make the Ricotta mixture up to 12 hours before frying, and refrigerate until you are ready to use.

Basilicata

Acqua e Sale
Soaked Bread with Sweet Onion, Tomato, and Basil

Foquazza di Matera
Vegetable-and-Cheese-Stuffed Focaccia from Matera

Bucatini al Fuoco
Bucatini in Fiery Chili-Garlic Paste

Grano con Ragù di Maiale
Wheat Berries in Savory Pork Ragù

Scorze d'Amelle con Cime di Rapa
"Almond Sliver" Pasta with Garlicky Broccoli Raab

Lagane e Ceci
Short Pasta Strips in Spicy Chickpea Broth

Minestra Maritata
Escarole, Fennel, and Sausage Soup Dusted with Pecorino

Agnello e Funghi al Forno
Roasted Lamb and Oyster Mushrooms

Patate Raganate
Baked Potatoes, Onions, and Tomatoes with Oregano
and Bread Crumbs

Grano Dolce
Plump Wheat with Pomegranate, Chocolate, and Nuts

I once taught a class on the cooking of Basilicata to a group of twenty-odd Italians and Italophiles. When I asked the students if they had been to Basilicata, not a single hand went up. One of the men in the class, a native of Milan, later told me he had been to every region of Italy—*except* Basilicata.

Basilicata is the region many people miss. Haunted by poverty until decades ago, racked by earthquakes, its woods and mountains and coastline as wild as when the Greeks arrived three thousand years ago, it quietly straddles the Tyrrhenian and Ionian seas. In Basilicata, it is still possible to imagine what life might have been like centuries ago. And in many of its mountain towns and hilltop villages, life *is* still very much as it was centuries ago. The craggy emptiness, the scorched, sun-burnished quiet, the stretches of coastline so blue they dazzle the eye . . . the land is as timeless as the olive groves planted by the Romans, as timeless as the vines that have borne fruit since the days of ancient Greece, as timeless as the wisdom lining the old shepherds' faces.

Known as Lucania before the Romans conquered it, Basilicata was named after the Lyki, an Anatolian tribe that settled in the area over three thousand years ago. After the Romans lost control, the Lombards, Byzantines, and Saracens took over; in the Middle Ages, the city of Melfi became the capital of a Norman dominion, leading Basilicata to play a pivotal role in the life of southern Italy until the thirteenth century. From the sixteenth to the eighteenth century, the Angevins and Spanish gained control; Basilicata later became part of the Kingdom of Naples, and was annexed to unified Italy in 1861.

The people of Basilicata are known as Lucani, after Lucania, and have struggled with poor soil and terrain for thousands of years. Wheat, rye, grapes, and olives are the major crops, yet agriculture is difficult in this intractable land. Many Lucani fled rural areas. Some moved to Potenza, the region's capital, or to Matera, a city dug in the tufaceous stone of a gorge; others sought their fortune in luckier cities elsewhere in Italy; and others still emigrated to North America. Potenza and Matera are the only cities with more than fifty thousand inhabitants; the rest of the region is made up of small towns perched high in the mountains, away from the coast, where malaria was once rampant and the threat of invasion by Turkish pirates a constant.

Meat was rare in the old days, since there was little land for grazing. So vegetables, along with wheat, olive oil, and sheep's or goat's milk cheeses, made up the bulk of the diet. Most families kept a pig or two, and the yearly pig slaughter remains an important event; skilled sausage-makers know how to conserve every last scrap of their pigs. Shepherds too learned to draw the most from nature's offerings, plucking herbs for the soup pot or the occasional *pignata,* a robust meat and vegetable casserole.

Favorite Restaurants, Shops, and Places

- CASA GROTTA DI VICO SOLITARIO, Sasso Caveoso, Piazza Sedile, Matera. Peek into life in the Sassi as it was until the 1950s in this Grotto Home Museum.
- FORNO A LEGNA CIFARELLI, Via Istria 17, Matera, 0835.385630. Matera's superb bread is baked daily here.
- HOTEL CHETA ELITE, Acquafredda di Maratea, 0973.878134. Outstanding food and hospitality along the most gorgeous stretch of coastline in Basilicata.
- HOTEL RISTORANTE PICCHIO NERO, Via Mulino 1, Terranova di Pollino, 0973.93170. The Golia-Genovese family cures Prosciutto and makes pasta daily for the restaurant.
- IL TERRAZZINO, Vico San Giuseppe 7, Matera, 0835.332503. The antipasti and *grano e ceci* are not to be missed.

- RISTORANTE FUORI LE MURA, Via 4 Novembre 34, Potenza, 0971.25409. *Strascinati al ragù* and *baccalà e peperoni* are marvelous.
- RISTORANTE LE BOTTEGHE, Via Sasso Barisano 8, Matera, 0835.344072. Try the *fusilli al ferro, scorze d'amelle,* and *arrosto misto.*
- SALUMIFICIO FRATELLI SILENO, Via Melfi 102, Venosa, 0972.35180. The owners make outstanding hams, sausages, and more in the winter.
- TRIMINEDD', Contrada Bucaletto, Potenza, 0971.55746. *Lagane e ceci, orecchiette e rape,* and *agnello in tortiera* are deftly prepared.
- ZA MARIUCCIA, Via Grotte 2, Località Porto di Maratea, Maratea, 0973.876163. The *ravioli dolci con ragù d'agnello* and *spaghetti alla Za Mariuccia* are a must-try.

Telephone country code: 011.39

Acqua e Sale

Soaked Bread with Sweet Onion, Tomato, and Basil

The Lucani, like their Apulian and Calabrese neighbors, are masters at turning vegetables into succulent antipasti and one-course meals: strips of fried peppers, coins of grilled eggplants, or a tomato-and-onion-topped bruschetta usher in most meals. Add a few slices of Soppressata, a ball of creamy Mozzarella, and a variety of oil-preserved vegetables, and you have the makings of a feast. Called acqua e sale ("water and salt"), the humble bruschetta below is what many farmers in Basilicata ate in the fields. When the same ingredients are cooked, they form a soup known as cialledda, the local equivalent of Tuscany's and Umbria's acquacotta.

SERVES 4

Eight ¼-inch-thick × 6-inch-wide slices day-old country bread
Sixteen ¼-inch-thick slices beefsteak tomatoes
1 small purple onion, sliced into paper-thin rings
¼ teaspoon salt
⅛ teaspoon freshly ground black pepper
16 basil leaves, torn
½ cup extra-virgin olive oil

Place the bread on a serving plate and sprinkle it with ½ cup of cold water. Set aside for 5 minutes, then drain off any water that has accumulated on the plate.

Top each slice of bread with 2 slices of tomatoes and a few onion rings. Sprinkle with the salt and pepper, top with the basil and olive oil, and serve.

PRESERVING THE HARVEST

Preserving food for the winter has been a way of life in Basilicata for millennia. Difficult mountain terrain, harsh winters, and poor roads meant isolation and little commerce with neighboring regions. The best tools for survival were self-reliance and careful planning, skills the Lucani honed to perfection. In the days of Cicero, they were already preserving their famed Lucaniche sausages in pork fat, salting hams, and smoking salami to better conserve them. Two thousand years later, these traditions persist, as do the customs of preserving vegetables in olive oil or vinegar and of sun-drying vegetables such as mushrooms, peppers, and tomatoes. Today you can still find *cardoncelli* mushrooms (page 309) spread out on a newspaper to dry in the sun, wreaths of chilies hanging over door frames, and ears of corn strung on wires in the larder.

THREE FARMHOUSE CHEESES

THE DRY, ROCKY SOIL OF BASILICATA is better suited to grazing sheep and goats than cows. As a result, most of the region's cheeses are made of sheep's or goat's milk, or a combination of the two. The following cheeses are available in North America (see Sources, page 372).

CACIORICOTTA, a dry-salted goat's and sheep's milk cheese, is soft, smooth, and white when it is aged two days and semi-firm, straw-yellow, and coated with a thin reddish rind when aged four months.

CANESTRATO DI MOLITERNO, a pungent goat's and sheep's milk cheese aged eight months, derives its compact texture from the pressing of the curds into baskets.

TOMA DI PECORA, made of raw sheep's or sheep's and goat's milk, is salt-brined and aged a minimum of two months.

Foquazza di Matera

Vegetable-and-Cheese-Stuffed Focaccia from Matera

Basilicata offers a range of savory pies whose fillings are usually more spartan than those of bordering Apulia or Campania. This foquazza (dialect for focaccia) from Matera is an exception: it features an abundance of oil-preserved vegetables, Mozzarella, and Pecorino. It owes its distinctive character to eggplants and mushrooms packed in olive oil; these oil-preserved vegetables can be found in specialty stores across the country (see Sources, page 372).

SERVES 6

1 recipe Yeasted Dough (page 371)
½ cup extra-virgin olive oil, plus extra for greasing the pizza pan
1 large yellow onion, thinly sliced
Unbleached all-purpose flour for the counter
½ pound fresh Mozzarella, thinly sliced, drained in a colander 30 minutes, and blotted dry
3 plum tomatoes, peeled (see page 369), seeded, and diced
1 cup pitted black olives, such as Gaeta
1 cup oil-preserved mushrooms, drained and chopped
1 cup oil-preserved eggplants, drained and chopped
¼ cup freshly grated Pecorino Romano
¼ to ½ teaspoon chili flakes

Make the dough and let it rise until doubled according to instructions on page 371.

Meanwhile, heat ¼ cup of the olive oil in a 12-inch skillet over a medium-high flame. Add the onion and cook for 15 minutes, stirring often. Remove from the heat and cool.

Preheat the oven with a baking stone in it to 425°F.

Cut the dough into 2 pieces, 1 twice as large as the other. Roll out the larger piece on a lightly floured counter into a 16-inch circle. Roll out the smaller piece into a 12-inch circle.

Generously oil a 10-inch pizza pan with high borders. Line it with the larger piece of dough, letting excess dough hang over the sides. Arrange the Mozzarella over the dough, then the tomatoes, sautéed onion (with its cooking oil), olives, mushrooms, eggplants, and Pecorino; dust with the chili. Cover with the smaller piece of dough and seal the edges with your fingers. Roll a rolling pin over the top of the pie to cut off excess dough and poke a hole in the middle (this allows air to escape). Brush the top of the foquazza with the remaining ¼ cup of olive oil and let rest 30 minutes (this allows the gluten to relax).

Bake directly on the baking stone in the preheated oven for 35 minutes, or until the crust is golden and lightly crisp. Serve hot.

PREPARATION TIPS: Make the dough up to 24 hours ahead and let it rise in the refrigerator; bring to room temperature before proceeding.

Bucatini al Fuoco

Bucatini in Fiery Chili-Garlic Paste

The ingenuity of Basilicata's kitchen is embodied in this simple pasta: three ingredients, easy to come by and inexpensive, are combined to make a formidably tasty sauce. The method of pounding garlic and chili peppers into a paste, then cooking the paste in olive oil, is common to Basilicata and Calabria and elevates the ordinary aglio, olio e peperoncino *of central and southern Italy to new heights of piquancy.*

SERVES 4

⅔ cup extra-virgin olive oil

4 garlic cloves, 3 peeled and 1 minced

6 small dried chili peppers or 1 teaspoon
  chili flakes

1 pound bucatini

2 tablespoons salt

Heat ⅓ cup of the olive oil in a small skillet over a medium flame. Add the peeled garlic and chili; cook 2 minutes, or until the garlic is golden and the chili peppers are swollen (or the chili flakes are aromatic). Cool the garlic and chili 5 minutes, then crush in a mortar with a pestle into a coarse paste.

Add the remaining ⅓ cup of olive oil to the skillet over medium heat and cook the minced garlic until aromatic, about 30 seconds. Stir in the prepared garlic-chili paste and cook 30 seconds.

Meanwhile, bring 5 quarts of water to a boil. Add the bucatini and salt and cook until al dente, about 8 minutes. Drain, reserving ½ cup of the pasta cooking water. Transfer the bucatini to a serving platter, fold in the chili-garlic sauce and the reserved cooking water, and serve hot.

Grano con Ragù di Maiale

Wheat Berries in Savory Pork Ragù

This dish is from Potenza, Basilicata's capital. Wheat berries are plentiful and cheap and offer a concentrated form of energy, so they are popular in poorer areas. Like many peasant foods, this preparation is both a first and second course rolled into one: The wheat berries are eaten as a first course, topped with the sauce in which the pork is braised; the pork is then served as a second course. You can, if you prefer, serve the pork alongside the wheat berries.

SERVES 6

1 cup chopped Italian parsley
2 garlic cloves, chopped
½ to 1 teaspoon cayenne pepper
½ teaspoon freshly grated nutmeg
⅓ cup cubed Pecorino Romano
1¼ cups freshly grated Pecorino Romano
3 pounds boneless pork loin, butterflied and
    pounded thin with a mallet
¼ pound thinly sliced Pancetta
½ cup extra-virgin olive oil
2 medium yellow onions, minced
⅔ cup dry white wine
6 cups canned chopped Italian plum tomatoes
1 teaspoon salt
2⅔ cups wheat berries, soaked 12 hours in cool
    water to cover

In a medium bowl, mix the parsley, garlic, cayenne, nutmeg, cubed Pecorino, and ¼ cup of the grated Pecorino. Place the pork, smooth side down, on a cutting board; spread the parsley mixture over it. Top with the Pancetta and roll lengthwise into a bundle, then tie with butcher's string.

Heat the olive oil in a 12-inch sauté pan over a medium-high flame. Add the onions and pork. Cook, deglazing every 5 minutes with 3 tablespoons of the wine and turning the

---

PORK FOR THE POT

The Lucani have a saying: *"Crisc'lu purch'ca t'ung'lu muss"* ("Raise a pig and you will grease your face with it," meaning you will eat it). Pork has been a favorite since the days of ancient Rome. Long, thin sausages called Lucaniche have been staples of the regional pantry for hundreds of years; today, they are flavored with sweet and spicy pepper, fennel seeds, and black pepper. On the day of the pig slaughter, various cuts of pork are cooked with preserved peppers, and every portion of the pig is put to good use: The fat is cooked down into a creamy lard that can be spiced and used in *focacce*; pork rind is stuffed with lard, parsley, garlic, and chili; a sweet-and-sour pork gelatin is flavored with cooked grape must, vinegar, almonds, and pine nuts; and a spicy salami called Soppressata is hung near the hearth to age and acquire a smoky aroma.

pork, until the wine is finished and the onions and pork are golden, about 15 minutes. Stir in the tomatoes and ½ teaspoon of the salt, reduce the heat to medium-low, cover, and cook for 2 hours, turning the pork every 15 minutes.

Meanwhile, drain the wheat berries and place in a 4-quart pot. Add the remaining ½ teaspoon of salt and 3 quarts of water. Bring to a boil and cook over medium heat until tender but not mushy, about 45 minutes. Drain.

Remove the pork and half of the sauce to a serving platter and cover with foil; set aside to serve as a second course (or serve the pork alongside the wheat berries). Spoon the wheat berries on a serving platter; top with the remaining half of the sauce and the remaining cup of grated Pecorino and serve hot.

PREPARATION TIPS: Stuff the pork up to 12 hours ahead and refrigerate.

BASILICATA'S WINES

ALTHOUGH BASILICATA HAS BEEN INHABITED since the Paleolithic Age, vines have only been planted in the area since a little over three thousand years ago. Greek and later Roman settlers improved viticulture, and wine soon became one of the most actively traded goods in the region, shipped from the main port of Metaponto to faraway lands. During the Middle Ages, the city of Melfi was especially renowned for its wines, but by the late nineteenth century, oenologists agreed that the best wines hailed from the fertile land at the foot of Monte Vulture, a volcano inactive since prehistoric times.

The rocky, mountainous, arid soil of Basilicata is a challenge for growing vines; production is therefore limited, ringing in at a low 13 million gallons annually, of which a mere 2 percent meets DOC regulations. Moscato, Malvasia, Aglianico, and Aleatico are the most important grape varietals. Aglianico del Vulture, dubbed "the Barolo of the South," is Basilicata's only DOC. Aglianico grapes, one of Italy's oldest varietals—likely planted on Italian soil by Greek settlers—form the basis for this intense, robust, spicy, almost chocolatey, berry-scented red. While most Aglianico del Vulture is dry, medium-sweet or sparkling versions exist.

Scorze d'Amelle con Cime di Rapa

"Almond Sliver" Pasta with Garlicky Broccoli Raab

Despite Basilicata's unyielding terrain, the region has a good supply of wheat, and pasta is the underpinning of its diet. Pastas include minuich *or* fusilli al ferro, *rolled around an iron rod;* strascinati, *pasta squares dragged across a stamp with a raised motif; and* scorze d'amelle, *shaped like teardrops. I tasted* scorze d'amelle *at Le Botteghe in Matera, where chef Angelo Giannello makes the almond sliver-shaped pasta by hand (*amelle *is dialect for* mandorle, *or "almonds"). The dough for this toothsome pasta is identical to that used for orecchiette, except it is pressed more forcefully, resulting in flattened ovals rather than concave shells.*

SERVES 6

For the scorze d'amelle:

3½ cups semolina flour, plus extra for the counter

¼ teaspoon salt

To cook and serve:

3 pounds broccoli raab, trimmed of tough stems and yellow buds removed, chopped

2 tablespoons salt

¾ cup extra-virgin olive oil

½ teaspoon chili flakes

4 garlic cloves, chopped

½ cup fresh bread crumbs

Make the scorze d'amelle according to instructions on page 370 using the ingredients listed above, adding enough cold water (about 1¼ to 1½ cups) to form a firm dough. Knead 5 minutes, or until smooth, adding a little water if the dough is dry or a little semolina flour if it is sticky. Shape into a ball, wrap, and let rest 30 minutes.

Cut the dough into 8 pieces. Working with 1 piece at a time and keeping the others covered, roll out each piece into a ¼-inch-thick log. Cut into ½-inch pieces and toss with semolina flour. Press each piece onto a semolina-dusted counter with your thumb, flicking it off with the middle finger of the same hand; it should resemble a slivered almond. Continue in the same manner with the remaining dough. Toss with semolina flour to prevent sticking and spread out in a single layer on a semolina-dusted tray; cover with a towel.

To cook, bring 6 quarts of water to a boil. Add the broccoli raab, scorze d'amelle, and salt. Cook until the pasta is al dente, about 12 minutes; drain thoroughly, reserving ½ cup of the pasta cooking water.

Meanwhile, heat ½ cup of the olive oil in a 6-inch skillet over a medium-high flame. Add the chili, garlic, and bread crumbs, and cook for 2 minutes. Transfer the pasta and broccoli raab to a serving platter. Fold in the warm bread crumb mixture and the reserved cooking water and serve hot, drizzled with the remaining ¼ cup of olive oil.

PREPARATION TIPS: Make the scorze d'amelle up to 12 hours ahead, spread out in a single layer on a semolina-dusted tray, and refrigerate, covered with a towel.

RICH VERSUS POOR PASTA

EVERY ITALIAN REGION makes some form of fresh pasta: diligently rolled out by hand, cut with a knife or highly specialized tools, shaped patiently by nimble fingers, Italy's pastas are the fruit of centuries of culinary evolution. And while every region identifies with specific pasta shapes, the ingredients from which the pasta is made are just as important to the pasta's final character.

In Basilicata and the rest of southern Italy, cooks have become adept at turning semolina flour and water into enticing pastas; egg pastas were reserved for special occasions. Compare the rustic flour-and-water pastas of Basilicata, its *lagane* and *cavatelli* and *minuich,* to the golden, egg-rich tagliatelle and lasagne that cooks in Emilia or Piedmont ritually make and you'll find the difference between a subsistence kitchen and a celebratory kitchen. Adding eggs to pasta dough reflects the status associated with pasta. In northern Italy, pasta was not just food for the masses: it was food for the courts, eaten at banquets, enclosed in golden crusts, stuffed with meat or cheese, laced with costly sugar, spiced with luxurious saffron and cinnamon, and presented with great pomp by cooks working for ruling families. It was only fitting that a rich food meant for rich people should include eggs, themselves a precious ingredient, which would give it a glorious golden color and elevate a simple combination of flour and water to the appropriate level of opulence.

But in Basilicata—just like in nearby Molise, Campania, Apulia, Calabria, Sicily, and Sardinia—pasta was one of the few foods that the masses could count upon, and most recipes do not call for eggs. One especially rustic pasta, called *miskiglio* (from *miscuglio,* meaning "mix"), combines chickpea flour, fava bean flour, semolina flour, and barley flour, a hint that even wheat was once costly and had to be stretched with more affordable grains.

Lagane e Ceci

Short Pasta Strips in Spicy Chickpea Broth

*L*agane are wide, short tagliatelle that find their roots in the laganum of ancient Greece. On March 19, Saint Joseph's Day, they are cooked with beans, lentils, or chickpeas and offered to the poor. You can use one 15.5-ounce can of chickpeas rather than dried chickpeas to make preparation quicker.

Drain the chickpeas and place in a 1-quart pot. Add water to cover by 3 inches and bring to a boil. Reduce the heat to medium, cover, and cook until tender, about 1½ hours. Drain, reserving 1 cup of the broth.

In a food processor, process all but ¼ cup of the chickpeas with the reserved broth until smooth.

Heat the olive oil, garlic, and chili over a medium-high flame in a 1-quart pot for 1 minute. Add the onion, oregano, basil, and bay leaves, and cook for 5 minutes. Add the puréed and whole chickpeas, tomatoes, salt, and pepper. Reduce the heat to medium, cover, and cook for 30 minutes.

SERVES 4

For the chickpeas:
½ cup dried chickpeas, soaked 12 hours in cool water to cover
¼ cup extra-virgin olive oil
2 garlic cloves, chopped
¼ teaspoon chili flakes
1 medium yellow onion, minced
1 tablespoon minced oregano
12 basil leaves, torn
2 bay leaves
4 plum tomatoes, peeled (see page 369), seeded, and diced
½ teaspoon salt
⅛ teaspoon freshly ground black pepper

For the lagane:
1½ cups semolina flour, plus extra for the counter
¼ teaspoon salt

To cook and serve:
2 tablespoons salt
¼ cup extra-virgin olive oil

Meanwhile, make the lagane according to instructions on page 370 using the ingredients listed above, adding enough cold water (about ½ cup) to form a firm dough. Knead 5 minutes, or until smooth, adding a little water if the dough is dry or a little semolina flour if it is sticky. Shape into a ball, wrap, and let rest 30 minutes.

Roll out the dough on a semolina-dusted counter into a 16 × 24-inch rectangle. Cut into four 4-inch-wide sheets. Cut each sheet into ¾-inch-wide strips and toss with semolina flour to prevent sticking. Spread out in a single layer on a semolina-dusted tray.

To cook, bring 4 quarts of water to a boil. Add the lagane and salt and cook 1 minute, or until half-cooked. Drain, reserving 1 cup of the pasta cooking water.

Fold the lagane into the chickpeas. Add as much of the reserved cooking water as needed to dilute the broth to a thick souplike consistency. Cook until the lagane are done, about 2 minutes, stirring constantly. Discard the bay leaves and serve hot, drizzled with the olive oil.

PREPARATION TIPS: Make the lagane up to 12 hours ahead, spread out in a single layer on a semolina-dusted tray, and refrigerate; cook the chickpeas up to 3 days ahead, refrigerate, and reheat while you boil the lagane.

FESTIVE PASTAS

A handful of greens or cauliflower florets and a dusting of Pecorino are enough to sauce Basilicata's everyday pastas, but festive meals call for hearty meat sauces. In Matera, orecchiette are baked with meatballs, Mozzarella, and tomatoes in a terra-cotta pot; in Potenza, the sauce calls for beef, onions, tomatoes, and basil instead. Stuffed pastas too are prepared for special meals: Ricotta- and Prosciutto-filled ravioli are served with pork ragù and Pecorino, while delicately sweet cinnamon-laced Ricotta *calzoncini* are sauced with a long-simmered lamb sauce.

Minestra Maritata

Escarole, Fennel, and Sausage Soup Dusted with Pecorino

Similar in name, but not in taste, to Apulia's *minestra maritata*, this chunky soup makes the most of Basilicata's beloved pork sausage, sheep's milk cheese, and flavorful vegetables. Like all *minestre maritate*, it features a number of vegetables; the season dictates what goes in the pot. If you have access to wild fennel, by all means use it instead of the fennel bulb.

SOUPS SEAFOOD AND NOT

The Lucani make soups out of any garden vegetable at its peak of freshness and any dried legume worthy of a slab of pork rind. Spring brings *ciaudedda*, a meal-in-one-pot that includes artichokes, potatoes, and fava beans. Rice, a virtual stranger to Basilicata's table, appears in a velvety mushroom soup. Beans star in numerous soups, including a dried fava bean purée with Swiss chard or chicory reminiscent of Apulia's *'ncapriata*. And along the short stretch of Tyrrhenian and Ionian coasts, especially in Metaponto and Maratea, fish soups laced with chili grace the table.

SERVES 8

1½ pounds escarole, washed thoroughly and chopped
1 tablespoon plus ½ teaspoon salt
16 Savoy cabbage leaves, chopped
2 fennel bulbs, quartered, cored, and thinly sliced
⅛ teaspoon freshly ground black pepper
¼ cup extra-virgin olive oil
1 pound spicy Italian sausage, casings removed and crumbled
4 cups (1 quart) Chicken Broth (page 368)
¼ pound Pecorino Romano, cut into ¼-inch dice
⅔ cup freshly grated Pecorino Romano

Bring 3 quarts of water to a boil over medium-high heat in a 4-quart pot. Add the escarole and 1 tablespoon of the salt and cook 5 minutes; remove with a slotted spoon to a bowl of cool water; keep the water boiling. Add the cabbage and cook 5 minutes; remove with a slotted spoon to the same bowl of cool water. Add the fennel to the boiling water and cook 5 minutes; remove with a slotted spoon to the same bowl. Drain the escarole, cabbage, and fennel, and season with the remaining ½ teaspoon of salt and the pepper.

Heat 2 tablespoons of the olive oil in a 2-quart pot over a medium-high flame. Add the sausage and cook 10 minutes, stirring often, or until lightly browned all over. Add the broth and bring to a boil, reduce the heat to medium, and cook 20 minutes, uncovered.

Preheat the oven to 400°F.

Arrange the escarole, cabbage, and fennel in a 10-inch cast-iron or terra-cotta baking dish. Add the broth and sausage and bake in the preheated oven for 20 minutes. Sprinkle with the diced and grated Pecorino and serve hot, drizzled with the remaining 2 tablespoons of olive oil.

Agnello e Funghi al Forno

Roasted Lamb and Oyster Mushrooms

Basilicata is a sheepherding region, and its preferred meats are the old shepherds' standbys: lamb, goat, and kid are slow-roasted in hermetically sealed clay pots called pignate, *often in the company of potatoes or other vegetables. In the Murgia Plateau, which stretches from Basilicata into Apulia, cooks forage for mushrooms called* cardoncelli *and toss them with chunks of lamb in a roasting pan; although similar to oyster mushrooms, cardoncelli have a stronger flavor and more compact texture. This lamb dish from Matera features oyster mushrooms (the closest thing to cardoncelli available in North America), olive oil, rosemary, and chili.*

SERVES 6

2 pounds boneless lamb shoulder, trimmed of fat and sinew, cut into 2-inch cubes

1½ pounds oyster mushrooms, rinsed and blotted dry, cut into 2-inch cubes

½ cup extra-virgin olive oil

4 rosemary sprigs

2 garlic cloves, chopped

¼ teaspoon chili flakes

1 teaspoon salt

Preheat the oven to 450°F.

Toss all the ingredients in a 10 × 14-inch roasting pan. Roast for 1 hour in the preheated oven, basting with the cooking juices every 15 minutes. Serve hot.

THE CITY OF STONE

It's been dubbed *La Città dei Sassi* ("The City of Stone"): Matera is an agglomeration of rock-hewn houses and churches built in a gorge dug over the millennia by a torrent. Inhabited continuously since the Neolithic Age, it is home to one of the oldest human settlements in the world. Until decades ago, the city was a symbol of poverty and deprivation: people lived, often with their pigs, horses, and cattle, in "grotto" homes that had been dug in the stone, without electricity or running water, in conditions that bred disease and dismay. The floor of one home served as the ceiling for the one below, since all dwellings in the Sassi (the area where the grotto homes are found) were interconnected. In the 1950s, the government cleared the Sassi and modernized the homes, leaving their structure intact. Matera is now on UNESCO's World Heritage List and the Sassi are once again teeming with life: twenty-first-century amenities are found within the soft tufa walls of the ancient homes, humming quietly along with the Lucani's unbreakable spirit.

Patate Raganate

Baked Potatoes, Onions, and Tomatoes with Oregano and Bread Crumbs

Cooking vegetables or seafood in a style known as *raganato* indicates the presence of bread crumbs, Pecorino, and herbs. The Lucani and Apulians make extensive use of the technique, applying it to mussels, sardines, tomatoes, peppers, zucchini, eggplants, and potatoes.

MAIN-COURSE VEGETABLES

In the old days, the Lucani reserved meat for feasts, serving vegetables as a main course instead. Baked or fried, these often-vegetarian dishes were once presented after the pasta or soup. While most of the region's soil is too mountainous or dry to yield plentiful crops, the mineral-rich volcanic land at the foot of Monte Vulture, where Basilicata's best wine is vinified, yields luscious vegetables, as does a fertile strip near Metaponto. Eggplants are especially significant; one variety, grown near the Parco del Pollino, boasts a red skin reminiscent of tomatoes. Red-skinned or mauve, long or fat, Basilicata's eggplants are delicious fried with potatoes, peppers, and tomatoes into a sultry *ciammotta* (similar to the *cianfotta* of Naples and the *caponata* of Sicily, page 345). Potenza is famous for its tiny lentils and Senise for its thin-skinned, elongated red peppers, ideal for adding vibrant flavor to cured meats.

SERVES 6

½ cup extra-virgin olive oil, plus extra for greasing the baking dish
1¾ pounds baking potatoes, peeled and cut into ⅙-inch-thick slices
3 large yellow onions, cut into ⅙-inch-thick slices
4 plum tomatoes, cut into ⅙-inch-thick slices
½ teaspoon salt
⅛ teaspoon freshly ground black pepper
½ cup freshly grated Pecorino Romano
½ cup fresh bread crumbs
2 tablespoons minced fresh oregano or 1½ teaspoons dried oregano

Preheat the oven to 400°F.

Generously oil a round 12-inch baking dish. Make a layer of potatoes, a layer of onions, and a layer of tomatoes in the baking dish, sprinkling each layer with a little of the salt and pepper and drizzling each layer with ½ tablespoon of the olive oil. Repeat with another layer of potatoes, onions, and tomatoes, again sprinkling each with a little of the salt and pepper and drizzling each with ½ tablespoon of the olive oil.

Top with the Pecorino, bread crumbs, oregano, and the remaining 5 tablespoons of olive oil. Bake in the preheated oven for 1 hour and 15 minutes, or until the potatoes are tender when pierced with a knife, and serve hot.

PREPARATION TIPS: Layer the ingredients in the baking dish up to 2 hours before roasting.

Grano Dolce

Plump Wheat with Pomegranate, Chocolate, and Nuts

Called cuccìa in dialect, this sweet is shared with Apulia and Sicily and is similar to Greek and Turkish desserts—after all, Basilicata was settled by the Greeks long before the Romans arrived. The pomegranate seeds likely find their roots in ancient pagan rituals: their ruby color and plump shape symbolized fertility in pre-Christian societies. The chocolate, on the other hand, is a post-Renaissance European touch that does not appear in Eastern versions of the dish. See Sources (page 372) to buy the vino cotto (cooked wine) needed for the sweet garnish.

A SWEET TASTE OF ANCIENT GREECE

Pastries in Basilicata, as in Apulia and Calabria, have Greek roots. Honey is frequently used as a sweetener, and frying remains a favorite cooking technique, even in today's fat-phobic world. Christmas brings chickpea-sized fritters called *cicirata* (similar to the *cicerchiata* of central and southern Italy) doused in honey and shaped like a wreath, and family feasts culminate in semolina-flour fritters dusted with confectioner's sugar, or sweet egg gnocchi scented with lemon zest.

SERVES 8

1½ cups wheat berries, soaked 12 hours in cool water to cover
¼ teaspoon salt
¼ cup sugar
1 ounce bittersweet chocolate, finely chopped
Seeds of 1 pomegranate
½ cup walnut halves, coarsely chopped
½ cup blanched almonds, coarsely chopped
½ cup vino cotto, plus extra if needed
1 cup whipping cream, whipped (optional)

Drain the wheat berries and place them in a 3-quart pot with the salt and 1½ quarts of water. Bring to a boil, reduce the heat to medium, and cook until tender but not mushy, about 45 minutes, stirring often. Drain.

Meanwhile, combine the sugar, chocolate, pomegranate seeds, walnuts, almonds, and vino cotto in a large bowl. Stir in the hot wheat berries and cool to room temperature. Serve in goblets, topped with the whipped cream.

PREPARATION TIPS: Make the dessert up to 12 hours ahead and hold at room temperature; do not refrigerate, or the wheat berries will become unpleasantly hard.

Calabria

Bruschetta di Pomodori Arrostiti
Roasted Tomato Spread on Grilled Bread

Pitta di Granoturco ed Olive
con Semi di Finocchio
Cornmeal, Fennel, and Olive Flatbread

Pitta con Broccoli di Rapa e Salsiccia
Broccoli Raab and Sausage Pitta

Vermicelli in Padella
Golden Pasta Pancake with Melting Cheese

Bucatini con Melanzane Spappolate
Bucatini in Chunky Eggplant Sauce

Zuppa di Cipolle
Long-Simmered Onion Soup

Tonno al Salmoriglio
Tuna in Herbed Olive Oil Bath

La Carne 'Ncantarata dei Fratelli Alia
Pork Loin in Honey-Chili Glaze

Peperonata
Braised Sweet Peppers and Onions

Fichi al Cioccolato
Chocolate-Covered Roasted Figs

People in Calabria are in love with chili peppers. The Calabresi can often be seen at the table or in the kitchen, bent over a chili, slicing it into slivers for a salad or crumbling it into bubbling olive oil. Yet as fiercely spicy as some of their dishes are, others show tremendous restraint and delicacy.

If Calabria's culinary repertoire ranges from the subtle to the intense, the region itself is just as diverse: High mountain peaks, hushed and snow-covered in winter, rise above tiny villages; to the east, the Ionian Sea glitters blue, while to the west, the Tyrrhenian Sea soothes the eye; and between these sprawling coastlines, the Calabresi cook as they have done for thousands of years, drawing out the best from the sea and land, oblivious to passing trends and fancies, caring only about freshness and flavor.

Calabria boasts the longest stretch of coastline in the peninsula: five hundred miles of rocky coves and sandy beaches. Largely mountainous, it was peopled by the Bruzi in antiquity, then settled by the Greeks as part of Magna Grecia. The boundaries of ancient Calabria encompassed areas of modern-day Apulia, which partly explains culinary similarities between the two. The Romans invaded in the third century B.C., and after the empire crumbled, the region passed to the Goths and Byzantines, who named it Calabria. Later the Lombards, Normans, Austrians, Angevins, Aragons, and Bourbons arrived, and Calabria shared the fate of other southern regions under the Kingdom of the Two Sicilies. In 1861, it was annexed to Italy.

Calabria's intractable terrain and frequent earthquakes, combined with rulers who often exploited the population, have made the region a poor one whose people had to struggle just to survive. Agriculture thrives in a small stretch of flatland, but Calabria's soil is difficult to cultivate: nearly one-third of it is covered in woods, and much of it is steeply mountainous. Only three cities have a significant population density: Cosenza, Reggio di Calabria, and Catanzaro, the capital. As in nearby Basilicata, there has been an exodus to luckier lands; one million people left in the last century alone. Today the economy is much improved, but people still recall their days of deprivation.

Anchored in ancient Greek cuisine and influenced by Albanian immigrants who arrived in the fifteenth century, Calabria's cooking includes some beguiling sweet-and-sour and sweet-and-spicy dishes. Fishing villages like Bagnara and Scilla still live by the old rules. Men fish or repair boats for a living and hold a festival every July during which they grill swordfish and throw a wreath of bay leaves into the water to honor drowned fishermen. Women prepare pasta from semolina flour and water, shaping the dough just as their mothers did, with nothing more than an iron rod or the force of a thumb pad.

Wheat is Calabria's primary crop, so pasta, bread, and savory pies are fundamental. These simple staples are transformed into festive dishes to mark special occasions: Ascension requires *lagane,* wide strips of pasta cooked in milk, and Carnevale calls for maccheroni with pork ragù. Fish is the *secondo* of choice in Calabria's coastal towns and cities, while inland, pork takes first place. In fact, the Calabresi have an adage: "*Amaru chi lu puorco non ammazza*" ("Unlucky is the person without a pig to kill"). Many Calabresi still raise their own pigs and are experienced pork butchers and *salumieri*. And while most weekday meals end with a platter of fruit—Sibari's clementines, for instance, are renowned across Italy—every feast brings its requisite sweet.

Favorite Restaurants, Shops, and Places

- AGORÀ, Grande Albergo Miramare, Via Fata Morgana 1, Reggio di Calabria, 0965.812444. Order the *linguine allo stocco* and *gratin di stocco e peperoni.*
- L'APPRODO, Via Roma 22, Vibo Valentia, 0963.572640. Sample the *tonno col fondo di cipolle di Tropea* and *tagliolini all'Approdo.*
- LA LOCANDA DI ALÌA, Via Vetticelle 69, Castrovillari, 0981.46370. Pino and Gaetano Alìa's gastronomic mecca; sample the *pasta con 'Nduja* and *carne 'ncantarata.*
- LA SCOGLIERA, Via Fosso, Località Le Castella, Isola di Capo Rizzuto, 0962.795071. Must-trys include *frittelline di lattuga di mare* and *quadaro,* a rich seafood soup.

- LA TERRAZZA, Via Nazionale, Gerace, 0964.356739. Home cooking and homemade ingredients in a rustic, no-frills setting.
- LATTICINI SANDRO LANZO, Via Daniele 10-12, Catanzaro, 0961.721593. Cured meats and cheeses are outstanding at this centrally located shop.
- ODOARDI, Contrada Campodorato, Nocera Terinese, 0968.91159. Call ahead to schedule a visit of this high-tech winery and olive oil estate.
- PELLICANÒ ANTONIO, Via Aspromonte 15A, Reggio di Calabria, 0965.92890. Regional foods for sale.
- REITANO, Via Circonvallazione 254-256, Taurianova, 0966.612059. The best torrone shop in a town famous for its torrone.

Telephone country code: 011.39

Bruschetta di Pomodori Arrostiti

Roasted Tomato Spread on Grilled Bread

Toasted bread rubbed with tomatoes, a handful of olives, a hunk of cheese: this is the way most meals start in Calabria. Near the coast, lemony anchovies and a spicy herring spread appear, while in mountain villages, a few slices of ham or salami are offered alongside thick slices of country bread. This recipe proves that the simplest things are often the best: sun-kissed tomatoes roasted over an open fire, crushed with chili and olive oil, and spread on grilled bread. If you have no wood fire, opt for a grill pan—less romantic, but functional.

CROTONE'S FAMOUS PECORINO

The ancient Greek town of Crotone lays two claims to fame: a massive Greek column and a pungent, sheep's milk cheese. Pecorino Crotonese can contain up to 20 percent goat's milk; dry-salted or soaked in a salt brine, it is aged three months to more than one year. See Sources (page 372) to buy it in North America.

SERVES 4

4 medium beefsteak tomatoes
1 tablespoon plus ½ teaspoon sweet paprika
1 teaspoon hot paprika
¼ teaspoon cayenne pepper
1½ teaspoons salt
¼ cup extra-virgin olive oil
Eight ½-inch-thick slices country bread
4 garlic cloves, peeled

Heat an outdoor grill or grill pan until blazing hot. Grill the tomatoes until they are scorched and soft but still hold their shape, about 25 minutes, turning often. Cool for 5 minutes, then peel; keep the grill or grill pan hot.

In a medium bowl, crush the tomatoes with a fork into a paste. Add the sweet and hot paprika, the cayenne, salt, and olive oil; set this spread aside.

Grill the bread until it is browned on both sides, about 2 minutes per side, turning once. Bring the bread, garlic, and tomato spread to the table; let everyone rub their bread with the garlic and spoon on the tomato spread.

Pitta di Granoturco ed Olive con Semi di Finocchio

Cornmeal, Fennel, and Olive Flatbread

Polenta, *seldom eaten in southern Italy, is a staple in Calabria. It is paired with chickpeas, broccoli raab, or sausages and beans, and baked into savory pies and breads like this cornbread from the town of Rende.* Pitta di granoturco *makes a wonderful antipasto in the company of cheeses and cured meats and is best savored hot out of the oven. A similar recipe exists in Basilicata, but it does not contain yeast and is much denser.*

YOU SAY PITTA, I SAY FOCACCIA

Pitta, Calabria's version of focaccia, is stuffed or flavored with whatever cooks have on hand, and baked in a variety of shapes and sizes: there are vegetable *pitte,* searingly hot pitte oozing spicy peppers, and rich winter pitte stuffed with fresh cracklings. The name *pitta* may originate in Greece, where it refers to savory pies and breads, although similar pies existed in Italy before the Greeks arrived. The most typical pitta stuffing is canned tuna, olives, tomatoes, and anchovies, but Ricotta, Prosciutto Cotto, parsley, and hard-boiled eggs make another favorite combination.

SERVES 8

2⅔ cups stone-ground coarse cornmeal

1½ cups unbleached all-purpose flour, plus extra for the counter and bowl

2 teaspoons instant yeast

½ teaspoon salt

¼ to ½ teaspoon cayenne pepper

½ cup plus 2 tablespoons extra-virgin olive oil, plus extra for greasing the pizza pan

1½ cups pitted green olives, such as Sicilian, minced

1 teaspoon fennel seeds

In a food processor, mix the cornmeal, flour, yeast, salt, and cayenne. With the motor running, add enough warm (110°F) water (about 1¼ cups) to make a soft dough that almost forms a ball; add a little water if the dough is dry or a little flour if it is sticky. Process for 45 seconds. Lightly flour a bowl and place the dough in it. Wrap and let rise at room temperature until doubled, about 1 hour.

Preheat the oven with a baking stone in it to 425°F.

Generously oil a 12-inch pizza pan with high sides. In a bowl, combine the olives, fennel seeds, and ½ cup of the olive oil. Knead into the risen dough on a lightly floured counter. Place the dough in the pizza pan, pat into a flat disk, brush the top with the remaining 2 tablespoons of olive oil, and cover. Let rest at room temperature for 30 minutes (this allows the gluten to relax).

Bake on the baking stone in the preheated oven for 35 minutes, or until the crust is golden and lightly crisp. Serve hot.

CALABRIA'S WINES

THE GREEK TOWNS OF SIBARI AND CROTONE were the site of important wine markets in classical Calabria, testimony to the ancient art of winemaking in this southern region. Calabria's rugged soil, similar to that of neighboring Basilicata, has made viticulture a difficult proposition. About 90 percent of the wine produced is red, and most of it is intensely colored and high in alcohol; less than 3 percent of the region's wine meets DOC standards. The major grape varietal is Gaglioppo, followed by Greco, Trebbiano, and Nerello.

Cirò is by far the most famous Calabrese wine, awarded to winners of the Olympics in classical Greece and still made from Gaglioppo grapes in red, rosé, and white versions; the red boasts a deep chocolatey flavor. But if Cirò is Calabria's most well-known wine, Greco di Bianco, an amber-hued, luscious dessert wine, is its most prized: vinified in the town of Bianco from what may be Italy's oldest varietal, the Greco grape, it is soft and ethereal, coppery, with a balanced flavor and airy bouquet, and is best three to five years from vintage. Like Cirò, red and rosé Savuto is based on Gaglioppo grapes; dry and full-bodied, it is named after a river that flows through its production zone. Lamezia, vinified in red, rosé, and white versions in the province of Catanzaro, is dry, balanced, and at times fruity.

Pitta con Broccoli di Rapa e Salsiccia

Broccoli Raab and Sausage Pitta

ork sausage mingles with broccoli raab between layers of rich, eggy dough in this hearty pie.

Heat the milk to 110°F. In a food processor, mix the flour, yeast, and 1 tablespoon of the salt. Add 1 cup of the warm milk and the egg. Process 5 seconds, then add enough of the remaining warm milk to make a soft dough that does not stick to the sides of the bowl (you may not need all the milk). Add a little flour if the dough is sticky. Process 45 seconds. Place the dough in an oiled bowl, wrap, and let rise at room temperature until doubled, about 1 hour.

SERVES 6

1½ cups whole milk

3½ cups unbleached all-purpose flour, plus extra
    for the counter

1½ teaspoons instant yeast

2 tablespoons plus ½ teaspoon salt

1 extra-large egg

⅓ cup plus 2 tablespoons extra-virgin olive oil,
    plus extra for greasing the bowl and pizza pan

2¼ pounds broccoli raab, tough stems and yellow
    buds removed, chopped

¾ pound spicy Italian sausage, casings removed
    and crumbled

¼ teaspoon freshly ground black pepper

Meanwhile, bring 8 quarts of water to a boil. Add the broccoli raab and 1 tablespoon of the salt; cook 2 minutes. Drain, plunge in a bowl of ice water, drain again, and squeeze dry.

Heat ⅓ cup of the olive oil in a 12-inch skillet over a medium-high flame. Add the sausage and cook for 5 minutes. Stir in the broccoli raab, the remaining ½ teaspoon of salt, and the pepper and cook for 10 minutes. Cool to room temperature.

Preheat the oven with a baking stone in it to 425°F.

Cut the dough into 2 pieces, 1 twice as large as the other. Roll out the larger piece on a lightly floured counter into an 18-inch circle. Roll out the smaller piece into a 14-inch circle.

Generously oil a 10-inch pizza pan with high borders. Line it with the larger piece of dough, letting excess dough hang over the sides. Arrange the broccoli raab mixture over the dough and cover with the smaller piece of dough. Seal the edges with your fingers. Roll the rolling pin over the top of the pie to cut off excess dough, then poke a hole in the middle (this allows steam to escape). Brush the top with the remaining 2 tablespoons of olive oil; let rest at room temperature for 30 minutes (this allows the gluten to relax).

Bake on the baking stone in the preheated oven for 30 minutes, or until the crust is golden and lightly crisp. Serve hot or warm.

PREPARATION TIPS: Let the dough rise in the refrigerator up to 24 hours; bring to room temperature before proceeding.

Vermicelli in Padella

Golden Pasta Pancake with Melting Cheese

Italians would never reheat pasta—they cook it just before serving and frown upon warming leftovers, except lasagna and other baked specialties. But they have developed an ingenious use for yesterday's pasta: the frittata. Beaten eggs and cheese are folded into cooked pasta, the whole is slipped into a pan, and there you have it: a crisp-on-the-outside, soft-on-the-inside first course that will have you looking forward to leftover pasta. If you are a fan of crunch, cook the pancake in a 12-inch skillet rather than an 8-inch one; you will have more of the crisp crust and less of the soft inside.

SERVES 4

½ pound vermicelli or spaghettini
1 tablespoon plus ½ teaspoon salt
¼ cup extra-virgin olive oil, plus 1 tablespoon
   if you are cooking the vermicelli ahead
3 extra-large eggs
⅛ teaspoon freshly ground black pepper
¼ cup freshly grated Pecorino Romano
¼ pound fresh Mozzarella or Caciocavallo,
   cut into ¼-inch dice

Bring 3 quarts of water to a boil. Add the vermicelli and 1 tablespoon of the salt and cook until al dente, about 6 minutes, then drain. (If you are not making the frittata immediately, toss with 1 tablespoon of olive oil to prevent sticking.)

In a large bowl, beat the eggs, the remaining ½ teaspoon of salt, the pepper, and the Pecorino. Fold in the Mozzarella and the cooked vermicelli.

Heat 2 tablespoons of the olive oil in an 8-inch skillet over a medium-high flame for 2 minutes. Pour in the egg and vermicelli mixture and cook for 10 minutes, or until golden and crisp on the bottom, shaking the skillet every minute to prevent sticking.

Pour the remaining 2 tablespoons of olive oil over the pancake. Flip the pancake over with 2 spatulas (or invert onto a 12-inch plate and return to the skillet) and cook until the bottom is golden and crisp, about 10 minutes, shaking the skillet every minute. Serve hot.

PREPARATION TIPS: Cook the vermicelli up to 2 days ahead and refrigerate; soak in warm water for 1 minute, blot dry, and fold into the eggs.

ABOVE: *Peppery Mussels with Lemon (Apulia)* • RIGHT: *Broiled Scallops with Oysters and Watercress (Friuli–Venezia Giulia)*

LEFT: *Braised Squid with Chili, Greens, and Tomatoes (Tuscany)* • BELOW: *Sea Bass in "Crazy Water" (Campania)*

ABOVE: *Baked Red Mullet Wrapped in Prosciutto (Marches)* • RIGHT: *Twice-Cooked Swordfish in Tomato, Pine Nut, and Caper Sauce (Sicily)*

ABOVE: *Chicken with Roasted Peppers and Onions (Abruzzo)* • LEFT: *Braised Chicken with Prosciutto and Fried Eggplants (Sicily)*

LEFT: *Pork Chops with Olives and Fennel Seeds (Tuscany)* • BELOW: *Pork Scaloppine in Caper and Red Wine Glaze (Umbria)*

RIGHT: *Pork Loin in Honey-Chili Glaze (Calabria)* • BELOW: *Veal Roast Stuffed with Spinach, Pancetta, and Frittata (Emilia-Romagna)*

ABOVE: *Braised Veal Shanks with Gremolata (Lombardy)* • RIGHT: *Fontina-Stuffed Breaded Veal Chops (Val d'Aosta)*

CLOCKWISE FROM LEFT: *Plum-Stuffed Buns (Trentino–Alto Adige)* • *Decadent Hazelnut-Chocolate Pudding (Piedmont)* • *Almond Paste Cookies (Sicily)*

The Best Caciocavallo

CACIOCAVALLO, A VERSATILE COW'S MILK CHEESE, is at its best in the Sila mountains of Calabria. This stringy, semifirm cheese belongs to the *pasta filata* ("plastic curd") family, which includes Mozzarella, Scamorza, and Caciotta. After the milk is coagulated with rennet, the curds are transferred to a vat of whey starter, where they ferment for a few hours; when the curd is stringy (*fila,* hence the name *pasta filata*), it is worked with a stick, kneaded by hand until smooth and shiny, and folded over itself into a taut oval or pear shape. A daylong soak in a salt brine follows and the cheese is ready to be tied, hung, and aged anywhere from fifteen days to four months.

Caciocavallo's most prized characteristic is its ability to melt, like other plastic-curd cheeses. The Calabresi grill it over an open fire as an antipasto, drop it into broths, and use it to stuff pastas, savory pies, and fritters. Its name is likely derived from the practice of hanging the cheese astride (*a cavallo*) a wooden rod as it ages, not from its shape, which recalls the sacks carried by horses (*cavalli*). See Sources (page 372) to purchase Caciocavallo Silano in North America.

Bucatini con Melanzane Spappolate

Bucatini in Chunky Eggplant Sauce

Eggplant is southern Italy's queen, and nowhere is her reign more sovereign than in Calabria. Plump, nearly seedless, with a thin skin and sweet flavor, Calabria's eggplants are the basis for many of the region's classic dishes, including a rendition of eggplant parmigiana that features hard-boiled eggs, meatballs, and battered and fried eggplant coins. Eggplant festivals are hosted across the region every summer; one of the most enjoyable is held in the town of Castrovillari, where local families gather to exchange a taste of their stuffed eggplants. In the dish below, strips of eggplant are fried, then crushed to create a chunky purée that coats pasta beautifully.

SERVES 4

½ cup extra-virgin olive oil

2 garlic cloves, chopped

¾ pound eggplant, peel on, cut into
   ¼ × ¼ × 3-inch strips

2 tablespoons plus ½ teaspoon salt

⅛ teaspoon freshly ground black pepper

1 pound plum tomatoes, peeled (see page 369),
   seeded, and diced

1 teaspoon minced oregano

12 basil leaves, torn

1 pound bucatini

½ cup freshly grated Pecorino Romano

Heat the olive oil in a 12-inch sauté pan over a medium flame. Add the garlic and cook 30 seconds, then add the eggplant, ½ teaspoon of the salt, and the pepper. Cook, stirring often, for 25 minutes, or until soft. Crush the eggplant with a fork into a coarse purée while it is still in the pan, then add the tomatoes and oregano and cook 5 more minutes. Stir in the basil and keep the sauce warm.

Meanwhile, bring 5 quarts of water to a boil. Add the bucatini and the remaining 2 tablespoons of salt and cook until al dente, about 8 minutes. Drain, reserving ½ cup of the pasta cooking water. Toss the bucatini and sauce in a bowl. Dilute with enough of the reserved cooking water to coat the bucatini and serve hot, dusted with the Pecorino.

THE ART OF PAIRING PASTA AND SAUCE

Every Calabrese pasta demands its perfect partner. *Ferrazzuoli,* long, hollow noodles shaped around a thin iron rod, are ideal with a bath of bread crumbs, olive oil, and anchovies; *scivateddi,* spaghetti-like noodles, are best with a pork and smoked Ricotta topping; and *fileja* or *itrya,* sheets that are turned into ever-thinner strings by skilled hands, are paired with lamb sauces. Long, hollow tubes called *candele* ("candles") are best with a spiced sausage called 'Nduja, while wheat berries—not a pasta proper, but treated the same way—are napped with ragù, as in Basilicata (page 302).

Zuppa di Cipolle

Long-Simmered Onion Soup

The Calabrese town of Tropea is renowned for its onions. Purplish and sweet, they are eaten with Pecorino, conserved in olive oil, pickled while still young, cooked into jam-like spreads, and turned into soups. A combination of purple and Vidalia onions approximates their delicate flavor in this simple soup.

SOUP, A SYMPHONY OF FLAVOR

A number of Calabria's soups recall those prepared in other regions. *Accia,* a celery soup with Soppressata, hard-boiled eggs, and Caciocavallo, is reminiscent of a soup made in Campobasso, the capital of Molise. *Maccu,* a purée of dried fava beans studded with spaghetti and tomatoes, finds resonant notes in Sicily's *macco* and Apulia's *'ncapriata. Millecosedde* ("one thousand things") is the Calabrese version of minestrone: beans, legumes (including *cicerchie,* or wild chickpeas), and short pasta are cooked until tender, then drizzled with olive oil before serving.

SERVES 6

1 pound purple onions, thinly sliced
1 pound Vidalia onions, thinly sliced
1 pound plum tomatoes, peeled (see page 369), seeded, and diced
2 garlic cloves, minced
¼ teaspoon chili flakes
½ cup extra-virgin olive oil
½ teaspoon salt
Four 1-inch-thick × 4-inch-wide slices country bread, cut into 1-inch cubes

Place all the ingredients except the bread in a 3-quart pot over medium heat. Cook 15 minutes, stirring often, then add 4 cups (1 quart) of water.

Bring to a gentle boil and cook over medium-low heat, covered, for 1½ hours. Stir in the bread and serve hot.

Tonno al Salmoriglio

Tuna in Herbed Olive Oil Bath

The word salmoriglio *refers to the salt that is an integral part of this olive oil bath for fish or meat. While salmoriglio most often relies on oregano, it can also call for mint; some cooks like to add lemon juice, especially when fish or seafood are to be soaked.*

Heat a grill pan for 5 minutes over a medium-high flame. Meanwhile, in a shallow container, combine the minced oregano, garlic, salt, pepper, olive oil, and 3 tablespoons of water. Dip the tuna in the olive oil mixture, turning to coat both sides.

Grill the tuna until it is seared on the bottom, about 2 minutes, then turn and cook the other side until it is also seared, about 2 minutes. (Cook longer, about 5 more minutes, for well-done tuna.) While you grill the tuna, dip the oregano sprig in the olive oil mixture and brush the tuna repeatedly with it. Serve the tuna hot, with the lemon wedges.

SERVES 4

2 tablespoons minced oregano or mint
2 garlic cloves, minced
½ teaspoon salt
¼ teaspoon freshly ground black pepper
¼ cup extra-virgin olive oil
4 tuna steaks (7 ounces each)
1 large oregano sprig (preferably with a long stem)
1 lemon, cut into wedges

CALABRIA MEETS SICILY

Calabria and Sicily share much when it comes to fish. Swordfish and tuna, plentiful in the Strait of Messina that separates Calabria and Sicily, are favorites in both cuisines. Both regions are also active in canning tuna, salting sardines, and, more recently, smoking swordfish. The Calabresi and Sicilians salt and dry tuna eggs, then grate them over pastas and salads; the Calabresi dub this salted tuna roe *ovotarica,* while Sicilians call it *bottarga.* But overlap between Calabrese and Sicilian cuisines is not limited to fish cookery. Rice, which appears seldom on Calabrese tables, is cooked in a complex rice *tortiera* that encases ragù, meatballs, sausage, Mozzarella, and hard-boiled eggs, much like Sicily's *sartù.* The Calabresi pair cauliflower, raisins, and pine nuts with pasta, and they boil their pasta with wild fennel, just like the Sicilians. And Calabria and Sicily both specialize in nougat, a legacy of Arab invaders who taught locals the art of turning honey, egg whites, and nuts into delectably soft or crunchy pastes.

La Carne 'Ncantarata dei Fratelli Alia

Pork Loin in Honey-Chili Glaze

Pino and Gaetano Alia, owners of La Locanda di Alia in Castrovillari, are two of Calabria's gastronomic heroes. The menu at their elegant restaurant revisits old recipes and proposes them in a lighter guise. A perfect example is this pork dish dating to the eighteenth century, which draws its name from the *canteros* (terra-cotta pot) used as a cooking vessel. Likely of Albanian origin given the combination of honey and chili, carne 'ncantarata was made with pork bones in the old days; today pork loin is used, but the meat is still packed with wild fennel, chili, and salt for months before cooking. Since you probably don't have access to salted pork in the Calabrese style (or the three months necessary for salting it yourself), like the Alia brothers, I suggest a quick-salted version. If you have wild fennel, use 2 tablespoons of it instead of the fennel seeds.

SERVES 4

1 tablespoon fine sea salt

½ teaspoon chili flakes

½ cup plus 1 tablespoon sweet paprika

1 teaspoon fennel seeds, crushed

1 pound boneless pork loin, cut into eight ½-inch-thick pieces

⅓ cup extra-virgin olive oil

⅓ cup fresh-squeezed orange juice

⅓ cup plus 1 tablespoon orange-blossom honey

In a shallow container, mix the salt, chili, 1 tablespoon of the paprika, and the fennel seeds. Add the pork and rub with the spices to coat both sides. Cover and refrigerate for 4 days.

Preheat the oven to 375°F.

Rinse the pork and blot it dry. Place it in a 12-inch terra-cotta pot or Dutch oven and add the olive oil and orange juice. Bake, covered, for 30 minutes in the preheated oven. Remove the pork with a slotted spatula to 4 plates. Whisk the honey and the remaining ½ cup of paprika into the liquid in the pot, pour over the pork, and serve hot.

A LITTLE MEAT GOES A LONG WAY

While sheepherding is less important than it used to be in Calabria, lamb and pork remain the region's preferred meats. No part of the animal goes to waste: kid's intestines are cooked with Pancetta, garlic, and rosemary, and pies stuffed with pork innards, tomatoes, and herbs form a hearty farmers' breakfast. There is a pork gelatin similar to one prepared in Basilicata, spicy rather than sweet, and a stew made of humble pig parts, much like Abruzzo's *'ndocca 'ndocca*. But best of all in Calabria are the cured meats made in the mountains, where the cool breezes and pristine air yield succulent, rosy hams and savory salami.

Peperonata

Braised Sweet Peppers and Onions

Calabria's peppers are famous for their fleshy texture and fruity taste, and in the summer, they are preserved in vinegar, roasted, and covered with olive oil, or dried under the blazing sun (these dried peppers, dubbed zafarani cruschi *because of their golden saffron color, are plumped in boiling water before cooking). Fresh peppers bursting with flavor and fragrance are also braised with onions and tomatoes, as in this peperonata. Serve this dish as an antipasto, as a side dish, or over pasta (in the last case, omit the vinegar).*

SERVES 4

½ cup extra-virgin olive oil
1 garlic clove, chopped
¼ teaspoon chili flakes (optional)
1 red bell pepper, cut into 2-inch cubes
1 yellow bell pepper, cut into 2-inch cubes
1 orange bell pepper, cut into 2-inch cubes
1 purple onion, cut into 2-inch cubes
6 plum tomatoes, peeled (see page 369), seeded, and cut into 2-inch cubes
1 tablespoon red wine vinegar
½ teaspoon salt
16 basil leaves, torn

Heat the olive oil in a 3-quart sauté pan over a medium-high flame. Add the garlic and chili and cook for 1 minute. Stir in the peppers and onion and cook for 15 minutes, stirring often.

Add the tomatoes, reduce the heat to medium-low, cover, and cook for 30 minutes. Uncover the pan, add the vinegar, salt, and basil, increase the heat to medium-high, and cook for 5 minutes. Cool to room temperature and serve.

PREPARATION TIPS: The peperonata keeps in the refrigerator for up to 5 days.

A HAUNTING NOTE OF BERGAMOT

There are as many legends surrounding the arrival of the bergamot tree in Calabria as there are uses for its fragrant fruit. Scholars speculate that the plant was brought by the Spanish or Arabs in the Middle Ages and that its name refers to the Spanish city Berga or the Turkish city Pergamo (not, as some believe, the Lombard city Bergamo). Whatever the origin, the Calabresi are the world's leading growers of this perfumed member of the citrus family. Today there are over 1,500 hectares devoted to bergamot cultivation in the region; the most highly prized specimens—with meatier flesh and richer fragrance—come from Pentadattilo. Bergamot's flesh is not edible, but its rind, flowers, and branches are packed with essential oils that are used in perfumes, liqueurs, candies, cookies, and teas (most famously Earl Grey).

Fichi al Cioccolato

Chocolate-Covered Roasted Figs

Calabria grows some of the best figs in the world: plump, juicy, and bursting with flavor. When fresh figs are not in season, the Calabresi indulge their fig craving with succulent dried fig sweets that recall those of Turkey, Greece, and the Middle East. Chocolate and cocoa are also used extensively in Calabrese pastries: There are boat-shaped almond and chocolate sweets from Cosenza; tartlets stuffed with almonds, cocoa, and vino cotto (page 204); hard-boiled eggs fried with a filling of cocoa, sugar, and cinnamon; fritters filled with Ricotta and chocolate; and even a chocolate blood pudding. The dessert below combines dried figs and chocolate to delectable effect and makes a splendid edible gift for the holiday season. See Sources (page 372) to buy Calabrese figs.

CELEBRATION SWEETS

Holidays usher in the most extravagant desserts in Calabria. Fried gnocchi dipped in honey and orange juice and fritters featuring *vino cotto* are among the most popular Christmas offerings. On New Year's Day, people curl bits of sugary dough around a rod to make fritters known as *scalille,* while Easter carries the scent of *cuzzupa* and *'nzuddi,* cakes shaped like animals or body parts.

SERVES 8

16 blanched almonds
¼ cup diced candied citron, minced
⅛ teaspoon ground cloves
16 large dried figs
3½ ounces bittersweet chocolate, chopped
1 cup loosely packed confectioner's sugar

Preheat the oven to 375°F.

Spread out the almonds on an 11 × 17-inch baking sheet and toast in the preheated oven for 12 minutes. Meanwhile, mix the candied citron and cloves in a small bowl.

Cut a vertical slit in each fig, being careful to leave the stem end attached. Stuff each fig with 1 almond and ½ teaspoon of the candied citron–clove mixture. Close up again so the figs look uncut and spread them out on the same baking sheet, stem side up. Bake in the oven for 15 minutes.

Meanwhile, in a stainless steel bowl set over a pot of boiling water, melt the chocolate with 3 tablespoons of water and the confectioner's sugar, stirring constantly; keep warm. If the chocolate thickens, stir in 1 more tablespoon of water.

Roll the warm figs in the warm chocolate, covering them completely. Place on a rack set over a tray to cool and dry for a few hours, and serve at room temperature.

PREPARATION TIPS: The figs keep in an airtight tin for up to 2 weeks.

Sicily

Olive Cunzate
Marinated Olives

Caciu all'Argintera
The Silversmith's Grilled Cheese

Insalata di Finocchi, Arance Sanguigne ed Olive
Fennel, Blood Orange, and Olive Salad

'Nfigghiulata Siracusana
Salami, Cheese, and Chive Flatbread

Busiati al Ragù di Maiale
Hollow Pasta in Rich Pork Ragù

Pesce Spada alla Ghiotta
Twice-Cooked Swordfish in Tomato, Pine Nut, and Caper Sauce

Involtini di Tonno delle Isole Eolie
The Aeolian Islands' Herb-Stuffed Tuna Bundles

Pollo con Prosciutto e Melanzane Fritte
Braised Chicken with Prosciutto and Fried Eggplants

La Caponatina
Simple Caponata

Biscottini di Mandorla
Almond Paste Cookies

There *is something magical about Sicily.* Maybe it's the volcanoes, Etna and Stromboli and a handful of smaller ones, forever threatening eruption, making every day seem like a gift. Maybe it's the perfume of jasmine and rosemary that hangs in the air, or the golden light that warms everything it touches. Maybe it's the way a Greek temple will suddenly appear on the skyline, or the way the vendors' voices at the open-air markets rise and fall like waves on the beach.

Whatever it is, Sicily's magic extends to its food, to its Baroque concoctions of pasta, its monumental seafood creations, its exuberant almond-laced pastries, its sweet, potent wines that taste like a distillation of the Sicilian sun.

One of Italy's five autonomous regions (along with Val d'Aosta, Trentino–Alto Adige, Friuli–Venezia Giulia, and Sardinia), Sicily is the largest island in the Mediterranean and has been inhabited continuously for ten thousand years. The Greeks colonized the area in the eighth century B.C., turning Agrigento, Siracusa, and Taormina into important towns and planting vines and olive groves across the island. Less than a thousand years later, the Romans made Sicily their first province and turned it into their main supplier of wheat and other grains, dubbing it "the granary of the empire." When the Roman Empire fell, the Vandals, Goths, and Byzantines vied for control, but it was the Arabs, who invaded in the ninth century and stayed on for two hundred years, that had the most lasting effect on the island's customs and gastronomy: they planted citrus, rice, jasmine, and melons, and introduced sugar as an alternative to honey, forever changing pastry-making in Italy. The Arabs were followed by the Normans, Angevins, Aragons, and Bourbons before Sicily was annexed to the newly formed Italian Kingdom in 1861.

These diverse influences are still apparent in a number of the island's most particular preparations: sweet-and-sour eggplant dishes show an Arab and Spanish imprint, complex meat creations like *farsumagru* (beef stuffed with ground beef, cheese, and onions, rolled up and braised in tomato sauce and wine) smack of French court cuisine, and jasmine- or orange blossom–laced sweets carry the scent of the Orient.

Sicily's capital is Palermo, a bustling cosmopolitan center that was already home to one hundred thousand people in the fourteenth century; the only European cities more densely populated at the time were Milan and Venice. As in southern Italy, the island's recently improved economic situation has put a stop to the mass exodus that decimated the Sicilian population in prewar years. The island's mountainous terrain, volcanic soil, intense summer heat, and low rainfall make Sicily perfect for the cultivation of olives, wheat, and grapes, a trio that has been the backbone of the economy and cuisine for millennia. Pasta and bread remain the basis of the Sicilian diet, and vegetables and sheep's milk cheese their fragrant companions.

Favorite Restaurants, Shops, and Places

- CAFLISH, Viale Margherita di Savoia 2, Palermo, 091.6840444. Palermo's most famous pastry shop, founded in 1800; try *gelo di melone.*
- FILIPPINO, Piazza Municipio, Lipari, 090.9811002. Sample the *ravioli di cernia in salsa paesana.*
- LA GIARA, Vico La Floresta 1, Taormina, 0942.23360. The *cannolini con Ricotta infornata e melanzane* are superb.
- MONDELLO PALACE HOTEL, Viale Principe di Scalea, Mondello, 091.450001. The *risotto al basilico e menta* is a delight.
- PANETTERIA GIOVANBATTISTA TUSA, Via Antonio Veneziano, Monreale, 0916.402689. Old-fashioned wood-burning oven bakery with an ample selection of breads.

- PASTICCERIA GIOVANNI DI PASQUALE, Corso Vittorio Veneto 104, Ragusa, 0932.624635. Traditional pastry shop with outstanding almond paste delicacies.
- PASTICCERIA MINOTAURO, Corso Umberto 8, Taormina, 0942.24767. The marzipan and almond cookies are out of this world.
- RISTORANTE DELL'HOTEL MODERNO, Via V. Emanuele 63, Erice, 0923.869300. The *busiati al pesto ericino* are a must, as is the *couscous di pesce.*
- SAN DOMENICO PALACE HOTEL, Piazza San Domenico 5, Taormina, 0942.23701. The *pesce spada alla ghiotta* is not to be missed.

Telephone country code: 011.39

Olive Cunzate

Marinated Olives

Every olive-producing region of Italy marinates olives with aromatic ingredients; in Sicily, favorite flavorings include celery, garlic, parsley or mint, and chili. Serve these olives as cocktail nibbles or as part of an antipasto selection, or toss with halved cherry tomatoes for a delightful salad. But remember that the character of the dish depends entirely on the character of the olives, so for best flavor, select sweet, plump olives cured in olive oil or a salt brine rather than vinegar.

THE SICILIAN ANTIPASTO TABLE

Whether it is a salad of sliced lemons, purplish olives, and tender mint, or a platter of raw anchovies marinated for days in lemon juice to "cook" without heat, a Sicilian antipasto never shies away from intense flavor. Nor does it shy away from pots of bubbling oil. The Sicilians are notorious for their love of fried foods like small-orange-sized balls of rice stuffed with ragù and hard-boiled eggs, aptly named *arancini di riso*; yeasted dough puffs flavored with anchovies and wild fennel; chickpea flour polenta strips; and fresh sardines stuffed with cheese.

SERVES 4

1 pound plain Sicilian green olives (not marinated with chili or other flavorings), pitted if desired
3 celery stalks from the heart, leaves on, stalks thinly sliced and leaves chopped
2 garlic cloves, minced
¼ cup Italian parsley or mint leaves, minced
1 tablespoon oregano leaves, minced
¼ to ½ teaspoon chili flakes
¼ teaspoon freshly ground black pepper
½ lemon, cut into 8 thin slices, seeded and halved
½ cup extra-virgin olive oil

Toss all the ingredients together in a large bowl. Marinate at room temperature for 1 hour or refrigerate for up to 3 days.

Serve at room temperature.

Caciu all'Argintera

The Silversmith's Grilled Cheese

Legend has it that this dish was born when an out-of-luck Sicilian silversmith had to make do without meat for the grill and resorted to thick slices of cow's milk cheese instead. For the tastiest results, be sure to use Sicilian Caciocavallo (labeled Caciocavallo Ragusano or simply Ragusano; see Sources, page 372).

SERVES 4

2 medium beefsteak tomatoes, cut into wedges
1/2 teaspoon salt
1/8 teaspoon freshly ground black pepper
1/4 cup extra-virgin olive oil
1 garlic clove, crushed
1 pound Caciocavallo Ragusano, cut into four 1/2-inch-thick slices
1 tablespoon fresh lemon juice (from 1/2 small lemon)
1 tablespoon minced oregano

In a medium bowl, toss the tomatoes with the salt and a pinch of the pepper. Set aside for 5 minutes.

Heat the olive oil and garlic in a 12-inch skillet over a medium-high flame. Add the Caciocavallo in a single layer and cook until browned lightly on the bottom, about 3 minutes. Turn and cook until the other side is also golden brown, about 3 minutes.

Sprinkle with the lemon juice, oregano, and the remaining pinch of pepper. Discard the garlic. Serve immediately, with the tomatoes.

CENTURIES-OLD SICILIAN CHEESES

MANY SICILIAN CHEESES have a long and distinguished pedigree. All the following cheeses are available in North America; see Sources (page 372).

PIACENTINU, the island's most interesting cheese, made since at least the sixteenth century, is an artisanal raw sheep's milk cheese scented with saffron and studded with black peppercorns. It is pressed, lightly cooked, and dry-salted, rubbed with the liquid it expels during the first weeks of aging, then aged from six weeks to six months; Piacentinu derives its name from the verb *piacere* ("to like"), because it is so well liked.

PEPATO SICILIANO, another unusual Sicilian cheese, is an aged sheep's milk cheese spiced with whole black peppercorns; it has a salty flavor, compact texture, and no rind.

PECORINO SICILIANO is also made of sheep's milk; dry-salted, aged from four to six months, it is grainy, sharp, with a biting, salty flavor and yellowish-red rind. When Pecorino Siciliano is sold immediately after production, it is called Tuma, and is soft, white, and bland; when it is aged ten days, it is known as Primo Sale ("first salt"), and is mild, lightly salty, and firm.

RAGUSANO (or Caciocavallo Ragusano) is made of cow's milk; excellent grilled when young or grated when aged, it is straw-yellow, smooth, and milky.

PROVOLA DELLE MADONIE, a pear-shaped plastic-curd cow's milk cheese aged from ten to fifteen days, is compact and mild; some dairies shape it to resemble animals.

Sicilians also produce a wide range of Ricottas: beside the ordinary fresh Ricotta (made of cow's, goat's, or sheep's milk), there is Ricotta Infornata, a baked Ricotta with a reddish-pink rind and creamy flesh flavored with black pepper, and Ricotta Salata, a salted Ricotta used for grating, especially over pasta.

Insalata di Finocchi, Arance Sanguigne ed Olive

Fennel, Blood Orange, and Olive Salad

Blood oranges grow across Sicily, where mild winter days and cold winter nights encourage the formation of anthocyanin, a substance that produces a gorgeous ruby hue. If you can't get your hands on blood oranges, you could simply opt for navel oranges, although the presentation will be less striking.

SERVES 6

4 large or 6 small blood oranges
2 fennel bulbs, trimmed, quartered, cored, and
    thinly sliced
1 purple onion, thinly sliced
½ cup pitted black olives, such as Gaeta
½ cup extra-virgin olive oil
½ teaspoon salt
⅛ teaspoon freshly ground black pepper

Cut the rind from each orange, removing the bitter white pith along with it. Working over a bowl to catch the juice, cut between the membranes, liberating the orange sections with a paring knife; reserve the orange juice. Arrange the orange sections and fennel on 6 plates.

Top with the onion and decorate with the olives. Drizzle with the reserved orange juice and the olive oil, season with the salt and pepper, and serve.

NO BETTER PLACE FOR AN ALMOND

There is no kitchen on earth that treats almonds better than Sicily's. In the town of Trapani, pesto is made with almonds and parsley, and cooks on the Aeolian Islands sauce their pasta with a thick tomato and almond sauce. Almonds are also ground and added to a veal and chocolate stuffing for savory pies, stirred into chicken stews, scattered over salads, and transformed into myriad sweets. Come February, when almond trees are in bloom, Sicilians celebrate spring with almond festivals that hark back to pagan days and host feasts featuring their beloved nuts in every guise imaginable.

'Nfigghiulata Siracusana

Salami, Cheese, and Chive Flatbread

Family festivities often start off with flatbreads and savory pies like the sfinciuni of Palermo, a yeasted dough topped with tomato sauce, anchovies, and Caciocavallo. Bursting with flavor, redolent of chives and laced with chili, the flatbread below is much simpler than sfinciuni, but just as delicious, and makes a splendid picnic lunch.

Make the dough and let it rise according to instructions on page 371. Roll out on a lightly floured counter into a 13 × 20-inch rectangle and brush with 2 tablespoons of the olive oil. Lightly oil a 14 × 20-inch baking sheet.

Scatter the Primo Sale over the dough, leaving a 1-inch border all around. Top with the tomato sauce and sprinkle with the chili and chives. Arrange the salami over the chives and dust with the fennel seeds and pepper. Fold in thirds to enclose by lifting the long side of the dough toward the middle and the other long side over the folded piece. Seal the edges with your fingers. Place on the prepared baking sheet, seam side up; brush the top with the remaining tablespoon of olive oil and let rest 30 minutes (this allows the gluten to relax).

Meanwhile, preheat the oven to 450°F.

Bake in the preheated oven for 30 minutes, or until the crust is golden and lightly crisp. Serve hot or warm.

PREPARATION TIPS: Make the dough up to 24 hours ahead and let it rise in the refrigerator; return to room temperature before proceeding.

SERVES 8

1 recipe Yeasted Dough (page 371)
Unbleached all-purpose flour for the counter
3 tablespoons extra-virgin olive oil, plus extra for greasing the baking sheet
¾ pound Primo Sale or young sheep's milk cheese, such as Marzolino or Fiore Sardo, thinly sliced
1 cup Tomato Sauce (page 369)
¼ teaspoon chili flakes
4 cups tightly packed snipped chives (4 bunches)
5 ounces thinly sliced mildly spicy salami, such as Napoli
1 tablespoon fennel seeds, crushed
¼ teaspoon freshly ground black pepper

SICILY'S WINES

SICILY, RESPONSIBLE FOR THE LARGEST PRODUCTION of wine in Italy after Apulia, had flourishing vineyards by the fifth century B.C. In classical times, Sicily exported a great deal of wine to Africa and beyond; the wines that best survived the lengthy sea voyage were sweet ones like Vernaccia, Mamertine, and Muscatello. To this day, dessert wines represent a large percentage of Sicily's output. The island's hilly and mountainous terrain, its dry, poor soil, hot summers, ample sunlight, excellent exposures, and low rainfall yield wines with real character. Sicily's trademark wines are:

ZIBIBBO, on the island of Pantelleria.

CATARRATTO and GRILLO, in Trapani, Marsala, and Alcamo.

PERRICONE and INZOLIA, mostly in the province of Agrigento.

NERO D'AVOLA and FRAPPATO, mostly in the provinces of Ragusa and Siracusa.

NERELLO MASCALESE, in the province of Messina, including the slopes of Monte Etna.

MALVASIA, in the Aeolian Islands, including Lipari.

MARSALA, a fortified wine vinified mostly in and around the town of Marsala, is Sicily's most symbolic wine. First vinified on a large scale in 1773, it is classified according to age; the Fine is aged one year, Superiore two, Superiore Riserva four, Vergine five, and Stravecchio ten. Marsala is produced in a dry, semi-dry, and sweet version in three colors: Oro (Gold); Ambra (Amber); and Rubino (Ruby).

Sicily's two other famed dessert wines are Malvasia delle Lipari, an amber-hued, grapey, sweet wine from the Aeolian Islands that also exists in a raisined and fortified version, and Moscato di Pantelleria, an alluringly sweet, golden wine vinified in still, sparkling, raisined, and fortified versions from Zibibbo grapes.

Notable reds include Cerasuolo di Vittoria, a full wine with an intense bouquet and good aging potential; Faro, a medium-bodied red with a delicate, persistent bouquet and dry, harmonious flavor; and full-bodied Nero d'Avola.

White wines of importance are Bianco di Alcamo, with a neutral nose and dry, slightly grapey, fruity flavor; full, spicy, slightly bitter Catarratto; citrus-flavored, earthy, astringent, ageworthy Grillo; and fruity, intense, light, fragrant Inzolia.

The slopes of Monte Etna, Europe's highest volcano, also yield intense wines.

Busiati al Ragù di Maiale

Hollow Pasta in Rich Pork Ragù

The Sicilians have a saying: "Cambia sempre, come la salsa" ("It always changes, like the sauce"). Pasta used to be the only dish Sicilian farmers ate most days, and it was tossed with every condiment available: simple tomato sauces, herbs both cultivated and wild, or beaten eggs and cubes of Caciocavallo. Hollow bucatini and perciatelli are among Sicily's favorite pastas, most often topped with sardines, wild fennel, and saffron, or with cauliflower, raisins, and pine nuts. Somewhat similar to these pastas, but much more toothsome, are busiati, long, hollow noodles that are shaped by hand, one by one, around a bamboo reed, knitting needle, or thin iron rod. If you don't have the time or patience to make busiati, substitute bucatini or perciatelli, or purchase dried *maccheroni al ferretto* (see Sources, page 372).

SERVES 4

For the ragù:

⅓ cup extra-virgin olive oil

3 garlic cloves, minced

1 large yellow onion, minced

16 basil leaves

¾ pound ground pork

¾ cup dry red wine

10 plum tomatoes, peeled (see page 369), seeded, and diced

½ teaspoon salt

¼ teaspoon freshly ground black pepper

For the busiati:

3 cups semolina flour, plus extra for the tray

¼ teaspoon salt

To cook and serve:

2 tablespoons salt

½ cup freshly grated Pecorino Romano

Make the ragù: Heat the olive oil in a 10-inch sauté pan over a medium-high flame. Add the garlic, onion, and basil and cook 5 minutes. Fold in the pork and cook until lightly browned all over, stirring often, about 10 minutes. Add the wine and cook for 5 minutes. Add the tomatoes, salt, and pepper, cover, reduce the heat to medium-low, and cook for 1½ hours.

Meanwhile, make the busiati according to instructions on page 370 using the ingredients listed above, adding enough warm water (about 1 cup) to form a firm dough. Knead 5 minutes, or until smooth, adding a little water if the dough is dry or a little semolina flour if it is sticky. Shape into a ball, wrap, and let rest 30 minutes.

Cut the dough into 4 pieces. Working with 1 piece at a time and keeping the others covered, roll out each piece into a ½-inch-thick log. Cut into 1½-inch-long pieces and toss with semolina flour. Roll each piece between your palms into a 3-inch log, then place on an unfloured counter and press a round ¹⁄₁₀-inch-thick iron rod or wooden skewer over it.

Place your right hand over the rod or skewer where the log of dough is and roll your hand gently back and forth over the rod; the dough will wrap around it, forming a hollow

6-inch-long tube. As the dough stretches over the rod, use both hands to roll the rod on the counter, without pressing too hard or the dough will stick to it. Slip the tube of dough off the rod onto a semolina-dusted tray (this will become easier with practice) and dust with semolina flour to prevent sticking. Continue in the same manner with the remaining dough. Spread the busiati out in a single layer on a semolina-dusted tray and cover with a towel until needed.

To cook, bring 5 quarts of water to a boil. Add the busiati and salt and cook until al dente, about 15 minutes. Drain, reserving ⅓ cup of the pasta cooking water. Transfer to a serving platter, fold in the ragù and the reserved cooking water, sprinkle with the Pecorino, and serve hot.

PREPARATION TIPS: Shape the busiati up to 4 hours ahead, spread out in a single layer on a floured tray, and cover with a towel until needed.

THE MYSTERY OF COUSCOUS

Couscous is associated with the Berbers of North Africa, for whom it is a staple. Most people assume that its presence in Sicily is a legacy of the Arabs; the same is also said of Sardinia's *fregola,* a semolina pasta reminiscent of couscous (page 359). It is possible, however, that couscous (and couscous-like preparations) predate the arrival of Arabs in Italy: perhaps the ancient Romans already cooked semolina-grain dishes, as Apicius' first-century cookbook indicates, and the Arab presence only anchored the habit more strongly in Sicily and Sardinia. Couscous with fish is also eaten in Livorno, Tuscany, partly—if not entirely—because during the Renaissance this port city was home to a sizable Jewish population whose links with Tunisian Jews made Tunisia's fish-topped couscous prevalent on Livornese tables. Interestingly, Sicily was also home to a considerable Jewish community before the Inquisition sent tens of thousands of Jews to mainland Italian cities such as Rome, Venice, and Livorno. Whether couscous is an Arabian, ancient Roman, or Jewish legacy, it is a delicious one to sample on Sicilian soil, especially near the town of Trapani.

THE MIGHTY CAPER

Ranging from a peppercorn to a hazelnut in size, capers—the immature buds of a flowering plant—are one of Sicily's most important products: 1.5 million pounds of the pungent buds are harvested every year on Sicilian soil. Caper plants grow spontaneously in rocks, sprouting wherever there is both stone and abundant sun. They have been prized since the days of classical Greece, when they were used for medicinal purposes on the Aeolian Islands. Capers are sorted by size: the smallest ones are packed in a vinegary brine, while the large, meaty ones grown a mere thirty miles off the coast of Tunisia on the island of Pantelleria are preserved with coarse sea salt.

Pesce Spada alla Ghiotta

Twice-Cooked Swordfish in Tomato, Pine Nut, and Caper Sauce

As the largest island in the Mediterranean, Sicily commands a considerable stretch of coastline. Many of its men earn a living by catching large fish—especially swordfish and tuna—and smaller ones like sardines and anchovies. In this recipe, Sicily's beloved capers, pine nuts, raisins, and olives mingle atop fried swordfish in tomato sauce. The trick to tender swordfish is two-fold, as Sicilian fishermen will tell you: choose a fatty part from the belly, and fry the swordfish first, then finish it in the oven.

SERVES 4

¼ cup raisins
Four ⅓-inch-thick swordfish steaks
   (6 ounces each)
½ cup unbleached all-purpose flour
½ cup extra-virgin olive oil
½ teaspoon salt
⅛ teaspoon freshly ground black pepper
4 bay leaves
1 medium yellow onion, minced
2 garlic cloves, minced
¼ cup pine nuts
1 celery stalk, minced
2 tablespoons salted capers, rinsed and chopped
¼ cup pitted black olives, such as Gaeta
16 cherry tomatoes, quartered

In a small bowl, soak the raisins in cool water to cover for 15 minutes. Drain and blot dry.

Dredge the swordfish in the flour, coating both sides and shaking off the excess. Heat the olive oil in a 12-inch skillet over a medium-high flame. Cook 2 of the swordfish steaks until golden brown on both sides, about 3 minutes per side, turning once. Transfer with a slotted spatula to a 10 × 14-inch baking dish. Cook the remaining 2 swordfish steaks in the olive oil left in the skillet in the same manner; remove with a slotted spatula to the baking dish. Season the steaks with ¼ teaspoon of the salt and a pinch of the pepper and top each with 1 bay leaf.

Preheat the oven to 400°F.

Add the onion and garlic to the olive oil left in the skillet over medium-high heat. Cook for 5 minutes, then stir in the pine nuts, celery, capers, olives, and raisins. Cook 5 minutes, then add the tomatoes, reduce the heat to medium, cover, and cook for 10 minutes. Season with the remaining ¼ teaspoon of salt and the remaining pinch of pepper.

Pour the tomato sauce over the swordfish in the baking dish and bake in the preheated oven for 15 minutes. Serve hot, warm, or at room temperature.

PREPARATION TIPS: The swordfish can be topped with the sauce up to 12 hours ahead and refrigerated, then baked before serving.

Involtini di Tonno delle Isole Eolie
The Aeolian Islands' Herb-Stuffed Tuna Bundles

The Aeolian Islands are a volcanic complex that includes the seven isles of Lipari, Stromboli, Panarea, Vulcano, Alicudi, Filicudi, and Salina. The land is rugged and the threat of eruption is constant, especially on Stromboli, where the volcano is permanently active. Until a few decades ago, tourism on these far-flung islands was practically nonexistent; now these outposts of Sicilian civilization have become trendy vacation spots, and the local cuisine is changing along with the landscape. Fortunately, some of the old dishes have survived: ravioli in grouper sauce, chestnut soup, black-eyed peas with wild cabbage, grape-must jellies, and the sage-scented tuna bundles below.

SERVES 4

1 small yellow onion, minced

¼ cup minced Italian parsley

¼ cup minced basil

2 tablespoons salted capers, rinsed and minced

1 extra-large egg

Four ¼-inch-thick slices tuna steak (¼ pound each)

¼ cup extra-virgin olive oil

4 bay leaves

8 sage leaves

½ teaspoon salt

¼ teaspoon freshly ground black pepper

½ cup dry white wine

3 tablespoons fresh lemon juice (from 1 lemon)

In a bowl, combine the onion, parsley, basil, capers, and egg. Top the tuna evenly with the mixture, then roll into bundles to enclose and spear each bundle with 2 toothpicks.

Heat the olive oil in a 12-inch skillet over a medium-high flame. Add the bay and sage leaves and cook 30 seconds. Add the tuna bundles and cook until they are browned lightly all over, turning to cook evenly, about 5 minutes. Remove the toothpicks; the bundles should hold together.

Season with the salt and pepper, deglaze with the wine, and cook until the wine almost evaporates and the tuna is done, about 3 minutes, turning it to coat with the sauce. Serve hot, sprinkled with the lemon juice.

PREPARATION TIPS: Stuff the bundles up to 12 hours ahead and refrigerate until needed.

TUNA, A SICILIAN STAPLE

Tuna has been big business in Sicily for thousands of years. Archaeologists on the island of Lipari even found a bowl dating back to classical Greece showing a fishmonger cutting tuna for an eager customer. Tuna is caught using an intricate set of underwater nets called *tonnare,* a legacy of the Phoenicians; the fish is cut into steaks and paired with an abundance of fried onions, cooked in tomato sauce with mint and garlic, or baked with tomatoes, bread crumbs, olives, capers, and basil. When it is dried and salted, it goes by the name of *mosciame* (until dolphin fishing became illegal, mosciame was made with dolphin). Mosciame is also common to Liguria, likely taken there by Sicilian sailors heading north. Canned tuna packed in olive oil is another Sicilian staple, used in salads, pasta sauces, savory pies, and sauces for cold chicken (page 344).

Pollo con Prosciutto e Melanzane Fritte

Braised Chicken with Prosciutto and Fried Eggplants

While most Italians are perfectly content to enjoy their meat as a simple roast or grill, Sicilians apply all their Baroque culinary wizardry to meat, stuffing it with savory ingredients and braising it in elaborate sauces. In this recipe, a duet of Prosciutto and tomato is paired with chicken and adorned by another typical Sicilian ingredient: eggplant.

THE ORIGIN OF TONNATO SAUCE

Sicily's *pollo alla messinese* (chicken in creamy tuna sauce) is strikingly similar to Piedmont's and Lombardy's *vitello tonnato* (page 69). While most people assume that Sicily's chicken is a variant on the north's veal, the opposite is more likely true: after all, tuna is indigenous to Sicily, not Piedmont or Lombardy. Perhaps the Piedmontese contingent from the House of Savoy, which ruled Sicily in the early eighteenth century, took a liking to the Sicilian chicken dish and carried the recipe north, where local cooks adapted it to veal.

SERVES 4

1 pound eggplant, peel on, cut into ½-inch cubes
1 tablespoon salt
1 cup extra-virgin olive oil
4 chicken legs, halved and skinned
1 garlic clove, minced
1 medium yellow onion, minced
12 basil leaves
1 cup dry white wine
5 plum tomatoes, peeled (see page 369), seeded, and diced
One ½-pound slice Prosciutto di Parma, cut into ¼-inch dice
¼ teaspoon freshly ground black pepper
1 tablespoon minced Italian parsley

Sprinkle the eggplant with the salt, place in a colander over a plate, and set aside for 30 minutes. Rinse lightly and blot dry. Heat ½ cup of the olive oil in a 12-inch skillet over a medium flame. Fry the eggplant in 2 or 3 batches until golden and soft, about 15 minutes. With a slotted spatula, remove to a plate and set aside.

Meanwhile, heat the remaining ½ cup of olive oil in a 12-inch sauté pan over a medium-high flame. Add the chicken and cook until browned all over, about 5 minutes per side, turning once. Add the garlic, onion, and basil and cook 5 minutes. Deglaze with the wine and cook for 5 minutes. Add the tomatoes, Prosciutto, and pepper. Reduce the heat to medium-low, cover, and cook until the chicken is tender, about 45 minutes, stirring once in a while and adding a little water if needed.

Stir in the reserved eggplant and cook, uncovered, 10 more minutes, or until the sauce thickens to a coating consistency. Fold in the parsley and serve hot.

La Caponatina

Simple Caponata

Caponata, Sicily's most famous vegetable medley, flavors eggplants, celery, and onions with a touch of sugar and vinegar. The original caponata is an elaborate affair and includes seafood (lobster, shrimp, and the like) as well as a rich, cinnamon-laced chocolate sauce. Often enjoyed as an antipasto, this simple caponata makes a lovely side dish and is quite delicious spooned atop crisp bread.

ISLAND VEGETABLES

If eating meat almost every day is a recent phenomenon in Sicily, eating plenty of vegetables certainly isn't. Until the 1950s, Sicilian farmers made a meal out of salad stuffed into a bread loaf. On the island of Lipari, boiled black-eyed beans were scooped up at the table with a wedge of onion rather than with a fork. Today cauliflower is still a main attraction at family meals—when it isn't paired with pasta, it is deep-fried or stewed with olives, anchovies, red wine, and Caciocavallo. And the Mediterranean quartet of zucchini, eggplants, peppers, and tomatoes animates much of Sicily's vegetarian cuisine.

SERVES 8

¾ cup extra-virgin olive oil
1¾ pounds eggplant, peeled and cut into ½-inch cubes
2 medium yellow onions, thinly sliced
4 celery stalks, thinly sliced
4 plum tomatoes, cut into ½-inch cubes
24 basil leaves, torn
½ cup pitted Sicilian green olives, chopped
¼ cup salted capers, rinsed and chopped
2 tablespoons red wine vinegar
1 teaspoon sugar
½ teaspoon salt

Heat ½ cup of the olive oil in a 12-inch sauté pan over a medium-high flame. Add half of the eggplant and cook until soft and golden on all sides, stirring often, about 10 minutes. Remove with a slotted spatula to a bowl. Cook the remaining eggplant in the same manner in the olive oil left in the pan and remove with a slotted spatula to the bowl.

Add 1 tablespoon of the olive oil and the onions to the pan and cook 8 minutes, stirring, then remove with a slotted spatula to the bowl. Add the remaining 3 tablespoons of olive oil and the celery to the pan and cook 8 minutes, stirring, remove with a slotted spatula to the bowl.

Add the tomatoes, basil, olives, and capers to the pan and cook until the tomatoes break down into a sauce, about 5 minutes. Add the vinegar, sugar, and salt and cook 3 minutes. Return the eggplant, onions, and celery to the pan; stir gently to avoid crushing the eggplant and cook for 1 minute. Transfer to a serving bowl and cool to room temperature, then serve.

PREPARATION TIPS: Make the caponata up to 3 days ahead and refrigerate.

Biscottini di Mandorla

Almond Paste Cookies

Given its varied cultural and culinary legacies, Sicily has developed one of the richest pastry-making traditions in Italy. Almonds,
pistachios, and honey are essential, and many of
the island's nut- or honey-based sweets have
cousins in the Orient and Greece. Almond paste
is so important to the Sicilian kitchen that it is
referred to as pasta reale ("royal paste").
Sicilians are skilled at making marzipan pastries—the nuns of the Martorana convent, for
instance, shape and color them like fruit—as
well as almond macaroons, cakes, and cookies.
The recipe for these chewy and dense almond
paste cookies is from Nuccio Cingari, owner of
Pasticceria Minotauro in Taormina.

MAKES ABOUT 40 COOKIES

1⅔ cups blanched almonds
1¼ cups granulated sugar
1 tablespoon honey
1 teaspoon almond extract
2 extra-large egg whites
1¾ cups confectioner's sugar

Preheat the oven to 375°F.

In a food processor, grind the almonds and
granulated sugar to a very fine powder, about 3
minutes. Pile the almond and sugar mixture on a
counter and stir in the honey and almond extract
with a fork. Beat the egg whites lightly, just to
blend, and stir in ¼ cup of the beaten egg whites; if the dough is not soft and tacky, add
more egg whites by the teaspoon (you will not need all of the egg whites; do not add too
much or the dough will be too wet).

Sprinkle 1½ cups of the confectioner's sugar on the counter. Roll the dough into a log
over the confectioner's sugar. Snip into walnut-sized pieces and roll each into a ball, coating
the outside well with the confectioner's sugar. The confectioner's sugar should remain on
the outside of the dough rather than be incorporated in it.

Line two 11 × 17-inch baking sheets with parchment paper. Place the cookies on the
baking sheets, about 1 inch apart. Bake in the preheated oven 6 minutes, or until the
surface cracks and blisters. The cookies will be pale and soft and will have flattened
considerably; do not overbake or they will be dry. While they are still warm and pliable,
gently press opposing edges of each cookie toward the center with both hands to obtain
a slightly conical mound. (This step is not traditional, but I have found that it makes up for
the natural flattening of the cookies as they bake, and yields a chewier consistency once
they cool.)

Cool the cookies to room temperature on a rack. Dust with the remaining ¼ cup of
confectioner's sugar and serve.

PREPARATION TIPS: The cookies keep in airtight tins for up to 4 days.

Cassata so Good Even the Nuns Got Distracted

Many of Sicily's cherished sweets were born in convents. The most famous of these is cassata, initially an Easter specialty created by nuns in Palermo. So consumed were the nuns by the task of cassata-making, in fact, that in the sixteenth century the religious authorities of Mazzara del Vallo forbade them from preparing it: it seems the nuns were letting their religious duties slide in order to make this rich cake. Most versions of cassata call for lining an oval mold (*quas'at* in Arabic, hence the name) with liqueur-soaked sponge cake, then spooning in a sweet Ricotta cream enriched with candied fruit and chocolate. Marzipan is sometimes wrapped around the cake, but a decorative topping of candied fruit, including squash, is a must. Frozen *cassate,* a recent phenomenon, feature a custard base, whipped cream, and almonds rather than Ricotta.

The Original Ice Cream

What to do with winter snow? Why, make *granita*—that's what the Sicilians who lived two thousand years ago would have told you. Scoop up snow near Monte Etna, mix it with crushed fruit or honey, and there you have it: the prototypical sherbet. Sicilian ices have come a long way since the days of ancient Rome, but an ingenious spirit and inventive streak (not to mention need for solace from the summer sun) have animated the Sicilian quest for frozen delicacies throughout the centuries. A native of Palermo named Procopio opened the first *gelateria* in Paris in 1670, and within one hundred years the French capital boasted two hundred and fifty ice cream shops. Sicilians have become renowned for their watermelon ice studded with candied squash and chocolate, jasmine ice, refreshing coffee and lemon *granite,* and dozens of frozen desserts that would make their snow-licking ancestors proud.

Sardinia

Insalata di Pomodorini, Sedano e Bottarga
Cherry Tomato, Celery, and Bottarga Salad

Melanzane in Pinzimonio
Smoked Eggplants in Mint-Basil Oil

Malloreddus con Ragù di Cinghiale
Saffron-Tinted Dumplings in Wild Boar Ragù

Ravioli di Melanzane al Pomodoro
Eggplant-Walnut Ravioli in Tomato Sauce

Fregola con le Arselle
Fregola Soup with Cockles

Aragosta Arrosto
Roasted Lobster with Parsley and Bread Crumbs

Muggine al Sale
Gray Mullet Baked in Sea Salt

Gallina al Mirto
Myrtle-Infused Hen

Agnello Arrosto con Finocchi
Roasted Lamb with Fennel

Seadas
Mint-and-Lemon-Laced Cheese Pillows in
Warm Chestnut Honey

M*ore than any other Italian region,* Sardinia is a land of mystery: ancient, rugged, impenetrable, floating undaunted in a soundless sea, the same as it was when the first Phoenician ships docked on its shores thousands of years ago.

The island's mystery has to do with its isolation from the rest of the country. Sardinians refer to the mainland as "the continent," speak a language utterly incomprehensible to other Italians (a combination of old Catalan, Arabic, and Italian), and proudly guard their traditions against encroaching modern ways. And just as they protect their culture and customs, they preserve their recipes and indigenous foods with a vengeance.

Inhabited since the Neolithic Age, Sardinia was settled by far-flung invaders: Etruscans and other Italic tribes in the north, Iberians in the center, and North Africans in the south. This varied pedigree meant that unity was impossible: the island was divided among tribes that fought one another for supremacy, and its thick, densely wooded mountains became the setting for bloody battles and ambushes. Shepherds lived in villages built at the foot of massive stone fortresses called *nuraghi*; the remains of seven thousand of these imposing structures can still be seen, some on strategic hilltops where they commanded a view of the countryside and, possibly, the approaching enemy.

The Phoenicians were the first to settle in large numbers, around 1000 B.C., followed by the Greeks and Carthaginians, who set up camp in the southern portion of the island, near the modern-day capital of Cagliari. The Romans invaded in 238 B.C., yet had difficulty infiltrating the central portion covered by the wild Barbagia mountains; so inaccessible is this area that, until mere decades ago, it was the domain of bandits. After the Roman Empire fell, the Barbarians stormed in. Next came the Vandals, Byzantines,

Saracens, Pisans, and Genoese, which explains why Tuscan and Genoese are still spoken in parts of Sardinia. But it was the centuries-long Spanish rule, from 1326 to 1708, that left the strongest imprint on local language, customs, and cuisine. In 1708, the Austrians took control, only to cede Sardinia to the House of Savoy a few years later. The island was joined to Piedmont and the two regions, along with Liguria, were annexed to France until Napoleon's empire crumbled; the Kingdom of Sardinia was soon reinstated. In 1861, Vittorio Emanuele, King of Sardinia, was proclaimed the first king of a unified Italy. Sardinia was decreed an autonomous region in 1948.

Today, much like in Vittorio Emanuele's day, nearly half of Sardinia's surface is devoted to grazing animals, especially sheep. Its cuisine is pastoral, drawing more heavily on the offerings of the land than those of the sea. Until recently, people lived far from the coast, out of reach of pirates and plunderers; as a result, lamb, kid, and offal have graced Sardinian tables more often than fish or seafood. Crackling disks of twice-cooked bread, hearty semolina pastas, creamy sheep's milk cheeses aged a mere day or two, tufts of wild fennel, orange threads of saffron, and just-slaughtered lamb are the basis of the region's cuisine, combined with the ingenuity and inventiveness of a people who have long relied on no one but themselves.

Favorite Restaurants, Shops, and Places

- AI TUGURI, Via Maiorca 57, Alghero, 079.976772. Catalan-influenced cuisine; try the *aragosta all' algherese*.
- CANTINA DEI GOLOSI, Via Arborea 13, Sassari, 079.237989. The *zuppa di granchi e patate* is a must-try.
- DAL CORSARO, Viale Regina Margherita 28, Cagliari, 070.664318. The *anghilla incasada* and *fregula con arselle* are outstanding.
- FRATELLI MANCA, Via Cima 5, Cabras, 0783.290848. *Bottarga* producer near the Cabras swamp.
- GALLURA, Corso Umberto 145, Olbia, 0789.24648. Mouthwatering seafood menu; order the *zuppa gallurese*.
- HOTEL RISTORANTE SU BARCHILE, Via Mannu 5, Orosei, 0784.98879. The *makkarones de busa* are handmade and the seafood is amazing.
- IL FARO, Via Bellini 25, Oristano, 0783.70002. The *muggine al sale* and *zuppa di fave con finocchietto e bietole* are marvelous.
- MANCA DOMENICO, Via Carrabuffas, Regione San Giuliano, Alghero, 079.977215. Torrone and other specialties for sale.
- SU GOLOGONE, Strada Oliena per Dorgali, Località Su Gologone, Oliena, 0784.287512. *Malloreddus* in wild boar ragù and spit-roasted meats are specialties at this elegant hotel and restaurant.
- VIDILI GIUSEPPINA, Via Santa Lucia 3, Paulilatino, 0785.55608. Near the *nuraghi* of Sant'Anna di Paulilatino, this bakery offers extraordinary ritual breads.

Telephone country code: 011.39

Insalata di Pomodorini, Sedano e Bottarga

Cherry Tomato, Celery, and Bottarga Salad

*C*abras, a town perched on a swamp so huge that it looks like a lake, is the best place to savor this beguiling salad. The gray mullet that thrive there are caught, and their eggs are retrieved, salted, and pressed under a weight for a week or so to obtain the flattened salami-shaped caviar that goes by the name of bottarga. Gray mullet bottarga, essential to Sardinian cuisine, is less salty and more delicate than tuna bottarga. I have enjoyed it grated over pasta, shaved over rice, tossed into salads, sandwiched between paper-thin slices of celery root, and accompanied by seedless grapes. For bottarga from Sardinia and pane carasau, a parchment-like flatbread, see Sources (page 372).

SERVES 4

4 half-sheets pane carasau or four ¼-inch-thick
   × 6-inch-wide slices of country bread
¼ cup plus 2 tablespoons extra-virgin olive oil
½ teaspoon salt
20 cherry tomatoes, halved
2 celery stalks from the heart, leaves on, stalks
   sliced paper-thin and leaves chopped
¼ teaspoon freshly ground black pepper
60 paper-thin slices gray mullet bottarga

Preheat the oven to 450°F.

Brush the smooth side of the pane carasau with 2 tablespoons of the olive oil. Sprinkle with ¼ teaspoon of the salt. Spread out in a single layer on an 11 × 17-inch baking sheet and bake in the preheated oven for 5 minutes, or until golden brown; watch the pane carasau so it does not burn. Now that it has been brushed with olive oil and toasted, the pane carasau is called *pane guttiau;* set aside. If using the sliced bread, proceed as above but bake 10 minutes, or until crisp.

Meanwhile, in a medium bowl, toss the cherry tomatoes, celery, and celery leaves with the remaining ¼ cup of olive oil, the remaining ¼ teaspoon of salt, and the pepper. Mound on 4 plates and sprinkle with the bottarga. Serve within minutes, accompanied by the pane guttiau or toasted bread.

Melanzane in Pinzimonio

Smoked Eggplants in Mint-Basil Oil

No Sardinian meal is complete without a vegetable or two: artichokes, zucchini, fennel, and eggplants are all favorites. This creamy purée of smoked eggplants hints at Arab roots, given its similarity to Middle Eastern salads. The best way to cook the eggplants is on an outdoor grill; failing that, a preheated broiler works very well.

SERVES 4

2 medium eggplants (1 pound each),
    pricked with a fork
2 garlic cloves, peeled
½ cup Italian parsley leaves
½ cup basil leaves
½ cup mint leaves
½ cup extra-virgin olive oil
1 teaspoon salt
¼ teaspoon freshly ground black pepper

Heat an outdoor grill or broiler. To cook the eggplants on the outdoor grill, grill until the skin is blistered and blackened all over, turning every few minutes, about 20 minutes. To cook in the broiler, place the eggplants on an 11 × 17-inch baking sheet and bake in the preheated broiler until the skin is blistered and blackened all over, turning every few minutes, about 20 minutes.

Remove to a platter, slit lengthwise, and cool to room temperature. Scoop out the flesh from the eggplant skin, discarding as many seeds as possible. Place in a sieve set over a bowl; drain at room temperature for 2 hours. Place the drained eggplant on a platter; it will be similar to a purée in texture.

In a food processor, combine the garlic, parsley, basil, mint, olive oil, salt, and pepper; process until nearly smooth. Pour over the eggplants and set aside at room temperature for 2 hours. Serve with pane carasau (page 352) or toasted bread.

THE SHEPHERD'S DAILY BREAD

Bread is as fundamental to Sardinian cuisine as pasta and sheep's milk cheese. Not only is it the staple that shepherds have long carried to the mountains for sustenance, it is the ingredient around which a battalion of their dishes is built. Sardinian breads are often made of nothing more than semolina flour, water, yeast, and salt. Some, like pane carasau, don't even call for yeast: disks of dough are baked until they balloon, then cut in half and baked again until crisp, the perfect food for long keeping. Pane carasau is made in small bakeries by women whose actions are as old and practiced as those of the shepherds tending their flocks in the craggy hills.

Malloreddus con Ragù di Cinghiale

Saffron-Tinted Dumplings in Wild Boar Ragù

Malloreddus and their shorter, rounder counterparts, gnocchetti sardi, are tiny dumplings made only of semolina flour and water. Sardinian families still prepare them by hand, using a metal screen to shape the malloreddus and give them their tapered edges and ridged exterior. Rather than add saffron to all the malloreddus, Sardinians aim for contrast: they add water in which saffron has been dissolved to a portion of the dough, resulting in a mountain of white dumplings and a hill of orange ones. The ragù below is a staple among Sardinian hunters; other toppings are a sausage ragù, a simple tomato sauce, and a chunky walnut and Pecorino purée. See Sources (page 372) to purchase malloreddus and wild boar. Substitute pork shoulder for the boar if boar is hard to find.

SERVES 4

12 basil leaves

3 bay leaves

6 juniper berries, crushed

2 thyme sprigs

1 cup dry red wine

½ pound boneless top round of wild boar, cut into ¼-inch cubes

2 carrots, 1 chopped and 1 minced

2 medium yellow onions, 1 chopped and 1 minced

2 garlic cloves, 1 peeled and 1 minced

⅓ cup extra-virgin olive oil

¼ teaspoon chili flakes

4 plum tomatoes, peeled (see page 369), seeded, and diced

2 tablespoons plus ½ teaspoon salt

1 pound saffron-tinted malloreddus

1 cup freshly grated Pecorino Sardo or Romano

Tie the basil, bay leaves, juniper berries, and thyme in a short piece of cheesecloth; place in a 1-quart pot with the wine and bring to a gentle boil over medium heat. Cool to room temperature. Transfer to a container; add the boar along with the chopped carrot, chopped onion, and peeled garlic. Refrigerate for 24 to 72 hours, tossing every few hours.

Drain the boar from the marinade and blot it dry, reserving the liquid and cheesecloth bundle; discard the chopped carrot, onion, and garlic. Heat the olive oil in an 8-inch sauté pan over a medium-high flame. Cook the boar until browned on all sides, turning with tongs to sear evenly, about 10 minutes. Add the minced carrot, minced onion, minced garlic, chili, and the cheesecloth bundle; cook until the carrot and onion are soft, about 5 minutes.

Deglaze with the reserved liquid from the marinade; cook 15 minutes, or until the liquid nearly evaporates. Add the tomatoes and ½ teaspoon of the salt. Bring to a gentle boil, cover, and cook over medium-low heat for 2 hours, adding water as needed. This is the ragù; discard the cheesecloth bundle and keep warm.

Bring 5 quarts of water to a boil. Add the malloreddus and the remaining 2 tablespoons of salt and cook until al dente, about 20 minutes. Drain, reserving ½ cup of the pasta cooking water; transfer to a bowl. Stir in the ragù, Pecorino, and reserved cooking water. Serve hot.

PREPARATION TIPS: The ragù can be cooked up to 3 days ahead and refrigerated; reheat as you boil the malloreddus.

SARDINIAN SOUP STAPLES

Wild fennel and semolina feature in many Sardinian soups. There is a *pasta e fagioli* with wild fennel, a wild fennel and chestnut soup, and a sausage soup scented with wild fennel. Semolina, on the other hand, provides bulk and structure to numerous soups. Semolina pasta is woven into fine strands called *filindeu* (from *fili,* meaning "strings") that are cooked in lamb broth and flavored with young Pecorino, a favorite in the Barbagia mountains for the feast of San Francesco di Lula. And coarsely ground semolina flour is cooked in milk and broth with fresh Pecorino to make a sustaining, rich soup known as *su-farri.*

Ravioli di Melanzane al Pomodoro
Eggplant-Walnut Ravioli in Tomato Sauce

Culingiones *and ravioli, Sardinia's stuffed pastas, are filled with a variety of foods depending on the season and the cook's mood. I particularly like this stuffing, which marries a good dose of fresh herbs with fried eggplants, creamy Ricotta, and chopped walnuts.*

FROM SPAIN'S EMPANADAS TO SARDINIA'S PANADAS

Sardinia's panadas, named after Spain's empanadas, are large, round pies stuffed with all manner of meat, fish, or vegetables. Pork, spinach, veal, eel, lamb, artichokes, boar, and more are used, alone or in varying combinations, by Sardinian cooks. When they are shaped into individual pies, they are called *impanadas* and served as antipasti or snacks.

SERVES 6

For the filling:
1/2 pound eggplant, peeled and cut into 1/2-inch-thick rounds
1 tablespoon plus 1/4 teaspoon salt
1/4 cup extra-virgin olive oil
6 ounces fresh Ricotta
2 extra-large eggs
1/4 cup finely chopped walnuts
1/4 cup minced Italian parsley
10 basil leaves, minced
5 sage leaves, minced
1/3 cup freshly grated Pecorino Sardo or Romano
1/4 teaspoon freshly ground black pepper

For the dough:
3 cups semolina flour, plus extra for the counter
1/4 teaspoon salt
1/4 teaspoon saffron pistils, dissolved in 1/2 cup warm water
2 extra-large eggs

To cook and serve:
1 tablespoon minced Italian parsley
1 tablespoon minced basil
1 recipe Tomato Sauce (page 369)
2 tablespoons salt
1/2 cup freshly grated Pecorino Sardo or Romano

Make the filling: Sprinkle the eggplant with 1 tablespoon of the salt; drain in a colander set over a plate for 1 hour. Rinse and blot dry. Heat the olive oil in a 12-inch skillet over a medium-high flame. Add the eggplant and cook until golden and soft, turning once, about 5 minutes per side. Remove with a slotted spatula to a plate lined with paper towels and blot dry, then cool.

Chop the eggplant and transfer to a large mixing bowl. Beat in the Ricotta, eggs, walnuts, parsley, basil, sage, Pecorino, the remaining ¼ teaspoon of salt, and the pepper. Set aside in the refrigerator.

Make the dough according to the instructions on page 370 using the ingredients listed opposite, adding a little water if the dough is dry or a little semolina flour if it is sticky. Knead 5 minutes, or until smooth, shape into a ball, wrap, and let rest 30 minutes.

Cut the dough into 2 pieces. Working with 1 piece at a time and keeping the other covered, roll out each piece on a semolina-dusted counter into a 20-inch circle, sprinkling both sides often with semolina flour to prevent sticking. Cut into 3½-inch disks with a round cookie cutter, top each with 1 heaping teaspoon of filling, moisten the edges with water, and fold in half to enclose. Seal the edges with your fingers, then with the tines of a fork. These are the ravioli. Spread out in a single layer on a semolina-dusted tray and set aside, uncovered, for 1 hour.

Preheat the oven to 375°F.

To cook, fold the parsley and basil into the tomato sauce in a medium bowl.

Bring 5 quarts of water to a boil and add the ravioli and salt; cook until al dente, about 3 minutes. Remove with a slotted spoon to a bowl. Layer the ravioli in a 10 × 14-inch baking dish with the herbed tomato sauce and the Pecorino. Bake in the preheated oven for 15 minutes and serve hot.

PREPARATION TIPS: Shape the ravioli up to 12 hours ahead, spread out in a single layer on a semolina-dusted tray, and refrigerate, covered with a towel.

PECORINO PARADISE

SARDINIA, WITH ITS MILLIONS OF SHEEP, is heaven for aficionados of sheep's milk cheese. The most renowned Sardinian sheep's milk cheese is Fiore Sardo, made of raw sheep's milk; soaked in a salt brine or dry-salted, it is rubbed with olive oil and sheep's fat, aged from two to eight months, and has a thick rind that ranges from yellow to brown.

Despite its appellation, Sardinia is an important producer of Pecorino Romano. Made with a whey starter according to a technique developed in ancient Rome, when

it was given to the legionnaires, Pecorino Romano owes its complex flavor to the milk of free-ranging sheep; it is dry-salted, rubbed with olive oil, and aged from five to eight months.

Pecorino Sardo, one of the island's proudest products, is aged up to two months when Dolce and up to a year when Maturo. The Dolce is white, compact, lightly acidic, with minute holes; the Maturo is yellowish, grainy, spicy, with a rind that becomes increasingly dark as the cheese ages, and can be smoked.

These three Sardinian sheep's milk cheeses may be purchased in stores across North America; see Sources (page 372).

Fregola con le Arselle

Fregola Soup with Cockles

Sardinia's soil, though difficult to cultivate, yields plenty of wheat—especially durum wheat, which is milled into semolina flour and transformed into an incredible diversity of pastas. Fregola is perhaps the most unusual and versatile of these: it is boiled in soups, tossed with tomato sauce, or baked with lard, Pecorino, and herbs. Made by sprinkling water onto semolina flour with the fingertips until pellets form, it has been dubbed Sardinian couscous, since the production method is similar for both. Some people add saffron to the semolina, tinting the fregola yellow; others add egg whites for a crisper texture. The most widespread way of cooking fregola is in soup with arselle, a clam variety indigenous to Italy that finds no equal in North America; New Zealand cockles make the best substitute. See Sources (page 372) to buy fregola.

SERVES 4

1½ pounds cockles or cherrystone clams
1 tablespoon plus ½ teaspoon salt
⅓ cup extra-virgin olive oil
2 garlic cloves, minced
⅛ to ¼ teaspoon chili flakes
3 bay leaves
2 tablespoons minced Italian parsley
24 basil leaves, torn
¼ cup tomato paste
5 ounces fregola

Soak the cockles in cool water to cover with 1 tablespoon of the salt for 1 hour; drain and rinse. Place in a 3-quart pot, cover, and cook over medium heat until they open, about 5 minutes; strain the cooking juices through a cheesecloth-lined sieve and reserve. Discard any unopened cockles.

Heat the olive oil over a medium flame in the same pot. Add the garlic, chili, bay leaves, parsley, and basil; cook 2 minutes, stirring constantly. Add the tomato paste and cook 2 more minutes, still stirring.

Pour in 4½ cups of water along with the reserved cooking juices from the cockles and bring to a boil. Stir in the cockles, fregola, and the remaining ½ teaspoon of salt. Cook until the fregola is al dente, about 10 minutes. Discard the bay leaves and serve immediately.

COUSCOUS IN CARLOFORTE

Couscous is a staple in Carloforte, a town on the island of San Pietro off the southwestern coast of Sardinia, where the descendants of Ligurian sailors taken captive by Arabs in the fifteenth century have lived for centuries. Not only do the people of Carloforte speak an ancient Ligurian dialect, they top couscous (locally known as *cascà*) with artichokes, peas, cardoons, cabbage, fennel, and other vegetables rather than with fish or meat, as the Sicilians and North Africans are wont to do.

Aragosta Arrosto

Roasted Lobster with Parsley and Bread Crumbs

Lobster meat is especially succulent in the Catalan-influenced city of Alghero and nearby Bosa. The simplest Sardinian recipes suggest poaching lobster and drizzling it with a whisper of olive oil, or baking it under a light coating of bread crumbs and herbs, as below, to highlight the sweet flavor of the shellfish rather than mask it. If possible, ask the fishmonger to cut up the live lobsters for you so that you can be spared the unpleasantness, and cook the lobsters within hours.

SERVES 2

2 live lobsters (1½ pounds each), halved lengthwise
¼ cup extra-virgin olive oil
¼ cup fresh lemon juice (from 1 large lemon)
2 tablespoons minced Italian parsley
½ teaspoon salt
¼ teaspoon freshly ground black pepper
2 tablespoons fresh bread crumbs

Preheat the oven to 375°F.

Extract the tail meat from the lobster shells and place in a 12-inch roasting pan (reserve claws for another use). Drizzle with the olive oil and lemon juice, sprinkle with the parsley, salt, pepper, and bread crumbs, and roast in the preheated oven for 15 minutes. Serve hot.

THE ISLAND'S HUMBLEST FISH

Sardines were named after Sardinia, given their abundance near its shores. Sardinians cook them in a variety of ways: battered and fried, marinated with lemon juice to be eaten raw, or baked with tomato sauce, wild fennel, and bread crumbs.

Muggine al Sale

Gray Mullet Baked in Sea Salt

Baking fish in a salt crust—a favorite technique around the Mediterranean—results in perfectly seasoned and marvelously moist fish: the salt forms a solid mass that flavors the fish and prevents it from drying out. If gray mullet is unavailable at your fish market, it can be purchased by mail-order (see Sources, page 372), but it can also be replaced by other large, meaty fish such as sea bass.

SERVES 2

3 extra-large egg whites, plus extra if needed
5 pounds coarse sea salt, plus extra if needed
1 gray mullet (2½ pounds), gutted, fins removed
½ cup extra-virgin olive oil
½ teaspoon freshly ground black pepper
2 lemons, cut into wedges

Preheat the oven to 375°F.

In a large bowl, beat the egg whites lightly, just enough to blend, and add the salt and ½ cup of cold water. Spread half of the salt mixture in a roasting pan that is 2 inches longer than the fish. Rinse the gray mullet, blot it dry thoroughly, and place it over the salt mixture in the roasting pan. Cover with the remaining salt mixture, making sure the fish is entirely covered by the salt and none of the skin shows through; if needed, make some additional salt mixture using the same proportions of salt, egg white, and water.

Bake in the preheated oven for 45 minutes. Turn off the oven and leave the roasting pan in the oven 15 more minutes. Bring the pan to the table and, using the back of a large knife or a mallet, crack the salt crust.

Lift the gray mullet fillets from the bone and drizzle with the olive oil. Sprinkle with the pepper and serve hot, passing the lemon wedges at the table.

SWAMP-CURED MULLET

The enormous swamp of Cabras, near the city of Oristano, is home to a unique specialty called *merca*: gray mullet is boiled with ample amounts of salt, shaped into a salami-like log, and wrapped in an aromatic grass that grows around the swamp. After a few days of drinking in the briny flavor of the grass, the mullet is unwrapped, sliced thin, and doused with olive oil as an antipasto.

Gallina al Mirto

Myrtle-Infused Hen

Myrtle is one of the plants that make up the macchia mediterranea ("Mediterranean brush"); others are rosemary, lentisk, broom, and oleander. In Sardinia, myrtle's purplish berries are distilled into a potent liqueur, and its pretty leaves and aromatic branches are thrown into the fire to perfume meat as it roasts. Florists in North America use myrtle branches in bouquets, so we need not travel to Sardinia to taste this cold poached hen infused with the heady scent of myrtle. However, commercial myrtle lacks the intense aroma of wild Sardinian myrtle, so I use an unorthodox myrtle-infused olive oil to underscore the myrtle flavor in the hen. When you purchase the myrtle branches from your florist, make sure that they are pesticide-free.

SERVES 4

16 cups (4 quarts) Vegetable Broth (page 34)
1 boiling hen, skin removed
24 myrtle branches
3 beefsteak tomatoes, thinly sliced
1 cup extra-virgin olive oil
2 garlic cloves, crushed
1 teaspoon salt
½ teaspoon freshly ground black pepper

Bring the broth to a boil in an 8-quart pot. Add the hen, reduce the heat to medium, cover, and cook until tender, about 45 minutes. Let the hen rest in the broth, covered, for 1 hour, then remove it with tongs to a plate. (Save the broth for soups or risotti.)

Arrange half of the myrtle on a 3-foot-long piece of sturdy aluminum foil. Top with the hen and cover with the remaining myrtle. Cover with another 3-foot-long piece of sturdy aluminum foil and wrap the foil around the hen tightly to enclose. Cool to room temperature, then refrigerate for 24 hours.

Unwrap the hen. Bone the breast and thighs and slice into ¼-inch-thick slices. Fan the slices out on a platter. Arrange a few myrtle branches around the sliced hen and decorate with the tomato slices.

Place the olive oil in an 8-inch skillet with the garlic, salt, pepper, and 3 of the myrtle branches, snapping the branches into 6-inch lengths first. Heat over a medium-low flame for 15 minutes. Strain the warm myrtle-infused olive oil over the hen, discarding the solids, and serve immediately.

Sardinia's Wines

Sardinia's intense sun and hot Mediterranean climate have made the island, along with Sicily and Apulia, one of Italy's most important sources for blending wines, given the staggeringly high alcohol content its wines have historically achieved. Spanish varietals like Vermentino, Cannonau, Carignano, and Bovale thrive across Sardinia. Although annual production hovers around a low 27 million gallons, the island offers a range of excellent wines.

VERNACCIA DI ORISTANO, the most Sardinian of the island's wines, is a sherry-like white with a dry, warm flavor, almond blossom notes, and clean, slightly bitter finish; like many Sardinian wines, Vernaccia di Oristano is vinified in dry, sweet, and fortified versions.

CANNONAU DI SARDEGNA, a robust, dry, full-bodied, muscular red, is vinified from Cannonau grapes; the best is from Oliena, in the province of Nuoro. A rosé version also exists.

CARIGNANO DEL SULCIS, an intense, dry red and harmonious rosé from the ancient Punic town of Sulcis, is also vinified in a *novello* and raisined version.

MONICA DI SARDEGNA is light, ruby-red, boasts an ethereal perfume, especially in wines hailing from Nuoro, and is best young; a sparkling version is also produced.

VERMENTINO DI GALLURA is the island's most characteristic white and its only DOCG; it has a subtle perfume, dry flavor, light bitter undertones, and high acidity.

MOSCATO DI SARDEGNA, a sparkling white, is light and frothy, with a spiced bouquet of Muscat and a delicate, fruity flavor.

Agnello Arrosto con Finocchi
Roasted Lamb with Fennel

The province of Nuoro has especially strong pastoral traditions, and one of its specialties is lamb braised with wild fennel. I have indulged in the Sardinian pairing of lamb and fennel both braised and roasted; the braised version is moister, but the roasted version is more intense, so it is the one I offer here. The recipe below is an adaptation of a dish I tasted at Su Barchile in Orosei, where the Chessa family offers traditional Sardinian food. Combining fennel bulb and a touch of crushed fennel seeds approximates the flavor—if not the romance—of wild fennel.

SERVES 4

1½ pounds boneless lamb shoulder, trimmed of fat and sinew, cut into 1½-inch cubes
6 garlic cloves, halved
2 teaspoons fennel seeds, crushed
¼ to ½ teaspoon chili flakes
1 teaspoon freshly ground black pepper
⅓ cup extra-virgin olive oil
2 fennel bulbs, stalks and fronds still attached
1 teaspoon salt

In a 10 × 14-inch roasting pan, combine the lamb, garlic, fennel seeds, chili, pepper, and olive oil. Refrigerate for 48 hours, tossing once in a while to distribute the flavorings.

Preheat the oven to 450°F.

Bring 4 quarts of water to a boil. Trim the fennel, discarding the stalks and reserving the fronds. Cut the fennel into quarters and remove the tough white core from each quarter. Slice each quarter into 4 wedges; drop the wedges into the boiling water. Cook 10 minutes, then drain. Coarsely chop the raw feathery fronds.

Add the boiled fennel wedges and raw fennel fronds to the lamb in the roasting pan, season with the salt, and toss. Roast in the preheated oven for 1 hour, and serve hot.

THE AUTHENTIC ROAST SUCKLING PIG

PORCEDDU IS THE DISH SARDINIANS are most proud of: a suckling pig weighing no more than ten pounds is threaded on a branch from a strawberry tree and slowly spit-roasted over a fire built on aromatic branches like bay, juniper, olive, myrtle, and lentisk. The meat is repeatedly rubbed with boiling lard as it roasts, and is eaten immediately or wrapped in myrtle leaves for a few days and then served cold. In true Sardinian spirit, no part of the pig is wasted: the skin, ears, trotters, and tail are all eaten. Suckling pig is sometimes buried under hot ashes instead, from which it emerges crisp and glistening. But few cooks on the island still take the time to dig the pit necessary for this style of outdoor cooking.

Seadas

Mint-and-Lemon-Laced Cheese Pillows in Warm Chestnut Honey

Pastries and sweets in Sardinia reflect Greek, Spanish, and Arab influences not only in method, but in flavor. Honey, saffron, almonds, citrus peel, orange-blossom water, semolina flour, and young sheep's milk cheese are within every Sardinian pastry cook's reach. Many sweets are long-keeping confections studded with dried fruit and nuts, the sort of food a lucky shepherd might have found tucked in his bag on long journeys away from home. Seadas, deep-fried cheese pillows drizzled with bitter honey, were offered by women to shepherds upon their return from winter pastures, and owe their melting texture to fresh sheep's milk cheese. Since days-old sheep's milk cheese is hard to come by in North America, I propose buffalo milk Mozzarella instead: its acidity and tang, as well as its exceptional melting ability, make it a good substitute. For a truly Sardinian touch, add a tablespoon of lard to the hot olive oil whenever you fry.

SERVES 8

½ pound buffalo milk Mozzarella, cut into
   ½-inch dice
Grated zest of 1 lemon
2 tablespoons minced mint
1 cup semolina flour, plus extra for the counter
¼ teaspoon salt
3 cups plus 1 tablespoon extra-virgin olive oil, or
   1 tablespoon extra-virgin olive oil and 3 cups
   peanut oil
1 cup chestnut honey (or orange-blossom honey
   for a milder version)

Place the Mozzarella in a 1-quart pot with ½ cup of water. Cook over medium-low heat, stirring constantly with a wooden spoon, until it forms a solid ball that separates from the liquid, about 15 minutes. Remove to a colander, discarding the liquid. While the Mozzarella is still hot, knead in the lemon zest and mint. Pour onto a counter, flatten into a 4 × 8-inch rectangle, and cut into eight 2-inch squares. Set aside, uncovered, for 2 hours.

Pour the semolina flour in a bowl. Work in the salt and 1 tablespoon of the olive oil, then add as much room-temperature water as needed (about ¼ cup) to make a supple, firm dough. Knead until smooth, about 5 minutes, adding a little water if the dough is dry or a little flour if it is sticky. Pat into a disk, wrap, and let rest 30 minutes.

Roll out the dough on a semolina-dusted counter into a 14-inch square. Cut into 3½-inch disks with a round cookie cutter; gather scraps, roll out again, and cut into more 3½-inch disks; you will need 16 disks in all. Top 8 of the dough disks with the Mozzarella squares, cover with the 8 remaining dough disks, and seal the edges with the tines of a fork. These are the seadas. Spread out in a single layer on a semolina-dusted tray.

Heat the remaining 3 cups of oil in a deep pan to 350°F, or until it is hot enough to brown a cube of bread in 1 minute. Fry 4 of the seadas at a time until golden and puffed, about 1 minute per side, turning once. Remove with a slotted spoon to a plate lined with paper towels, blot dry, and continue in the same manner with the remaining 4 seadas, maintaining the temperature of the oil by regulating the heat.

Meanwhile, heat the honey in a 1-quart pot over a medium flame for 2 minutes. Serve the seadas hot, drizzled with the warm honey.

PREPARATION TIPS: Shape the seadas up to 2 hours ahead, spread out in a single layer on a semolina-dusted tray, and set aside at room temperature, covered with a towel.

A TASTE FOR HONEY

Italians in general take honey seriously. Sardinians, on the other hand, revere honey. They pour it over fritters, dredge pastries in it, brush it over cookies, and drizzle it over fresh sheep's milk Ricotta, then whip the whole mass into a sweet white cloud. For every one of these characteristic desserts, Sardinians pick among a number of varietal honeys: mild and fragrant orange-blossom honey; astringent honey from strawberry trees; pungent, dark chestnut honey; intensely floral lavender honey; earthy cardoon honey; bracing eucalyptus honey; ultrabitter lentisk honey. Each of these honeys lends its distinctive aroma and flavor to Sardinia's most traditional pastries, sweetening them in a way sugar never could.

Basic Recipes

Brodo di Pollo
Chicken Broth

The most flavorful, rich broth is made from a whole chicken, but chicken legs or backs (or, lacking that, wings) make very good broth too. The broth can be refrigerated for up to 5 days or frozen for up to 2 months.

MAKES ABOUT 6 CUPS (1½ QUARTS)

2 pounds chicken parts
1 celery stalk, chopped
1 carrot, chopped
1 medium yellow onion, quartered
1 leek, green part only, halved and rinsed
2 garlic cloves, crushed
1 bunch Italian parsley, stems included
8 thyme sprigs
2 bay leaves
1 tablespoon black peppercorns

Rinse the chicken parts and place in a 6-quart pot. Add the remaining ingredients and pour in 12 cups (3 quarts) of cold water.

Bring to a gentle boil over medium-high heat, skimming the surface often with a slotted spoon to get rid of the scum that rises to the surface. Lower the heat to medium-low and cook, uncovered and without stirring, for 6 hours. The liquid in the pot will have reduced to half of its original volume.

Strain through a cheesecloth-lined colander into a large bowl; discard the solids. Allow the broth to cool, then refrigerate until the fat solidifies, about 12 hours. Skim off the fat with a slotted spoon, and transfer the broth to smaller containers.

Brodo di Manzo
Beef Broth

Unlike chicken broth, beef broth requires that the bones be blanched before the cooking truly gets underway; this prevents the broth from turning cloudy. The broth can be refrigerated for up to 5 days or frozen for up to 2 months.

MAKES ABOUT 6 CUPS (1½ QUARTS)

2 pounds beef bones, cut into 3-inch pieces
1 celery stalk, chopped
1 carrot, chopped
1 medium yellow onion, quartered
1 leek, green part only, halved and rinsed
2 garlic cloves, crushed
1 bunch Italian parsley, stems included
8 thyme sprigs
2 bay leaves
1 tablespoon black peppercorns

Rinse the beef bones and place them in a 6-quart pot. Add cold water to cover by 3 inches and bring to a boil over medium-high heat. Cook for 5 minutes, then drain. Return the beef bones to the pot, add the remaining ingredients, and pour in 12 cups (3 quarts) of cold water.

Bring to a gentle boil over medium-high heat, skimming often with a slotted spoon to get rid of the scum that rises to the surface. Lower the heat to medium-low and cook, uncovered and without stirring, for 6 hours. The liquid in the pot will have reduced to half of its original volume.

Strain through a cheesecloth-lined colander into a large bowl; discard the solids. Allow to cool, then refrigerate until the fat solidifies, about 12 hours. Skim off the fat with a slotted spoon; transfer the broth to smaller containers.

Brodo di Pesce
Fish Broth

Salmon and other fatty fish should not be used for fish broth; select white fish and those with a relatively delicate flavor, such as turbot, snapper, and bass, and add shells from shrimp, scampi, or lobster if you have them on hand. The broth can be refrigerated for up to 3 days or frozen for up to 6 weeks.

MAKES ABOUT 8 CUPS (2 QUARTS)

2 pounds fish trimmings
2 cups dry white wine
1 celery stalk, chopped
1 leek, green part only, halved and rinsed
1 medium yellow onion, quartered
1 fennel bulb, stalks and fronds only
2 garlic cloves, crushed
1 bunch Italian parsley, stems included
8 thyme sprigs
1 bay leaf
1 teaspoon black peppercorns

Discard the gills, livers, brains, and other entrails from the fish trimmings. Rinse the trimmings and place in a 6-quart pot. Add the remaining ingredients and pour in 8 cups (2 quarts) of cold water. Bring to a gentle boil over medium-high heat, skimming often with a slotted spoon to get rid of the scum that rises to the surface. Lower the heat to medium-low and cook, uncovered and without stirring, for 30 minutes. The broth will not have reduced.

Strain through a cheesecloth-lined colander into a large bowl; discard the solids. Allow to cool, then refrigerate until the fat solidifies, about 12 hours. Skim off the fat (there will barely be any) with a slotted spoon and transfer the broth to smaller containers.

Sugo di Pomodoro
Tomato Sauce

This all-purpose sauce is ideal for pasta, savory pies, meat and poultry stews, and more. The sauce can be refrigerated for up to 5 days or frozen for up to 2 months.

MAKES ABOUT 4 CUPS (1 QUART)

3 pounds plum tomatoes, or 3 cups canned
    chopped Italian plum tomatoes
1/3 cup extra-virgin olive oil
1 small yellow onion, minced
2 garlic cloves, minced
12 basil leaves, torn
1/2 teaspoon salt

If using fresh plum tomatoes, bring 4 quarts of water to a boil. Cut a small ✕ on the bottom of each plum tomato and drop into the boiling water. Cook 2 minutes, or until the skin starts to loosen, then remove with a slotted spoon to a large bowl filled with ice water. Drain, slip off the skin from each tomato, cut in half along the width, scoop out the seeds, and dice, then set aside.

Heat the olive oil in an 8-inch sauté pan over a medium flame. Add the onion, garlic, and basil; cook 5 minutes, stirring often. Stir in the reserved tomatoes and salt. Bring to a boil, then reduce the heat to medium-low and cook for 30 minutes, covered.

Use immediately, or cool to room temperature before refrigerating.

Besciamella
Béchamel

*T*his creamy white sauce is used in lasagne, can-nelloni, and many oven-baked dishes. It can be refrigerated for up to 3 days. It will thicken in the refrigerator; whisk in a little cold milk before using to return it to a flowing consistency.

MAKES ABOUT 4 CUPS (1 QUART)

6 tablespoons ($^3/_4$ stick) unsalted butter
$^1/_2$ cup unbleached all-purpose flour
4 cups (1 quart) whole milk
$^1/_4$ teaspoon salt
$^1/_8$ teaspoon freshly ground white pepper
Pinch freshly grated nutmeg (optional)

Melt the butter in a heavy-bottomed 1$^1/_2$-quart pot over medium-low heat. Pour in the flour, stirring with a wooden spoon. Cook for 5 minutes, stirring constantly; do not allow the flour to take on any color.

Meanwhile, heat the milk in a 1$^1/_2$-quart pot until it is nearly boiling.

Pour the hot milk into the butter-flour mixture, beating vigorously with a wire whisk to prevent lumps. Bring to a boil, still whisk-ing; cook over medium-high heat, whisking often, until thick, about 10 minutes. Season with the salt, pepper, and nutmeg. If needed, strain through a fine sieve to eliminate lumps.

Use immediately, or cool to room tempera-ture before refrigerating.

Pasta all'Uovo
Pasta Dough

*M*aking pasta is an easy enough task once you've done it a few times. The recipe below is for the most basic wheat flour and egg pasta, but the same procedure can be applied to semolina and egg, semolina and water, wheat flour and water, or any type of flour and liquid. This is the basic method you will need to follow to make all the pasta recipes in this book, regardless of ingredients used. The dough can be made up to 24 hours ahead and refrigerated; return to room temperature before rolling, cutting, and shaping.

MAKES 1$^1/_2$ POUNDS FRESH PASTA

2$^2/_3$ cups unbleached all-purpose flour, plus
   extra for the counter
$^1/_4$ teaspoon salt
4 extra-large eggs

Place the flour on a counter and add the salt; combine with a fork. Make a well in the cen-ter of the flour and add the eggs to the well. Using a fork at first, draw the flour little by little into the eggs.

When almost all of the flour has been incorporated into the eggs, begin kneading the dough by hand; knead until it is smooth and firm, about 5 minutes, adding a little water if the dough is dry or a little flour if it is sticky. (Alternately, mix the flour and salt in a medium bowl and stir in the eggs with a fork, then turn the resulting dough out onto a counter and knead as above; this method is easier for beginners.)

Shape the dough into a ball, dust with flour, wrap in plastic, and let rest at room temperature for 30 minutes. This relaxes the gluten and makes rolling easier later; some pasta recipes do not call for a rest, but most do. Follow instructions in individual recipes for rolling out, cutting, and shaping pasta.

Pasta Lievitata
Yeasted Dough

This dough can be used in numerous ways. If you let it rise slowly in the refrigerator rather than quickly at room temperature, its flavor will be more complex. It can be made up to 24 hours ahead and allowed to rise in the refrigerator; return to room temperature before proceeding.

MAKES ENOUGH FOR ONE 15-INCH FOCACCIA

3¼ cups unbleached all-purpose flour
1 teaspoon instant yeast
1 tablespoon fine sea salt
¼ cup extra-virgin olive oil, plus extra for greasing the bowl

Combine the flour, yeast, and salt in a food processor. With the motor running, add ¾ cup of warm (110°F) water. Add the olive oil with the motor running and then add enough warm water to make a soft dough that does not stick to the sides of the bowl (you will need about ¼ to ⅓ cup of water). Process 45 seconds. Turn out onto the counter and shape into a ball.

Lightly oil a bowl and place the dough in it; wrap and let rise at room temperature until doubled, about 1 hour. Follow instructions in individual recipes for shaping, second rise, and baking.

Polenta
Polenta

Experiment with this recipe to create infinite variations: Use less water for a firmer polenta or more water for a softer polenta; combine white cornmeal and yellow cornmeal for a lighter color and flavor; and try different grinds of cornmeal (coarse, medium, or fine) for a grittier or smoother texture. Once cooked, cooled polenta can be refrigerated for 3 days until needed for grilling, frying, or baking.

SERVES 8

¼ teaspoon salt
2 cups yellow cornmeal
Extra-virgin olive oil for greasing the baking sheets if you are frying, grilling, or baking the polenta

Bring 8 cups (2 quarts) of water to a boil in a heavy 4-quart pot. Add the salt. Pour in the polenta in a thin, steady stream, beating with a whisk all the while to prevent lumps. Lower the heat to medium-low and cook, uncovered, stirring constantly with a wooden spoon, until the polenta is creamy and smooth, about 45 minutes. (See below for a no-stir method.)

If you are serving the polenta immediately, spoon it onto individual plates. If the recipe suggests stirring in flavorings, do so before serving: try unsalted butter, grated Parmigiano, a touch of cream, or Mascarpone.

If you are frying, grilling, or baking the polenta, spread it out onto 2 oiled 11 × 17-inch baking sheets to a thickness of ⅓ inch; smooth the top, allow to cool, and cut into the required shape.

For the no-stir method, whisk the polenta into the boiling water as above, then pour it into a 4-quart stainless steel bowl, cover with foil, and set it over a pot of simmering water. Cook without stirring for 2 hours. Uncover, stir, and serve or use as above, whisking in a little hot water if needed to thin it.

Sources

Most of the stores and importers below will ship anywhere in the country with sufficient notice. Those marked with an asterisk (*) rarely mail-order but have such a good selection that they are worth mentioning for those who can actually visit.

LEGUMES, GRAINS, AND PASTAS

Bread flour: 15
Buckwheat flour: 8, 14, 15
Cicerchie (wild chickpeas): 1
Cornmeal: 1, 2, 5, 8, 14, 21
Dried beans: 1, 2, 6, 8, 14
Fagioli di Lamon (Lamon beans): 1
Farro: 1, 2, 5, 8
Lenticchie di Castelluccio (Castelluccio lentils): 1
Pastas (including pizzoccheri, garganelli, malloreddus, fregola, taccozze, pappardelle, cavatelli, maccheroni al ferretto, and maccheroni alla chitarra): 2, 3, 5, 6, 8, 9, 14, 18, 21
Rice (Arborio, Vialone Nano, Carnaroli, Vialone) 1, 2, 5, 14, 21
Wheat berries: 2, 8
White cornmeal: 5

CONDIMENTS, DRIED GOODS, AND LUXURY ITEMS

Balsamic and wine vinegars: 1, 2, 3, 5, 6, 8, 10, 14, 18, 21
Bottarga (gray mullet and tuna): 22
Canned Italian plum tomatoes: 1, 2, 3, 5, 6, 8, 10, 14, 21
Galette del marinaio: 5, 21
Oil-preserved vegetables: 1, 2, 5, 8, 14, 21
Olive oil: 1, 2, 3, 5, 6, 8, 10, 14, 18, 21
Pane carasau (Sardinian flatbread): 2, 5, 21
Porcini mushrooms (dried, fresh, and frozen): 4, 22
Salted anchovies: 1, 2, 3, 5, 14
Salted capers: 1, 2, 3, 5, 21
Spices: 8, 19
Tomato paste: 2, 3, 5, 6, 8, 10, 14, 21
Truffles and truffle products: 4, 22

BAKING

Boiled chestnuts: 14
Calabrese figs: 2
Candied fruit (including candied citron): 14, 15
Varietal honeys (chestnut and others): 1, 5, 8, 13
Vino cotto (cooked grape must): 6, 13

PERISHABLES (MEAT, FISH, AND PRODUCE)

Game (wild boar, hare, etc.): 6, 8, 12
Fish and seafood (including gray mullet, sturgeon, eel, Mediterranean sea bass, Mediterranean red mullet, and pike on special order): 6, 23
Produce: 8, 14, 17
Specialty meats (goat, sheep, rabbit): 6, 8, 12

CURED MEATS AND CHEESES

Bufalina del Matese: 11, 13
Buffalo milk Mozzarella: 2, 8, 11, 14, 21
Burrata: 13, 14
Caciocavallo Silano: 5
Caciocavallo Ragusano: 2, 6, 10, 13
Caciotta al Tartufo: 2, 13, 14
Crescenza: 2, 21
Cured meats (including Pancetta; Speck; Prosciutto Cotto, di Parma, di Carpegna, and di San Daniele): 2, 8, 14, 21
Firm fresh Ricotta (sold as Ricottone): 2
Formaggio di Fossa (also known as Pecorino di Fossa): 10, 11, 13
Full range of cheeses: 2, 6, 8, 10, 11, 14, 18, 21
Pecorino Crotonese: 5, 10, 13
Pecorino Sotto le Foglie di Noci (Pecorino in walnut leaves): 13

Robiola (fresh): 2, 21
Scamorza: 2
Sheep's milk Ricotta: 5, 10, 21
Smoked Ricotta from Abruzzo: 11
Toma delle Langhe from Piedmont: 13

KITCHENWARE
Baking supplies (baking stones, baking peels, and more): 15, 20

Farinata pans, polenta pots, risotto pots, and other copper products: 7
Spaetzle press: 20
Specialty kitchen items: 20

WINES
Di Majo Norante's wines: 24
Full range of Italian wines: 16, 24
Walter De Battè's Sciacchetrà: 16

1. A.G. FERRARI FOODS
   3490 Catalina Street
   San Leandro, CA 94577
   (510) 346-2100

2. AGATA & VALENTINA*
   1505 First Avenue
   New York, NY 10021
   (212) 452-0690

3. WWW.ALIMENTITALIA.COM

4. BOSCOVIVO USA
   107 East 31st Street, 3F
   New York, NY 10016
   (212) 448-1892 or
   (877) TARTUFO
   www.boscovivo.com

5. BUONITALIA*
   75 Ninth Avenue
   New York, NY 10011
   (212) 633-9090

6. CITARELLA
   2135 Broadway
   New York, NY 10023
   (212) 784-0383

7. COPPER PRODUCTS OF
   ITALY
   413 Industrial Drive
   North Wales, PA 19454
   (215) 661-2000
   www.cpi-inc.net

8. DEAN & DELUCA
   121 Prince Street
   New York, NY 10012
   (212) 254-8776
   www.deandeluca.com

9. DELVERDE USA
   1901 Research Boulevard,
   Suite 160
   Rockville, MD 20850
   (800) 222-4409, ext. 525
   www.delverde.com

10. DiBRUNO BROTHERS
    HOUSE OF CHEESE
    930 South Ninth Street
    Philadelphia, PA 19147
    (215) 922-2876
    www.dibruno.com

11. WWW.ESPERYA.COM

12. ESPOSITO'S PORK SHOP
    500 Ninth Avenue
    New York, NY 10018
    (212) 279-3298

13. FORMAGGIO KITCHEN
    244 Huron Avenue
    Cambridge, MA 02138
    (888) 212-3224

14. GRACE'S MARKETPLACE
    1237 Third Avenue
    New York, NY 10021
    (212) 737-0600

15. KING ARTHUR FLOUR
    P.O. Box 876
    Norwich, VT 05055
    (800) 827-6836
    www.bakerscatalogue.com

16. LIVIO PANEBIANCO
    IMPORTS
    1140 Broadway, 5th floor
    New York, NY 10001
    (212) 685-7560

17. MELISSA'S WORLD
    VARIETY PRODUCE
    P.O. Box 21127
    Los Angeles, CA 90021
    (800) 588-1281

18. WWW.PASTACHEESE.COM

19. PENSEYS SPICES AND
    SEASONINGS
    P.O. Box 933
    Muskego, WI 53150
    (414) 574-0277

20. SUR LA TABLE
    1765 Sixth Avenue South
    Seattle, WA 98134
    (800) 243-0852

21. TODARO BROTHERS
    555 Second Avenue
    New York, NY 10016
    (212) 532-0633

22. URBANI USA
    2924 Fortieth Avenue
    Long Island City, NY 11101
    (718) 392-5050
    www.urbani.com

23. WILD EDIBLES
    318 Grand Central Terminal
    New York, NY 10017
    (212) 687-4255

24. WINEBOW
    22 Hollywood Avenue,
    Suite C
    Ho-Ho-Kus, NJ 07423
    (201) 445-0620

Glossary

Amaretti di Saronno Almond macaroons from the town of Saronno in Lombardy whose dough includes ground bitter almonds. Most commonly used in pasta stuffings, savory pies, and desserts.

Arborio Short-grain rice variety most commonly used for risotto, rice dishes, soups, and even rice-based desserts. Overcooks fairly easily.

Asiago Firm cow's milk cheese from the Veneto; available young and full-fat (Pressato) or aged and semifat (d'Allevo).

Balsamic Vinegar The precious vinegar of Modena in Emilia-Romagna, obtained by aging vinegar from local grapes in various wooden barrels for as long as one hundred years. Complex, sweet, and rich, it is good in salads and meat glazes, over ice cream and strawberries, and more.

Bottarga Pressed salted roe, usually of gray mullet (in Sardinia) or tuna (in Calabria and Sicily). Shaved over cooked beans, salads, or pastas, it adds a pleasantly intense fish taste.

Bucatini Spaghetti with a hole (*buco*) in the middle; common in Latium and Sicily.

Buckwheat Flour Nutty, light brown flour obtained from buckwheat groats; a staple in the Valtellina area of Lombardy and other cool areas, where it is used to make pasta, bread, and polenta. Refrigerate to prevent it from turning rancid.

Buffalo Milk Mozzarella Fresh Mozzarella made from the milk of water buffaloes; the most prized is from Campania and Latium. Best eaten the day it is made; if necessary, conserve it in salted water in the refrigerator for up to 24 hours, then soak in warm water for 15 minutes before serving. Typically consumed raw, as it lets out a lot of water when cooked.

Caciocavallo Cow's milk cheese shaped like a pear and slung over a wooden board to age; melts beautifully.

Carnaroli Short-grain rice variety; along with Vialone Nano (see below), the best for risotto.

Cavatelli Short, concave, sometimes-ridged semolina-flour gnocchi; common to Apulia, Calabria, and Basilicata.

Chestnut Flour Gray-beige flour obtained from dried chestnuts; used to make polenta, flat-breads, breads, and pasta. Refrigerate to prevent it from turning rancid.

Chickpea Flour Golden flour obtained from dried chickpeas, utilized in polenta and fritters; look for untoasted chickpea flour. Refrigerate to prevent it from turning rancid.

Crescenza Creamy, fresh cow's milk cheese from Lombardy; used for stuffing savory pies, eating at the table, and serving with salads.

Durum Flour Finely ground durum wheat, a strong variety of wheat; best for bread-making. Not to be confused with semolina flour, which is the coarser grind meant for making pasta.

Extra-Virgin Olive Oil Olive oil with less than 1 percent acidity. The oil of choice for everything: dressing salads, sautéing, deep-frying, and even baking certain desserts.

Farro Emmer, an ancient form of wheat, not to be mistaken for spelt; whole berries are cooked into soups, salads, or risotto-style first courses, while ground farro is used to make bread, polenta, and pasta.

Fontina Firm cow's milk cheese from Val d'Aosta; essential to *fonduta*.

Fregola Small Sardinian semolina pasta, obtained by sprinkling semolina flour with water until pellets form; a cousin of couscous, it is used in soups, salads, and casseroles.

Gorgonzola Italy's most famous blue-veined cheese; typical of Lombardy, as good melted over gnocchi, pasta, pizza, risotto, or meat as it is eaten at the table.

Grana Padano Crumbly cow's milk cheese from Lombardy; used for grating, cooking, or at the table.

Grappa Potent aquavit distilled from the seeds and stalks (and, more commonly now, the pulp) of grapes left over from wine-making.

Maccheroni alla Chitarra Square spaghetti shaped on a stringed wooden instrument; typical of Abruzzo and Molise.

Malloreddus Tiny ridged semolina gnocchi-flour from Sardinia.

Mascarpone Creamy, full-fat cow's milk cheese from Lombardy; used in desserts (including tiramisù) and pasta sauces and stuffings.

Montasio Firm cow's milk cheese from the region of Friuli–Venezia Giulia.

Orecchiette Ear-shaped pasta (from *orecchia,* meaning "ear"); standard fare in Apulia, Calabria, and Basilicata.

Pancetta Unsmoked pork belly, spiced and aged; meant for cooking, it can be rolled or flat. Bacon can be substituted, but it is smoked.

Pane Carasau Crisp, crackling flatbread from Sardinia; used in soups, salads, desserts, and pasta sauces and eaten at the table.

Parmigiano-Reggiano Grainy, firm cow's milk cheese from Emilia-Romagna; made from raw milk, it is Italy's most prized grating cheese.

Pecorino Sheep's milk cheese; the most common is Romano, from Latium and Sardinia, although nearly every region makes its own. Varies from mild when young to sharp when aged.

Polenta Cornmeal; ground more or less finely depending on the region. Used to make polenta, soups, breads, fritters, cakes, and cookies. All the recipes in this book call for regular (not instant) polenta.

Prosciutto Ham; can be smoked (Affumicato), unsmoked, or cooked (Cotto). The most famous is the unsmoked ham of Parma, with the one from San Daniele a close second.

Prosciutto Cotto Cooked ham; it is not sweet, so be careful if substituting a domestic ham for Prosciutto Cotto.

Provolone Cow's milk cheese, usually shaped like a pear and hung to age; can be unsmoked or smoked (Affumicato) and is ideal for melting.

Robiola This family of cheeses has many members: The most readily available is made from cow's milk and is creamy and fresh; other Robiole (some from cow's milk, others from goat's and cow's milk) are aged, therefore crumbly and sharp.

Salted Anchovies Anchovies packed in salt; the best are from Liguria, Sicily, Sardinia, and Calabria. Rinse, gut, and debone before using.

Salted Capers Capers conserved with coarse salt rather than in brine; essential to Sicilian cuisine. Rinse before using.

Scamorza Cow's milk cheese, unsmoked or smoked (Affumicata); melts beautifully.

Semolina Flour Coarsely ground durum wheat, a strong variety of wheat; used for making pasta. This flour is not to be confused with durum flour, which is ground more finely and is used for making bread.

Smoked Ricotta Ricotta smoked over aromatic wood; drier than fresh Ricotta, meant for cooking and grating over pasta.

Speck Smoked ham from Trentino–Alto Adige; eaten as an antipasto, incorporated in pasta stuffings, bread dumplings, and more.

Stracchino Creamy, fresh cow's milk cheese similar to Crescenza (see above); typical of Lombardy, it is used in pasta stuffings, in risotti, in savory pies, and at the table. It is the mold-free predecessor of Gorgonzola (see above).

Truffles Fragrant fungi that grow spontaneously near certain types of trees. The most prized are white winter truffles, best raw; black truffles are better cooked.

Vialone Nano Short-grain rice variety from the shores of Lago di Garda, obtained by crossing Vialone and Nano varieties; ideal for risotti and soups.

Acknowledgments

IT SEEMS IMPOSSIBLE, on one page, to thank all those who were instrumental to the making of this book. In Italy, the following people offered insight and recipes: Maurizio Grange, Gignod; Giuseppina Bagliardi and Piero Fassi, Asti; the Asti Chamber of Commerce; Pierangelo Cornaro, Bergamo; the Martinis, Mantua; Maurizia and Olga Dasso, Guido Porrati, the Bajs, and Luciano Benedetti, Rapallo; Luigi Miroli, Portofino; Mario Suban, Trieste; the Aizzas, Aquileia; Marlene Zisser, Bolzano; the Campeols, Treviso; Melania Facciani, San Vittore di Cesena; Paolo Sari, Lucca; Sandro Argilli, Spoleto; the di Marcos, Spoleto; Marco Gabbiotti, Spello; Gabriele Monti, Urbino; Marco Capponi, San Felice Circeo; Celestino Le Donne, Sulmona; Massimo Mastrangelo, Termoli; the Di Majo Norantes, Campomarino; Sergio Serva, Palinuro; Mimmo Ciuffreda, Vieste; the Golias, Terranova di Pollino; Angelo Giannello, Matera; Eustacchio Persia, Matera; Pino and Gaetano Alia, Castrovillari; Nuccio Cingari, Taormina; Giovanni Brai, Oristano; and the Chessas, Orosei.

This book would have been a different animal if not for Judith Riven; more than an agent, Judith has been a friend and a guide, helping me shape the book with her astute advice. At Clarkson Potter, I owe a debt of gratitude to so many fine professionals: Pam Krauss, the acquiring editor who bought not only my book, but my vision of it, and who is as sagacious as she is kind; Chris Pavone, my editor, who skillfully transformed my vision into a reality with an unwavering dedication to quality, a sense of humor, and much patience for my idiosyncrasies; Marysarah Quinn, creative director, and Maggie Hinders, designer, who did a beautiful job with the visuals; Mark McCauslin, the production editor, and Jane Searle, the production supervisor; Leigh Ann Ambrosi, the publicist; and Ronnie Grinberg, for being so helpful.

I thank Jerry Ruotolo, whose splendid photos of the recipes light up the book; Mark Ferri, who photographed other recipes so beautifully; and Margarita Villaquiran, who cooked and helped me style Jerry's dishes. In Manhattan, I thank Julie Gaynes, owner of Fishs Eddy, for lending tableware, and Gracious Home, for lending linens.

In the food world, I am indebted to: Nick Stellino, a friend above and beyond the call of duty; Rozanne Gold, a consummate professional with a big heart; Biba Caggiano, a true inspiration; Jacques Pépin; André Soltner; Mary Ann Esposito; Michele Scicolone; Lynne Rossetto Kasper; Anne Nurse; Anna Teresa Callen; Cesare Casella; Walter Potenza; Luigi Diotaiuti; Laura Maioglio; Dennis Caldarola; Fran McCullough; Rick Smilow, President of the Institute of Culinary Education in Manhattan, and his wonderful staff, for welcoming me into their family; and Einav Gefen, Culinary Director of the Jewish Community Center, also in Manhattan. In Montreal, I am thankful to my catering clients and my teachers at the Institut de Tourisme et d'Hotellerie du Québec.

For their support, I thank: Susanna Saarinen, for always being there; Jerry Ruotolo, for his heart; Margarita Villaquiran, for giving so much of herself; Sal Rizzo, for making me laugh; Julie Brasil, for being who she is; Jennifer and Uli Iserloh, for the fondue; Ouathek Ouerfelli, for the tomato jokes; Karen Chandross and Ric Cohen, for their long-time friendship; Beth Goslin, for sharing dumplings; Laura Niccolini, for six memorable years; Charles Pennino, Helena Lonergan, Slava Petrakov, Nathaniel Harrison, Lisa Merlini, Nicole Rial, Laura Crocenzi, Julie Byun, Barbara Ragghianti, Sabina Galli, Gisella Ingraffia, Chiara Carfi, Natasha Lardera, Paolo Modigliani, and Anna Canepa, former colleagues who have remained true friends.

My parents gave me the greatest gifts of all, unconditional love and friendship, and for this I am grateful every day of my life.

And I am more thankful than words can express to my husband, Dino De Angelis: He has traveled across Italy with me and took many of the photographs on these pages; he tasted every dish in this book and has been my most helpful critic; he drew a map of Italy that far exceeded my hopes; but most of all, he is my best friend and my greatest inspiration.

Bibliography

Accademia Italiana della Cucina. *Ristoranti d'Italia 2001*. Milan: Arnoldo Mondadori Editore, 2000.

Artusi, Pellegrino. *La Scienza in Cucina e l'Arte di Mangiar Bene*. Florence: Bemporad-Marzocco, 1962.

Barbero, Emma Enrica. *Liguria Maestra in Cucina*. Genoa: Coedital, 1996.

Bini, Bruno. *Torte Ripieni Focacce Polpettoni Farinata*. Genoa: Il Secolo XIX, 1993.

Blason Scarel, Silvia. *At Table with the Ancient Romans*. Aquileia: Andrea Moro Publishers, 1999.

Boni, Ada. *Cucina Regionale Italiana*. Milan: Arnoldo Mondadori Editore, 1988.

Bugialli, Giuliano. *Bugialli on Pasta*. New York: Stewart, Tabori & Chang, 2000.

Calvetti, Emerico Romano. *La Vera Cuciniera Genovese Facile ed Economica*. Bologna: Arnaldo Forni Editore, 1992.

Cardella, Antonio. *Sicilia e Isole*. Bologna: Edizioni Mida, 1989.

Celant, Enio. *Valle d'Aosta in Cucina*. Edizioni Gulliver, 1998.

Contini, Mila. *Friuli e Trieste*. Bologna: Edizioni Mida, 1989.

Davidson, Alan. *The Oxford Companion to Food*. Oxford: Oxford University Press, 1999.

Erler-Zanol, Anna, and Daniela Kofler. *La Vera Cucina Casalinga nelle Dolomiti*. Bolzano: Casa Editrice Athesia, 1993.

Fava, Franco. *Cucina Regionale*. Milan: Libreria Meravigli Editrice, 1993.

Field, Carol. *The Italian Baker*. New York: Harper & Row Publishers, 1985.

Gosetti della Salda, Anna. *Le Ricette Regionali Italiane*. Milan: Casa Editrice Solares, 1967.

Gosetti, Fernanda. *La Grande Cucina Regionale Italiana: I Primi Piatti*. Milan: Fabbri Editori, 1989.

Grazietta, Butazzi. *Toscana*. Bologna, Edizioni Mida, 1989.

Guarnaschelli Gotti, Marco. *Grande Enciclopedia della Gastronomia*. Milan: Selezione dal Reader's Digest, 1990.

Guide to Italian Regional Specialties, A. Rome: Ismea, 1999.

Joseph, Robert. *The Book of Wine*. New York: Smithmark Publishers, 1996.

Kagan, Donald, Steven Ozment, and Frank M. Turner. *The Western Heritage*. New York: Macmillan Publishing Company, 1987.

Kasper, Lynne Rosetto. *The Splendid Table*. New York: William Morrow and Company, 1992.

Kompatscher, Anneliese. *La Cucina nelle Dolomiti*. Bolzano: Casa Editrice Athesia, 1995.

Lanterna, Alberto. *Piemonte in Bocca*. Bologna: Edizioni Mida, 1988.

Marchese, Salvatore, Giorgio Mistretta, Piero Palumbo, and Maria Tempestini. *Sapori d'Italia: Guida ai Prodotti Tipici Regionali*. Novara: Istituto Geografico De Agostini, 1999.

Martini, Fosca. *Romagna*. Bologna: Edizioni Mida, 1989.

Molinari Pratelli, Alessandro. *La Cucina Ligure*. Rome: Newton & Compton Editori, 1996.

Noro Desaymonet, Elida, Luciana Faletto Landi, Maria Luisa Di Loreto, Bianca Marcoz Calchera, and Gemma Ouvrier. *Cucina di Tradizione della Valle d'Aosta*. Aosta: Pheljna, 1997.

Petroni, Paolo. *Il Libro della Vera Cucina Fiorentina*. Florence: Edizioni Il Centauro, 1994.

Ploner, Richard, and Cristoph Mayr. *Il Pane: 100 Ricette Tradizionali nelle Dolomiti*. Bolzano: Casa Editrice Athesia, 1991.

Plotkin, Fred. *Recipes from Paradise*. Boston: Little, Brown and Company, 1997.

Redon, Odile, Françoise Sabban, and Silvano Serventi. *The Medieval Kitchen: Recipes from France and Italy*. Chicago: The University of Chicago Press, 1998.

Robinson, Jancis. *The Oxford Companion to Wine*. Oxford: Oxford University Press, 1994.

Roden, Claudia. *The Book of Jewish Food: An Odyssey from Samarkand to New York*. New York: Alfred A. Knopf, 1997.

Roman Cookery of Apicius, The. John Edwards, translator. Great Britain: Random House, 1988.

Rotraud, Michael-Degner. *The Cheeses of Italy*. Rome: Edizioni Abete, Italian Institute of Foreign Trade.

Sada, Luigi. *Puglie*. Bologna, Edizioni Mida, 1989.

Santich, Barbara. *The Original Mediterranean Cuisine: Medieval Recipes for Today*. Chicago: Chicago Review Press, 1995.

Saracco, Carlo, Mauro Gaberoglio, and Ercole Zuccaro. *Guida sui Vini e Piatti Tipici Regionali*. Bologna: Edagricole, 2000.

Servi Machlin, Edda. *The Classic Cuisine of the Italian Jews, Volumes I and II*. Croton-on-Hudson: Giro Press, 1981 and 1992.

Tannahill, Reay. *Food in History*. London: Penguin Books, 1973.

Testa, Itala, and Andrea Porcu. *La Cucina della Sardegna*. Quartu S. Elena: Progetto Sardegna, 1998.

Valli, Emila. *La Cucina del Friuli–Venezia Giulia*. Rome: Tascabili Economici Newton, 1999.

Vaona, Martino. *La Cusina de Milan*. Milan: Libreria Meraviglia Editrice, 1995.

Varvaro, Aurora, Luigi Bernabò Brea, and Pietro Lo Cascio. *Aeolian Cooking*. Palermo: Edizioni Novecento, 1998.

Willan, Anne. *La Varenne Pratique*. Toronto: Macmillan of Canada, 1989.

Wright, Clifford A. *A Mediterranean Feast*. New York: William Morrow and Company, 1999.

Index

Index • 383